Prolegomena to the Study of Islam

W. Arthur Jeffery

Edited by Ruth J. Nicholls

Editor's Introduction: The Prolegomena
Ruth J. Nicholls

Arthur Jeffery Centre for the Study of Islam
Melbourne School of Theology

An affiliated college of the Australian College of Theology

PROLEGOMENA to the STUDY OF ISLAM
W. Arthur Jeffery
© 2023 Melbourne School of Theology Press. All rights reserved.

ISBN 978-0-9876401-3-0

Editor
Ruth Nicholls

Production and cover design
Ho-yuin Chan

Publishing Services
Published by MST Press
Thank you to Richard Shumack for his publishing services.

Arthur Jeffery Centre for the Study of Islam
Melbourne School of Theology
5 Burwood Highway, Wantirna,
Victoria, 3152, Australia.
Ph: +61 3 9881 7800
Email: mst@mst.edu.au
www.mst.edu.au

> Opinions and conclusions published in this book are those of the authors and do not necessarily represent the views of the Arthur Jeffery Centre for the Study of Islam or its Editors. This publication is purely an information medium, to inform interested parties of religious trends, discussions and debates. The Arthur Jeffery Centre for the Study of Islam affirms the free expression of the religious convictions of its authors but rejects hatred towards any persons or religious group.

William Arthur Jeffery (1892 – 1959)

PUBLICATIONS BY ARTHUR JEFFERY

(This list does not include Jeffery's book reviews which are extensive. Since some of Jeffery's books have been republished, only the original date of publication is listed here.)

1911 (1328), التزام عبد الرحمن محمد،), جفري، آرثر) قرآن كريم, al-Darb al-Aḥmar, Miṣr (Egypt).

1932, *Su due recenti traduzioni musulmane inglesi del Corano* (Italian), Roma, Istitute per l'Oriente.

1934, *The Muslim Point of View,* [Egypt?] pp1-12
Address given at the Egypt Inter-mission Conference, Radstock Hall, Ezbet el-Zeitoun, March 20th, 1934.

1937, *Materials for History of the text of the Qur'an*, Leiden, Brill.

1938, *The Foreign Vocabulary of the Qur'an,* Baroda, Oriental Institute.

1951 (?), *Al-Biruni's contribution to comparative religion*, Iran Society, Calcutta.

1951, *Index of Qur'anic Verses to the English part of Materials for the History of the Text of the Qur'an,* Leiden, E.J. Brill.

1952, *The Qur'an as scripture*, New York, Russell F. Moore.

1954, *Two muqaddimas to the Qu'ranic sciences: the Muqaddima to the Kitab al-Mabani and the Muqaddima of Ibn 'Atiyya to his Tafsir* (Arabic), Cairo, Al-Khaniji.

مقدمتان فى علوم القرآن و هما مقدمة كتاب المبانى و مقدمة ابن عطية, 1954, مطبعة سنة محمدية,قاهرة,

1954, Muqaddimatan fi 'ulum al-Qur'an wa-huma muqaddimat Kitab al-Mabani wa-muqaddimat Ibn 'Aiyah, Maktabat al-Xangi.

1958, (Translator), *The Koran,* New York, The Heritage Press.

1958, *The Koran: selected suras,* New York, Limited Editions Club.

1958, *The Koran. Selected Suras.* Translated from the Arabic by Arthur Jeffrey and decorated by Valentini Angelo, New York, Heritage Press.

1959, *Ibn al-'Arabi's Shajarat al-Kawn,* Paris, Larose.

1962, *A Reader on Islam; Passages from standard Arabic writings illustrative of the Beliefs and Practices of Muslims,* 's-Gravenhage, Mouton.

Written with others, or as Editor.

1933, Abd Allah ibn Sulayman Sijistani
Materials for the History of the Text of the Qur'an: the old Codices: The Kitab al-Maṣaḥif of Ibn Abi Dawud, together with a collection of the variant readings from the codices of Ibn Ma'sud, Ubai, 'Ali, Ibn 'Abbas, Anas, Abu Musa and other early Qur'anic authorities which present a type of text anterior to that of the canonical text of 'Uthman, Leiden, Brill.

1942, I. Mendelsohn, (Author), L. Carrington Goodrich, C. Martin Wilbur, *The Orthography of the Samarqand Qur'an Codex,* Extract from the Journal of the American Oriental Society, v. 62, p. 175-195.

1948, *The Qur'an readings of Ibn Miqsam,* (From Ignace Goldziher memorial volume, part 1), (no publication details), pp38.

1958, *Islam; Muḥammad and His Religion,* New York, Liberal Arts Press.

Journal Articles

1922, "Eclecticism in Islam", *The Muslim World*,[1] Vol. 12, no. 3, Jul, pp230-24

1924, "The Presentation of Christianity to Moslems", *International Review of Mission*, 13 no 2 Apr, pp174-189

1924, "The Mystic Letters of the Koran", *The Muslim World*, Vol. 14, no. 3, Jul, 247-260

1925, "The Mecca Pilgrimage in the Life of Islam," *International Review of Mission*, Vol. 14, no 1, Jan, p73-91.

1925, "A Reference to the Ishtar-Cult in the Qur'an", *The American Journal of Semitic Languages and Literatures*, Vol. 41, No. 4 (Jul), pp. 280-282

1925, "A Collection of Anti-Christian Books and Pamphlets Found in Actual Use among the Mohammedans of Cairo", *The Muslim World*, Vol 15, no.1, Jan, pp26-37

1925, "A Moslem Torah from India". *The Muslim World*, Vol. 15, no. 3, Jul., pp232-239

1926, "The Anti-Christian Moslem Press", *The Muslim World*, Vol. 16, no. 4, Oct, p425

1926, "The Quest of the Historical Mohammed", *The Muslim World*, Volume 16, no. 4, Oct, pp232

1929, "The Real Muhammad and the Ideal: A Study of One Phase of Modern Muslim Apologetic", *International Review of Mission*, Vol. 18, no 3, Jul, pp390-400.

1929, "Christians at Mecca", *The Muslim World*, Vol. 19, no.3, Jul, pp221-235

---

[1] Originally titled "The Moslem World"

1932, "Three Cairo Modernists", *International Review of Mission,* Vol. 21, no. 4, Oct, pp498-515

1932, "The Suppressed Qur'an Commentary of Muḥammad Abu Zaid", *Der Islam*, Vol. 20, no. 4 pp301-308.

1934, "Il Modernismo Musulmano Dell'Indiano "Sir" Mohammad Iqbal", *Oriente Moderno,* Anno 14, nr. 10, Ottobre, pp. 505-513

1937, "The Qur'an Readings of Zaid.B.'Ali, The Qur'an Readings of Zaid B. 'ALI, *Rivista degli studi orientali,* Vol. 16, Fasc. ¾, Gennaio, pp249-289

1938, "Abu 'Ubaid on the Verses Missing from the Qur'an", *The Muslim World*, Vol 28, no 1, Jan, pp61-65

1938, "The Prophet of Islam", *The Muslim World* Vol. 28, no. 2. Apr, pp180-186

1939, "A Variant Text of the Fatiha", *The Muslim World*, Vol. 29, no. 2, Apr) pp158-162

1939, "Further Qur'an Readings of Zaid B. 'Ali", *Rivista degli studi orientali,* Vol. 18, Fasc. 2, (Agosto), pp218-236

1940, ✠ David Samuel Margoliouth ✠, *The Muslim World*, Volume 30, Issue 3, Jul ,pp295-298

1942, "Gregory of Tathew's 'Contra Mohammedanos", *The Muslim World*, Volume 32, Issue 3, Jul, pp219-235

1942, "The Political Importance of Islam", *Journal of Near Eastern Studies*, Vol 1, no. 4, Oct, pp383-395

1943, "Present Day Movements in Islam", *The Muslim World,* Vol. 33, no. 3, Jul, pp165-186

1945, "The Arab Heritage", *Thought,* Vol. 20, p147

1945, "Three Documents on the History of Christianity in South Arabia", *Anglican Theological Review,* Vol. 27, no 3, Jul, pp185-205.

1945, "The Patience of Unanswered Prayer", *The Muslim World,* Vol. 35, no. 4, Oct, p273-280

1946, "Christianity in South Arabia", *The Muslim World,* Vol. 36, no. 3, Jul, pp193-216

1950, "The Qur'an as Scripture", *The Muslim World,* Vol. 40, no. 1, Jan, pp41-55.

1950, "The Qur'an as Scripture", II, *The Muslim World,* Vol. 40 no 2 Apr, pp106-134.

1950, "The Qur'an as Scripture", III, *The Muslim World,* Vol. 40, no. 3, Jul, pp185-206

1950, "The Qur'an as Scripture", IV, *The Muslim World,* Vol. 40, no 4, Oct, pp257-274.

1951, "Professor Schoeps on Judeo-Christianity", *Anglican Theological Review,* Vol. 33 no 3 Jul, pp169-173

1956, "Christian Approach to the Religions of the East", *Union Seminary Quarterly Review,* Vol. 11 no 2 Jan, pp13-24.

1959, "Ibn al-Arabi's "Shajart al-kaun", *Studia Islamica,* No. 10, pp43-77

1959, "Ibn al-Arabi's "Shajart al-kaun", (Concluded) *Studia Islamica,* No. 11, pp. 113-160

1960, "History of Religions", (Bibliography), *Union Seminary Quarterly Review,* Vol. 15, no 3, Mar, pp239-244

ARTHUR JEFFERY CENTRE FOR THE STUDY OF ISLAM, Melbourne School of Theology, Australia

Formerly known as the Centre for the Study of Islam and Other Faiths it was renamed the Arthur Jeffery Centre for the Study of Islam in 2016. William Arthur Jeffery was an Australian Methodist missionary who first went to India and ultimately developed proficiency in 19 languages. A contemporary of Samuel Zwemer, Jeffery became a recognized scholar of Islam who was invited to join the staff of the American University in Cairo. His book, "The Foreign Vocabulary of the Qur'an" which was first printed in 1938, still stands as the standard text in the field.

The Arthur Jeffery Centre for the Study of Islam is the only such Centre in Australia. Through its team of expert scholars and teachers of Islam it provides a variety of resources at both academic and public levels for those involved in or desiring to be involved in loving and meaningful engagement with Muslims.

The Centre is responsible for designing, preparing and teaching subjects approved by the Australian College of Theology at undergraduate and postgraduate levels relating to Islam. The Centre also aims for academic excellence through its publications which include not only scholarly works but also information for those who desire to increase their understanding of Islam. As part of its public engagement the Centre also holds open seminars and events, often joining with others sharing a similar vision and ethos. Staff are also available to speak at public programs.

In 2018 the Centre celebrated 10 years of operation and has established itself as a major centre for postgraduate studies in Islam.

For further information about the Centre and its activities, as well as opportunities to study Islam in a Christian context at both undergraduate and postgraduate levels, email: info@JefferyCentre.mst.edu.au

TABLE OF CONTENTS

EDITORIAL COMMENT	xix
ABBREVIATIONS	xxvii
LIST OF JOURNALS	xxx
EDITOR'S INTRODUCTION:	xxxiii

PROLEGOMENA TO THE STUDY OF ISLAM

PRIMARY SECTIONS

INTRODUCTION	3
PHYSICAL BACKGROUND	8
THE TRADE ROUTES	16
ETHNOLOGICAL BACKGROUND	19
HISTORICAL BACKGROUND	57
A. SOUTH ARABIAN CIVILIZATION	58
B. THE ARAB KINGDOMS	68
C. THE OUTSIDE EMPIRES	88
D. THE LEGENDARY TRIBES	100
TRIBAL ORGANISATION	117
THE QURAISH	130
MECCA	138
RELIGIOUS BACKGROUND	140
ARABIAN PAGANISM	144
SABIANISM	190
SABAEAN RELIGION	202
ZOROASTRIANISM	206
JUDAISM	212
CHRISTIANITY	219

APPENDICES
    A COMPARATIVE TABLE   229
    TIMELIE   231
    BYZANTIUM AND THE KINGS OF AXUM   235
    EPIPHANIUS COMMENT   237
    ETHIOPIAN WAR ELEPHANTS   238
    LANE-POOLE – POETICAL CONTESTS   239
    PERSIAN INTERVENTION IN YEMEN   240
    PRE-ISLAMIC CONTACTS WITH PERSIA   242
    REVENUE FROM PILGRIMAGE CROWDS   243
    THE PROBLEM OF THE PROPHET HUD   244
    ZOROASTRIANISM   248

BIBLIOGRAPHY   249

MAPS and TABLES

MAPS
1	MIDDLE EAST: POLITICAL GEOGRAPHY 21ST CENTURY	6
2	GREEK DIVISIONS OF ARABIA	7
3	ARABIA AND ITS REGIONS	7
4	PHYSICAL FEATURES OF ARABIA	9
5	SIGNIFICANT CENTRES	15
6	TRADE ROUTES IN AND AROUND ARABIA	17
7	MINAEAN	60
8	SABAEAN	60
9	HADRAMAUT	60
10	HIMYRAT	60
12	OUTSIDE EMPIRES ABOUT 600 CE(AD)	89

TABLES
1	EARLY SEMITIC MIGRATIONS	26
2	LIST OF SEMITIC LANGUAGES	27

EDITORIAL COMMENT

William Arthur Jeffery (1892 – 1959), a contemporary of such well known Islamic scholars as Samuel Zwemer, David Margoliouth, Andrae Tor and Julius Wellhausen, was himself a noted scholar of Islam. Today he is possibly best known for his work *The Foreign Vocabulary of the Qur'an* which is still the standard in its field. He lectured at various times, it would seem, from the several extant outlines available on 'An Introduction to Islam' as they were named. However, this particular set of notes, was titled *A Prolegomena to the Study of Islam*. A Prolegomena according to the Merriam-Webster internet dictionary is "a formal essay or critical discussion serving to introduce and interpret an extended work". To Jeffery, then, these lecture notes were intended to introduce his students to the world of Islam and to lay the foundations for further study.

Over sixty years have passed since Jeffery died and since that time Islam has violently exploded into world consciousness with the attack on the World Trade Centre in New York, 9th September 2001, though prior to that event and even subsequent to it, there have been many terrorist attacks with bombings, suicidal attacks, knifings and shootings. In some places it has also included abductions. The reports of the ravages of ISIS in the Middle East filled our TV screen, all of which kept Islam at the forefront of people's minds, though attention to Islam has decreased significantly in the 2020s. As a consequence, for some time there was a greater interest in Islam. This led in some areas to a growth in the number of colleges and universities providing courses on the study of Islam. For those already providing such courses, their curricula have been strengthened and widened as students have expressed greater interest. Jeffery, though, and the many scholars with whom he shares an interest and a passion, belong to those who for years have grappled with understanding Islam. Not surprisingly since Jeffery's day studies of Islam have taken various routes, though current studies have been particularly focused on the question of whether terrorism is or isn't Islamic and the question of Islam and politics. Western modern critical analysis techniques have also had their impact on the current study of Islam. On the other hand, since Islam is to the Muslim the best religion and divinely inspired, asking questions about certain sensitive topics and engaging in critical evaluation of basic dogma can be seen as blasphemy.

In 2016, in honour of this great Australian-born scholar the Melbourne School of Theology, Victoria, Australia renamed its Centre for the Study of Islam and other Faiths, the Arthur Jeffery Centre for the Study of Islam. Islam has been a subject of study at the school for many years, with many of its students finding their way to lands where Islam was a significant religion and where they were involved in Christian service. When Jeffery moved to India during World War I it was both as a Methodist minister and a missionary. Some of that sense of calling is found in the closing paragraph of the section on Christianity in this *Prolegomena*. Melbourne School of Theology is an affiliated college of the Australian College of Theology through which it offers courses in the study of Islam from undergraduate studies through to various levels of postgraduate courses, with students presenting master projects and doctoral theses relating to Islam.

It was about the time of the renaming of the Centre that the Centre became aware of these unpublished lecture notes of Jeffery. It was on his death, that Columbia University, where Jeffery was the Professor of Semitic Languages, a post he first held at the School of Oriental Studies, Cairo, became the custodian of Jeffery's materials. It was from that University that the Arthur Jeffery Centre acquired these lecture notes with the view to publishing them. A search was made for Australian relatives of Jeffery. While one (an eighty-year old) was initially contacted to seek their permission which was verbally offered, subsequent attempts of further conversations with this relative have not been successful so further exploration has been suspended. Nevertheless, recognising the historical significance of these lecture notes, the Arthur Jeffery Centre for the Study of Islam has taken upon itself to publish them.

The world has changed in many ways since Jeffery prepared these notes. Some of the words that Jeffery uses reflect the academic world of his time. When Jeffery was writing it was believed that cultures, following the Darwin theory of evolution had gone through various stages. A word like 'primitive' was an accepted academic term describing what was understood as an earlier stage in evolution that appeared to reflect a very basic form of lifestyle. Islam was referred to as Muhammadanism, a term which is no longer considered acceptable. Where Jeffery used this term in the *Prolegomena* it has been changed to M[uslim]: the brackets indicating that this was not the original word. Some of his phraseology also sounds strange to modern ears: some may today even be considered politically incorrect but given that this was to be a reproduction of Jeffery's work his terminology has been maintained.

Jeffery was obviously a great scholar whose understanding of Islam was wide ranging and detailed. In preparing his notes for publishing it did not take long to realise that Jeffery had read extensively and deeply, readily acknowledging his sources. Consequently, recognising that in his *Prolegomena* there were extensive research sources of earlier works on Islam the decision was made to include a bibliography. In many ways that has proved to be very demanding and time consuming. Many of Jeffery's sources are no longer in circulation so finding the year of printing and the publisher often required extensive searching. I am indeed very grateful to Dr Denis Savelyev who is now the Administrator of the Arthur Jeffery Centre for the Study of Islam as well as lecturer in Islam for his great help in finding many of the works I failed to locate. Some however still have not been definitively identified. In many cases Jeffery only referred to the title of the book while at other times only the author. If that author has published a number of relevant works relating to the subject, those works are also included in the bibliography. Since the bibliography is ordered by authorship, in the footnotes the author's name has been added to facilitate locating the reference in the bibliography. At times Jeffery refers to a source, notes it but for some reason has not completed the details in the footnotes. Such instances are indicated with an editorial note of 'details not given' in the footnotes.

Jeffery also used journals extensively, some of which are no longer published. While there has been an attempt to create a comprehensive list of the journals to which he referred, his journal references, while mentioned in the footnotes, have not been included in the bibliography.

When Jeffery referenced many of the works of the writers of the early days of the current era he left no record as to which source he was using. In identifying calendar years, Jeffery used the then current system of AD and BC. The modern usage prefers CE to denote the years that were formerly identified by AD with BCE, replacing BC. Jeffery's practice has been maintained. Added to this complexity, Jeffery, at various places, added extra handwritten notes, obviously to supplement his lectures. While very neat and tidy his writing is incredibly small – magnifiers and zooms on the computer have sometimes helped – but at other times questions have remained. These are indicated in the text by a question mark in brackets (?). In relation to those notes – written on the page opposite his typed notes — it was also difficult on occasions to decide the particular place where Jeffery would have included the extra information. Nevertheless, every endeavour has been made to place the notes appropriately. These have been clearly indicated by the words 'handwritten note'. On the occasion when Jeffery's footnotes were extensive, these have been transferred to the Appendix. These too are clearly indicated.

Jeffery's proficiency in other languages is also evident in these lecture notes: works in Arabic, Hebrew, Greek, Babylonian, Ethiopic, Syriac, German and French are not only referenced but also quoted. Interestingly, it is said that Jeffery was proficient in 19 languages and these lectures notes go some way in supporting that comment. While computer technology has been an added advantage in reproducing Jeffery's quotes, sadly, modern alphabets do not reproduce some of the older characters, nor are they easy sources of older scripts. This means that some of the words that he had handwritten into his typed notes are missing from this reproduction. However, those places, where he wrote down words in these various older languages but which are not reproduced in this edition, are clearly marked using a modern symbol – a computer keyboard ⌨.

One of the challenges that faces a student of the Middle Eastern area is the variant methods of the transliteration not only of Arabic words but also Semitic words: indeed, of any language that has its own script. In some ways it would seem that Jeffery had his own method of transliteration. Consequently, many of the same words appear with different spellings. Since these differences often occur in quotes there has been no attempt to standardize the spelling – noting that Jeffery himself isn't always consistent. Interestingly, Jeffery always used ā when spelling Islām: a practice which has not been followed in this reproduction. Various publishers have also developed their own particular style of transliteration. Today there are a number of systems in operation with each recognised publisher of works relating to Islam and Arabic, having their own preferred standard. Detailed transliteration of Arabic terms and phrases in the original manuscript has been eliminated to facilitate the task of reproduction using a standard keyboard.

To reprint such a work as this required a number of decisions. The vast number of references and quotes in Jeffery's manuscript are reproduced without being checked against his sources; for some the actual source that Jeffery was using is not identified in the original manuscript. Where possible, the foreign language terms and phrases used by Jeffery have been checked, but in certain cases this has proven unfeasible because of Jeffery's facility with so many languages and given the fact that some of the scripts that he has used could not be reproduced. Jeffery's manuscript is located along with other materials of his, in the Arthur Jeffery Papers, Rare Book & Manuscript Library, Columbia University in the City of New York.

Also, in reproducing this work, as far as possible I have followed Jeffery's divisions, subdivisions and at times even further subdivisions. Even with computer technology, this has presented a challenge in terms of formatting the document in such a way, that the spirit of his work is represented. Thanks to the versatility of computer programs, I trust, I have been able to reproduce that spirit.

While Jeffery's work did not include any maps or charts, one can assume that he would have used them in his lectures. So, a number of hand drawn maps and charts have been incorporated into this edition, with the aim of aiding those for whom knowledge of the areas to which Jeffery refers is limited. It must be remembered though that in ancient times boundaries were rarely delineated and any attempt to identify areas of influence can only be considered estimates and approximations. In addition, several timelines have been included. The first is a comparative table of Early South Arabian Kingdoms while the second outlines the historical events mentioned throughout Jeffery's notes.

In preparing this work, I am indebted to a number of people for the idea of bringing this work to the attention of those for whom the study of Islam is their interest and passion. It is to Joshua Lingel we owe our thanks for alerting us to these lecture notes, 'A Prolegomena to the Study of Islam'. Particular thanks also goes to: Dr Richard Shumack, the Director for the Arthur Jeffery Centre for the Study of Islam, Melbourne School of Theology, Melbourne, Australia. Both Dr Shumack and Prof. Peter Riddell (former Director of the Arthur Jeffery Centre) have provided the encouragement to continue on with it, especially when it was challenging. A number of the staff of the Melbourne School of Theology have also provided assistance in various ways: Richard Coomb (Early Church History); Gillian Asquith, (Greek); Andrew Brown (Early Church History, Hebrew and Greek);[1] Michael Bräutigam[2] (German), and Prof. Peter Riddell, an expert in Islam in his own right has also checked the French. Once again, I am deeply grateful to Denis Savelyev who has been such a great help in compiling the bibliography. Grateful thanks goes to Yvonne Ritchie, Vera McIlroy, Margaret Rickard and Peter Riddell who have read the manuscript with critical eyes and picked up on some of those errors that can be easily missed. My

---

[1] Referenced as AB in footnotes when proofing the copy of Jeffery's manuscript.
[2] Referenced as MB in footnotes when proofing the copy Jeffery's manuscript

thanks also goes to the Melbourne School of Theology for its time and resources and to the Australian College of Theology under whose auspices the college can offer courses on Islam and so foster the Arthur Jeffery Centre for the Study of Islam, whose desire is with this edition to honour the Australian scholar after whom it is named.

The limitations that have occurred in reproducing the text, compiling the bibliography, creating the maps and charts are mine. Nevertheless, I have been honoured to bring this very informative work of such a great Australian Islamic scholar to publication status. In the process I have understood how this scholar of Islam rose to such prominence.

Ruth J. Nicholls
Editor
Adjunct Research Fellow
Arthur Jeffery Centre for the Study of Islam
Melbourne School of Theology

ABBREVIATIONS

JOURNALS

Abr	*Life of Abraham*, Philo
AOF	*Altorientalische Forschungen*, Leipzig: Verlag von Eduard Pfeiffer, 1893-1905.
AJSL	*American Journal of Semitic Languages and Literatures*
APAW	*Abhandlungen der Preußischen Akademie der Wissenschaften*
BA (?)	*Lexicon Syriacum of Bar Ali*
	Biblical Archaeologist
BGA	Bibl. Geog. Arab
	Michael Jan de Goeje, *Bibliotheca Geographorum Arabicorum*
CIL	*Corpus Inscriptionum Latinarum*, Berlin
CIS	*Corpus Inscriptionum Semiticarum*, Paris
DCB	*Dictionary of Christian Biography*
DCG	*Dictionary of Christ and the Gospels*, vols I & II, ed. James Hastings, Edinburgh, T & T Clark, 1908
E. Britt	*Encyclopaedia Brittanica*
EI	*Encyclopaedia of Islam*, First Ed. 1913-1938
ERE	*Encyclopaedia of Religion and Ethics*, ed. James Hastings, 1908
GGA	*Göttingische Gelehrte Anzeigen*
HDB	*Hastings Dictionary of the Bible*, Edinburgh, T & T Clark, 1989
JA	*Journal Asiatíque*
JAOS	*Journal of the American Oriental Society*
JE	*The Jewish Encyclopaedia*
JPOS	*Journal of the Palestinian Oriental Society*
JRAS	*Journal of the Royal Asiatic Society*
KAT	*Die Keilinschriften und das Alte Testament* (Schrader)
KAT	*Die Keilinschriften und das Alte Testament mit Ausdehnung auf die Apokryphen, Pseudepigraphen und das Neue Testament,* revised 3rd edition, edited

	by Hugo Winckler; Heinrich Zimmern, Friedrich David Heinrich
MAL	*Memorie della Reale Accademia dei Lincei*
MFOB	*Mélanges de la Faculté Orientale de l'Université St Joseph de Beyrouth.*
MGWJ	*Monatsschrift für die Geschichte und Wissenschaft des Judenthums*
MVAG	*Mitteilungen aus der Vorderasiatischen Abteilung der Staatlichen Museen zu Berlin,* Berlin: Curtius H. 1.1922
MW	*The Muslim World,* (Journal)
NSI	Cooke's *North Semitic Inscriptions*
OLZ	*Orientalische Literaturzeitung* Weisbaden
RB	*Revue Biblique or*
Rev. Bibl.	*Revue Biblique*
REJ	*Revue des études juives*
RGG	*Religion in Geschichte und Gegenwart*
RHR	*Revue de l'histoire des religions, Paris*
RS	*Revue sémitique d'Epigraphie et d'Histoire ancienne*
SBAW	*Sitzungsberichte der königl. Akad. D. Wissenschaft.* (Berlin or Wien)
ThStKr	*Theologische Studien und Kritiken*
VMKA	*Verslagen en Mededeelingen der Koninklijke Akademie van Weternschappen*
WZKM	*Weiner Zeitschrist für Kunde des Morgenlandes*
ZA	*Zeitschrift für ägyptische Sprache und Altertumskunde*
ZDMG	*Zeitschrift der Deutschen Morgenländischen Gesellschaft,* lit. "Journal of the German Oriental Society"
ZfE	*Zeitschrift für Ethnologie*
ZWT(h)	*Zeitschrift für wissenschaftliche Theologie*

THE BIBLE

When citing Bible references, various publishers use different though similar abbreviations for the various books that constitute the Bible. Those listed here are the ones used throughout this work. The books are listed in order of their occurrence in the Bible. Chapter references are given in Roman numbers with verses given in standard numbers. (Note: This is not a complete listing of the Books found in the Bible, only the ones referenced in this work.)

Old Testament

Genesis	Gen.
Exodus	Exod.
Leviticus	Lev.
Joshua	Jos.
Judges	Jud.
Samuel (I & II)	Sam.
Kings (I & II)	Ki.
Chronicles (I & II)	Chron.
Ezra	Ezra
Nehemiah	Neh.
Job	Job
Psalms	Ps.
Isaiah	Isa.
Jeremiah	Jer.
Lamentations	L.
Ezekiel	Ez.
Hosea	Hos.
Joel	Joel

Septuagint (also Catholic Bible - Apocrypha)

Maccabees (I & II)	Mac.

New Testament

Acts of the Apostles	Acts
Galatians	Gal.

LIST OF JOURNALS

Al-Mashriq (al-Machriq)
American Journal of Semitic Languages and Literatures (AJSL)
Annales de l'Académie Royale d'Archéologie de Belgique
Annales de Geographie
Annali dell'Islam
Assyriologische Bibliothek
Babylonia and Oriental Record
Contemporary Review
Das Ausland
Der Islam
Gnomon, on Kritische Zeitschrift für die Gesamite Kussische Altertunswissenschaft
Göttingische Gelehrte Anzeigen
Hebraica
Jahrbuch für deutsche Theologie
Journal of the American Oriental Society (JAOS)
*Journal Asiatigue (*JA)
Journal of the Palestinian Oriental Society (JPOS)
Journal of Religion
Journal of the Royal Asiatic Society (JRAS)
Journal of the Royal Asiatic Society of Great Britain and Ireland
Kyrkohistorisk Årshrift
L'Année sociologique
Mannus
Mélanges de la Faculté Orientale de l'Université St Joseph de Beyrouth (MFOB)
Mémoires de l'Académie des inscriptions
Memorie della reale accademia dei Lincei
Ser. 3-6, 8- issued as Atti della Accademia nazionale dei Lincei
Monatsschrift für die Geschichte und Wissenschaft des Judenthums (MGWJ)
Muslim World (MW)
Nachrichten von der Gesellschaft der Wissenschaften zu Göttingen, Mathematisch-Physikalische Klasse,
Nineteenth Century
Oesterreichische Monatsschrift für den Orient

Orientalia
Petermanns Mitteilungen.
Proceedings of the Society for Biblical Archaeology
Religion in Geschichte und Gegenwart
Repertorium für biblische und morgenländische Litteratur
Revue Biblique (Rev. Bib / Rev Bibl, or RB)
Revue d'Assyriologie
Recueil des Travaux
Studien über die vorislamischen Religion der Araber
Theologische Studien und Kritiken
Verslagen en Mededeelingen der Koninklijke Akademie van
Vienna Oriental Journal
Vivre et Penser
Weternschappen (VMKA)
Zeitschrift der Deutschen Morgenländischen Gesellschaft, (lit.
"Journal of the German Oriental Society". (ZDMG)
Zeitschrift für Ethnologie (ZfE)

EDITOR'S INTRODUCTION:

Prolegomena to the Study of Islam

"A Prolegomena to the Study of Islam" was, as the name suggests, an introduction to the study of Islam which, as originally conceived, would appear to have been a series of lectures. But even that has a more specific focus, for the materials present the reader with a detailed study of the Arabian scene prior to the advent of Muhammad, the Prophet of Islam, with a particular focus on its impact on what developed into Islam. The lecturer was none other than William Arthur Jeffery (18 October 1892– 2 August 1959). Arthur Jeffery, as he was best known, was born in Melbourne, Australia and graduated from the University of Melbourne, with a B.A. (1918), M.A. (1920) and BD (1926), winning several scholarships during his course of studies.[1] He also gained his PhD (1929) and his D. Litt (1938), both from Edinburgh with honours. Jeffery's more formal interest in Islam and Arabic began when he encountered these fields of study in India where he went early in his career during World War I as a Methodist minister and missionary to be a lecturer at the Madras Christian College. During his time there he became a noted linguist, Orientalist and scholar of Islam. His ability in languages and his interest in Islam resulted in his being asked to join the staff of the School of Oriental Studies, Cairo, Egypt, a department within the newly formed American University there, which he did in 1921. Initially the School of Oriental Studies (SOS) operated as the Language Study Centre of the American Mission serving Christian missionaries who made their way to Egypt.

---

[1] William Arthur Jeffery, Memorial Minute, Methodist Minutes of 1959 Conference, via Synod Archivist, Missions Resourcing Unit, Uniting Church in Australia, Melbourne, p52

Not surprisingly, while in Egypt his interest, his knowledge and his interaction with Islam grew and developed. In Egypt, as a lecturer at SOS, he taught Arabic and lectured on Islam to those who attended the Centre. One of the students named Whitehouse, a former Melbourne School of Theology student, was there in the 1930s; he wrote[1]

> Of course, we were greatly privileged at being introduced to Arabic and Muslim culture at the School of Oriental Studies (SOS) at the American University. ... And who could forget Arthur Jeffery's inimitable style of teaching and his interspersed anecdotes? But above all I remember his mastery of who knows how many Semitic languages, and how he used the parallel between Hebrew, Aramaic and Arabic to emphasise a point – sometimes to jolt our understanding of Biblical texts.

In 1938, Jeffery joined Columbia University, Manhattan, New York as head of the department of Near and Middle Eastern Languages becoming the Professor of Semitic Languages. He was concurrently an adjunct Professor of Semitic and Comparative Religions at the Union Theological Seminary also in New York. He held both positions until his untimely death in August 1959.

Sadly, there is no record of when Jeffery prepared these lectures, though a scan of the dates of the resources used, would suggest that it was early in his career. In a tribute to Jeffery in *The Muslim World,* January 1960, Eric Bishop comments about these lecture notes.

> "... his typed lectures on "Prolegomena to the Study of Islam" were left in Jerusalem for others less instructed to use. These lectures were given in the evenings without the typescript in the courtyard at the back of the house. People came night after night to fill our hundred and more chairs. There were friendly Muslim scholars and one such remarked as he left: "This man knows more of the beginnings of Islam than most of us."[2]

So it would seem that they were originally conceived in Egypt. One suspects that the handwritten notes that were subsequently added to the typed ones, were either clarification of a point made or

---

[1] Aubrey Whitehouse, *Do you remember ...?* 2017, Melbourne, MST Press, pp22,23
[2] "Arthur Jeffery – A Tribute", *The Muslim World,* vol 50, no1. 1960, pp49-54, p52.

additional information he had recently accessed. Among his notes though, there were various outlines which suggest that he consciously modified, re-shaped and reordered them over time. Did he ever plan to publish these notes? Of that there is no record, but one thing is for sure, these notes are well-documented, though he often uses abbreviations which, in some cases, have been a challenge to decipher and reference. Perhaps Jeffery did not consider it necessary to publish his notes. A fellow Professor, Philip Hitti, holding the seat of Semitic Literature at Princeton University, published "History of the Arabs: From the Earliest Times to the Present" in 1937 though enlarging it in 1951. In part I of this work, the first seven chapters raise many of the issues that Jeffery covers in these notes. Since Jeffery does not refer to Hitti's work in his *Prolegomena* it may be that he used these notes primarily when he was living and working in the Middle East.

ISLAM in CONTEXT

Central to Jeffery's approach is his understanding that the Prophet of Islam became so within a context. In other words, even before the Prophet began his role as a preacher of Islam he had not only imbued the culture and its worldview, into which he was born and out of which he thought, spoke and lived, but it was also from out of that underlying framework that he formed his attitudes, responded and preached. Also, the Prophet grew, lived and worked within a specific time frame in which peoples, tribes, countries and empires were all impacting each other to greater or lesser degrees. To Jeffery this was not only the backdrop to the Prophet's life, but it also formed the foundation out of which Muhammad responded and reacted during his life as the Prophet and also later as 'ruler' at Medina. This was also the context out of which the Prophet would have understood the 'divine revelations' that were to provide the directions which he took and would have determined not only his actions but those of the many who follow him.

Also underlying Jeffery's presentation would have been his awareness of the many foreign words which are found in the Qur'an. His work on the foreign words in the Qur'an, the study of which was the basis of his thesis,[1] is still recognised as the standard

---

[1] *The Foreign Vocabulary Of The Quran*, Oriental Institute, Baroda, 1938

text in that area. Why so many foreign words? Why such a breadth of different words? Was it just that Muhammad was a travelling camel-caravan merchant, (though there are those who question the extent of his travels),[1] who had acquired these words on his travels? Some may have been, but other words it would appear were a part of everyday life in Mecca and Medina where he lived. Others obviously were not, for in those cases the Qur'anic exegetes are uncertain of their origin or meaning.

ECLECTICISM

A further claim that Jeffery makes, which is offensive to those who regard the Prophet as having restored the true religion of Abraham, is that it is 'an eclectic religion which borrowed almost all its religious conceptions and a majority of the elements of its cult from the religious life of its environment'.[2] Not surprisingly then throughout these lecture notes Jeffery details those concepts and cultic elements which were already part of Arabian tribal religious practices or imported from those religions which were impacting the area.

So then, Jeffery's focus is the 'context' and 'eclecticism' and he takes a whole series of lectures in which to explore the issues he identifies as important. Indeed, many of the sources to which Jeffery refers are those covering the life of Muhammad and the surrounding influences. This approach is in contrast to my own learning experience and many recent books and lectures on Islam which begin with the tenets of Islam and its practices. Some of the introductory material found in Jeffery's work may be incorporated incidentally or may be mentioned in passing to illustrate an issue later in the work or when dealing with a difficulty or problem. In some publications, there is an initial chapter briefly covering some of the material Jeffery presents. Of course, the question can be raised, is it necessary to know this background material? Interestingly, in Muslim terminology the period before the coming of the prophet was known as the times of ignorance – *jahiliyya*. As

---

[1] Patricia Crone, 1987, *Meccan Trade and the Rise of Islam*, Princeton NJ, Princeton University Press
[2] A. Jeffery, *Prolegomena*, p4

such to Muslim historians[1] it was not worthy of remembering or recording: if a reference was made it was interpreted through their 'Muslim' eyes — a fact, Jeffery laments on a number of occasions.[2] This has also impacted Qur'anic exegesis with the result that exegetes have not been able to explain some of the terms and references which the Prophet used and which were obviously understood by those with whom he interacted. Still the question remains: Can person's life, attitudes, accomplishments and work be understood without exploring the context in which it arose? Jeffery, it would appear, did not believe so. Yet for Jeffery while there was a spread of scholarship on Islam of which he was eminently aware – his knowledge would appear almost encyclopaedic - he was also aware of its limitations. It would also seem that Jeffery, in his notes, has borrowed extensively from others. At the same time, it would also appear that he has well documented his sources. For Jeffery there were still many questions which he believed needed to be explored or which at that time had no answers.

Jeffery's approach, then, is essentially an examination of the past to understand primarily the cultic features of Islam as it has emerged. Today, however, studies on Islam and women including genital mutilation, slavery, the place of magic, the Prophet's ascetic tendencies and tribal politics are some of the issues that would also benefit from an examination of past roots. There are hints of some of these in his notes but Jeffery does not explore them.

Certainly, during Jeffery's life there were both World Wars with their disruptions to life and also to scholarship as well as being a stimulus for many worldwide political changes, including the resurgence of Islam. Indeed, since Jeffery's day, scholarship relating

---

[1] The Islamic understanding of history includes hagiography as well as a number of biographical genres many of which have arisen in association with the development of the Hadith. Cf 'Biography and Hagiography', Islamicus.org and 'Hagiographic Literature', iranicaonline.org sited 20 September, 2018

[2] Volker Popp also notes this in his article, 'The Early History of Islam, Following Inscriptional and Numistamic Testimony', pp17-124 in *The Hidden Origins of Islam* ed Karl-Heinz Ohlig and Gerd-R Puin, New York, Prometheus Books, 2010.
Stephen Humphreys in *"Islamic History: A Framework for Inquiry"* rev ed., Princeton, Princeton University Press, 1991, devotes his Chap 3 to this issue.

to Islam has taken many different paths.[1] More recently the rise of terrorism, with its claimed origin to be within the fold of Islam has given rise to a greater interest in Islam and Islamic studies, though that tide may be waning.

PEOPLES and LANGUAGE

It must also be remembered that Jeffery was a scholar of his time and generation. Since that time, such issues as political correctness, especially in terms of use of words, gender issues and questions of racism and racial discrimination have become important issues with their own implications. This is most significant when it comes to dealing with issues in the Middle East and especially the question of the use of the term 'Semitic'. Some consider that the word was originally coined to be discriminatory though it could be argued that it was meant as a descriptive and classificatory term to identify people living within the geographical area of the Middle East sharing languages that appeared to be related. The term is still used largely in this linguistic sense as is reflected in the *Journal of Semitic Studies* which focuses primarily on issues related to the Semitic languages. That group of languages includes Ugaritic, Arabic, Hebrew, Syriac to name just a few. The questions, which naturally arise from this, are who are the people who speak this group of languages, where do they live, have they always lived where they are based now, and what changes have taken place in this language group over time? These were questions, that Jeffery, from his time and in the cultural milieu in which he lived attempted to answer from the scholarship that was then available.

The issue of language also includes with it a question of people grouping: — be it at a level of clan, tribe, ethnic cluster, community, or population or what has been termed race. The question of racial groupings is a difficult one, especially since the

---

[1] Stephen R. Humphreys, "Islamic History: A Framework for Inquiry", rev. ed., Princeton NJ, Princeton University Press, 1991, is 'a practical guide to the bibliography and research skills required for productive work in this area', pix; though dated it is a valuable resource. Michael Cook and Patricia Crone in "Hagarism; The Making of the Islamic World", Cambridge, Cambridge University Press, 1977 attempted to recreate the development of Islam using non-Arabic sources. "Crossroads to the Study of Islam", Yehuda D. Nevo and Judith Koren, New York, Prometheus Books, 2003, also critically examines a wide range of traditional interpretations.

means for classification in the past have revolved around mainly physically observable features such as the colour of a person's skin, facial features including hair types and cultural practices including language and perhaps to a much lesser degree on a particular worldview. Historically, it would seem that physically distinguishable groups were located in particular geographical spaces which in turn influenced and were reflected in their culture and their interpretation of the world around them. With the discovery of the human DNA and the resultant human genome research, the question of 'race' is now being explored from that perspective though that too is thwart with accusations of potential racial discrimination. Current research on the question using genome research would claim that 'Indigenous Arabs are descendants of the earliest split from ancient Eurasian populations'[1]. That research suggests that the "Arabian Peninsula was the initial site of the out-of-Africa migrations that occurred between 125,000 and 60,000 yr [sic] ago".[2] While that scholarship points to an African origin for the indigenous Arabs one notes that it appears to have been done on a relatively small sample. The study is also based on a number of presumptions that at this stage have the backing of the current state of scientific studies. However, it also needs to be acknowledged that there are 'still gaps of understanding' and who knows what future studies may bring to light. On the other hand, the question still arises — What is the relationship between the Arabs as a people and the Semitic language? However, in terms of current Islamic studies it would appear that such questions as to the origins of the Arabs and their language attracted only limited interest.[3] Given Jeffery's focus it is not surprising that he asks the questions 'who are the Arabs' and 'where is Arabia?'

To answer these questions Jeffery refers to ancient sources, mostly non-Muslim and notes that the word 'Arabia' previously

---

[1] "Indigenous Arabs are descendants of the earliest split from ancient Eurasian populations", Juan L Rodriguez-Flores, Khalid Fakhro, Francisco Agosto-Perez et al, Genome Res, 2016 Feb;26(2):151-62. doi: 10.1101/gr.191478.115. Epub 2016 Jan 4; National Centre for Biotechnology Information,
 https://pubmed.ncbi.nlm.nih.gov/26728717/, cited 20 July 2020
[2] Juan L Rodriguez-Flores, Khalid Fakhro, Francisco Agosto-Perez et al - Abstract
[3] Humphreys "Islamic History" makes no reference to these two issues.

applied to a much wider geographical area in contrast to the present day where it is more limited to the Arabian Peninsula, today's Saudi Arabia. The designation 'Arabia' apparently was descriptive of those areas where 'Arabs' were living. Understanding what constituted Arabia does provide insight into possible reasons for the early advancement of Islam in the Middle Eastern area.

Jeffery indicates that the term 'Arab' means 'bedouin – nomad'. He notes that their earliest mention appears to be in an Assyrian inscription dating from about 800BC. Naturally, the question that also arises is 'what language do they speak?' While the answer might appear obvious, *Arabic,* the question of the origin of *Arabic* becomes more complex since Arabic belongs to the Semitic group of languages. From Jeffery's analysis, there appear to be three primary areas where the Semitic languages have been located: one in what was North Arabia, covering much of the area known as the fertile crescent; the second 'Peninsula Arabia' extending from the Mediterranean to the Arabian Sea and the third area in what is currently Ethiopia in Africa. However, many maps including that found on Encyclopaedia Britannica website also has the Semitic language grouping spreading across the North of Africa, a fact of which Jeffery is also aware. One current study on the Semitic languages claims:

> The origin of Semitic and the nature of dispersals by Semitic-speaking populations are of great importance to our understanding of the ancient history of the Middle East and Horn of Africa. Semitic populations are associated with the oldest written languages and urban civilizations in the region, which gave rise to some of the world's first major religious and literary traditions.[1]

Obviously, then the question of the Semitic language of which Arabic is a part is still an important issue and one that is still being explored, though perhaps not with the intensity and fervour that marked the studies by various scholars at the end of the 19th and

---

[1] "Bayesian phylogenetic analysis of Semitic languages identifies an Early Bronze Age origin of Semitic in the Near East", Andrew Kitchen and Christopher Ehret et al, Proc Biol Sci. 2009 Aug 7; 276(1668): 2703–2710, Published online 2009 Apr 29, doi: 10.1098/rspb.2009.0408, PMCID: PMC2839953; PMID: 19403539

the beginning of the 20th centuries. In his discussion of the development of the Semitic language, the scholarship of his day had varying suggestions based on various studies that were then available. These included Turkestan, Mesopotamia, Africa and Arabia. Even Jeffery acknowledged that some of those studies had their weaknesses and were far from conclusive. In the study mentioned above, Kitchen and Ehret

> ... estimate an Early Bronze Age origin for Semitic approximately 5750 years ago in the Levant, and further propose that contemporary Ethiosemitic languages of Africa reflect a single introduction of early Ethiosemitic from southern Arabia approximately 2800 years ago.[1]

Jeffery's study though is not simply concerned with issues of language. He also examines a number of cultural practices such as divorce, blood revenge[2] and plagiarism that are common among this particular group who share a similar language background. He highlights these issues for they have found their way, in a variety of expressions, into current Islamic practice.

Jeffery also spends a significant amount of his study in relation to the ethnic origins of the area especially identifying various historical migrations. He suggests that these were precursors to those which occurred after the death of the Prophet, initiating the spread of Islam. From the scholarship available at that time, he identified six migrations: The Semitico-Hamitic;[3] the Babylonian; Amoritic; Canaanitish or Aramean; Nabataean and the South Arabian into Abyssinia. This latter migration helps to give credence to the Prophet's action of sending some of his followers there for their safety. In focusing on this South Arabian migration, it gives Jeffery the opportunity to examine some of their customs: — marriage, traditions and law — particularly in terms of their impact on Islamic practices. Jeffery also suggests that this

---

[1] Andrew Kitchen and Christopher Ehret et al
[2] Ed. Note: Some writers use the term blood feud.
[3] Ed. Note: The term 'Hamitic' was derived from the name of one of Noah's sons who is referred to in a 'table of nations' found in the Bible. (Gen 10) In an earlier incident, Ham's actions (Gen 9:22) resulted in a curse which even to this present day has influenced attitudes toward African nations. Because of the negative connotations associated with the word, it is rarely used now.

relationship with Abyssinian can possibly account for words of Ethiopic origin that have found their way into the Qur'an.

Current studies would confirm that over the ages, human beings have migrated across the face of the earth. However, it seems that most of the studies at present are more concerned with the 'long distant' migrations of various humanoid groups than with migrations within the smaller area of the Middle East. That human migration has occurred within the Middle East is fairly certain with various forms of evidence confirming the proposition, though it does not appear to be a focus of study at the present. Jeffery postulates some of the reasons for these migrations. The primary one is that of the 'drying' of the Arabian Peninsula causing both economic and population pressures which forced Arab tribes to move beyond their 'homeland'. It was these movements, Jeffery postulates which gave rise to Arab dynasties in areas distant from Peninsula Arabia.

THE STRUCTURE of the PROLEGOMENA

Jeffery's *Prolegomena* lecture notes follow an ordered structure with main sections, subsections and at times further subpoints. His first section outlines the "Physical Background" to which he adds a section on "Trade Routes". Since Jeffery wrote, further studies on the role of the trade routes, especially those associated with numismatic evidence, have provided interesting insights while others have raised questions as to its importance.[1] Early sources suggest that both the Roman and Greek Civilizations were aware of the trade routes that wended their way through, or was it around the Arabian Peninsula.[2] One of his outlines also mentioned climate as well as flora and fauna but they do not appear in this set of notes.

While the geo-political world in which Jeffery lived and which was impacted by both World Wars has changed considerably

---

[1] Patricia Crone, *Meccan Trade and the Rise of Islam*, Princeton NJ, Princeton University Press, 1987 would suggest that the role of trade has been overplayed. She also questions the extent to which the Prophet was a travelling merchant.
[2] cf. "The Chronology of Roman Trade in the Indian Ocean from Augustus to Early Third Century CE", Matthew Cobb, *Journal of the Economic and Social History of the Orient,* Vol. 58, No. 3 (2015), pp. 362-418

since those times, the natural features of mountains, valleys, rivers — the temporary ones of an arid environment — the deserts of rock and sand have changed little. Though, as mentioned earlier, the extent of the desert does appear to have increased over the centuries. Still, it is even these physical features that have largely determined the lifestyle of the Arabs, necessitating their wandering lifestyle with its dependence on camels and horses. Since opportunities for agriculture are minimal, foraging for the basic necessities requires constant moving. For Jeffery, the question of climate change was a real one and over historical time Jeffery could suggest that it has been impacting not only the Arabian Peninsula but the 'greater Arab area' as well.

More interestingly, Jeffery refers to various ruins which dot the desert landscape. Some of these have provided archaeological evidence of the times that have passed. However, while Jeffery's resources were limited, there is a growing body of various forms of archaeological evidence which can be studied.[1] Of this, Humphreys writes,

> 'Islamic archaeology ... has not as yet made the contributions of historical studies which we might hope for.',

he concludes that section with this comment

> 'In any case, there is obviously a rich and rapidly growing fund of archaeological data and interpretation for those historians who are prepared to learn how to use it.'[2]

Yehuda and Koren have an extensive section within their book that deals with 'religious inscriptions in Classical Arabic' (p297-335) with an extensive appendix of this material (p365- 425) but the material they reference is essentially 'post-Islam'. Humphreys does not refer to any of the earlier inscriptions to which Jeffery makes reference. A

---

[1] Though the title is somewhat exaggerated, the article, 'Before Islam: When Saudi Arabia Was a Jewish Kingdom' refers to a recent inscription found in rocks not far from Najran which was a known centre of Jewish and Christian populations. Haaretz Com. Archaeology, https://www.haaretz.com/archaeology/.premium-before-islam-when-saudi-arabia-was-a-jewish-kingdom-1.5626227 cited 3 Aug. 2020.
[2] Humphreys, p63 and p65

more recent work by Robert G. Royland, "Arabia and the Arabs: From the Bronze Age to the Coming of Islam" which covers many of the topics covered by Jeffery's *Prolegomena* has made extensive use of the advance in archeological finds and the interpretation of inscriptions which were not available to Jeffery.[1]

Ethnological Background

Jeffery's next section, and the one that these days is possibly the most controversial and which we have already briefly discussed, is where he deals with what he calls the "Ethnological Background". In this section he attempts to identify the Arabs which leads to questions relating to the origin of Semitic stock and the spread of the Semitic language as well as some of the Semitic cultural practices. This is followed by the section on Historical Migrations to which reference has already been made.

Historical Background

Following on from those sections Jeffery examines the "Historical Background". This section covers a number of varied topics, including those 'empires' that predate the Prophet in Arabia itself. To begin, he surveys Muslim sources available to him. For Muslim scholars, since this material belonged to the days before Islam or as they understand it 'the times of ignorance', it seems as though there was little incentive for exploratory study for the Prophet's aim was to 'restore the true Abrahamic religion'. Interestingly now, there are a growing number of scholars from a Muslim/Arabic background who are exploring some of these issues. For this section Jeffery's aim was to go back to original, ancient sources both Muslim and non-Muslim, a fact verified in Lingel's article and reflected in Jeffery's references. However, Jeffery rarely identifies in detail which of these early resources he was using, though a search of the materials housed at Columbia University may well identify the physical copies, since Jeffery deliberately endeavoured to obtain such resources. While Jeffery (and others) clearly recognise the limitations of the historical accounts of the early Muslim writers, he also on occasions refers to them. Nevo and Koren, however, would question the treatment of

---

[1] Robert G Royland, "Arabia and the Arabs: From the Bronze Age to the Coming of Islam, London, Routledge, 2001

such Muslim resources by western scholars[1] suggesting that most do so uncritically.

Arabian Civilizations

Following the overview of the ancient empires that existed on the Arabian Peninsula he explores the later Arab Kingdoms which arose in various parts of 'Arabia'. In investigating these South Arabian civilizations, he notes in some detail their incursions further north into the Mecca and Medina areas which would have ultimately impacted the Prophet's understanding of the past, his interpretation of the then present and guided his thinking regarding the future and shaped his understanding of the revelations he received. Jeffery then demonstrates how the migration of these South Arabians northward were instrumental in the creation of some of the dynasties that rose and fell in North Arabia.

The six ancient South Arabian kingdoms to which Jeffery refers are: the Minaean Kingdom that appears to date from between the sixth to the fourth Century BCE[2]; the Sabaean Kingdom which is often considered as the home of the Queen of Sheba of King Solomon fame (cf. Bible-I Kings 10:1, approximate dates 970-930 BCE); the Himyaritic; Katabanian (Qatabanian); Hadhramaut and Geban. More recently Andrey Korotayev and Kenneth Kitchen[3] have done further research on the Minaean and Sabaean Kingdoms and would suggest that their history and their use of terminology is more complex than Jeffery has suggested.[4] There appears to have been some more recent studies on the Himyaritic and Katabanian Kingdoms but there seems to be no further information on either the Hadhramaut or Geban Kingdoms. On the other hand it would seem that another kingdom, Awsan, has also been identified in that area[5].

---

[1] Nevo & Koren, p1ff
[2] Ed. Note. Some estimates would suggest that this kingdom was much earlier.
[3] Andrey Korotayev, "Ancient Yemen", Oxford: Oxford University Press, 1995 and "Pre-Islamic Yemen" Wiesbaden: Harrassowitz Verlag, 1996.
Kenneth A. Kitchen: The World of Ancient Arabia Series. Documentation for Ancient Arabia. Part I. Chronological Framework & Historical Sources. Liverpool, 1994
[4] Andrey Korotayev p2-5
[5] 'The Art of Himyar and the Mountain Kingdoms of Yemen', Professor Lily Filson of Tulane University, New Orleans. Spring 2018.

Humphreys makes no reference to this kingdom in his work. For Jeffery the importance of these kingdoms is varied. With the Sabaean there are not only suggestions of trade but in the section on religious influences he details many of their beliefs and practices. The Himyaritic Kingdom is important, for during this time, Abyssinian, Christian and Jewish influences had significant impact in that Yemeni area and beyond. Recent archeological exploration is adding to the information available regarding that influence.[1]

However, it was from about 570CE onwards the area came under Persian influence. The consequences of that Persian influence are still impacting life in those areas today and represents one of the underlying factors in the early 21st century conflict between Saudi Arabia and Yemen. Yet Jeffery sums up his exploration of these early kingdoms with this comment,

> the full significance of this South Arabian civilization has yet to be fully estimated. As we will see in our further studies, bands of these southern Arabs, owing to the decline of the prosperity of South Arabia, migrated in pre-Islamic times into various parts of the Arabian Peninsula ... had a very important share in the development of pre-Islamic Arabia. Their religion, also, ... had a profound influence on the religion of the Arabs.[2]

Having discussed the South Arabian Civilizations, Jeffery then focuses on the various Arab dynasties that rose to prominence in various locations outside peninsula Arabia. He begins with a study of Palmyra (Tadmor) with its famous ruler Zenobia.[3] Jeffery notes that

> The one important thing to note is that the story of this way, where the peasants of Syria and Palestine fought with enthusiasm on the side of Aurelius, shows clearly that the Palmyra's empire was that of a small Arab aristocracy

---

https://filsonarthistory.wordpress.com/2018/03/07/13-the-art-of-himyar-and-the-mountain-kingdoms-of-yemen/ cited 13 August, 2020

[1] Ahmad Al-Jallad, "Jesus in Arabia: Tracing the Spread of Christianity into the Desert,' pp40-46, *Biblical Archeological Review,* vol 48, no 1, Spring 2022.

[2] Jeffery, *Prolegomena*, p67

[3] An interesting article on Zenobia can be found in the Ancient History Encyclopaedia, https://www.ancient.eu/static/about/ cited 30 July, 2020

dominating a quiet, peaceable, peasant population, despising them with true Bedouin contempt of agriculturists and heartily hated by them in turn.[1]

Jeffery then refers to two other rulers, one from the clan of Sahil and another Jadhima. Of the former there appears little new information while that regarding Jadhima varies. As Jeffery portrays him, he is of South Arabian descent which some scholars would question. Of greater significance though was the growth and development of the town of Hira from about the third century CE. This led to the rise of the Lakhmid dynasty that controlled an area encompassing the Euphrates for a significant period of time including the early years of the Prophet's preaching. He also comments on the Ghassan and Kinda empires. The former was a Christian Arab dynasty which stretched from about Damascus in the north to the Sinai Peninsula in the south and generally supported the Byzantines. Of the Kinda Kingdom little is known though it was located in Central Arabia, extending its control as far as the Persian Gulf. However, it was possibly one of the first attempts to unite a number of disparate Arab tribes and no doubt one on which the Prophet was able to build. It too was founded by Arabs who had migrated from the South and were also considered Christians. Humphreys also does not mention them. More recently an article by Michael Lecker examines in some details the tribal constitution around the Kinda 'Ridda'.[2]

Surrounding Empires

This is followed by a study of the Empires of the surrounding areas: Byzantine, Sasanian and Abyssinian as well as an excursus into an extensive section that he entitled 'Primitive Tribes'. Given the political correctness of current times, the expression Indigenous or Original or even Pre-Islamic Tribes would be preferred. Essentially these are tribal groups, or Legendary Peoples as Jeffery refers to them in another outline, that are mentioned in the Qur'an. Many of them, the Prophet claimed, had perished because they failed to respond to the message of a prophet who had been sent to warn

---

[1] Jeffery, *Prolegomena* p72
[2] Michael Lecker, 'Kinda on the Eve of Islam and during the "Ridda"', *Journal of the Royal Asiatic Society*, Third Series, Vol. 4, No. 3 (Nov, 1994), pp. 333-356

them. Obviously though, knowledge of these tribal groups was still part of the living memory or at least part of the oral history of those who were listening to the Prophet. While these tribes form part of the Arabic tradition, Jeffery notes that outside of that tradition they are basically unknown. He refers primarily to 'Ad and Thamud as well as a number of lesser tribes.

Pre-Islamic Tribal Organisation

He then discusses in some detail the nature of what could be derived from the then current state of scholarship on the Pre-Islamic Tribal Organisation. This includes a consideration of a possible earlier matriarchal system which included both polyandry and a form of contract wives. Jeffery also explores a possible totemistic organisation which may account for many of the 'animal' tribal names, references to animal worship and some of the food taboos that have found their way into current Islamic practice.

Since the prophet was a Quraish, Jeffery examines what historical evidence there was for their importance. He dismisses the Abraham-Ishmael connection as legendary, noting that the form of their names is not of Arabic origin. He also examines the Quraish's role as the 'protectors' of the Ka'ba. This gives rise to an exploration of idol worship and the various deities that were part of Arabian worship, though that is dealt with in further detail in the section on Religion. This leads Jeffery to spend some time on considering Mecca, though the knowledge of its early history is limited. Doubts still remain as to its reference in early works. Its religious importance, Jeffery suggests, relates to its association with astronomical worship, the importance of the Ka'ba and that it (was) is a site of pilgrimage. Of the limited number of recent resources that I have surveyed, except for the reference to various idols and explorations into the possible origin of the word 'Allah', most of the material Jeffery mentioned is not included and much of it was new to me.

Religious Background

Possibly the largest section of these lecture notes is that covering the Religious Background. First Jeffery deals with Arabian Paganism in some detail – in so doing, he no doubt will arouse the ire of many Muslims. His first concern is to examine what evidence there is for developing an understanding of religious practices prior to the emergence of Islam. Jeffery looks at evidence from inscriptions, classical authors, the Talmud, the Qur'an, pre-Islamic literature, current Islamic practice and philology. This is followed by an examination in some detail of the types of religion suggested by those sources, which include a more detailed study of astrologically, totemically, Euhemerism and monotheistic religious evidence. He notes that the incorporation of 'stones' into religious ritual appears to be an accepted early practice which may have its association with blood smearing and worship associated with sacrifice. Jeffery also explores in some detail the issue of the 'Hanif', noting that the prophet's emphasis on monotheism did not arise within a vacuum.

The next section, which for some would be controversial, is an examination of current Islamic practices that appear to be expressions of various forms of pre-Islamic paganism. Not surprisingly this is a fairly detailed section covering such topics as sacrifices, the 'aqiqa' ceremony, the sacred stones (the black stone of the Ka'ba and the three pillars in the valley of Mina), the concept of 'haram' in relation to a place, pilgrimages and festivals. Another area that Jeffery explores for pre-Islamic influences is the Prophet's understanding of eschatology which includes the future life, belief in angels including jinn, prophecy (soothsaying), magic and cosmology. The mention of magic is an interesting one, for it has a significant place in Sufi-type, popular practices but is disputed and denied by those holding a more orthodox interpretation of Islam. He concludes this section by references to the month of fasting, practices of prayer and food regulations.

His final subsection within this section is an overview of the significant religions known at the time. In discussing Sabianism he includes excurses into the Mandaeans, Harranians and Elkesites[1]. He then examines in greater detail aspects of the Sabaean religion including its astronomical orientation, totemism, sacrificial system, pilgrimages and temples. His next consideration is Zoroastrianism. He first outlines its development before reflecting on its dualism, its understanding of revelation. However, it is aspects of its eschatology

---

[1] Humphreys makes no mention of these

such as *houris*, bridge *sirat*, *mi'raj* and what may have influenced what is now termed the 'light of Muhammad' in greater detail.

Interestingly Jeffery's section on Judaism is surprisingly brief given the many references to Jews in the Qur'an and their opposition to the prophet's teaching. He notes that Jewish sources have Jews moving to Arabia after the destruction of Jerusalem in 70CE though those in what is Yemen today, he suggests, may have come via Egypt. Interestingly, Jeffery notes that names of the 'Jews', as recorded in Arabic sources from the Medina area, were Arabic in form, which raises the question as to whether they were Judaised Arabs rather than Jews who had migrated. Jeffery also notes that these Jews seemed to be more acquainted with the Talmud rather than the Jewish scriptures. Perhaps one of the reasons for the brevity is that Jeffery notes that information is complicated and in his day knowledge about them in Arabia was limited. Berkey, in his *The Formation of Islam*, notes that information about the Jews of that time is still limited but deals with the question from a different, but also informative perspective, from that of Jeffery's.[1] Humphrey's references to the Jews primarily relate to the time of the Prophet and afterwards.

The final section deals with Christianity. Jeffery indicates sources regarding the early origins of Christianity in the area are also limited and to use his word 'obscure'. Jeffery begins by attempting to identify the ways in which Christianity entered the area and how it spread and the possible impact of its spread. By the time of the Prophet, Christianity was characterised by various theological debates mainly revolving around questions concerning the nature of Christ in relation to his divinity and humanity. These debates were identified by the particular emphasis proposed, such as monophysite and/or by the name of the particular church father, for example Nestorius, who was espousing a particular interpretation.

These debates were primarily ecclesiastical. However, from the time Constantine formally accepted Christianity as a religion

---

[1] Jonathan P Berkey, *The Formation of Islam, Religion and Society in the Near East, 600-1800,* Cambridge, Cambridge University Press, 2003, pp10-19

and then from the time of Theodosius I whose adoption of Nestorian Christianity associated it with the Byzantine Empire, these debates entered the political arena. Consequently, during this period many church councils were called, usually with the backing of the Emperor who often appears to have supported a particular interpretation. Interpretations not accepted by the council were considered heresies and, in some cases outlawed by the Emperor, often resulting in the persecution of those whose views were not accepted. Almost simultaneously there was the rise of aesthetic Christianity which took various forms, including the development of monasteries and convents. Some individuals adopted extreme forms of a disciplined lifestyle, either living in the desert and/or caves while becoming recognised as spiritual guides and informers. One of them was Simeon the Stylite who sat on top of a pillar for most of his life and for whom a church was also built. Practically it would seem that much 'Christian' practice was debased. So called Christian rulers were known for their cruelty and oppression. Generally speaking, there appeared to be a significant lack of knowledge of their Scriptures.[1] So, it is little wonder that the Prophet of Islam sought to restore and reform the 'Christians' he encountered to what he believed was 'true worship'.

In some respects, the lecture notes finish abruptly. There is no conclusion to parallel the introduction nor is there any overall summary with which the notes conclude. Was there meant to be more? That is a question that will remain forever unanswered. In reading through the lecture notes, one has a much firmer grasp of the context out of which Islam grew and which nurtured, formed and also informed the Prophet. Moreover, it was out of that context that Muhammed became the founder of a religion and a political movement that has spread worldwide.

In essence, Jeffery's material is an exploration of the scholarship that was then available and was dependent on the known sources of his day. In referring to those sources his work is in a sense timeless. The interpretations of scholarship can and do change over time. Some modern scholarship would even

---

[1] It would appear that the form of the Bible with its 39 Old Testament books and 27 New Testament books was known by about 400CE. The degree to which it was available as a 'unit' and the extent to which it was circulated are still uncertain.

question the existence of a 'Muhammed' as the Prophet of Islam.[1] While the word 'amd' (meaning 'most praised one') appears in the Qur'an four times Durie notes that in the context it appears more as a title than a personal name.[2] Studies into the development of the Qur'an and its text have seen the introduction of a computer programme providing extensive material on variant readings within the text as well as having concordance type capabilities.[3] Women in Islam is another area that has seen a growth in studies. The rise of Islamic terrorist groups and the ISIS movement have led to a focus on Islamic studies, especially political Islam, while others are exploring the great diversity of regional expressions of Islam.

Still, as Jeffery notes, the exploration into 'Arabia: pre-Islam' has much scope for research. Hopefully this edition will prompt further studies in this area as well as providing for others a foundation for an understanding of the Prophet and his message.

Ruth J. Nicholls

---

[1] Yehuda D. Nevo and Judith Koren, *Crossroads to Islam: The Origins of the Arab Religions and the Arab State,*, Amherst, Prometheus Books, 2003, p11.

[2] Mark Durie, 'Problems with the Qur'an Origin Story' in *Understanding and Answering Islam,* April 2017, Melbourne, ed. Ruth Nicholls, Melbourne, MST Press, 2018, pp45-63, p48

[3] "The Qur'an Gateway", The leader on the website reads, "A world of Qur'anic research and analysis at your fingertips. Explore a powerful tool for the critical study of the Qur'anic text and its early manuscripts. With advanced search functions and a simple-to-use interface, Qur'an Gateway empowers your analysis of Islam's founding text."

Bibliography

Berkey, Jonathan P,
The Formation of Islam, Religion and Society in the Near East, 600-1800, Cambridge, Cambridge University Press, 2003

Brown, Daniel W.
A New Introduction to Islam, 2nd ed., Chichester, Wiley-Blackwell, 2009

Humphreys, R. Stephen,
Islamic History: A Framework for Inquiry, rev. ed., Princeton NJ, Princeton University Press, 1991

Kitchen, Andrew and Christopher Ehret et al
"Bayesian phylogenetic analysis of Semitic languages identifies an Early Bronze Age origin of Semitic in the Near East", *Proc Biol Sci.* 2009 Aug 7; 276(1668): 2703–2710., 2009, Published online 2009 Apr 29, doi:10.1098/rspb.2009.0408, PMCID:PMC2839953; PMID:19403539, https://www.ncbi.nlm.nih.gov/pmc/articles/PMC2839953/ cited 20 July, 2020

Lingel, Joshua,
nd, *Arthur Jeffery Memorial*, An Essay submitted to Dr. Geoffery King, School of Oriental and African Studies, University of London, unpublished document

Nevo, Yehuda D and Judith Koren,
Crossroads to Islam: The Origins of the Araba Religion and the Arab State, New York, Prometheus Books, 2003

Rodriguez-Flores, Juan L, Khalid Fakhro, Francisco Agosto-Perez et al
"Indigenous Arabs are descendants of the earliest split from ancient Eurasian populations", Genome Res,2016 Feb;26(2):151-62. doi: 10.1101/gr.191478.115. Epub 2016 Jan 4.; National Centre for Biotechnology Information, 2016,

https://pubmed.ncbi.nlm.nih.gov/26728717/, cited 20 July, 2020

Whitehouse, Aubrey,
    Do you remember ...? Recollections, Reflections and Valuable Insights, Melbourne, MST Press, 2017

Additional Reference Materials:
Brockopp, Jonathan E., ed.,
    The Cambridge Companion to Muhammad, Cambridge, Cambridge University Press, 2010

Crone, Patricia,
    Meccan Trade and the Rise of Islam, Princeton NJ, Princeton, University Press, 1987

Crone, Patrician & Michael Cook
    Hagarism: The Making of the Islamic World, Cambridge, Cambridge University Press, 1977

Donner, Fred. M
    Muhammad and the Believers, At the Origins of Islam, Cambridge, Belknap Press (Harvard University Press), 2010, (includes an easy read section of the Byzantine and Sasanian Empires)

Fisher, Greg
    Kingdoms or Dynasties? Arabs, History, and Identity before Islam, *Journal of Late Antiquity; Baltimore* Vol.4, Iss.2, (Fall): 245-267, 2011.

Hitti, Philip K.,
    History of the Arabs: From the Earliest Times to the Present, sixth ed., London, Macmillan & Co., 1958

Hoyland, Robert G.,
    Arabia and the Arabs: From the Bronze Age to the Coming of Islam, London, Routledge, 2001

Ibrahim Mumayiz,

'Imru' al-Qays and Byzantium', *Journal of Arabic Literature*, Vol. 36, No. 2005, 135-151

Kennedy, Hugh,
The Prophet and the Age of the Caliphates: Islamic Near East from the Sixth of the Eleventh Century, London, Longman, 1986. (Deals with the economic conditions, trade and empire relations)

Kitchen, Kenneth A., "Hagarism: The Making of the Islamic World", *The World of Ancient Arabia Series. Documentation for Ancient Arabia: Part I. Chronological Framework & Historical Sources*, Liverpool, Liverpool University Press, 1994

Korotayev, Andrey
Ancient Yemen, Oxford: Oxford University Press, 1995
Pre-Islamic Yemen, Wiesbaden: Harrassowitz Verlag, 1996

Küng, Hans
Islam: Past, Present and Future, Trans John Bowden, Oxford, Oneworld, 2007. (gives an introduction into geography and empires (pp25-45) and has a section on the religions in the area, especially, Jewish, Christian and Manichaeans (32-45))

Lecker, Michael,
'Kinda on the Eve of Islam during the "Ridda"', *Journal of the Royal Asiatic Society*, Third Series, Vol. 4, No. 3 (Nov.), 1994, pp 333-356

Rippin, Andrew,
Muslims: Their Religious beliefs and Practices, 3rd ed., London, Routledge, 2005. (Asks the question of how to approach the study of Islam)

Shahid, Irfan
"Pre-Islamic Arabia", *The Cambridge History of Islam,* vol 1A, *The Central Islamic lands from Pre-Islamic Times to the*

First World War, Ed P.M. Holt, A.K.S Lambton, B. Lewis, Cambridge, Cambridge Uni Press, 1970, p3-29

Tobi, Yosef,
> The Jews of Yemen in light of the excavation of the Jewish synagogue in Qanī' (poster), *Proceedings of the Seminar for Arabian Studies*, Vol. 43, Papers from the forty-sixth meeting of the Seminar for Arabian Studies held at the British Museum, London, 13 to 15 July 2012 (2013), 2013, pp. 349-356

Prolegomena

to the

Study of Islam

W. Arthur Jeffery

INTRODUCTION

Islam, like Christianity, Buddhism, and Zoroastrianism owes its existence to a personal founder. In the case of none of these historical religions, however, can we take the founder as a starting point for our attempt to understand the significance of the movement, for in every case the movement had its source or sources away back in long antecedent religious conditions. In fact, it may be said that what we find in the founder, is the blossoming forth of a life impulse which had its birth in the far dark past and had for long been growing in intensity and complexity, awaiting the propitious moment for its sudden bursting forth before the eyes of men.[1]

In the case of Christianity, the student hardly needs reminding that through all the long weary history of Israel, the Messianic hope had been fostered, the Messianic ideal progressively purified and defined[2], until at last, after several *ébauches qui avortent*[3], suddenly when *the fullness of the time was come* (τὸ πλήρωμα τοῦ χρόνου)[4] the Incarnation embodied what all those years of yearning had dimly symbolized. The studies of recent years have been gradually leading us to understand how

---

[1] "Les grands mouvements d'idées sont généralement précédés d'une période obscure où, à l'insu de tous, ils se preparent. L'esprit nouveau est en gestation. Il se manifeste par des symptômes que l'on ne comprendra que plus tard, à la lumière des événements. L'âme des temps imminents semble s'essayer d'abord en des ébauches qui avortent. Puis, tout à coup, c'est l'explosion." de Faye, *Gnostiques et Gnosticisme,* Paris, 1913, p 415.

[2] Cf., the section "Die Messianische Hoffnung" in the third edition of Schürer's *Geschichte des Jüdischen Volkes*, ii, p497-556 or the art, *Messiah* by Whitehouse in DCG, ii, p171-179.

[3] Vide Volz, *Jüdische Eschatologie,* p209-210. The pages of Josephus show how one rival Messiah followed another and succeeded in kindling more or less passionate enthusiasm for revolt against Roman authority, and it is interesting to note how the Messianic expectancy travelled to the West. (Angus, *Environment of Early Christianity, p136-139*).

[4] Which naturally reminds one of Philo's πλήρωμα χρηστῶν ἐλπίδων *de Abr.*, 46 (ii, p39).

Christianity was likewise the fruition of the religious strivings of the Graeco-Roman world.[1]

Buddhism and Jainism, again, can only be explained in light of the barren philosophical Brahmanism against which they were movements of revolt,[2] and Zoroastrianism cannot be understood without a knowledge of the matrix of Indo-Iranian polytheism in which it was born.[3] In a word, to understand the growth and success of these religions we need to know the religious milieu in which they were planted.

What is true of these religions is true in a much wider sense of Islam, an eclectic religion which borrowed almost all its religious conceptions and a majority of the elements of its cult from the religious life of its environment.[4] It becomes of first importance, therefore, for the student of Islam to study in some detail the world into which Islam was born. Naturally this study will deal particularly with the religions which were professed in Arabia at the time when Muhammad began his preaching, but it is scarcely less important to study in some detail the physical, ethnological, social and historical conditions of pre-Islamic Arabia. If the preaching of Muhammad be considered the seed, these conditions were the soil, and in this case the soil is of greater importance for this understanding of what grew than the seed. Our purpose in this study then is to examine the soil, to picture the early environment, and when we have painted the background, with its vividly contrasted lights and shadows, it will be evident that Islam more than any other historical religion, is explainable in terms of its early environment.

---

[1] Vide particularly Angus' recent volume *The Mystery Religions and Christianity*, London, 1925.
[2] Farquhar, *Crown of Hinduism*, 1915, p225, p235.
[3] Moulton, *Early Zoroastrianism*, 1913, Lecture ii.
[4] See the writer's art. "Eclecticism in Islam" in *MW*, 1922, vol XII, no.3, July, p230-247. (Currently available at
https://onlinelibrary.wiley.com/doi/10.1111/j.1478-1913.1922.tb01905.x
cited January 2019.)
There is an interesting chart (not at all exhaustive however) in Zwemer's *Arabia, the Cradle of Islam*, 1912, p178 showing the borrowed elements and their sources. Unfortunately, one cannot recommend a more recent study of this subject *The Sources of Islam*, Madras, 1925, Rev. John C Blair.

Our plan will be first to discuss the physical background, the Arabia which was Islam's original home, and then pass to a consideration of the ethnological background, the Arab tribes among whom the new doctrine was first preached. This leads naturally to a consideration of the social conditions of the time and prepares the way for an examination of the political conditions, giving some account of the history up to this period, and the conditions of the great Empires which were politically interested in Arabia when Islam was born and against which Islam as a political and national force had to fight its first battles. Having thus sketched in the great outlines of our picture we are ready to paint in the bright colours by describing in some detail the conflict of religions in the Arabian Peninsula at the time when Muhammad began to preach.

MAP 1: MIDDLE EAST –
POLITICAL GEOGRAPHY 21st CENTURY

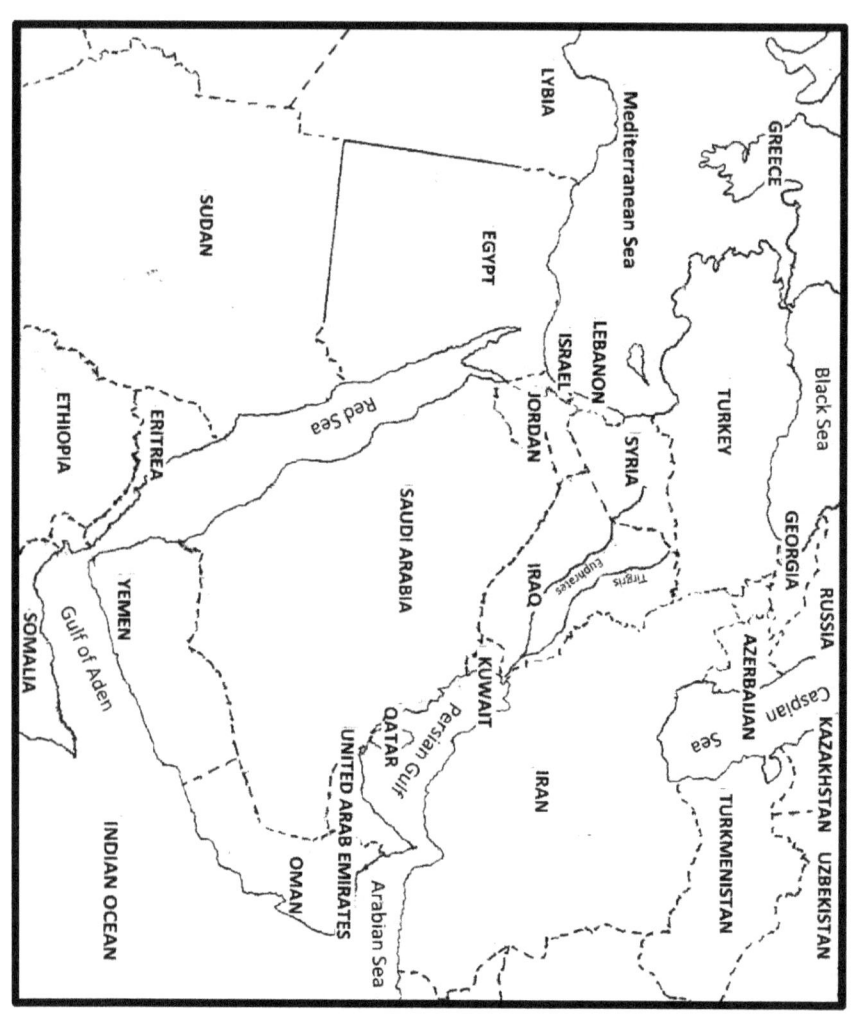

MAP 2: GREEK DIVISIONS OF ARABIA

MAP 3: ARABIA AND ITS REGIONS

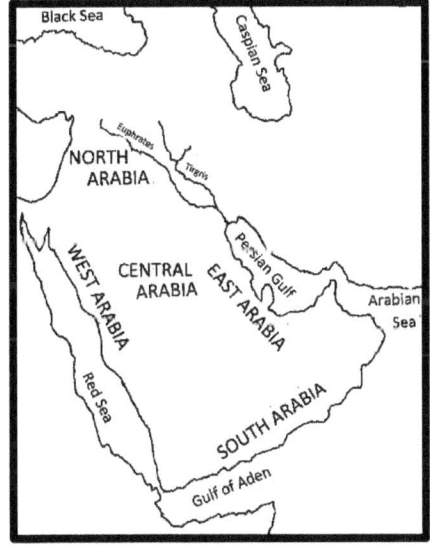

PHYSICAL BACKGROUND

Islam was born in Arabia, and Arabia has ever been its stronghold. Its founder claimed that it was to be a religion of Arabia.[1] Its Holy Book was written in plain Arabic language that the people might understand:[2] its Holy Cities are pre-eminently those in Arabia, and the background of the thinking of early Islam is in the Arabian desert.

It is difficult, however, as Hogarth has pointed out[3], to define exactly what one means by Arabia; for as an historical regional name it has both a wider and a more limited acceptation, and the wider acceptation may be of varying widths. Dealing with it however, as the physical background of Islam, we need to take in a fairly wide acceptation, and include the northern apex between Syria and Mesopotamia, as well as the actual peninsula, the Jazirat-al-'Arab.

Ancient Arabs appear not to have recognised any definite scheme of geographical division in their country, dividing it simply according to the names which had grown customary in different parts,[4] e.g. the desert of Najd[5] in the midst, the Hijaz overlooking the Red Sea, the Jauf and Yemauna in the Northwest and the Yemen and Hadramaut in the South.

The Greek geographers divided it into three parts:[6]

---

[1] Vide, Hurgronje, *The Moslem World of Today*, 1925, ed. Mott, pp81,82.
[2] Sura xii.1.
[3] *Arabia*, 1922, p1. Lammens, however, denies that there is any geographical, physical or ethnographical unity; and calls the term *Arabia* 'une abstraction fallacieuse' *Berceau*, 1914, p9. Even if this is so it need not prevent us from using the term as a convenient appellation for the entity, even if only a logical one, which we desire to study as a background of [Islam].
[4] cf. Cheikho, *L'Histoire du Christianisme dans l'Arabie pré-islamique*, Beirut, 1912, p4
[5] alt. spelling Nejd
[6] *Dictionary of Greek and Roman Geography*, (ed. William Smith) 'Arabia'.

MAP 4: PHYSICAL FEATURES OF ARABIA

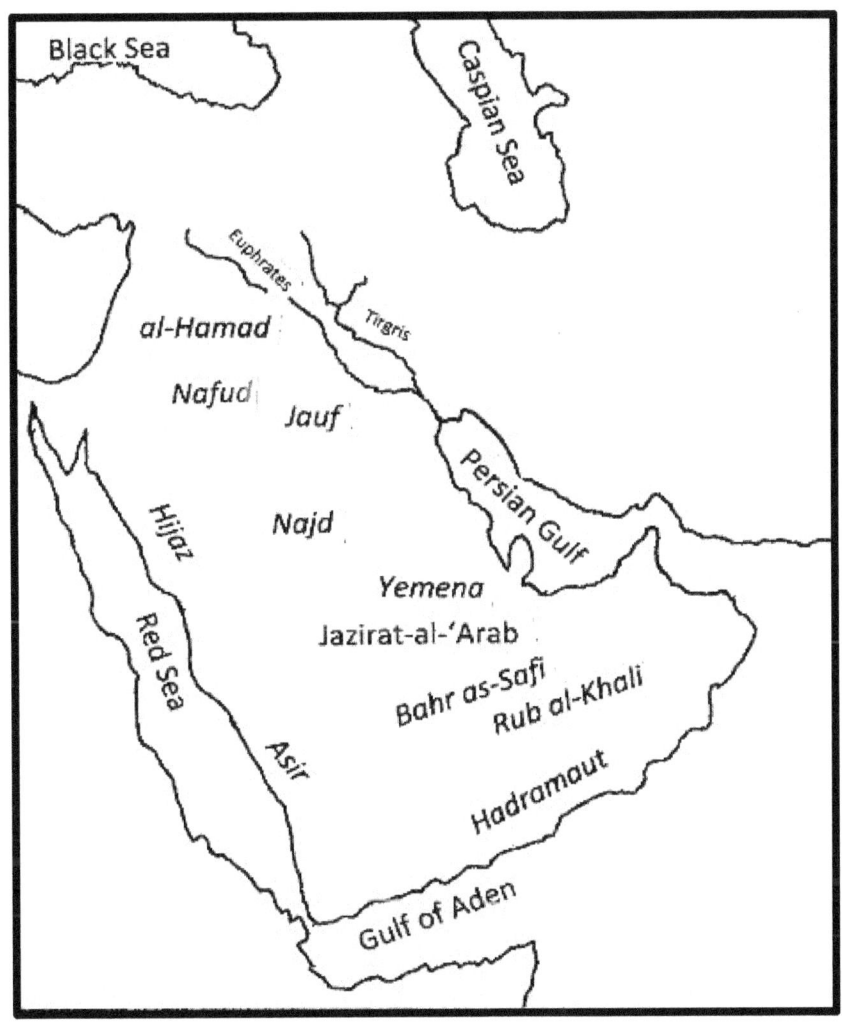

- Arabia Petraea (ἡ πετραία Ἀραβία) including the peninsula of Sinai, the mountain range of Idumaea and the rocky country of Transjordania. It was named from its capital Petra סלע though the sense of 'stony' Arabia came later to be attached to the term.
- Arabia deserta (ἡ ἔρημος Ἀραβία) including the great northern desert between Syria and the Euphrates, with offshoots into Palestine and Central Arabia.
- Arabia Felix (ἡ εὐδαίμων Ἀραβία) which included the rest of the peninsula, but later came to be applied particularly to the fertile region of Yemen.

A more practical division is the more modern one into five great parts[1].

(i)   North Arabia, i.e. the territory bordering on Syria and Palestine, bounded on the north by the Anti-Lebanons and stretching across from Sinai to the head waters of the Lebanons. It is mostly of the nature of calcareous steppe land interspersed with hills. This is the Hamad.[2]

(ii)   West Arabia, or the Hejaz[3] and Asir, which as containing the Holy Cities, Mecca and Medina, is the best-known sector of Arabia, stretches along the Red Sea coast from the Gulf of 'Aqaba

---

[1] The division into seven provinces – Hejaz, Yemen, Hadramaut, 'Oman, Hasa, 'Irak, and Nejd, - found in many books, is merely a concession to political geography.

[2] Ed. note: While Jeffery had intended to add a footnote, the information was not included. The following has been adapted from the 'Syrian Desert', Wikipaedia (January 2019). The Hamad or al-Hamad is considered one of the world's largest desert areas covering some 500,000 square kilometers (200,000 square miles) of the Middle East, including parts of south-eastern Syria, northeastern Jordan, northern Saudi Arabia, and western Iraq. The desert is bounded by the Orontes Valley and volcanic field of Harrat al-Shamah to the west, and by the Euphrates to the east. In the north, the desert gives way to the more fertile areas of grass, and the south it runs into the deserts of the Arabian Peninsula.
Some sources equate the Syrian Desert with the *"Hamad Desert"*, (https://en.wikipedia,org/wiki/Syrian_Desrt - cite_note-britannica41.9) while others limit the name *Hamad* to the southern central plateau, and a few consider the Hamad to be the whole region and the northern part the *Syrian Desert* .

[3] The name Hejaz (احجاز - the Barrier) really stands for the range separating the coast land (Tihama تهامه) from the plateau (Najd – نجد) but in common parlance stands for the whole area: so Goeje in *EI*, p367.

to the borders of Yemen. It may be divided¹ into three longitudinal areas –

- A dry coastal strip
- A cooler valley
- A hilly strip approaching the character of the central plateau.

Some scholars limit all their enquiry as to the background of [Islam] to this coast area of the Hejaz. Lammens e.g. in his *Berceau* (p10) makes this limitation for the reason that,

> Les habitants du Hijaz seuls ont créé l'Islam: l'élaboration de l'indigente et primitive dogmatique du Qoran constitue leur travail exclusif, reprise en sous-oeuvre at complété par les races conquises.²

Asir, between the Hejaz and Yemen is a more mountainous country and consequently more fertile. Its latest explorer claims to have proved that it is the Biblical "land of Ophir" and the gold coast of antiquity.³

(iii) <u>South Arabia including Yemen and Hadramaut.</u>
Yemen has from time immemorial been famous for its fertility and wealth. It alone abounds in perennial streams which water its fields and groves, which render it worthy of its name Arabia Felix.⁴ It is mostly highland intersected by numerous valleys

---

[1] As by Caetani, *Studi di Storia Orientale,* i, 1911, pp 293-295.
[2] So also, Huart Histoire des Arabes i. p2 "Le Hejaz est le berceau du Mahometisme." Translation by Peter Riddell: "The inhabitants of the Hijaz alone created Islam: the elaboration of the poor and primitive dogmatics of the Qur'an constitutes their exclusive work, taken as a foundation and completed by the conquered races."
[3] B. Moritz Arabien, Hannover, 1923. He certainly makes out a more plausible case than Burton did for a N. Arabian site in his Gold Mines of Midian in 1879. Descriptions of the Hejaz and Asir country will be found in Euting's Tagbuch.
[4] The Latin 'Arabia Felix' is just a translation of Strabo's Ἀραβια εὐδαίμων, which as a matter of fact is based on a mistranslation of the word Yemen, which has been wrongly taken to be from يُمْن "good fortune, prosperity". It really means the "South Land". Cf. (Heb. יָמִין [Jeffery includes the Syriac word here] the South', a derivative from 'the right hand': (Ed. Handwritten note) يمين of course comes from the sense of 'right hand'. This being the lucky side. Cf. ZMDG xxi 601ff and Wellhausen Reste, p202.

sloping away to the central desert. It has been the most visited and most described portion of the peninsula.¹

Hadramaut stretches away to the East of Yemen. It is still mountainous country, but not so fertile. It probably was at one time very much more fertile and prosperous than it is at present for the name was familiar to the ancient writers. In the form חַצְרְמָוֶת it occurs in the Old Testament (The Bible: Gen x:26) which in the Sabaean inscriptions is חצרמות which is in all probability the home of the Χατραμωτῖται (chatramōtîtai) of Strabo (xvi.4.2). Ptolemy knows the Adramitae in this region² and Margoliouth suggests that the name is preserved in the Ἀδραμύττιον (Adramyttium) of Mysia.³ This celebrity could not have arisen from anything like the present arid ranges, so we are justified in inferring a more prosperous past.⁴ Many interesting suggestions in this direction will be found in Von Maltzan's account of Wrede's travels.⁵

(iv)   <u>East Arabia</u>, i.e. Oman and the coast lands of the Persian Gulf.

Oman again is fairly fertile, mountainous country, and the coastline is tolerably well supplied with harbours, which, but for the almost unbearable heat, might be important centres of trade. This region is the great camel-country of Arabia, that Arabs themselves call the Umm al-Ibl (أُمّ الإبل) and all travellers in Arabia are agreed that the best of dromedaries are the Omani breed. Thus, Palgrave writes,⁶

---

¹ A list of earlier travellers is given in Zwemer's Cradle 1912, p 53m. Niebuhr's description still deserves attention, but more recent studies are in Seetzen's Travels in Yemen, 1810 and Manzoni's El Yemen: tre anni nell Ἀrabia felice, 1884.
² Ed. note. Jeffery has brackets here. Obviously, he was going to add a word here later.
³ Margoliouth, *The Homer of Aristotle*, 1923, p88. See also the article by Rendel Harris in *Contemporary Review*, August 1925. (Ed. As at December 2020 have not been able to trace this journal.)
⁴ For descriptions see Bent's essay in the. *The Nineteenth Century*, Vol. 36 (211), Sept, 1894, 419-37: Van den Berg's *Hadhramaut*, 1886; L Hirsch's *Reisen in Süd-Arabien, Mahraland und Hadramaut*, Leiden, 1897; and the useful summary by Schleifer in *EI*, ii, p207.
⁵ H.F. von Maltzan, *Adolph von Wredes Reise in Hadhramaut*, 1873.
⁶ *Central and Eastern Arabia*, 1908 ed. p196.

> To see real live dromedaries, my readers must, I fear, come to Arabia, for these animals are not often to be met with elsewhere, not even in Syria: and whoever wishes to contemplate the species in all its beauty must prolong his journey to Oman, the most distant corner of the Peninsula, and which is for dromedaries what Nejed is for horses, Cashmire for sheep, and Thibet, I believe, for bulldogs.

(v) Central Arabia, the Najd is a great sandy plateau with granite outcrops, dissected by innumerable valleys, habitable in the central portion where the water supply is good, but merging into the trackless desert (the *Bahr as-Safi* and the *Rub al-Khali*) to the South, and again (the *Nafud*) to the North. Travellers have commented on the surprising fertility of this plateau when sources of water are available, but the encircling bands of desert which cut it off from the coastline form an almost insuperable barrier to its commercial prosperity.[1]

This is the horse country. "In Nejed", says Palgrave[2]

> ... is the true birthplace of the Arab steed, the primal type, the authentic model. Thus at any rate I heard, and thus, so far at least, as my experience goes, it appears to me: although I am aware that distinguished authorities maintain another view. But at any rate, among all the studs of Nejed, Feysul's was indisputably the first; and who sees that has seen the most consummate specimens of equine perfection in Arabia, perhaps in the world.

Our main impression then of the physical Arabia is that of a high tableland surrounded by great stretches of burning trackless desert fringed on all sides by a strip of fertile land, the least fertile portion of the fringe being to the N.W. and the most fertile to the S.E. and N.E. i.e. in Yemen and the Mesopotamian border. Although it is not correct to think of Arabia as nothing but a burnt up desert plateau as it figured in many of the older geographies, it is nevertheless true that the dominant feature of the country is the sand of the desert, and as we contemplate this physical background of

---

[1] Perhaps the best description of that is in Palgrave's *Central and Eastern Arabia*, London, 1868.
[2] Op. cit. (ed. cf. 1908. p305).

Islam we are prepared for the thesis covered by the names of Renan[1] and Leon Gauthier[2] that

> 'desert, Semite, and the Unity of God are inseparable terms' and that Islam ever appears as the religion of the deserts where it was born.'[3]

---

[1] Renan *Langues Semitiques*.
[2] Gauthier *La Philosophie Musulame*, 1900, p19.
[3] Vide also an essay by W. H. Norton "The Influence of the Desert on Early Islam', in *Journal of Religion,* iv, 1924, p4.

MAP 5: SIGNIFICANT CENTRES

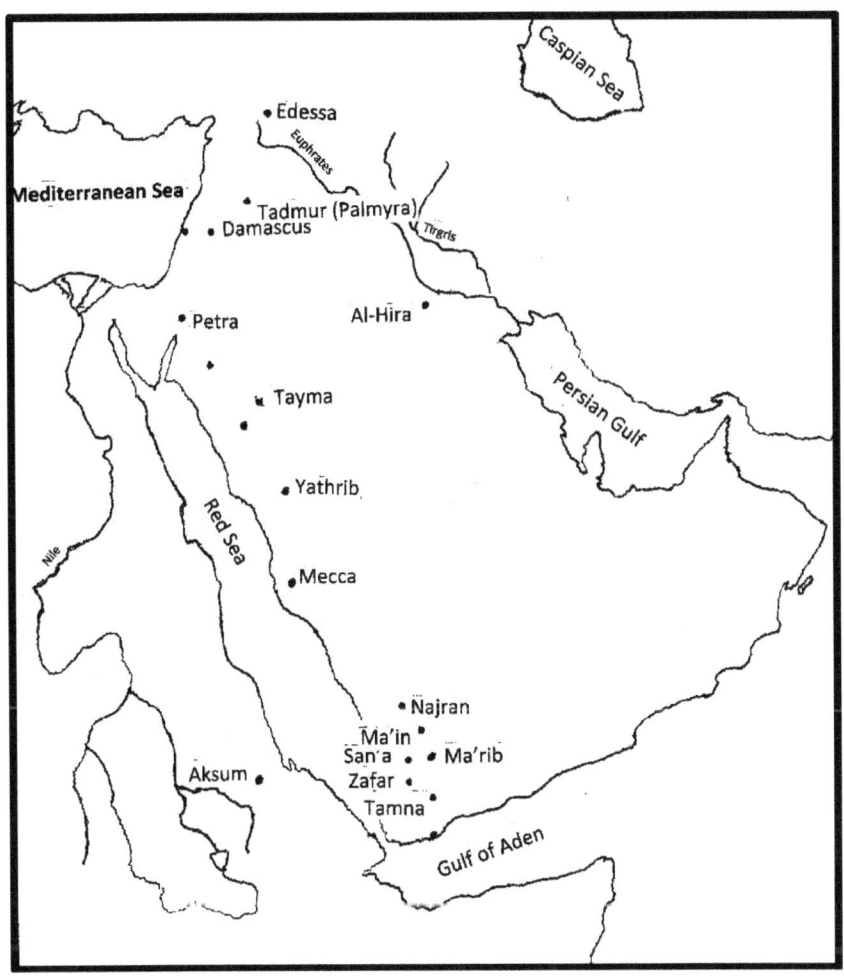

THE TRADE ROUTES

The one thing that made this desert land important in pre-Islamic times, was the fact that through it ran the great caravan routes carrying trade between the rich lands of Persia and India and the East, and the Western markets in Syria and Palestine and the West.

Sea travelling in those early days was a precarious thing and the sea was dreaded. Such shipping as was done followed routes that hugged the land closely the whole way, and though there is clear evidence that hundreds of years before our era there was considerable sea traffic between India and South Arabia[1] the water route through the Red Sea was very treacherous and greatly to be feared,[2] so that from Yemen to Syria the land route was preferred. Now, was this land journey altogether a simple or pleasant task? Given the nature of the country we have already seen, and as the long caravans travelled slowly through the inhospitable country, it was of the first importance that there should be well marked stages where there was certainty of shelter and water at the end of the day's journey: that there should be well known tracks that offered protection from the attacks of marauding nomads: that there be definite landmarks to indicate the way lest inexperienced travellers go astray. Thus grew up the customary trade routes which were followed year by year through the centuries by the going and coming caravans. As Heeren points out in his *Asiatic Researches*:[3]

---

[1] A. Müller *Der Islam im Morgen - und Abendland*, pp24ff. A most interesting illustration of this is found in the number of Dravidian loan words in the ancient languages (cf. Caldwell, *Comparative Grammar of the Dravidian Languages*, 1913, pp88ff. The most interesting are the Hebrew תֻּכִּיִּים - 1 Ki. x.22 (תּוּכִיִּים- 2 Chron. Ix:21 -The Bible) for *peacock*, derived from the Dravidian *tokei* and the Grk κάρπιον–cinnamon, which is derived from the Dravidian *karuppu*.
[2] On the perils of this sea route see Nicholson *Literary History*, p5 suggests that the overcoming of these difficulties to sea traffic about the first century A.D. was a main cause of the decline of the Sabaean prosperity in South Arabia. See further p66 and Muir's LIFE pxci.
[3] A.H.L. Heeren, Vol I, Part 1, *Historical Researches into the Politics, Intercourse, and Trade of the Carthaginians, Ethiopians, and Egyptians*, Oxford, D.A. Talboys, p 23.

MAP 6: TRADE ROUTES IN AND AROUND ARABIA

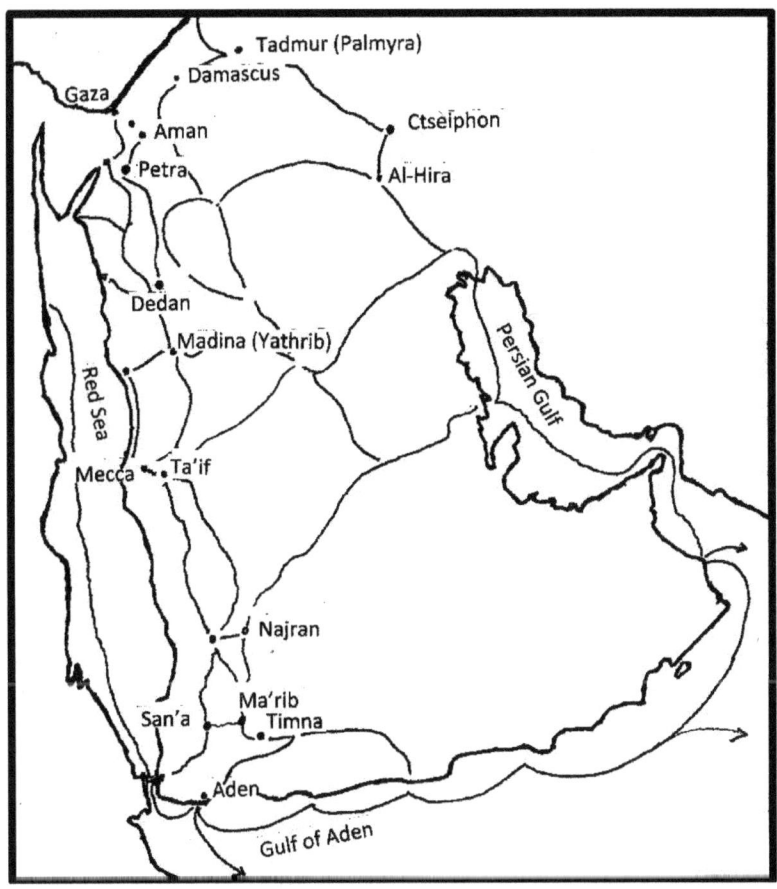

This map is based on several trade maps of the early centuries of the Common Era, though it is primarily a reflection of 'The main pre-Islamic trade routes and cities of Arabia',
http://pic50.picturetrail.com/VOL487/153479/295264/16923904.jpg
cited 20 November 2017

The course of the caravan was not a matter of free choice, but of established custom. In the vast steppes of sandy desert, which they had to traverse, nature had sparingly allotted to the traveller a few scattered places of rest, where under the shade of palm trees, and beside the cool fountains at their feet, the merchant and his beast of burden might enjoy the refreshment rendered necessary by so much suffering. Such places of repose became entrepôts of commerce, and not infrequently the sites of temples and sanctuaries, under the protection of which the merchant prosecuted his trade, and to which the pilgrim resorted.

The pioneer student in the investigation of these ancient Arabian trade routes is Sprenger whose work *Die Post- und Reiserouten des Orients* (Leipzig, 1864), first placed the study of this problem on a scientific basis. The great route was the Western one which ran parallel to the Red Sea, between the craggy hills of the coastline and the parched deserts which fringe the central plateau. The early writers are witness to the importance of the trade that came by this route. The passage in 1 Kings. x.15 (The Bible) that tells us of the sources of Solomon's wealth mentions the traffic of the spice merchants and all the kings of the רַב whom the Chronicler (2 Chron. ix.14 – The Bible) interprets as the עֲרָב; and in Ezekiel's well-known account of the commerce of Tyre (Chap xxvii. 22, 23 – The Bible) he mentions the merchants of Saba (Sheba) and Raama.[1]

    Hogarth, however, thinks that the amount of overland traffic down the "Spice Road" has been exaggerated by modern historians of ancient economics, who are apt to forget how good the evidence is for very early use of Red Sea ports connected by short desert roads with the middle of the valley of the Nile.[2]

---

[1] שְׁבָא, of course, is the S. Arabian, ▫, the Arabic سَبَأ (Gen 10:7, 28 [The Bible) רַעְמָה (twice רַעְמָא) e.g. Hommel *Süd-arabische Chrestomathie* p131. Dillmann thinks it refers to the ῥαμμανῖται of Strabo, xvi. 4, 24.

▫ Please note this symbol is used throughout to indicate that Jeffery had written the word in the appropriate script.

[2] Hogarth, *History of Arabia*, p7.

ETHNOLOGICAL BACKGROUND

Not only was the founder of [Islam] born in Arabia, but he was born of Arab stock, an Arab of the Arabs so that our next enquiry deals with the inhabitants of Arabia, the people from whom he came, and to whom he preached his new doctrine of Allah.

As far back as 800B.C. we hear in Assyrian inscriptions of *Matu arbaai,* of *land of the Arabs*[1] but there is little information about the land or the people to be gleaned from these early records.

The name Arab probably means Bedouin. In a South Arabian inscription, the first of the Mound of Ma'rib, we find the word Arab used in this sense. The ruler there (5th century AD) describes himself and his father as kings of certain regions and all their Arabs, i.e. all their nomadic population. In other South Arabian material they are referred to as raiders, and there can be little doubt that the name was once used to distinguish them from the peaceful dwellers of the South Arabian Kingdoms,[2] a theory which is supported by the Qur'anic use of the word, and by the fact that the ערב of the Old Testament is associated specially with Bedouin.[3]

Now these Arabs belong to that racial stock known as the Semites, a stock which also includes the Hebrews, Assyrians and Babylonians, Phoenicians, Aramaeans, Abyssinian and others.[4] This word Semite was first used by Schlözer in 1781 in Eichhorn's

---

[1] Winckler *A.O.F.*, ii, p456, and Weber in *M.V.A.G.*, vi. p58. The word probably went from Babylon to the Persians and from them on to the Greeks, who gave the name Ἀραβία to the peninsula.
[2] Margoliouth, *Schweich Lectures,* 1924, pp2, 3.
[3] Margoliouth ibid, p40. It is interesting that the author of II Macc.xii.10 makes Arabs and nomads synonymous. Vide also Zaidan, p31.
[4] Paton, *Syria and Palestine,* 1902, p3. "The fact that all the branches of this race Assyro-Babylonian, Canaanitic, Aramaean, Ethiopic and Arabian, are closely similar to one another, both in physiological structure and in language, points to their being descendants of a single primitive stock." (Primitive here means early or original.)

Repertorium. (viii, p161)[1] on the basis of the Table of Nations in Gen. x (The Bible). This Table of course is not ethnologically exact, for it includes the Elamites and Lydites as Semitic, when they certainly are not, and excludes the Phoenicians, who as certainly are[2] and one must remember that in its scientific use the term is confined to those peoples who spoke one or other of the so called Semitic languages.

It is of the first importance for us now to consider the position which the Arabs hold in this group of Semitic peoples, and that position will only become clear to us as we discuss in some detail the vexed question of the original home of the Semitic peoples, the Cradle of the Semites.

In historical times we find them occupying but a small area centering around the south west corner of Asia. Roughly the boundaries of this area are Mt Taurus and the Armenian Mountains on the North, the highlands of Kurdistan[3] and the Persian Gulf on the East, the Indian Ocean and the Abyssinian hills to the South, and the Sahara and the Mediterranean on the West. At different times we do indeed find colonies going out from this area, such as the Phoenicians to North Africa and Sicily, but such sporadic cases do not affect the general truth of the statement that in historic times the Semitic family has been practically confined to this area.[4]

---

[1] Ed. Note: "Von den Chaldäern" in Johann Gottfried Eichhorn *Repertorium für biblische und morgenländische Litteratur* Vol. VIII, Leipzig: Bei Weidmanns Erben und Reich, pp.113-176. In searching for Eichhorn's *Repertorium* and while looking for Schlözer's article, I found this comment by Martin F.J. Baasten, *A Note on the History of "Semitic"* ... "Stefan Weninger noted in passing that it was not A.L. Schlözer who first used the designation 'Semitic languages' in an essay from 1781, but that as early as 1710 G.W. Leibniz had preceded him in coining this term.'.
https://www.academia.edu/11807673/A_note_on_the_history_of_Semitic cited 18 March 2019.
(However, neither Schlözer's article nor Eichhorn's work have been cited March 2019.)
[2] Brockelmann, *Semitische Sprachwissenschaft,* 1916, pp14,15.
[3] Ed. Note: The term Kurdistan refers to that area where the Kurdish speaking people with their own culture are located. Currently they are located, often tenuously within various political boundaries such as Turkey, Syria, Iraq and Iran and at times have been considered to occupy an area stretching, arc-like from the Mediterranean to the Persian Gulf. Not surprisingly both their presence and the extent of the physical location of these people has been hotly contested.
[4] W. Wright, *Comparative Grammar*, p4.

There is increasing evidence, however, that the Semites were not autochthones in all this area,[1] and this forces on us the problem of ascertaining the centre from which they spread to the various points we find them occupying in historical times, a problem whose solution, as we shall see, is not without an important bearing on the origins of Islam.

Up to the present time no unanimity has been reached by scholars on the solution of this question, and at different times various theories have been put forward as to the original home.

a) <u>Turkestan</u>. In 1875 Von Kremer following the line of *linguistic palaeontology,* which had proved so fruitful in the investigations in search of the primitive home of the Indo-Europeans, published two articles in the Journal *Das Ausland* (vol iv. 1875, first two numbers), on *Semitische Kulturentlehnungen aus dem Pflanzen und Thierreiche.* By a careful, but somewhat limited, examination of the names of the plants and animals borrowed by the different Semitic dialects from outside sources, and a collection of the names that the Semitic dialects have in common, he found that while, for example, they have a common word for *camel,* they have no common name for *ostrich,* nor for any part of the *date palm.* His conclusion then is that the Semitic people, before the formation of the various dialects, lived in a region where the camel was a common animal but where ostriches and date palms were unknown. Where is such a region to be found? Von Kremer says, in the tableland of Turkestan around the sources of the Oxus and the Jaxartes. From there, he thought, possibly under the pressure from advancing Indo-Europeans, they first moved down into Mesopotamia, where he finds the earliest traces of Semitic civilisation.

---

[1] The Sumerians in Mesopotamia, for example, were undoubtedly a pre-Semitic people, (cf. Pinches in *ERE* xii, p40) and of the primitive tribes we find inhabiting Palestine before the coming of the Hebrews, such as the Nethinim, (נתינים) 'Anakim (ענקים), Zamzammin (זמזמים), Rephaim (רפאם), Horim (חורים), etc. not all were Semites. The great megalithic monuments found to the East of Jordan and which are similar to those found in Western Europe and N. Africa also point to a pre-Semitic population in that area. Non-Semitic place names are common in Central and North Syria, see *AJSL* xli p74. Also, the dominant physical type in Syria is non-Semitic.

The objections to this theory are that Von Kremer had not made a sufficiently wide survey of the *palaeontological* evidence, much of which does not in the least fit in with his theory, and that he failed to take into account other types of evidence which, as we shall see later, point distinctly in another direction.[1]

b) Mesopotamia. As Von Kremer noticed, the earliest traces of Semitic civilisations that have been revealed to us by the work of the excavators are in Mesopotamia. This has led other scholars to seek the original home somewhere in the fertile land between the Euphrates and the Tigris. Renan in his *Langues Semitiques*[2] had sought the *premier séjour historique des Semites* in the mountains of Armenia near the upper reaches of the great rivers. In 1879, the Italian scholar Ignazio Guidi, carried the investigation along this line a step further in his monograph *Della Sede primitive dei popoli Semitici*[3]. Guidi's method is also that of *linguistic palaeontology* but his range of examination is much wider than that of Von Kremer and his contention is that the geographical, botanical, and zoological conceptions which are expressed in the different Semitic languages by the same word, point to the lower Euphrates as the primitive Semitic home, though he is inclined to think that they earlier migrated there from a region to the South West of the Caspian Sea.[4]

Guidi's argument is much more cautious than that of Von Kremer, and is worked out with great ingenuity; but, as Nöldeke points out,[5] the line of argument is an unsafe one, for e.g. the ordinary words for *man, old man, boy, tent, black* and

---

[1] See also *AJSL* xli 75 for later theory.
[2] Renan, *Langues Semitiques,* 6th edition, 1901, pp31-32.
[3] In the *Memorie della Reale Accademia dei Lincei,* Ser.III vol. iii, 1879. His position was for a time favoured by de Goeje and by Driver (*Hebrew Tenses*, 1881, p250 n.) and from the Arabic side was defended by Jacob, *Altarabisches Beduinenleben,* 1897, p28ff.
[4] It is to be remembered that Guidi had in mind in all his argument the position already set forth by Sayce, Sprenger & Schraeder, that Arabia was the cradle of the Semites. His essay may be considered as a definite attempt to combat the Arabia theory.
[5] *Die Semitischen Sprachen,* 1899, p14.

many others, are different in the different dialects, and yet there can be no doubt that the original Semites had these ideas.

Guidi's position, however, was taken up afresh, and his arguments vigorously defended with great diligence by Krall in 1899, in the first volume of his *Grundriss der altorientalischen Geschichte,* (Wein, 1899, p31ff), and have been more recently defended by his countryman Caetani.[1]

Fritz Hommel has also defended the Babylonian home in a series of writings on the subject, basing his arguments on much the same type of material as was utilized by Guidi.[2] In his earlier treatises he argued for a lower Mesopotamian site, but later he shifted it to upper Mesopotamia.

Still more recently a form of the same theory has been vigorously, though unconvincingly, urged by American Assyriologist Clay.[3] Clay's object in his writings is to refute the theory long held by students of the Old Testament that the origin of a great many customs and beliefs of the Hebrew people is to be found in Babylonia. One step in this process of refutation is to deny that the Hammurabi Dynasty at Babylon was of Arabian origin. To do this it is necessary to find some other source for the Semitic influence that becomes soon so prominent, and to find another site other than Arabia as the original Semitic home. The first he secures by postulating a

---

[1] *Studi di Storia orientale,* I. p98. Tkatsch holds the same view *EI* 'Saba' p4.
[2] Hommel's discussions will be found in *Die Namen der Saugsethiere bei den Südsemitischen Völkern,* Leipzig, 1879, p406. *Die Semitischen Völker und Sprachen,* 1883, i63 & 80ff; an article 'Über den Grad der Verwandtschaft des Altägyptischen mit dem Semitischen' in *B.A.* ii. 342 ff (1891-2); an article 'Die Genealogie unter der babylonischen und ägyptischen Götter-genealogie und der babylonische Ursprung der ägyptischen Kultur' in *Oriental Congress Transactions,* v 2., London 1892 pp218, 224; (Ed. Note.) The title in that volume is slightly different: "Die Identität der ältesten babylonischen und ägyptischen Göttergenealogie und der babylonischeUrsprung der ägyptischen Kultur" in his article 'Babylonia' in *HDB,* 1898; the second edition of his *Gundriss der Geographie und Geschichte des Alten Orients,* 1904. His view was defended by Vlock, vide *Hebraica* ii, p147ff.
[3] Clay's theory is worked out in *Amurru the Home of the Northern Semites,* 1915; *The Empire of the Amorites* 1919; *A Hebrew Deluge Story in Cuneiform, 1822, The Origin of Biblical Traditions,* 1923; a pamphlet *The Antiquity of Amorite Civilisation,* 1924; and *JAOS,* 1925.

great 'Empire of the Amorites' in North West Mesopotamia, and of course this now becomes the original home of the Semites.

c) Africa. The question of the relationship between the Semitic and the Hamitic[1] language groups has not yet been definitely settled, but there is a growing mass of evidence to show that they are both of one family, though the wide morphological and lexical differences between them would seem to show that they must have been separated at a very early age. The study of this question has led some scholars to look to Africa as the original home of the Semites, the Hamites representing that part of the original stock which stayed behind and became gradually largely intermixed with other African races. Nöldeke gave his allegiance to this theory in his pamphlet *Die Semitischen Sprachen,* Leipzig, 1887[2] and he has been followed by many other scholars.

The most important contribution that has since been made to this argument is that of Meinhof, who in an article *Das Ful in seiner Bedeutung für die Sprachen der Maiten, Semiten und Bantu* in the *ZDMG* for 1911 and later in his book *Die Sprachen der Hamiten* (Hamburg, 1912), has shown from a careful examination of the Hamitic languages that they may be graded in a series stretching from the Ful in the Western Sudan to the Bishari in the Eastern Nilotic desert, with a gradation which shows nearest to Semitic in its eastern end and furthest from it

---

[1] Ed. Note: The word "Ham" comes from the Table of Nations given in Gen x (The Bible). However, because of the negative associations of the word it is rarely used today.

[2] See also the later edition, Leipzig 1899, p11, and his art. 'Semitic Languages' in E. Britt. IXth ed. Grimme also favours this theory, vide the early pages of his *Muhammad,* 1904, and Brinton has gathered a lot of material in favour of it in his *Cradle of the Semites,* Philadelphia, 1890. See also *AJSL*, xxxiv, p81ff: *Recueil des Travaux,* xl. 64ff: Sethe, in *ZDMG,* 1923, p207: and François Lexa, "Comment se revèlent les rapports entre les langues Hamitiques, Sémitiques et la langue Egyptienne dans la grammaire des pronoms personnels, des verbes et dans les numéraux cardinaux", 1- 9, Prague, 1922.

in its western end.¹ When we remember that the Semitic languages can be similarly graded, stretching from South Semitic (Arabia, Sabaean and Ethiopic) near the Red Sea, through North Semitic (Aramaic, Hebrew and others) to East Semitic (Babylonian and Assyrian), being closest to the primitive Semitic form at the eastern and furthest from it at the western end, the conclusion would seem to be that there has been a development from one type into another through a number of intermediates, each of which is a little further from the original than its predecessors.² Those members which explain their successors are the more original, and the original here would be around the Red Sea.

The question, however, as to which side of the Red Sea was the original home is not definitely indicated by this discussion. Some of the philologists, however, think that the more primitive forms are found on the African side, and that therefore the original home would be there.³ With this general conclusion a number of ethnologists also agree. Gerland, for example, in his article on *Ethnography* in the *Iconographic Encyclopaedia*, vol. 1,⁴ thinks that the physical characteristics of the Semites point to their beginnings in a North African region, and Palgrave claims⁵ that the strong racial resemblances between the Arabs, Berbers, Abyssinians, and others especially in the form of the jaw and the small calf of the leg, together with their social affinity and linguistic similarity, would point to an African home.

---

[1] He carries the western end even further than we have mentioned, linking it up with the large Bantu family of central Africa. Brockelmann admits at least the possibility of this connection, vide his *Semitische Sprachwissenschaft*, 1916, pp17, 18, and *ZDMG*, lxvii, but the point cannot yet be regarded as more than an interesting hypothesis.
[2] See *JPOS*, 1920 p16.
[3] cf. F. Müller, *Grundriss der Sprachwissenschaft, 1884, iii,* 225.
[4] Heck, J. G., ed. *Iconographic Encyclopaedia of Science, Literature, and Art* v. 1, trans. Spencer Fullerton Baird, New York, R. Garrigue, 1852.
[5] Art. *Arabia* in *Encyclopaedia. Britannica*, ix[th] ed.: so, G. Elliot Smith, *Ancient Egyptians,* 1923, claims that the pure Hamites type is practically indistinguishable from the Arab.

TABLE 1:	EARLY SEMITIC MIGRATIONS*	
	Name	**Location of migration**
1st	Later known as Babylonians	Mesopotamia Syria Palestine
2nd	Amoritic	Babylon Palestine Egypt Yemen
3rd	Canaanitish or Aramean	Egypt Palestine Syria Mesopotamia
4th	Nabataen	Syria Palestine
5th	South Arabian	Abyssinia
6th	Safaite	Syria

* This list is based on Jeffery's text pp 35-41.

TABLE 2:	LIST OF SEMITIC LANGUAGES*	
Approx Date	**Name**	**Semitic Type**
2500BC	Akkadian	Eastern
2000BC	Babylonia	Eastern
2000BC	Assyrian	Eastern
1500BC	Ugaritic	Northwest
1500BC	Old Hebrew	Northwest
1000BC	Aramaic	Northwest
1000BC	Old Ethiopian	West
1000BC	Sabaean	Southern
1000BC	Minaean	Southern
1000BC	Qatabanic	Southern
1000BC	Hadramatic	Southern
500BC	Syriac	North Central
500BC	Safiatic	South
500AD	Palmyrene	Northwest\West

* It would appear that Jeffery was literate in a number of these Semitic Languages.

This view has been accepted by Brinton[1], Ripley[2] Keane[3], Barton[4] and others; but to the present writer the facts of the case have always been much more simply explained if the original home was situated on the eastern side of the Red Sea, and the Hamites considered as the earliest body of emigrants from the deserts of Arabia to more fertile lands across the sea.

d) Arabia. This brings us to the theory that Arabia was the cradle of the Semites, a theory which has always found most favour among Semitic Scholars. The advocates of the African theory are themselves compelled to assume that the Semites must have dwelt long in Arabia and developed there their peculiar characteristics, before they were radiated into other lands.[5] This theory of the Arabian home was elaborated by Sprenger in his *Das Leben und der Lehre des Muhammad* (1861) vol i, p241ff and later in his *Alte Geographie Arabiens* (1875) p293, and has been held by a succession of scholars such as Sayce, de Goeje, Schrader, Wright,[6] Winckler, Ed. Meyer, Luckenbill, Macalister, L. W. King, Paton, Caetani, Hogarth, de Morgan, Montet, Robertson Smith, Thiele, Geden, G. A. Smith, Weber, and so on.

The case for the Arabian home may be briefly summarized.

(i) Semitic traditions all point to Arabia as the original home of the race, and it is the only place which has remained exclusively Semitic.[7]

(ii) Arabia is the hub of the Semitic World.
'If we leave out of account,' says Robertson Smith,[8] 'settlements made over the seas — the South Arabian colonies in East Africa, and the Phoenician colonies on the coasts and isles of the

---

[1] *Cradle of the Semites,* Philadelphia, 1890 and *Races and Peoples,* New York, 1890, p132.
[2] *Races of Europe,* 1899, p376. See also Luscham in Meinhof's *Hamiten.*
[3] *Ethnology,* 1896, p392 and *Man Past and Present,* 1899, p490.
[4] *Sketch of Semitic Origins,* 1902, p24.
[5] Barton, op.cit. p24.
[6] Jeffery does not identify to which Wright he is referring.
[7] Sayce, *Assyrian Grammar for Comparative Purposes,* 1872, p13.
[8] *Religion of the Semites,* pp9,10.

Mediterranean — we find that the region of Semitic occupation is continuous and compact. Its great immoveable centre is the vast Arabian Peninsula, a region naturally isolated and in virtue of its physical characters almost exempt from immigration or change of inhabitants.'

A glance at the map of the distribution of the Semitic languages will make clear how the Semitic people in historical times have been grouped round Arabia. There are no great complications here as there are in the case of the Indo-European family, and it seems plain that Arabia is the hub of the Semitic area.

(iii) During the historic period wave after wave of Semites has been passing from Arabia into the surrounding more fertile lands, and as there is not a scrap of evidence of the contrary process, the probability is that the migration has always been that way and that not vice versa.[1]

(iv) Semites in historical times are found in the fertile lands around Arabia as well as in Arabia itself, and it is axiomatic among ethnologists that migration is from unfertile to more fertile, and not the reverse.[2] Thus we can easily conceive of migrations from the inhospitable land of Arabia to the fertile lands surrounding it, but the contrary process is inconceivable.

De Goeje adds a point to this by pointing out that mountaineers never became inhabitants of the steppe nor agriculturalists nomad shepherds; but it is true that nomads are continually passing over into agriculturalists with settled habitations.[3]

(v) The Arabic language has preserved more fully than any of the other dialects, the characteristics of primitive Semitic speech, e.g. the 'l' of the article, the distinction between the ع

---

[1] Sprenger, *Alte Geographie Arabiens* p293; Margoliouth, *Schweich Lecture*, 1924, p1.
[2] See Dussaud, *les Arabes en Syrie,* p6 and Augustin Bernard, 'Essai sur le nomadisme' in *Annales de Geographie,* 15, 80, 1906, p152-165.
[3] *Het Vaderland der Semitische Volken,* 1882 (Michael De Goeje delivered a 307th Dies Natalis lecture, University of Leiden).

and غ; and the ح and خ and so on¹ are preserved only in Arabic. Moreover, as Margoliouth points out² as compared with say Hebrew, the Arabic represents a stage further back, and can explain things which have no explanation in Hebrew itself. Now the isolated and protected position of Arabic will explain this, if we can assume Arabia to have been the original home.³ Moreover, on the analogy of Lithuanian in the Indo-European family, we expect the more primitive characters to be preserved in the language which has moved least from the original home.⁴

(vi) Ethnologically the Arabs have preserved better than the other branches of the family the Semitic racial characteristics of exclusiveness, ferocity and intensity of faith.⁵ This fact has been so well recognised that investigators into primitive Semitic religions have ever turned to Arabian desert life for their illustrations. Thus Curtis writes,

> "If then we wish to discover the ancestor of Semitic Religions, whose lineaments are to be found in the beliefs and usages of Assyria, Phoenicia and Israel, we shall pursue our investigations among Syrians and Arabs, who observe the same religious rites as did their progenitors from the earliest dawn of history."⁶

---

[1] Ethiopic it is true also preserves the distinction between ح and خ, eg ሐ and ኀ but as will be seen later, of all the many offshoots, the Abyssinians remained longest in the original home.

[2] *Schweich Lectures*, p5.

[3] See also Schrader in *ZDMG*, xxvii, p417 and Vlock in *Hebraica*, (Encyclopaedia Hebraica?) ii, p419. Weber thinks it can explain also the persistence of the Semitic type. He says *Arabian von dem Islam*, 1904, p6 '*Es muss eine unerhörte Lebenskraft an den Boden dieses eigenartigen Landes gebunden gewesen sein. Auch andere Rassen haben den Versuch gemacht, in Vorderasien sich zur Geltung zu bringen und hin und wieder einen Ansturm auf die alten Kulturzentren unternommen. Sie haben es nicht vermocht, sich dauernd zu behaupten und mehr als flüchtige, nur von politischem Einfluss getragene und mit ihm wieder schwindende Spuren ihres Wesens der semitischen Kultur aufzudrücken.*

[4] Ed. note: No details given for this footnote.

[5] Sayce, *Assyrian Grammar*, p13; Nicholson *Literary History of the Arabs* pxvi.

[6] *Primitive Semitic Religion Today*, 1902. So Ditlef Nielsen, *Der Dreieinige Gott*, 1922 p6ff claims that in Arabia we have Neolithic Semite religion preserved virtually intact. Vide *AJSC* xii, 77.

But if it is granted that Arabia is the cradle of the Semites, we have gained a most important point for our interpretation of Islam. The founder of Islam claimed to be an "Arab of the Arabs": we now see that his claim really has a wider meaning, and practically means "Semite of the Semites", and whatever we can learn of the social and religious background of these Semitic peoples will help us both in our interpretation of the life of Muhammad, and of the history of his movement. As Cook says, "In their broad outlines all the Semitic religions are the natural expression of the Semitic temper and modes of thought".[1] It becomes plain then that our main canon of interpretation[2] when we are dealing with Muhammad and his movement must be to insist rigidly on viewing them in the light of this Semitic background, rather than from our western point of view.

One or two illustrations of this will bring out the significance of the point.

(a) Divorce Legislation

To the Western student, one of the darkest features of the whole Islamic system is its extremely low view of the marriage tie, with the fatal facility of divorce and the legislation granting practically unlimited sexual licence to the male. In this respect Islam compares most unfavourably with every other social or religious system, Eastern or Western. The authority for the Islamic system is found in the life of the Prophet himself and in many passages of his revelation, the Qur'an, but its origin is much further back. It lies in the conditions of primitive Semitic society, concerning which there is a great mass of evidence, as Barton points out to show –

> '...that the primitive Semitic marriage tie was an evanescent bond. These facts are abundantly attested by the Old Testament, the Babylonian contracts, the Qur'an, by numerous instances in

---

[1] *Cambridge Ancient History, (ed J. B. Bury)* p108-198.
[2] ie. We must constantly remind ourselves in connection with Muhammad's message, what McCurdy asks us to remember in connection with the Bible, that it "was not merely conveyed to the world through an outward Semitic channel; it was moulded in Semitic minds, coloured by the genius of Semitic speech, and put to the proof for the education of the world, in Semitic hearts and lives." HDB v. p83.

Arabic life, and by the condition of Abyssinian society at the present day'.¹

And the root of this must also be found in primitive Semitic religious conceptions, where we find, as Cook points out – 'sensual grossness alternatives with reverence, and both asceticism and sensuality have been pursued to the extremest lengths.'²

(b) Fatalism

Kismet has become a household word in Europe in association with Muslim belief, and the Qur'an contains an abundance of passages teaching a fatalistic attitude to life.³ This, however, derives from a remote origin in primitive Semitic life, as Cook has pointed out –

> 'Semitic religion is coloured throughout by a rather crass determinism and the sense of man's nothingness before an arbitrary God.'⁴

*(b) Blood revenge*⁵

A particularly revolting episode in the life of Muhammad is that of the cold-blooded slaughter of the Beni Kuraiza after the siege of Madina in 627AD. The story may be read in Muir's Life (Chap xvii).⁶ This Jewish tribe had surrendered at discretion on the understanding that they were to be judged by their friends of the tribe of 'Aus. Muhammad accepted this, but then chose as their judge the one man of the 'Aus who was their bitter enemy, and who was even at that moment rankling with a wound received in the combat with them.

---

[1] Barton, *Sketches of Semitic Origins*, 1902, p44ff. The facts as to nomad Arab life can well be illustrated from the pages of Doughty's *Arabia Desesta* where he again and again comments on it.
[2] *Cambridge Ancient History*, vol i., p200.
[3] This material has been carefully studied in the second chapter of Bakker's *De verhouding tusschen de almacht Gods en de zedelijke verantwoorde lijkheid van den mensch in den Islam*, Amsterdam, 1922.
[4] *Cambridge Ancient History*, vol.i. p200.
[5] Ed. Note: also referred to as blood feud.
[6] (Ed Note: Jeffery planned to add information later.) The Arabic sources include Sahih al-Bukhari, 4:52:68; 4:57:66; 4:57:66; 4:59:443; 4:59:44, 4:52:280 and many others. A reference is also found in Sunan Abu Dawood, 38:4390 (This information was cited on 14 May, 2015 (http://en.wikipedia.org/wiki/Invasion_of_Banu_Qurayza).

As Muhammad anticipated, this man condemned the men to slaughter and the women and children to slavery, and when the judgment was thus given, Muhammad had it straightway carried out, and even had Rihana, the most beautiful of their women, taken to his own tent. From our Western point of view the whole thing was an unspeakable abomination, but to a Semitic chieftain such a transaction would seem nothing out of the ordinary, and the biographers of the Prophet hand down the story without any sense of its moral reprehensibleness.

O. Procksh has made a special study of this question of blood revenge in his pamphlet *Die Blutrache bei den vorislamischen Arabern*, Leipzig, 1899 and the information he has there collected is very suggestive for an understanding of the conditions of early Islam.

(c) *Plagiarism*
It has already been pointed out (p4) how eclectic a religion Islam is, and no student of the Qur'an can fail to be struck by the large amount of material it has borrowed from other sources. Not infrequently hard words have been written about Muhammad's plagiarism[1] but here again he was only representative of his people, for as is well known 'the Semites are middle-men, copying foreign models, reshaping what they adopt, and stamping themselves upon what they sent out'[2] and the Arabs as Dozy points out[3]

'Manifest the same lack of creative power. They translated and commented on the writings of the ancients, they enriched certain branches of science by their patient, accurate, and minute observations: but they made no capital discoveries, and we are not indebted to them for a single great and fruitful idea.'[4]

(d) *Semitic Migrations*
Undoubtedly the most important fact, however, that this consideration of the Semitic background has brought out, is that which links up the great outburst of the Arabian people after the

---

[1] Zwemer, *Arabia, The Cradle of Islam* p170 and the unfortunately expressed remarks occurring throughout Blair's recent book, *The Sources of Islam*, Madras 1925.
[2] *Cambridge Ancient History*, I, p203.
[3] Reinhardt Dozy, *Spanish Islam*, 1912, pp8,9.
[4] Many would hotly contest Dozy's comments.

death of the Prophet, with the great series of similar migrations which in historical times have been passing out from Arabia to the more fertile lands surrounding it.

We have already noted the fact of these migrations. It is now time to look at them more closely. Hugo Winckler in 1892 in his *Geschichte Babyloniens und Assyriens,* first drew attention to these periodical wave-like migrations from Arabia and suggested that they were due to overpopulation. Later writers have gone into the question more fully, and at the present stage of investigation we can recognise six definite waves of migration moving out from Arabia, with suggestions of certain others, and we may be fairly sure that there were yet others of which we have at present no evidence.

It will be best to commence with two of these as yet indefinite suggestions, before proceeding to discuss the six well recognised historical migrations.

a) We have already noticed in discussing the Semitico-Hamitic relationship, that while many scholars hold that the original home was in Africa, there is yet reason for holding the opposite view. If this proves well-founded we may regard the presence of Semites on the African side of the Red Sea, as evidence of a very early migration. Erman, e.g. in the Introduction to his *Ägyptische Grammatik,* 1894[1] thinks the philological evidence strongly supports the view that the peculiarities of Hamitic are best explained as the result of a small body of conquering invaders imposing their language on an alien population with the result that the language becomes changed almost beyond recognition. Other scholars such as de Morgan, in his *Recherches sur les Origines de l'Egypte,* Paris, 1897, vol ii, p219ff, Wiedermann[2], Ember[3] and Geden[4] point out that the ethnological characteristic of the ancient Egyptians and the curious mixture of Semitic astronomical cult with the native animal worship of Africa, which we find in their religion, is best explained by considering the Semites as an

---

[1] See also his article in *SBAW* 1900 xix, p350ff.
[2] In de Morgan's *Recherches,* ii, p219ff.
[3] *ZÄ,* 1911, vol xlix-li.
[4] *Studies in the Religions of the East,* p64ff.

invading ruling class who mingled with the negroid inhabitants of the Nile Valley.[1]

b) The second suggestion is that there was an early migration into Asia Minor. Dr Margoliouth in his *Homer of Aristotle* (1923) p88 writes:

'Of some prehistoric immigrations or immigrations from Arabia, traces have been found in names which figure on the map of Asia Minor, and to some extent even on the that of Hellas itself. The most striking is doubtless Ἀδραμύττιον – Adramyttium, whose identity with Hadramaut does not seem doubtful. Abydos, found in the Iliad, cannot well be separated from the 'Abbas of Arabia and Larissa seems in ancient and modern times to be an accommodation to European pronunciation of the Arabic al-'Arish – the hut'.

This is a question that merits much further investigation. Dr. Rendel Harris in an article in the *Contemporary Review*, Aug 1925[2], has carried a little further the research into the spread of the fame and commerce of Hadramaut in the Mediterranean area, and further study may bring interesting results.

But to return to the migrations of historical times, with which we can deal with greater certainty.[3]

Historical Migrations

(i) The first great migration in the historical period is that which brought the Semites, later known as Babylonians, into the fertile lands of Mesopotamia[4] and also doubtless spread over parts of Syria and Palestine.[5] The earlier inhabitants of the lower valleys of the Euphrates and Tigris were the Sumerians, a Mongol-like race who were, so far as we can discover, the inventors of the cuneiform

---

[1] This theory, however, has been strongly opposed by Max Müller in *OLZ*, I, p78 and by Sergi, *Mediterranean Race*.
[2] James Rendel Harris, 'Adramyttium', *The Contemporary Review*, V.128 (1925), pp. 194–202.
[3] The simplest account of these migrations will be found in Patons' *Syria and Palestine*, 1902.
[4] See Caetani, *Studi*, i, p180ff.
[5] Winckler, *Völker Vorderasiens*.

system of writing.[1] Hordes of Semites from North Arabia came down upon this people, partially conquered them and largely intermarried with them, so that the result of the absorption of Sumerian culture by these Semites gives us beginnings of what we know as Babylonian civilisation. The incoming Semites apparently did not conquer the whole of the Mesopotamian valley. They were supreme in the North and the Sumerians held their own for a considerable period in the South[2], but the Semites appear to have been the virile section, while the Sumerians were the more cultured, and gave to their conquerors of the best that their civilisation had to offer.

> 'This statement is that which seems to the present writer the best reading of the evidence at present available, though he is of course aware that it is not by any means universally accepted. Brünnow, many years ago, from an examination of the bilingual inscriptions, suggested that, as in his opinion the originals were always Babylonian, that fact pointed to the Semites being the original inhabitants whom the Sumerians later conquered, and whose civilisation they absorbed. (*Revue d'Assyriologie*, vol. xviii), Ed Meyer held that same view[3], basing his conclusions, however, on the very uncertain criteria of the representations of gods and men on the monuments.'
>
> 'Beyond the fact that these arguments rest on very precarious foundations, there is the further important consideration that Pumpelly's researchs in Russian Turkestan, in the region of Merv and Anau[4], have brought to light traces of a Sumerian civilisation there. Contenau, in his account of these discoveries (*La Civilsation Assyro-babylonienne*, 1922, pp26-27) points out that this civilisation is much older than that of the Mesopotamian area, for different stages of it can be traced right back to the Stone Age, and there are traces of the different stages in the process of the acclimatization of domestic animals. Pumpelly's discoveries also link on with those made in 1913, of Sumerian traces in

---

[1] Vide Meissner, *Die Keilschrift*, 1913, pp16,17. It is impossible any longer to treat seriously the attempt of Halevy (cf. his essay "Sumériens et Sémites en Babylonie" *R.S.* 1907 pp239-254) to maintain that Sumerian is merely a system of secret writing used by the Babylonian priesthood for writing their own language in a form unintelligible to the masses.
[2] Delaporte *La Mesopotamie: les civilisations babylonienne et assyrienne*, 1923, cap.ii.
[3] E. Meyer, *Sumerier und Semiten in Babylonien*, 1907.
[4] R Pumpelly, *Excavations in Turkestan*, Washington, 1906 in Publications of the Carnegie Institute of Washington.

South Russia, so that conclusion seems fairly obvious that the Semites took over a culture from them and not they from the Semites: from which it follows that they must have been the earlier inhabitants in Mesopotamia, to which they came from the hill country of Turkestan.'

'That their original home was somewhere in Turkestan is also favoured by the philological evidence. Although it is no longer possible to hold with Lacouperie[1] and Ball[2], that there are numerous affinities between the Sumerian syllabus and Chinese ideograms, a home somewhere about the region of Turkestan is indicated whether we class Sumerian with the older scholars Oppert, Lenormant, Shrader and Delitzsch as a Ural-Altaic speech,[3] or follow the more recent scholars such as Hein and Autran, in considering it Indo –European.'[4]

Just when the Semites came into the country we cannot tell. Winckler points out that the fact that a Semitic type of civilisation was flourishing there by 3,500 BC and was a civilisation stable enough to last down to the Christian era, points to a considerable development before the date at which we first get traces of it.[5] But when Winckler wrote research had not gone far forward distinguishing exactly between what was Sumerian and what was Semitic.[6] It cannot be claimed that we can make many hard and fast distinctions even now, but we should hesitate more about calling the type of civilisation we find there in 3500B.C. a distinctly Semitic type.

---

[1] *Babylonian and Oriental Record*, vols. i & ii.
[2] Articles in *PSBA* for 1890, 1891 and his book *Chinese and Sumerian*, 1913.
[3] See also Langdon *Sumerian Grammar*, 1911, p22-32 i.; Hommel *Grundriss*, p 18 and Meissner *Die Keilschrift*, 1913.
[4] (Ed. *Handwritten note*:) See Hein, 'Sumerer und Indogermanen", *Mannus zeitschrift für vorgeschlchte*, 11/12, 183-204, Leipzig, 1919-20: *Sumerisch-Indogermanisch?* in Steindruck Altona, 1919: 'Die Ältesten indogermanischen Sprachreste' in *OLZ*, 1921, Autran, *Sumérien at Indo-Européen* 1925.
[5] See his article 'Die politische Entwicklung Altmesopotamiens' in *AOF* I, 1893 and *Geschichte Israels*, p 128.
[6] A good example of this difficulty is seen in the religious texts. Many of the Sumerian religious texts may be Semitic in origin as Zimmern admits for the Sumerian Penitential Psalms (*Babylonische Busspsalmen*, Leipzig, 1885), and much of the Sumerian religious conception and cultus as we know it at this time may also be Semitic. All the earliest documents however are in the Sumerian language, the earliest inscriptions all refer to Sumerian kings, and when the bilingual inscriptions begin to appear, it is always the Sumerian text that comes first. So we are fairly safe in concluding that the earlier we get, the more certainly Sumerian our documents are.

Probably, however, we may judge that Pinches is right in placing the Semitic coming to power about 4000 B.C. and suggesting a thousand years earlier for the entrance of the Sumerians into Mesopotamia.[1]

ii.) We have seen that the first Semitic migration into Mesopotamia, only partially subdued the Sumerians; it was a second great wave of migration, known as the *Amoritic* migration, which definitely established the Semitic ascendancy.[2] The earliest evidence for this is the new type of names which suddenly appear in the inscriptions[3] (sometimes accompanied by a Babylonian translation)[4], and a large borrowing of Canaanitish idiom into the language.[5]

Part of this migration also reached Egypt and drove the Pharoahs of Memphis southwards[6] and if some evidence in the South Arabian inscriptions can be trusted, another wave of it invaded Yemen.[7] It was this migration that brought the famous Hammurabi dynasty to power in Babylon and the Canaanitish tribes into Palestine, and a later wave of it is supposed to have carried the Hyksos into Egypt.[8] The date of the migration is given as roughly 2500-2230 B.C..

The Biblical student is interested in the fact that it was this migration that brought Abram into Palestine. In that curiously

---

[1] Art. 'Sumero-Akkadians' in *ERE* vol xii.
[2] Delaporte op. cit. p18: Hogarth *Ancient East,* p22 cf. also Paton's *Syria and Palestine,* cap.iii, Hommel's *Ancient Hebrew Tradition, 1897,* and review in *ZDMG* xlix of Meissner's work in Bd (vol). xi of the *Assyriologische Bibliothek,* ed Friedrich Delitzsch and Paul Haupt 1893.
[3] Pognon, *JA,* 1888, p543ff; Winckler *AOF,* ii, p396-400. Particularly noteworthy are the forms compounded with *Abi* and *'Ammi.*
[4] Hommel, *Ancient Hebrew Tradition,* p88.
[5] Winckler says these borrowings are as numerous as in the Amarna Tablets, op. cit. article, 'Hamustu'.
[6] A glance at the Table of Kings on p598 of Breasted's *History of Egpyt,* 1920, will show how this period of migration corresponds with the sudden decline of Egypt under the VII to X Dynasties. See also Petrie, *History of Egypt, I,* p120.
[7] The evidence here is from the forms of personal names which appear in forms closely similar to the new names appearing on the Babylonian monuments (See Hommel in *ZDMG* xlix.) One uncertainty here, is whether these South Arabian inscriptions can be dated so far back, and it is also of course possible to argue that the wave of migration started from South Arabia and carried these names with it. See *AJSL,* xli p77.
[8] Hogarth, *Ancient East,* p 22. They also founded a dynasty at Larsa.

ancient fragment Genesis xiv (The Bible) we find him described as the contemporary of Eri-aku (Arioch – אריוך) and living at the same time of the Elamite supremacy, which followed on the weakening of Babylonian control in the struggle against these invading elements. He is also brought into relationship with 'Amraphel, king of Shinar, and there is considerable probability that this אמרפל is Hammurabi.[1]

      iii.)   The third wave of migration is known as the *Canaanitish* or *Aramean* migration. It is still uncertain whether this was a separate migration, or just a late wave of the previous Amoritic migration. Paton, for example[2], argues that this migration was the one which brought the Hyksos into Egypt. The later phases of this migration are best known from the Amarna letters[3] which contain appeals to Amenhoteph IV of Egypt from his garrison in Palestine for help against the *Habiri* and other tribes who were invading Syria and Palestine. It was part of this Aramaean migration which from about 1500-1250 B.C. carried various tribes, including the Hebrews, Moabites, and others into Palestine, Syria and Mesopotamia.[4]

      (iv.)   Next is the Nabataean migration which culminated about 500BC and overflowed a large part of Syria and Palestine. Unfortunately, little is known about the Nabataeans until, in 312 BC they came into conflict with the Greeks,[5] but although they used an Aramaic dialect in their inscriptions[6] we know that they were an Arab race.[7] Their capital was Petra[8] in the old Edomite country, and their

---

[1] (Ed. *Handwritten note:*) But against the equation of 'Amraphel with Hammurabil see Johns' *Schweich Lectures*, 1912. Hall, however, in the *People and the Book*, 1925 p18 holds to it.
[2] *Syria and Palestine*, cap.viii. On the 'Hyksos' see Breasted op. cit caps xi and xii.
[3] On the Tell-el-Amārna Tablets see Winckler *Der Thontafelfund von el-Amarna*, 1889-90 and in vol 5 of the *Keilinschriftliche Bibliothek* (ed. Schrader) which appeared in an English translation. The student may also consult Bezold and Budge, *the Tel-el Amarna tablets*, 1892.
[4] See map in Caetani's *Studi*, i, p192.
[5] See the account of Antigonus' expedition in Diodorus Siculus, cap.xix.
[6] A number of these are collected in Cooke's *North Semitic Inscriptions*, Oxford, 1903 and in the Paris *Repertoire d'epigraphie semitique* (Chabot).
[7] Dussaud lays it down as a general rule that we may normally expect to find that nomads who settle down to a sedentary life lose their language (*Arabes en Syrie*, p21).
[8] On Petra see Brünnow and Domaszewaki, *Die Provincia Arabia*, Strassburg 1904; Musil, *Arabia Petraea*, Vienna 1907-8; Dalman, *Petra und seine Felsheiligtümer*, Leipzig, 1908.

little kingdom lasted until merged by Trajan in 106 AD into the Roman Province of Arabia.[1]

(v.) Next came the migration of the South Arabians into Abyssinia. The fact of this migration is certain enough on many grounds[2] but the date of its commencement is very uncertain. The early conjectures of Ludolf[3] and de Sacy[4] were the merest guesses, and though, as Littmann points out[5] we can find some reason for believing that the bulk of the immigrants came over in the last centuries B.C., but there is no doubt that there had been a 'gradual infiltration'[6] for a considerable time before that. Our lack of evidence is almost complete, for all the extant Ethiopic literature is of late date, and the earliest inscription so far known, goes back no further than 350 AD[7] and tells us nothing to the point.

We have to rely then on such evidence as the following:

(a) The ancient Ethiopic language, parent of the modern vernaculars (Amharic, Tigré and Tigrinya) and still used as a liturgical language in the Abyssinian Church, belongs to the South Semitic group, and is demonstrably a later form of the language of the South Arabian inscriptions.[8]

(b) The Ethiopic alphabet is demonstrably derived from that used in the South Arabian inscriptions.[9]

---

[1] Dio Cassius, lxviii, 14; Cooke's article 'Nabataeans' in *ERE* gives a concise account of their later history.
[2] Vide Renan, *Langues Sémitiques,* pp323-4.
[3] *Historia Aethiopica,* (Ludolf) cap i, 3.
[4] *Mémoires de l'Académie des Inscriptions,* vol. i, p278ff.
[5] Littmann 'Abyssinia', *ERE*, 1908.
[6] The phrase is Renan's.
[7] If we can accept the authority of Cosmas Indicopleustes there is an inscription dating from somewhere in the first century AD but it tells us no more than the Aizanas inscription of 350AD about the date of their entry.
[8] Brockelmann *Grundriss der vergleichenden Grammatik der semitischen Sprachen,* i, p30; Hommel, *Südarabische Chrestomathia.*
[9](Ed. *Handwritten note:*) In Jeffery's notes he included a hand written Ethiopic Alphabet as well as a hand written copy of the Ethiopic alphabet as found in Hommel's *Südarabische Chrestomathia.*

(c) The most ancient remains of Abyssinian civilisation as found in the ancient settlement at Axum, bear close resemblances to the monumental types found in South Arabia by Glase and Halévy and their followers.[1]

(d) The Greek geographers knew of the connection and regard the Ἀβασσηνόι [2] as of Yemenite origin.[3]

(e) Ethnological connections have been observed, though the Abyssinians have so closely intermarried with native African stocks that this is frequently difficult to recognize.[4]

(f) The Abyssinian tribes still preserve the traditions of their having lived originally in Arabia.[5]

(g) Recent research into the traditional law and customs of some of the outlying tribes who have not yet accepted Islamic law and practice, reveals many curious similarities with Semitic law and practice such as we imagine they must have followed in the old Arabian home.[6]

Very much work remains to be done on the question of the early history of Abyssinia, and it is not at all unlikely that diligent research would enable us to fill up many of the gaps which at present disfigure our picture of this interesting period. Further light may also come from the South Arabian inscriptions, for the migration was almost certainly due to the break-up of the South Arabian Kingdoms.

(vi.) Dussaud[7], would on the ground of the Safaite inscriptions at Safa, south-east of Damascus, have us count a sixth or Safaite migration in the 1st Century A.D.

---

[1] Renan, op. cit. 323.
[2] (AB) Ἀβησσυνοί? Can't find the text itself, but this spelling would mean those from Abyssinia, i.e. Ethiopia
[3] Herodotus, iii, p94; vii, 70.
[4] vide art. 'Aethopia' in the *Dictionary of Greek and Roman Geography* (ed W. Smith).
[5] Rodén, *Le Tribu dei Mensa,* 1913, cap i..
[6] Rodén, op. cit.
[7] *Les Arabes en Syrie avant l'islam,* Paris 1907, esp. i..

(vii.)   The seventh great migration from Arabia is the [Islamic]. During the lifetime of the Prophet, the Arab tribes, united under his rule, had practically conquered the whole of Arabia. Under his immediate successors, band after band of desert Arabs poured out, conquering the fertile lands of Syria and Mesopotamia, moving on to Persia and Egypt, extending then further into Turkestan and India in the East, and across North Africa as far as Spain in the West. Then the force spent itself, and the tribes of Arabia lapsed back into the state of barbarism in which they were before Muhammad came, and in which they have remained ever since.[1]

The question now arises as to the cause of these migrations, that we may see whether or not this [Islamic] migration is of the same general nature as the others with which we have dealt. We noticed above that Winckler,[2] who first drew attention to the fact of these periodic migrations, also made a suggestion as to their cause, vis that in common with the migrations of peoples studies elsewhere,[3] they were due to overpopulation. This suggestion of Winckler's has been worked out in some detail by Caetani in the first volume of his *Studi di Storia Orientale* (Milan, 1911)[4], who basing his study on a theory of the gradual desiccation of Arabia, has shown that all the Semitic migrations, the [Islamic] included, have been brought about by the stress of economic conditions. As it is strikingly put in the Hebrew story of Abraham and Lot,[5] 'the land was not able to bear them', so at such times as the pressure became too acute, bands would move off to 'peaceably penetrate', or conquer by force of arms, more fertile territory.

---

[1] (Ed. *Handwritten note.*) It is, of course true that large tracts of Syria and Palestine had been thinly occupied by Arabs before Islam, eg. the people of Ghassan, who might be called the forerunners of the [Islamic] migration.   The present *fellah* population of Palestine (southern and central) owes its origin to a migration of Arab tribes which followed the Crusades.
[2] supra page 34.
[3] Vide Haddon *Wanderings of People*.
[4] Vide also the second volume of his *Annali dell' Islam,* 1907, pp831-861.
[5] Genesis xiii (The Bible).

Caetani's argument is partly geological and climatological, based on the researches of Croll, de Morgan, Krapotkin[1] and others in which he works out the proof of the gradual drying up of Arabia since the last glacial period,[2] and partly historical, dealing with the facts of the actually known migrations, including the [Islamic].

Without following rigidly Caetani's argument we may set forth the evidence as follows:

(i) The Encroaching Desert
The evidence for this is geological and climatological, and goes to show that since the last glacial period, the climate of Arabia has changed, and little by little the sands have crept down like an incoming tide, driving civilisation before them, and necessarily decreasing the productivity of the peninsula.[3]

Most interesting sidelights have been thrown on this fact by the studies of the geologist Ellsworth Huntington. His theme worked out in several books is the influence of climatic conditions on civilisations. In his first volume, *The Pulse of Asia* 1907 (new edition, 1919) he studied the climatic pulsations in the deserts of Turkestan, which are closely connected in this respect with those of Arabia and North Africa. As a result of his investigations, it became possible to construct a graph illustrating the successive wet and dry periods over this desert area, a graph which shows a striking correspondence between the excessively dry periods marked by the geologist, with the dates for the Semitic migrations arrived at by the historian.[4]

(ii)   Evidence of Extinct Civilisation in Arabia
Evidence is steadily accumulating to show that in Arabia, where now there is only waterless desert and where human

---

[1] Ed. Note: It is assumed that Caetani refers to these works.
[2] (Ed. *Handwritten note:*) There is good geographical evidence for the former greater fertility of central Arabia in the now quite dry river valleys running towards the coast. On one of these see Cheesman *In Unknown Arabia*, p238ff.
[3] (Ed. *Handwritten note*): That the process is still going on is evidenced by Cheesman, op. cit. p249.
[4] Serious objections, however, have been raised against Huntington's theory by Olmsted and others. See *AJSL* xli. p76.

habitation is impossible, once there were flourishing civilisations.

a) Princeton Expedition of 1904, describes the mass of ruins dating from the beginning of the Christian era that was found in North Arabia some three hundred miles south of Lake Gouldjik[1], evidencing the existence of a considerable civilisation in an area that is now quite barren and uninhabitable.

b) The South Arabian antiquities[2] with which we shall deal in more detail later on, reveal to us the remains of a very flourishing civilisation which has now been largely blotted out, and apparently it stretched far away along the coasts of Hadramaut where now no such civilisation is possible.

c) Palmyra, the ancient Tadmor, in the third century of our era was the centre of an important civilisation, which was powerful enough to defy for a time the might of Rome.[3] The encroaching desert, however, has gradually destroyed it. In 1741 when Wood and Dawkins visited it, there were still mighty and imposing ruins, pictures of which can be seen in their work,[4] and there was still a considerable population of Arabs on the spot. In 1894 Deville found but little of the grandeur remaining, and the Arab population considerably decreased.[5] When the present writer visited the ruins in 1924 there was very little of the ancient ruins standing and the Arabs had dwindled to a few families depending on the one well of sweet water that remained.

---

[1] See the account by F. A Norris in *Publications of Archaeological Expedition to Syria*, 1904-5 and 1909, Leiden.
[2] Vide infra p58ff.
[3] Lucien Double Syrie, *Les Césara de Palmyra*, 1877.
[4] *Les Ruines de Palmyre,* Paris 1812. The English edition appeared at London in 1753 but I have not seen it.
[5] *Palmyra, souvenirs de voyage et d'histoire,* Paris, 1894.

d) Philby the explorer of the great Southern desert, the *Rub'al-Kali,* notices that in depressions in this great desert waste

> the wind blowing over the piled up sand lays bare from time to time some relic of man's handiwork of past ages, bits of statuary – a severed head or arm or trunk of a stone or marble figure, at which they marvel.[1]

It is true that these remains which have been found in various parts of the country are not so very ancient, but they sufficiently illustrate our thesis that there is evidence of the country becoming more and more uninhabitable, and there can be little doubt that it was the same at even earlier periods.[2]

(iii) The Migrations

We have already considered the great historical migrations, but it needs to be remembered that temporary migrations are still going on, as they apparently have for untold ages in the past. At the present day we find clans of Arabs such as the 'Aniza migrating for the summer months across the borders into Syria, just as the Midianites used to do in Gideon's day[3] and returning in the autumn.[4] As we have already noticed, migrations are always from less fertile to more fertile lands, which of itself suggests that economic causes largely govern the migrations, and Myers writes of these migrations:

> 'In the moister spells, such people multiply over the widening grassland more rapidly than any alien can habituate himself to a pastoral life, or to precarious agriculture between the desert and the sown. On the other hand, in spells of drought, Arabia erupts like a volcano, pouring floods of highly organized and mobile tribes across its land frontiers.'[5]

---

[1] *The Heart of Arabia,* London 1922, ii, 221.
[2] Hommel has made the very interesting suggestion (*Grundriss* p272) that the Hebrew description of the Garden of Eden points to an Arabian location, and this would be a memory of the once flourishing home from which they had been driven out.
[3] Judges iv:3 (The Bible).
[4] George A. Smith, *Historical Geography of the Holy Land,* p8. So Dussaud says *Arabes en Syrie,* p2 'la pénétration des nomads Syrie est un phenomène et normal'.
[5] *Cambridge Ancient History, I,* 38.

A second point to notice, is that certain of these migrating bands from Arabia quickly adopted the civilisation of the lands into which they came, rather than attempting to force their own civilisation on the conquered,[1] which is explainable if they entered these countries as desperate hordes driven by dire economic necessity to seek new homelands, but hardly explainable if they marched out as the advance guards of a conquering civilisation[2]. The case resembles that of the Norman invaders of the English, rather than that of the English conquest of India where a mere handful of the conquering race by sheer force of culture have imposed their language and culture on the native inhabitants.[3]

The third point is the little information we can gather from the facts of the migrations themselves, which uncertain as much of it is, seems to picture them to us as hungry hordes anxious above all else to devour the country they had encroached upon.

Take for example the Hebrew account of the entry of the tribes into Palestine as we have it in Joshua and Judges.[4] The persistent tradition in all this account is that they had been

---

[1] In the first migration in our list e.g. we find the Akkadians (i.e. the Semites later known as Babylonians and Assyrians accepting the civilisation of the Sumerians whom they conquered. So the Hythos (Hyksos?) absorbed contemporary Egyptian culture and we have seen the Nabataeans, who were Arabs, adopting the Aramaic language for their inscriptions.

[2] Margoliouth, however, has a demur to make on this point. He says (*Schweich Lectures* p 25) "We are learning to think of the immigrations not as nomads in the savage or semi-savage state, but as colonists carrying with them to their new homes the memories of a developed political organisation, with usages and practices having a history behind them.

[3] Compare also the Scandinavians in Normandy with the Spaniards in America, and note how the Bulgarian tribes accepted the Slavic tongue of the peoples they conquered (Bryce, *International Relations* p55).

[4] Thorny problems of Old Testament (The Bible) criticism at once raise their heads when one approaches this subject, but for the purposes of our argument it does not matter much whether we accept the theory that only a few Hebrews were in Egypt, the others in that time being engaged in struggling for a footing into Palestine, or whether we follow the Orthodox position that Joshua's account of the conquest is in no disagreement with that of Judges. In either case the tradition on the point under our consideration is the same.

promised by their God, a 'land flowing with milk and honey', and the stories of their expeditions to secure this

אֶרֶץ זָבַף חָלָב. וּדְבָשׁ

are given boldly enough in the narrative. It is especially striking to read in the account in the 5ᵗʰ Chapter of Joshua:

> 'And they did eat of the old corn of the land on the morrow after the Passover, unleavened cakes, and parched corn on the selfsame day. And the manna ceased on the morrow after they had eaten of the old corn of the land: neither had the children of Israel manna any more: but they did eat of the fruit of the land of Canaan that year.' (v11,12)

The narrative had carefully given the story of the miraculous provision of food for the Hebrew tribes on their journey through the wilderness, but now that they reach Canaan this miraculous supply stops: from then on they are to live on the land they have reached.

Similar evidence is borne by the little we know of the Hyksos period in Egypt. The story of Manetho as preserved by Josephus[1] may be only the substance of a "folk tale" as Breasted calls it[2] but it doubtless preserves good tradition as to the actual conditions during their invasion, when it relates their ravages among the people, devouring the land as they came, until at last they settled down and appointed kings over themselves in true Egyptian fashion.

Now Caetani holds that the [Islamic] outburst in seventh century A.D. was precisely similar to these previous outbursts, and was brought about by similar economic causes. We may gather up the evidence as follows.

I POLITICAL PRESSURE

The political condition of Arabia at the time when Muhammad was born, was bad. Three great Empires were pressing in on the Arab tribes from three directions, little by little depriving them of the most fertile parts of the land, and continually forcing

---

[1] *Contra Apion*, I, 14.
[2] *History of Egypt,* 1920, p45.

them back on to the central desert and plateau. We have already remarked that the greatest part of the fertile land of Arabia is on its fringe, the northern fringe at Syria and Palestine, the southern at Yemen and Oman, the eastern at Mesopotamia and the shores of the Persian Gulf. At the time all these fertile sections were under the domination of foreign powers.

> a) To the North, Syria and Palestine, and much of Mesopotamia were under the control of the Byzantine Empire, which also controlled Egypt to the West. Heraclius was the Emperor at Constantinople and he was busily pushing his power away down through Palestine. In the stress of his struggle with Chosroes of Persia, he had endeavoured, more or less successfully, to link up the Arab tribes of Syria as sources of strength to himself. In the north of Arabia he had made the great and powerful Arabian Kingdom of Ghassan tributary to his crown, and there is reason to believe that but for the stress of the war with Persia, he would have a more persistent attempt to push Byzantine influence further down the Hejaz coast.[1]

> b) To the east was the Persian power of the Sasanian monarch Chosroes, engaged as already noted, in a desperate struggle with the Byzantines, and like them, gradually extending his power in Mesopotamia, and along the shores of the Persian Gulf. Like the Byzantines, he also enlisted the neighbouring Arab tribes for his support. At this time the Persians had become the dominant power in 'Oman and along the southern coast of Arabia as far as Yemen, where they finally cast out the Abyssinian Governor. The powerful Arab Kingdom of Hira on the western Euphrates was also more or less under Persian control.

> c) To the south west was Abyssinia, at this time a considerable power, and always more or less interested in Yemen, which as we have seen was the original homeland of the Abyssinian Semites. We shall discuss their occupation of Yemen at a later

---

[1] There is a tradition that 'Uthman ibn Huwairith became Governor of Mecca by aid of the Romans, but the Meccans, fearing this Roman influence, drove him away. See Muir's *Life*, p 38. There is some reason also for thinking that the great Kinda tribe were in touch with the Byzantines, see Nicholson *Literary History* p 104.

stage of our investigations; it is sufficient to note at present that when Muhammad was born the Abyssinian power was at war with the Arab tribes[1] and was preparing for the coming conflict with the Persians.

II. ECONOMIC CONDITIONS

Not only was there this continued restlessness of the Arab tribes caused by the encroachment of the surrounding foreign powers, but the economic conditions of Arabia itself at the time were very bad. Living conditions, particularly in the south, had steadily been growing from bad to worse. Early evidence of this is given in the continual process of infiltration of Arabian bands into the spheres of influence of Rome and Persia, two of which crystalized into the petty Kingdom of the Ghassanids and the Lakhmids, and will come under our notice again in a later section of our work. With the decline of political power the public water-works had fallen into disrepair, causing still further economic distress.

III. EXCESS OF POPULATION

One of the things which modern apologists for Islam claim as a matter of great credit to their Prophet, is that he put down the killing of female infants.[2] That the practice was common at the time there is abundant evidence,[3] and the reason for the practice is no secret: it was economic. Similar causes have given rise to similar practices in other parts of the world, and wherever we find it, we can safely use it as evidence of overpopulation, and a consequent economic distress leading to mechanical reduction of possible sources of increase in the population.

---

[1] After the Persian conquest of Yemen, however, the Abyssinians would seem to have become more or less reconciled with the Arabs, for Muhammad sent there some of his persecuted Meccan followers and they were well received.
[2] Qur'anic references are Qlxxxi.8 & 9: xvi.61: xvii.33: vi.152. The two latter are especially interesting as they distinctly mention poverty as the reason for the killing of the children.
[3] e.g., *Musnad (*Ahmad ibn Hanbal), i.389: Wellhausen's 'Die Ehe bei den Arabern," *Nachrichten von der Gesellschaft der Wissenschaften zu Göttingen, Mathematisch-Physikalische Klasse,* 11, 1893, pp. 431-81, p458.

Putting all the pieces of evidence together, it becomes plain that just at the time of Muhammad everything was ripe for another outburst. As Dr. K.H. Becker puts it –

> 'The sudden surging forward of the Arabs was only apparently sudden. For centuries previously the Arab migration had been in preparation. It was the last great Semitic migration connected with the economical decline of Arabia. Such a decline is indisputable even though we may not be disposed to accept all the conclusions which have in recent times been connected with this oft-discussed thesis.'[1]

All that was wanted was some factor that would unify the Arabian tribes and provide them with the inspiration that would keep them together. This Muhammad did. To quote Becker again –

> 'The expansion of the Saracens is thus the final stage in a process of development extending over centuries. Islam was simply a change in the watchword for which they fought, and thus arose at the same time an organisation which, based on religious and ethical principles, and crowned with unexpected success was bound to attain an historical importance quite different from that of buffer states like Hira and Ghassan.
>
> Under these circumstances it would be a mistake to regard the Arab migration merely as a religious movement incited by Mahomet. The question may in fact be put whether the whole movement is not conceivable without the intervention of Islam. There can in any case be no question of any zealous impulse towards proselytism. That strong religious tie which at the present time binds together all Muslims, that exclusive religious spirit of the later world of Islam, is at all events not the primary cause of the Arab migration, but merely a consequence of the political and cultural conditions caused by it.
>
> The importance of Islam in this direction lies in its masked political character, which the modern world has even in our own time to take into consideration. In the outset, Islam meant the supremacy of Medina, but it soon identified itself with Arabianism, i.e. it preached the superiority of the Arabian people generally. This great idea gives an intellectual purport to

---

[1] *Cambridge Mediaeval History*, (ed Gwatkin) vol ii, Chap xi, 331.

the restless striving for expansion and gives a political focus of the great Arabian state of Medina, founded on religion. Hunger and avarice, not religion, are the impelling forces, but religion supplies the essential unity and central power. The expression of the Saracen's religion, both in point of time and in itself, can only be regarded as of minor import and rather as a political necessity. The movement itself had been on foot long before Islam gave it a party cry and an organisation. Then it was that the minor streams of Arabian nationality, gradually encroaching on the cultivated territory, united with the related elements already resident there, and formed that irresistible migratory current which flooded the older Kingdoms, and seemed to flood them suddenly.'[1]

When we study the movement of Islam itself during these early years, and its early development after the Prophet's death, we discover several pieces of evidence that lend force to Dr. Becker's conclusions.

a) The Political and Social Emphasis

We find Muhammad, at the commencement of his mission, standing forth as a Prophet with a burning message from God, calling on men to repent and to forsake idolatry. In an amazingly short time we find him changed from a Prophet to a Legislator, laying down minute regulations as to inheritances and the division of the spoils. This change is characteristic of the whole movement. The emphasis suddenly shifts from the religious note to the political and social notes. It would seem as though the religious note had been the introductory one, which when it had served its purpose, was dropped in favour of the more important notes to which it had merely served as a prelude. This second emphasis is so strong that at least one biographer of Muhammad[2] has been led to see in it the key note of the whole life of the Prophet, and has written of him as the first Arabian socialist.

---

[1] Op. cit. ii, 332. See also Dussaud *Les Arabes en Syria,* who says (p.2.) *En d'autres termes, se la conquête musulmane au VIIe siècle de nôtre ère, apparait comme un événement anormale par son ampleur, elle repong, en realité, à un movement normale des populatiens arabes qui tendent continuellement à pénétrer, et mêne, à s'installer en terrirorie sêdentaire."*
[2] Hubert Grimme, *Mohammed*, 1904.

b) The Lure of Plunder

Looting caravans is an old established custom of the Bedouin of Arabia, practiced since the time of Abraham as it is today.¹ It fell to Muhammad, however, to give it a divine sanction. The need of it occurred early in his own mission. But a few months after his flight to Medina, both he and his followers were in direst poverty. Attempts to remedy this by honest methods had failed, so Muhammad began to organize and send out expeditions to plunder rich caravans going between Mecca and Syria.² If such expeditions were commanded by Muhammad in person they were known as Ghazwas (غزوة): if he appointed one of his assistants as leader it was called a Sariya (سرية), and divine legislation was forthcoming to legalize the robbery.³ Thereafter the lure of plunder was ever before the eyes of the Arabs who followed the Prophet's banner, and after his death it was the same lure that bound the Arab tribes together, so that "forthwith the whole Arabian people, both town and Bedawi, were riveted to Islam by a common bond – the love of rapine and the lust of spoil."⁴

c) Muhammad's Picture of Paradise⁵

However modern rationalistic interpreters, and their English sympathisers, may explain away the sensuous delights of the Muslim Paradise as figurative representations of spiritual

---

¹ See ample evidence in Doughty's *Arabia Deserta*, passim.
² See the whole story with references to the original authorities, in Margoliouth's *Mohammed*, 1905, p234ff. Simpler accounts will be found in Canon Sell's *Battles of Badr and Uhud*, 1913 and *Ghazwas and Sariyas*, 1911: both in the *Islam Series*.
³ Vide Sura ii:212ff, and on the division of booty, Sura viii.1 and 42.
⁴ Muir, *Caliphate*, p42, see also p12 and his statement, p41 *Convictions so shallow and aspirations so low, as those of the Bedawin would soon have disappeared, force and fear would not long have availed to hold together such a disintegrated materials as go to form the Arab nation.* It is curious also to remember that it was held against 'Uthman, that the civil wars in his reign had made an end to the distribution of booty. Mir Khwand, quoted in Sell's *Four Rightly Guided Khalifas*, 1913, p48
⁵ (Ed. Handwritten note:) Hamasa (Freytag) p792 v.3 *"Thou hast not left home for the sake of Paradise, but for the sake of the bread and the dates. (*Ed. Note: The *Hamasa* is a collection of poems gathered together in the 9ᵗʰ Century by Abu Tamma: Another collection of poems with the same name was compiled by the poet al Buthari.)
https://encyclopedia2.thefreedictionary.com/Hamasa cited Oct. 2019)

delights,¹ there is no doubt that the contemporaries of the Prophet and all the early Muslims took them literally², and that as Sir Wm. Muir says

> 'The soldier's imagination was inflamed by tales of heaven opened on the very battlefield, and the expiring warrior tended by two virgins wiping away the sweat and dust from off his face, and with the wanton graces of Paradise drawing him upwards to their fond embrace.'³

Let the student ponder over Sura lvi. 10-40 and the parallel passages, with their promise of fountains of flowing limpid waters, gardens of luscious fruits, ewers of wine, and dark-eyed damsels, and ask himself of what such a picture of Paradise is evidence.⁴ We know that when the cultured Persians, who were used to every luxury, became Muslims, they could not understand how anyone could believe in such a picture of Paradise, and so made the first attempts to spiritualize them away. To them, as to us, such a picture could make no appeal, but can we imagine a picture that would make a greater appeal to the poverty-stricken, ever thirsty, rude⁵ sons of the desert who lived among the parched sands on a minimum of food and drink and whose only comforts were those of their dreams? The enthusiasm which such a picture of Paradise evoked among contemporary Arabs is sufficient commentary on the economic pinch of their common life.

(d) The Shu'ubiyya Movement

---

¹ Lane's friend likened them to the descriptions in the Apocalypse (Lane: *Modern Egyptians*, Everyman's Ed., p68, n4). The commentator Baidawi explains the love for the Houris of Paradise as purely Platonic affair and explains the wine as a draught which intoxicates only with a desire for the Beatific Vision. It will be remembered that Al-Ghazzali was accused by ibn Rushd of going too far in his matter of spiritualization.
² *Miskat al Masabih* (al-Tabrizi) xxiii.13 contains sufficient detail to convince anyone.
³ *Calipate*, p69. An interesting instance is given in *Nur al-Yaqin*, Cairo, 1326, p 121 (? Author ash-Shaykh Muhammad al-Khudhari).
⁴ See also in Nöldeke's *Beiträge zur Kenntniss der Poesie der alten Araber*, 1864, p 183ff *Die Beduinen als Beiträger ihrer Gläubiger*.
⁵ Ed Note: In Jeffery's day this word would have meant uncultured, or lacking sophistication.

Theoretically Islam was the completest of socialisms, every Muslim being considered as an exact equality with every other.[1] This was theoretically the Prophet's own doctrine, and the first Caliph, Abu Bakr, more or less faithfully attempted to carry it out. But it did not last, for such equality of all believers became galling to these Arab tribes who had just tasted the joys of conquest, and bitterly resented the claim of foreigners to share on equal terms in all that was theirs. They were the free sons of the desert of whose race the Prophet had been. They were the chosen people who spoke the divine Arabic tongue in which God's book was revealed. They had borne the brunt of the fighting in the way of Allah, and why should these miserable victims, conquered by Arab prowess in battle, who Islamised only out of craven fear and to save their own skins, whose tongue was barbarous, and whose hands yet smelt of incense offered to other gods, be on an equality with the true children of the desert, and share an equal amount of the spoil?

Under 'Umar, therefore, we find the position defined that although all Muslims are theoretically equal yet the Arabs, the people of the Prophet, are the aristocracy of Islam[2] and everyone who could claim pure Arab descent could draw a stipend from the State.[3] For this purpose a great register was kept in which the genealogies were entered,[4] and the Arabs were thus enrolled as the dominant race. Muslims of other races could then only aspire to become clients[5] of some Arab family, and shine in their reflected glory. A natural corollary of this was that all the best posts and offices in the Islamic State were reserved for Arabs, and most of the emoluments fell to their share. Now among these non-Arab Muslims were many, particularly Persians, who were

---

[1] Vide von Kremer's *Culturgeschichtliche Streifzüge auf dem Gebiete des Islam*, Leipzig, 1873, p 22 for the tradition of the Prophet's pronouncement as to this.
[2] Note the significance of II Chron.viii:9 (The Bible) in this connection.
[3] A simple account will be found in Muir's *Caliphate,* cap. XX: See also *Al-Fakhri* ed Derenbourg p 116-117; Tabari I, 2751 (Ed.Note: Tabari wrote two works; *Tafsir al-Tabari* ('Commentary of al-Tabari'), a Qur'anic commentary (tafsir); and *Tarikh al-Rusul wa al-Muluk* (History of the Prophets and Kings), an historical chronicle. Jeffery is more likely to be referring to the *Tafsir.*)
[4] Large numbers of these genealogies were artificial in the extreme.
[5] i.e. Mawali. (Ed. Note: non-Arabs) A masterly study of their struggle will be found in Wellhausen's *Das Arabische Reich under Sein Sturs,* Berlin, 1902.

in every way superior to the best of the Arabs, and out of their natural efforts to obtain recognition in the State, grew the Shu'ubiyya movement,[1] which led ultimately to the fall of the 'Umayyads.

Here again comment is hardly necessary. As one reads the story of struggle, the suggestion is continually forcing itself upon one, that the theoretical demands of the religious system, which are supposedly the *raison d'etre* of the Islamic movement have every time to give way to the practical demands of providing economic satisfaction for the Arabian tribes. Such an illustration of our thesis is sufficiently obvious.

The question still remains as to why Muhammad chose religion as the force which was to bind these roaming, restless Arab tribes into an all-conquering nation. Numerous observers have commented on the naturally irreligious nature of the Arab[2] which makes it all the more curious that religion should have been chosen as the unifying principle and inspiring force. That most acute of all Muslim historians, Ibn Khaldun, recognised that religion alone was the force that could have inspired the Arabs to unite to found a kingdom[3] though he does not know exactly why. Some have seen in this fact the strongest evidence that Muhammad must have been a god-sent Prophet, but their error has been in not understanding what we have emphasized above, viz that Muhammad was essentially a Semite and the people to whom he preached were the purest of Semites.

Now the simple fact is the religious appeal of what Hogarth calls "Super-monotheism",[4] has been the one force that all through history has been able to bind their loosely knit social organisation in

---

[1] The classical account of the Shu'ubiyya movement is that in Ignaz Goldziher's *Muhammedanische Studien*, vol 1, Halle 1890. A simple account in English based on Wellhausen and Goldziher will be found in Khuda Bukhsh's *Essays Indian and Islamic*, London 1912 and the student should consult Hurgronje's article "Islam and the Race Problem" in the *Moslem World View of Today*, (ed Mott) 1925 especially pp87-89.
[2] Vide Palgrace *Eastern and Central Arabia*, p 23, 24, 109, 152, 201, 342: Cook in *Cambridge Ancient History*, I, 197: Burton, *Pilgrimage* ii, 109: de Goeje, *Ency Islam* i.376.
[3] *Prolégomènes:* tr. De Slane, i.313; cf. Muir's *Life*, p.xciv.
[4] *The Ancient East*, p 23.

any sort of unity. Prone as they were to the development of local cults, the Semites responded to this call of the Super-monotheism. Students of the Old Testament (The Bible) will remember an excellent example of this which is preserved in the Elhoist document in Joshua xxiv (The Bible) (and which can still be clearly seen under Deuteronomistic colouring at chap XXIII), where, before his death, the great national leader Joshua, enthuses the people to cast out other gods and in the name of Yahweh press on to complete the conquest of the Promised Land.

Assyrian history is full of examples of the same kind. The forces of union against tyrannical oppressors was "God's House" at Babylon, and the prestige of the great Ninevite war-lords largely depended on their relations with the far away Babylonian Marduk.[1] The same is true of the Phoenicians at Carthage.

Muhammad was thus simply obeying a true Semitic instinct when he chose this call of the "Super-Monotheism", as expressed by Allah, to be the uniting and driving force of the new movement.

---

[1] Hogarth, op.cit. pp 61, 62.

HISTORICAL BACKGROUND[1]

SOURCES

The outstanding fact about the sources for our knowledge of the history of Arabia in pre-Islamic times, is their paucity. The Greek and Syriac historians provide us with a certain amount of material, but always very fragmentary and disconnected. Arabia has very little interest for the world with which they deal, and practically no part in the great events in which they were interested. The Persian chronicles from which we might have expected more, in reality provide us less, and very little has been preserved in Jewish writings. Inscriptions have contributed their quota, but they are not numerous and save in the case of South Arabia, have not been very helpful for the purposes of historical reconstruction. We may, however, confidently expect that more information will come from this source. A little, but very little may be gleaned from the Qur'an. The pre-Islamic poets might have been expected to prove a rich mine, but in reality they contribute very little, and in recent years very serious doubts have been raised as to their genuineness.[2] For the rest we are dependent on the Muslim historians, who are untrustworthy in the extreme as regards everything that occurred in the "times of ignorance".[3]

The chief Muslim historians whose works come under our survey are –

Ibn Wadih al-Ya'qubi, 890AD

Tabari, 922 AD whose *Tarikh ar-Rusul wa'l-Muluk* is one of the most important monuments of Muslim learning.

---

[1] (Ed. *Handwritten Note.*) 'It is the fact that with the Moslems real and continuous history commences with the Prophet's migration: what precedes that date is a mass of fiction wherein some facts may be buried and occasionally appear. It can indeed be used in illustration of matter which happens to be known from some trustworthy source; but for other purposes it is worthless. Margoliouth, *Early Development*, p231.

[2] See Margoliouth's essay in *JRAS* 1926 on the early Arabic poetry; conclusions which are largely accepted by the Egyptian scholar Taha in his little volume فى الشعر الجاهلى.

[3] It would appear that, when Islam arose, there were no chronicles in existence dealing with the affairs of Central Arabia, and for some generations the days of paganism were regarded with a sort of horror, which prevented the preservation of precise information concerning them. Margoliouth in *ERE*, viii. 511.

Ibn Duraid 934 AD whose *Kitab al-Ishtiqaq* deals with the genealogies of the Arab tribes.

Mas'udi, 956 AD, author of the *Muruj ad-Dhahab,* and called the Herodotus of the Arabs.

Ibn al-Athir, 1234, whose book *al-Kamil,* is for early part mostly a summary of Tabari.

Abu'l-Fida, 1331 who again for the early part is little more than a summary of Ibn al-Athir.

Ibn Khaldun, 1332-1406, the greatest historical thinker in Islam.

Hamza of Isfahani who wrote in Baghdad in the early part of the tenth Century, and being a Persian by birth was mostly interested in the early Persian side of the history, will be a help at times; as also the *Book of Creation* of Al-Balkhi, recently edited by Huart.

A   SOUTH ARABIA CIVILISATION

The Arab historians knew well of the existence of a great and mighty civilisation in the South of Arabia, an ancient civilisation that was in striking contrast with anything that had developed in North Arabia. But their accounts are so obviously legendary that we might well despair of building any historical structure on such a basis. The discovery and gradual accumulation of inscriptions from South Arabia, has, however, provided us with a solid foundation for an attempt at historical reconstruction of this Himyaritie, or Sabaean, or South Arabian civilisation of Yemen and Hadramaut.

In 1772 the Danish explorer Carsten Niebuhr in his *Beschreibung von Arabien* brought to the knowledge of European scholars the existence of inscriptions from the ruins of Zafar, in what Niebuhr conjectured to be the Himyaritic language. It was not till 1810, however, that any copies were made of these inscriptions, and those made then by Seetzen, the German Orientalist, were very inexact and quite useless for the purposes of scholarship. It was left to the English officers employed on the coastal survey of South and Western Arabia, and particularly to Lieut. Wellsted, to bring to scholars the first reliable copies of these interesting inscriptions.[1] They

---

[1] See his *Travels in Arabia,* London, 1838, vol ii, p424

were followed by Arnaud, who discovered the ruins of the ancient capital at Ma'rib[1], and by Parisian Jew, Halévy, who at the peril of his life, disguised as a Yemeni Jew, managed after suffering almost unbelievable hardships to return to France with almost 800 precious inscriptions.[2] Another Jew, Eduard Glaser, followed in his steps, and by a similar disguise penetrated far into the country and returned with a harvest of about 2000 inscriptions.[3] Additions have been made since then from various sources, but little in comparison with that (which) was brought back by these pioneers.

The first attempts at interpretation were made by Roediger and Osiander,[4] but the great names associated with interpretation of this material are, besides Halévy himself, D. H. Müller,[5] J.H. Mordtmann and F. Praetorius. The language proved itself to be the parent of Ethiopic which of course is a well-known Semitic tongue, and the alphabet in which the inscriptions were written is obviously an older form of the Ethiopic script. There are two distinctively marked dialects used in the inscriptions, which have been named Minaean and Sabaean. The inscriptions are still in course of publication, and the few living scholars who are working at the material are Rhodokanakis of Vienna, Margoliouth of Oxford, Ditlef Nielsen of Copenhagen, Hommel of Munich, Grehmann of Prague and Tkatch of Vienna. It must be remembered that this study is yet in its infancy, and further discoveries may completely change many

---

[1] "Relation d'un voyage à Mareb dans l'arabie méridionale" in *JA*, 1845.
[2] See his "Rapport d'ure unr Mission archeologique dans le Yemen" also in *JA* 1872. See further his *Etudes Sabéennes*, Paris, 1872.
[3] Of Glaser's journeys there is an interesting account by O. Weber, *Eduard Glasers Forschungsreisen in Südarabien*, Leipzig,1909. Glaser's own account may be seen in Petermann's *Mittheilungen*, vols xxxiv & xxxvi. The best account of the earlier explorations is to be found in another little brochure by O. Weber, *Forschungsreisen in Südarabien bis zum Auftreten Eduard Glasers*, Leipzig, 1907 which has interesting illustrations.
[4] "Zur himjarischen Alterthumskunde von Dr. Ernst Osiander" by M. A. Levy, Vol. *ZDMG*, Vol. 20, No. 2/3 (1866), pp. 205-287, 470 (84 pages),
Studien über die vorislamischen Religion der Araber. by Ernst Osiander, *ZDMG,* Vol. 7, No. 4 (1853)
[5] His important works are *Die Burgen und Schlösser Südarabiens*, Vienna, 1879: *Epigraphische Denkmäler aus Arabien*, 1888, and in collaboration with Mordtmann, *Sabäische Denkmäler,* Wien, 1883.

EARLY SOUTH ARABIAN KINGDOMS

MAP 7: MINAEAN

MAP 8: SABAEAN

MAP 9: HADRAMAUT

MAP 10: HIMYRAT

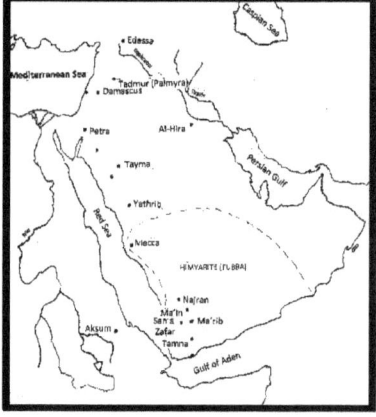

Ed. Note: These maps are based on a number of sources. However, at best they are only estimations and approximations. There are no extant maps of the period and the definition of boundaries even then appeared fluid.

of the conclusions which may be drawn from such evidence as is available at the present time. It is known by report that there are yet many thousands of inscriptions to be gathered,[1] and till more information is available one's conclusions can only be tentative at best.

One result of the greatest importance has however been gathered at the outset, and that is that the information found in the inscriptions has largely confirmed what we had from Greek sources, and shown that the Arabic accounts of South Arabia are utterly unreliable.[2,3] They may thus well be said to have revolutionized our study of the history of early Arabia.

Our starting point for our attempt at reconstructing the history of South Arabia, must be from the statement of Eratosthenes (as quoted by Strabo), writing about 240 BC. He tells us that there were four kingdoms at that time sharing South Arabia between them: that of the Minaeans with its capital at Karna, that of the Sabaeans with its capital at Mariaba, that of the Kattabanians with their capital at Tanna, and that of Hadramaut with the chief city Katabanon.[4]

As to the chronological sequence of these kingdoms there has been much dispute, and equally as much as to the earliest date at which we can place them. Glaser, whose epigraphical discoveries have meant so much to investigators on this question, was certain that the Minaean Kingdom precedes the others, and he argued for a date

---

[1] See Hommel, *EI* i, p377.
[2] See Tritton in *ERE* x 880. Further works which should be consulted on this important line of study are Glaser *Skizze der Geschichte und Geographie Arabiens, 1890: Zwei Inschriften 1897; Altjemenische Nachrichten, 1906:* Hommel's *Südarabische Chrestomathie,* 1893: Weber, *Studien zur südarabischen Altertumskunde,* 1908 and in *MVAG,* 1901; Mordtmann, *ZDMG* xlviii: Hartmann, *Der Islamische Orient,* ii, 1909.
[3] (Ed: *Handwritten Note:*) Note Amir 'Ali's gross misstatement on this point. *History of Saracens,* p5.
[4] The passage (Strabo xvi, 4, 32) reads 'Κατοικεῖ δὲ τὰ μέγιστα τέτταρα ἔθνη τὴν ἐσχάτην λεχθεῖσαν χώραν. Μιναῖοι μὲν ἐν τῷ πρὸς τὴν Ἐρυθρὰν μέρει, πόλις δ' αὐτῶν ἡ μεγίστη Κάρνα ἢ Κάρνανα. ἐχόμενοι δὲ τούτων Σαβαῖοι, μητρόπολις δ' αὐτῶν Μαρίαβα. Τρίτοι δὲ Katταβανεῖς, καθήκοντες πρὸς τὰ στενὰ καὶ τὴν διάβασιν τοῦ Ἀραβίου κόλπου, τὸ δὲ βασίλειον αὐτῶν Τάμνα καλεῖται πρὸς ἕω δὲ μάλιστα Χατραμωτῖται, πόλιν δ' ἔχουσι Σάβαταν.
(AB: cf: https: https://archive.org/details/in.gov.ignca.2919/page/n319/mode/2up)

as far back as 2000BC for the early period of the Minaeans.¹ Hommel carried further the same line of argument and arguing for the identification of the *magan* of the Babylonian inscriptions with *Ma'in* through an earlier form *'Ma'an,* held that we have a reference to the Minaean Kingdom in South East Arabia as early as the third millenium BC. He also thought that the Sabum mentioned in inscriptions of the times of the Kings of Ur, about 2500 BC is the Biblical Sheba, i.e. Saba' of South Arabia.² The great antiquity of the Minaean Kingdom has also been defended by Winckler[3] and Weber.[4] There are very serious difficulties, however, in supposing that the Minaean inscriptions are of any great antiquity, though it is possible that Saba' is mentioned in a Sumerian inscription of Aradnannar as early as the second half of the third millenium, BC.[5] The prevailing opinion also at the present time is that the Minaean and Sabaean Kingdoms were contemporary, and the Minaean Kingdom, so far from having come to an end about 500 BC as the older theory supposed, is found existing at least down to the second century BC.[6]

---

[1] *Skizze der Geschichte und Geographie Arabiens,* 1889, i.5
[2] Hommel has developed his views in *Aufsätze und Abhandlungen,* 1892-1901, especially pt.ii: *Die altisraelitische Überlieferung,* 1897: *Südarabische Chrestomathie,* 1893: in his essay in Hilsprecht's *Explorations in Bible Lands,* 1903: *Grundriss der Geographie und Geschichte des alten Orients,* 2nd ed. 1904: *Geschichte des alten Morgenlandes,* 1908: .*EI,* i. 399ff.
[3] In *MVAG* for 1898, and 1906: in *KAT* p140ff: in his AOF.
(Ed. Note: There are two volumes that are identified by the initials *KAT* one of which is edited by Winckler. It is assumed that the abbreviation AOF refers to Winckler's *Altorientalische Forschungen.*)
[4] *Arabien vor dem Islam,* 1904: and in his accounts of Glaser's journeys already mentioned.
[5] On this Sabu (Saba') see Tkatsch in *E. I.* art *Saba.*
[6] D. H. Müller in his *Burgen und Schlösser,* ii, had suggested that the Kingdoms were contemporaneous, and repeated his views in *WZKM,* viii. Halévy was the first to take up arms against Glaser's theory and he was followed by Meyer *Geschichte des Altertums,* ii, 382: Mordtmann in *ZDMG,* xlvii: "Beiträge zur minäischen Epigraphik", 1897 (in *Semitische Studien,* Bezold, pt. 12: Lidzbarski, *Ephemeris fur semit, Epigraph: 101:* Hartmann, *ZA.* x. (Note: This reference not identified.) and his *Die Arabische Frage,* 1909 passim.

Tkatsch points out that the inscription on the Minaean sarcophagus of Gizeh, shows they were still supplying spices for Egyptian temples in the Ptolemaic era, and the Minaean and Greek inscription at Delos of the second century BC is similar evidence of their existence at that date. See art: *Saba* in *E. I.* and Praetorius in *ZDMG,* lxiii.220.

It is convenient however to take the kingdoms in the order in which they are mentioned by Eratosthenes.

a) Minaean Kingdom

Inscription evidence for the Minaean Kingdom may be said to begin with the *Musri* in the cuneiform inscriptions of Tiglath Pileser III and Sargon II,¹ which refers to a Minaean colony in Northern Arabia in the land of Midian, probably founded to protect the trade routes from the South to Syria, and whose presence has been verified by Euting's discovery of Minaean inscriptions at El 'Ola in that territory. The Biblical record as we read it in I Chron. iv:41, tells us that the people of Ma'in were defeated by the Simeonites who seized their settlements in South Palestine, and in II Chron. xxvi:7 we find them among the enemies defeated by Uzziah.²

b) Sabaean Kingdom

Cuneiform evidence again begins with certainty in the records of Tiglath-Pileser III and Sargon II (i.e. between 745-705 BC). In the Annals of Sargon II for the year 715 BC we read

> 'I received the tribute of Pharoah the King of Egypt, of Shamsiyya the Queen of Arabia, of Iti'amar the Sabaean – gold, spices, slaves, horses, camels.'³

Sheba (שְׁבָא, LXX (Septuagint), Σαβα) is well known in the old Testament as the country of a wealthy trading people, who supplied Syria and Egypt with spices such as frankincense and exported gold

---

¹ See the inscriptions in Schrader *Die Keilinschriften und das Alte Testament, (KAT)*. This *Musri* is of course to be equated with the *Musran* of the South Arabian inscriptions. It appears to have been in a state of decline at this time from the fact that it is in dependency on Sargon's empire.
² There can be no doubt about the identification of the המעונים (Septuagint (LXX) Μειναιοί) of these passages with the Minaeans.
³ Schrader *KAT* p57. Kiepert, *Lehrbuch der alten Geographie,* p187: and Delitzsch *Paradies,* p303 have sought to situate the Saba' of these inscriptions in North Arabia: but the contrary view is rightly insisted on by D. H. Müller *Burgen,* ii p989, and in *Sabäische Denkmäler,* p108. Grimme, *Muhammad,* 1904, p 18, points out that the tribute mentioned consists of characteristic South Arabian products. The Iti'amar mentioned is rightly equated with the name Yath'iamar frequently found in Sabaean inscriptions.

and jewels (vide Ezek. xxvii:22: xxxviii:13; Isa. lx:6; Jer.vi:20: Job vi:19: Ps. lxxii:10,15: Joel iii:8)[1], and the familiar story is told of the visit of the Queen of Sheba to Solomon (I Ki.x:1-13: II Chron.ix:1-12)[2]. The Greek and Latin writers also know of Saba as the land of Spices,[3] and the descriptions of the geographers gave rise to the later popular conception of it as a remote Eldorado.

Of the beginnings of the Sabaean Kingdom we have no more definite information than on that of the Minaeans. At the period of the later inscriptions they appear to have eclipsed in power and glory all the other Kingdoms, and their rulers call themselves Kings of Saba, Dhu Raidan, Hadramaut, and Yamanet. In the early period the ruler is called a *mukarrib* which perhaps means "priestking", and it is noticeable that in Sargon's inscription he does not give the title "King" to the Sabaean ruler. Later, the word *malik* is used, but as in some of the inscription it would appear that three of these *Kings* were reigning at one and the same time, we are driven to conclude that the word is used in a somewhat different sense from our usual use of the word. The state of their society has been likened to that of feudal Europe[4], the great families possessing towers and castles and exercising sway over large areas of land. The prosperity of the Kingdom appears to have been considerable, for the information we gather from the inscriptions agrees with both the picture in the Old Testament and the Classical authors that it was a country to be associated with abundance of gold, ivory, precious stones, spices and perfumes of all sorts, horses and camels.[5] There was apparently a very considerably developed system of irrigation for agricultural purposes,[6] and the Arab writers (including the Qur'an) put down the ruin of the Kingdom to the breaking of the great irrigation dam at Ma'rib.[7] It is of unusual interest to notice that women seem to have lived on practical equality with men, taking apparently a full share in the public life of the community.

---

[1] These references are to be found in The Bible.
[2] These references are also to be found in The Bible.
[3] Theophrastus, *Historia Plantarum (Enquiry into Plants)*, ix.4.
[4] Margoliouth *H.D.B.* iv, 481.
[5] See the accounts in Müller's *Burgen*, vol. ii and *Südarabische Alterthümer*.
[6] The ruins of dams on which inscriptions have been found provide sufficient proof of the importance of this irrigation.
[7] Vide Sura xxxiv. The Arab legend is given by Nicholson, *Literary History*. p15ff.

(c) **Himyaritic Kingdom**[1]

This does not figure in Eratosthenes' enumeration of the South Arabian Kingdoms,[2] but came into prominence later, and in fact is the one Kingdom of South Arabia of which the Muslim historians have preserved much tradition. It represents the Homeritae ('Ομηρίται) of the classical authors. Their country lay apparently between Saba and the sea, and their capital at Zafär, later at San'a. It is supposed that about the end of the second century BC the hegemony passed from the Sabaeans to the Himyarites, who may perhaps be considered a younger branch of the same stock. Their rulers were called *Tubba'*, a designation which the Arab writers apply to all rulers of South Arabia. During the reign of the Emperor Constantine II (337-361) Christianity was introduced among them[3] from Byzantium, and apparently was fairly widely accepted. About the middle of the fourth century AD we find traces of an Abyssinian invasion of the country, though there may have been incursions of Ethiopians into South Arabia a century earlier. The Himyarites raised a revolt against this Abyssinian control in 521, under a native leader Dhu Nawas, whom tradition makes a convert to Judaism.[4] It seems certain in any case that he persecuted the Christians which led to new armies coming from Abyssinia and seems certain that there was a definite Axumite[5] occupation of the country in 526 AD.[6] About the year 570, the Himyarites invited help from the Persians against these Axumites, help which the Persians were only too willing to

---

[1] (Ed. Jeffery included various handwritten notations on HIMYAR apparently copied from various sources.)
[2] Tkatch thinks that this is evidence it did not exist as a separate kingdom in the time of Eratosthenes *EI* ii, 810.
[3] See article "Elsebaan" in *DCB* p471, and Philostorgius *Ecclesiastical History*. iii, and supra p220.
[4] See supra p213.
[5] Ed. Note: Axum or Aksum (Tigrinya: ፡/Axsum/, Amharic: ፡/Aksum/) is a kingdom located in the Horn of Africa rising to importance about 350CE and extending its influence over Yemen, then called Himyar. "The ancient city of Axum (sometimes called Axumis) is located at an altitude of over 2,000 metres (6800 ft) in the north of the Ethiopian highlands (in the modern province of Tigray), close to the River Tekeze, a tributary of the Nile."
(https://www.worldhistory.org/Kingdom_of_Axum/ cited 11 July, 2022)
[6] See Mordtmann in *EI*. ii, 310-11.

give,[1] as the Byzantines had been using their influence with Axum to hold South Arabia against the Persians. The Persians were successful against the Axumites, but far from granting freedom to the Himyarites, Chosroes I set up a governor of his own at San'a, and the Persians remained in control till the Muslim conquest.

(d) **Katabanian Kingdom**

This is the third of the Kingdoms mentioned by Eratosthenes and is referred to by the Greek botanist Theophrastus as one of the spice producing localities of South Arabia.[2] Its territory was to the South and South West of Saba, stretching from Hadramaut to the straits of Bab al Mandab. Apparently the Kingdom is as old as that of the Minaeans, and it is probable that it once included what later became the Himyaritic Kingdom. Its capital was at Tamna, and we gather from the inscriptions that it had a monarchical constitution much the same as that of the Minaeans. The language of the inscriptions is much nearer Minaean than Sabaean. It is unfortunate that the Katabanian inscriptions are so few, for while we can gather from them that for a time they seem to have been the strongest power in South Arabia and had other kingdoms depending on them, and while we can construct a list of some eighteen rulers, we have no certain guide to the history and can only conjecture that about the beginning of our era they became merged in the Kingdom of the Himyarites.[3]

(e) **Kingdom of Hadramaut**

Of this fourth Kingdom of Eratosthenes we know even less than of the Katabanians. Some few inscriptions have been found, but they do not assist us greatly. From the Greek geographers we gather that this was an independent Kingdom existing alongside those of the Sabaeans and Minaeans, and that the Kingdom was situated further to the South-west. The ancients knew of Χατραμωτῖται with their capital at Sabbata in the frankincense country as one of the most powerful kingdoms of South Arabia. The Kingdom would seem to have come into some state of subjection to Ma'in at one period, and

---

[1] (Ed. *Handwritten note.*) 'Antara *Mu'allaqa* 28 has a reference to this Persian occupation of Yemen.
[2] *Historia Plantarum* ix.4.
[3] The best account at present is that of Tkatch in *EI*, article *Kataban*.

the inscriptions like those of Kataban are in a dialect closer to Minaean than to Sabaean. It would seem to have been included in the Himyaritic Kingdom.

(f) **Kingdom of Geban**

Strabo mentions among the people of South Arabia the Γαβῖοι (xvi.786) who are doubtless the Gebanitae of Pliny (vi. 153; xii.63, 68ff., 87ff, 93). The inscriptions also refer to the Gaba'an, but we are unfortunately not able in a positive way to say very much about them. Sprenger thought that they were an invading horde who drove the Katabanians out of South-west Arabia[1] and settled in their place. Glaser took them to be a subdivision of the Katabanians.[2] The most recent writer, however, Dr Tkatch,[3] inclines to the opinion that they were a smaller Kingdom situated on the borders of Katabanian territory. Later they were, like the others, included in the Himyaritic Kingdom.

The full significance of this South Arabian civilisation has yet to be fully estimated. As we shall see in our further studies, bands of these southern Arabs, owing to the decline of the prosperity of South Arabia, migrated in pre-Islamic times into various parts of the Arabian peninsula,[4] and some of these tribes, such as the Tayyi', Kinda, and Tanukh, had a very important share in the development of pre-Islamic Arabia. Their religion, also, which we shall study later in another section of this present investigation, had a profound influence on the religion of Arabia. Naturally the migrating bands from the south would take with them their divinities, and in later times we find all over the peninsula traces of the worship of divinities, eg. 'Uzza and Nasr, whose names are now revealed to us in these South Arabian inscriptions. As we get more and more inscriptional evidence available, it is not improbable that we shall be able to clear up many points that are at present obscure in the early development of Islam. It is noteworthy that Dr. Margoliouth has recently been able

---

[1] *Alte Geographie Arabiens* (Sprenger)256, 268, 282. Cf. Also Müller *Burgen,* ii. 1028 ff.
[2] "Punt und die südarabischen Reiche", *MVAG*, 1899.
[3] Article "Kataban" in *EI,* ii 812 and articles "Gabaioi" and "Gebbanitae" in *Pauly Raelenzyk,* ed. Wissowa.
[4] cf. Blau's article "Die Wanderung der sabäischen Völkerstämme" in *ZDMG,* 1868

to explain from South Arabian material the origin of *shirk* which plays so large a part in the theology of the Qur'an.[1]

B   THE ARAB KINGDOMS

Arabic literature presents us with a confused mass of poetry and legend concerning the *Jahiliyya*[2] or "Times of Ignorance" before Muhammad, but so little reliable history that it were profitless for us to deal with it here save to pick out certain points where we have independent confirmation of the Arabic stories from outside sources. The Arabic material may be studied, as it is admirably set out, in the monumental work of Caussin de Perceval *Essai sure l'Historire des Arabes avant l'islamisme*, 3 vols, Paris, 1847-48[3] but the student should always remember that this work is quite uncritical and can only be used with the greatest caution for historical purposes.

(a)   Palmyrene

The city of Palymra rose from an oasis in the Syrian desert some 150 miles out from Damascus, half way between the Orontes and the Euphrates, in the direct line of the caravan routes which in ancient as in modern times connected the Persian Gulf with the Mediterranean. The trade routes from Petra, Northern Syria and Central Arabia converged on Palmyra, and there can be no doubt that in very ancient times its fine supply of water, made it an important post on the caravan routes.

The earliest (?)[4] mention of the city is in II Chron. viii:4 (The Bible) where Tadmor (תַּדְמֹר = תדמור) of the Palmyrene inscriptions),

---

[1] Margoliouth *Schweich Lectures*, p 68.
[2] On the word *Jahiliyya* (جاهلية) see Goldziher, Muhammedanische Studien, i. 25.
[3] This edition is now unprocurable, but the work is available in an anastatic reprint in 3 volumes, Paris, 1902 (Ed. Note: So wrote Jeffery, however it is now available on many sites on archive.org).
[4] This sign of a question mark in brackets (?) indicates that Jeffery himself was uncertainty about this statement. His small handwriting has been very difficult to decipher on occasions. Where there is any doubt this symbol has also been used.

which is the Semitic name of the town even at the present day,[1] is said to have been built by Solomon. This is certainly a mistaken reference to the תָּמָר of I Ki. ix:18, (The Bible) which refers to the Judaean city mentioned also in Ez. xlvii:19; xlviii:28 (The Bible), but the very mistake shows that it must have been well known at the time the Chronicler wrote. Its origin may have been in very remote antiquity, but its coming to prominence may with some certainty be placed at the time of the Nabataean migration. These Arab tribes who came in and possessed themselves of the partly cultivated lands East of Canaan gradually settled down to a stable occupation, learned settled habits, acquired the civilisation of the surrounding Arameans, and quickly became masters of the Eastern trade. It will be obvious how important such a center as Palmyra would be for them, especially as we remember that it was on the direct route northward from Petra which was a capital center of the Nabataean control. This is borne out by the inscriptions from Palmyra, which are in the Nabataean dialect of Aramaic, and which show us a characteristic civilisation which was a mixture of Arabic, Aramaic, Greek and Roman elements.[2]

There is no further reference to Palmyra in history until in 42 BC, we learn from Appian[3] that the account of the riches of the city stirred the cupidity of Mark Anthony, but the inhabitants by a quick removal of their wealth to the other side of the Euphrates, frustrated his attempts. When the Romans conquered Syria, Palmyra seems for some time to have maintained its independence on the border between the Roman and Parthian empires. In such a precarious position its independence could not last long, especially when

---

[1] Palmyra (the Παλμύρα of Ptolemy: Παλμίρα of Josephus; and the *Palmira* of Pliny) is of course only a transliteration of the Semitic name, תַּדְמֹר=תַּתְמֹר = "city of Palms". It is curious that the Arabs who conquered Spain called the Spanish city Palma by the name تدمير.
(Ed. *Handwritten note*) Tiglath Pileser calls the city Tadmor. It is suspected that the etymology connecting it with Tamar and date is only fanciful. See *AJSL* xli.74n.
[2] The names of leading families are unmistakably Arabic as are many of the deities. It dates its era by the Greek method, but uses the Macedonian calendar, and makes use of the western Aramaic square character for its writing.
[3] Bell, civ.v.9 (Ed. Note: It would appear that Jeffery is referring to the 1899 edition of Appian's *Civil Wars* translated by Horace White and printed by Bell (London) 1899).

relations between Rome and Parthia grew strained. Thus, we are not surprised to find it referred to as a *colonia* on the coins of Caracalla.

Its one period of glory, however, was during the Parthian wars in the third century AD.[1] The overthrow of Petra in 105 AD had left it without a commercial rival, and under its ruling class of Arab aristocracy,[2] it quickly came into prominence, and a little later, probably under Septimus Severus[3] it received the *ius italicum* and became a Roman colony. When Rome became engaged anew in her struggles with Parthia and Persia, the nobles of Palmyra had new careers open to them in the legions of the imperial army. One family in particular seems to have attained fame in this direction and received Roman citizenship, apparently under Septimus Severus. As has not infrequently happened under similar circumstances increase of honour under Roman administration inspired this family to attempt to throw off Roman control. An attempt was apparently made by Septimus Odenathus about 250 AD but was frustrated by a Roman officer named Rufinus, who procured the assassination of the Palmyrene leader. He left two sons, Hairan, who succeeded him in office, and a younger son Odenathus[4] who inherited his father's ambitions and took upon himself the task of avenging his father's blood.

The historians tell how he spent his youth among the mountains and deserts, learning to endure every sort of hardship to prepare himself for the fatigues of war, and more particularly to bind himself by ties of personal affection, to the Bedouin tribes on whom he was to rely when the hour came to strike for himself. It would seem that he first made overtures to Sapor King of Persia, offering to help him against the Romans, but Sapor was offended that Odenathus

---

[1] Greek and Latin sources become available now and we have accounts of it in Zosimus, Vopiseus, and Trebellius Pollio.
[2] *The true Arab despises agriculture: but the pursuit of commerce, the organisation and conducting of trading caravans, is an honourable business which gives full scope to all the personal qualities which the Bedouin values, and cannot be successfully conducted without widespread connections of blood and hospitality between merchants and the leading Sheikhs on the caravan route. An Arabian merchant city is thus necessarily aristocratic, and its chiefs can hardly be other than pure Arabs of good blood.* W. Robinson Smith in *Ency. Britt.* xviii, 199.
[3] Or possibly under Caracalla.
[4] Ὀδαιναθος.

did not come in person to bring his offer, and rejected his gifts. He then bent all his energies to helping the Romans to subdue the power of Persia, a policy which would strengthen his hands when he gained his own independence. Gallienus was emperor at the time and readily fell in with the plans made by Odenathus and thus enabled him amply to revenge himself on the arrogance of Sapor. Odenathus, profiting by the weakness of Rome at this time, when every general was aiming for the purple, set himself to concentrate in his own hands the supreme authority over Syria. In 264 AD he was made supreme commander in the East, and though to the Romans he appeared as a subject of the empire, he was fully recognized in the East as an independent prince exercising undisputed sway from Armenia to the deserts of Arabia.

In this struggle for independence Odenathus was nobly seconded by his wife Zenobia,[1] whose name has been remembered in history where his has been forgotten. She was Palmyrene by birth and her native name was Bath Zabbai. Pollio describes her as of unusual beauty, dark with black flashing eyes and pearly teeth, of unusual physical endurance and with a frank commanding personality. She was also apparently a woman of unusual culture, speaking Greek[2] and Coptic as well as Syriac and having some knowledge of Latin. During her husband's absences in the camp she held the reins of government in the city, and some historians both ancient and modern have been of the opinion that she and not Odenathus, was the ruling spirit in the brief day of Palmyra's glory. Odenathus and his son Herod were assassinated just at the zenith of their success and while Zenobia was engaged in directing the conquest of Egypt, her second son Wahballat was proclaimed his father's successor, but Zenobia really ruled behind the figurehead of this beardless youth.

By the time the Emperor Aurelian had restored the unity of the Empire in the West, and with a fine army, well disciplined by the wars in Gaul, he turned his attention to straightening out the East. Palmyra now had to choose quickly whether to strike a blow for

---

[1] (Ed. *Handwritten Note.*) There is a זַבַּי in Ezra x:28 and Neh. iii:20 (The Bible) but it is suspected to be an error for זַכַּי.
[2] The famous rhetorician Longinus was her teacher.

freedom and face war with Rome, or make submission anew to an Emperor who would insist on real subjection, not a mere show such as had satisfied Galienus. She chose to bid for freedom. In 271 Wahballat took the title of Augustus and dropped the name of Emperor from his coins. He was assassinated almost immediately after in the town of Emesa where Roman influence was strong and Zenobia, supported by her two generals Zabdai and Zabba faced the Roman invasion. Her position was strong, for she had control of Egypt, Syria, Mesopotamia and Asia Minor, with a moral certainty that the Armenians and Arabs would support her.

The story of the struggle which ended in the triumph of Aurelian in 272 and the capture of Zenobia to grace his triumph in Rome, does not fall to be recounted here. The one important thing to note is that the story of this war, where the peasants of Syria and Palestine fought with enthusiasm on the side of Aurelian, shows clearly that Palmyra's empire was that of a small Arab aristocracy dominating a quiet, peaceable, peasant population, despising them with true Bedouin contempt of agriculturalist and heartily hated by them in turn.

Legends have clustered thick around Zenobia, who with Semiramis and Cleopatra has captured the imagination of the ages as among the great queens of the past. Jewish accounts mention her with reverence as the protectress of the Palmyra Rabbis.[1] Christian Chroniclers relate tradition of her theological discussions with Paul of Samosata,[2] and Arab memory never forgot how Arabs had once marched forth under her leadership to do battle with the Roman legions. In the Arab legends,[3] however, we only find an obscure and distorted story in which her name is confused with that of her general Zabbai.

---

[1] *Yer, Ta'anith*, viii.46b. On the other hand, there are several references in the Talmud which would go to show that the ruling class at Palmyra was not in good odour with the Jews viz *Yer.Ta'an*, iv.8 Yeb.16.17. (Ed. Note: Both these Talmudic references are to *Talmud Yerushalmi*, often just cited as *Yerushalmi*.) See also Graetz, *Geschichte der Juden*, iv.273-276; vi.241.

[2] Athanasius – *Historia Arianorum*, cap lxxi: Eusebius *Historia Ecclesiastica* (*Church History*) vii.30. The Palmyrenes would seem to have embraced Christianity in some numbers about the time of Constantine.

[3] See e.g. Zotenberg's *Tabari* ii, 17ff; Caussin de Perceval, *l'Histoire des Arabes* ii.28ff.

(b) Sahil سليح

Legend brings us information of a clan by the name of Sahil, who came north from South Arabia, and have come to have the name among the Arabs of being the first Arabs to found a Kingdom in Syria. Our information about them is very badly confused, but Krenkow[1] would seem to be right in thinking that there is an historic basis[2] for the legends, and in placing the period of their kings at about 400AD. Some authorities say that they belonged to the people of Ghassan,[3] others to the tribe of Quda'a[4] and they are said to have formed part of the army of Zenobia. The cause of their war with Ghassan is said to have been an attempt they made to impose tribute upon the Ghassanids who revolted and conquered them.[5] This ended their Kingdom, but they appear to have survived as a tribe and to have been among the Arabs who fought with the Greek armies at the time of the [Muslim] invasion in 634 AD.[6] There is some reason for thinking that they were Christians and held official positions in Syria under the Byzantine Emperors.[7]

---

[1] *EI*, iv.114. cf. also Nöldeke, *Geschichte der Perser und Araber*, 1879, p35: and *Die Ghassanidischen Fürsten*, 1887, p8.

[2] (Ed. *Handwritten note:*) Ibn Rashiq, *Umdah* ii. 177 After repeating Ibn Qutaibah as to them being the first Arabs in Syria and have only three rulers, definitely states that they held sway till the coming of the 'Amr b Muzaiqiya.
(Ed. *Handwritten note:*) Ibn Qutaiba *Ma'arif*, Egyptian edition p215 gives them only three kings: Amr 'Nulman b 'Amr b. Malik; Malik b. Amr Nulman (his son); Amr b. Malik (his son) and he says clearly that the Byzantines appointed them to power there and they consulted the Byzantines (?) powers on matters of policy.

[3] Ibn Qutaiba, 313: Ya'qubī, 1:235: Hamza, 115. See also Dussaud *Arabes en Syrie*. p9.

[4] (Ed. *Handwritten note:*) Ibn Qutaiba, Egyptian ed.(?), p215 gives it differently in his story of the Azdite Jadha' b Sinan.

[5] (Ed. *Handwritten note:*) *As the antagonist of Hugr (Akil al murar) we find consequently in most versions one of the princes of the Daga'ima of B.Salih. These were, earlier than the Gassanites, the vassals of Byzantium in Syria, where, from the end of the fourth century for about 100 years, they had a dominion, which gradually yielded to the Gassanites.*" Olinder, *Kings of Kinda*, p45.

[6] The Arab sources are Ibn Duraid, *Kitab al-Ishtiqaq*, 314; Ibn Qutaiba, *Kitab al-Ma'arif*, 51; Ibn Khaldun, *al-'Ibar*, ii, 278: *Kitab al-Aghani*, (al -Isfahani) xi, 161: Abu'l-Fida *Tarikh* (Ed.Note: Reference missing); Hamza al-Isfahani, *Annales*, 115: Ibn Rashiq *'Umda*, 11, 177: Qalqashandi, *Nihayat al-Arab*, 243.

[7] That they represented the Byzantine government as Phylarchs seems to be the conclusion to be drawn from the story of their imposing tribute on Ghassān. The

(c)   Jadhima

Another of the legendary kings brought into contact with Zenobia, by Arab legend, is Jadhima,[1] who founded a Kingdom on the lower Euphrates, at a period earlier than the famous Lakhmid Kingdom in the same district. He became very popular in Arabic story and proverb and in later literature we find frequent reference to the story that he was so proud that he would have no boon companion save two stars. Zenobia is said to have lured him to Palmyra and killed him. We have no certainty as to his origin, though if the tradition which makes him an Azdite is correct, he must have been originally from South Arabia.[2]

The star-companion story has become so famous that it is worth quoting. He was called al-Abrash *the speckled* as a polite euphemism for al-Abras *the leper,* and about the year 230 AD became the vassal of Ardashir the Sasanian Monarch of Persia. Jadhima was so proud of his position and so full of the sense of his own superiority over the Arabs that he refused to have any man as his drinking companion, but conferred this honour on two stars of the firmament, known as *al-Farqadani*[3] and whenever he drank a cup for himself he would pour out a cup for each of them. The winning of him back to human companionship was in this wise. His sister[4] had fallen in love with one of his pages named 'Abi b. Nasr and one day in his cups they extorted his consent to their marriage. When he became sober and learned how he had been tricked he was furious, immediately beheaded the page and heaped shame on his sister for having degraded herself to marry a servant. However, when she gave birth to a son, 'Amr, Jadhima adopted the boy, brought him up as his own

---

Daja'ima mentioned there would seem to be plural of Doj'om, ie Ζδκμος, the Christian Phylarch mentioned by Sozomen, *Historia Ecclesiastica,* vi.38.
[1] (Ed. *Handwritten note:*) Ibn Qutaiba, *Ma'arif,* Egyptian ed. says Jadhimah b. Malik al Abrash came from those Azd who after getting tired of being at Mecca, journeyed to the Sawad and came to rule there.
[2] Sources are *Kitab al-Aghani,* xiv, 72-76: Tabari, *Annales,* I, 746-61: Ya'qubi *Historia,* i.237: Mas'udi *Prairies d'Or* iii.181-194: Ibn Qutaiba *Kitab al-Ma'arif,* 53, 274. The story can be found in Caussin de Perceval *l'histoire des Arabes,* ii.16-34: Zotenberg's, *Tabari* ii, 7-19. There is also inscriptional evidence for Jadhīma. See *Florilegium* de Vogüé, p586.463ff.
[3] Also as *al-Daizanani* or *al-Daribani:* vide Buhl in *EI,* i.992.
[4] She is called Riqash (alternate spelling Rasqash) in the poets.

son and treated him with the greatest affection. One day, however, 'Amr disappeared, and no trace of him could be found. After some time two brothers named Malik and 'Aqil[1] found him running wild in the desert, clothed and cared for him, and when he was presentable brought him to the King. Jadhima was so overjoyed at the return of 'Amr that he promised the two brothers anything they might care to ask even to the half of his Kingdom. They chose to take the place of *al-Farqadani* and be his boon companion, which for his oath's sake he had to grant.[2]

Both Arabic tradition and evidence from non-Arab sources, however, agree in finding the acme of pre-Islamic Arabian civilisation in the Kingdoms of Hira, Ghassan, and Kinda, all of which must probably be regarded as but developments of the old South Arabian civilisation, by tribes which had been forced out of their ancient home by economic distress consequent upon the failure of the water supply and the influence of outside political pressure.

(d) Hira[3]

About the beginning of the third century AD when internal troubles had weakened the Persian Empire to such an extent that its outlying provinces were left inadequately defended, certain tribes of South Arabian origin took advantage of the situation[4] to establish themselves in the fertile lands to the west of the Euphrates near Lake Najaf where the country was rich in cornfields and date groves and intersected by numerous canals. Joining together they formed the confederacy of Tanukh.[5] Part of these tribes continued their nomadic life, living in their tents and caring for their herds. Others settled down to an agricultural life and were joined by Arabs of other stocks. Soon towns began to grow up amidst this settled life, the most famous of which was Hira, situated in a fine healthy position some three miles

---

[1] They are said to have belonged to the tribe of Qoda'a.
[2] Cf. Caussin de Perceval ii, 20-22.
[3] Arabic حيرة is the Syric ܚܝܪܬܐ, meaning originally an enclosure (cf. Heb חצר) and would refer primarily to the fenced camp of the Arabs and later be applied to the walled town.
[4] (Ed. *Handwritten note:*) Ibn Hisham *Sira*, tells the tale of Rabi'a b. Nain who was terrified of the coming fate of Himyar and sent his family to Iraq with a letter to Sopher b. Khurnazed, who gave them leave to settle in al-Hira where they founded the family from which was descended an-Nu'man b. Munidhir.
[5] On 'Tanukh' see Dussaud, *Arabes en Syrie*, p9.

south of the site of the later city of Kufa, and not far from the ancient Babylon, where the salubrity of the air was so noted as to give rise to the proverb – 'A day and a night at Hira work more good than attending doctors for a year.' Under the happy conditions thus enjoyed the population grew from year to year, and naturally the town dwellers came to exercise the governmental authority. The main portion of the tribes who settled in the towns were Christians, though of the origin of Christianity among them we have no record. These Christian Arabs called themselves '*Ibadites*[1] and apparently took great pride in their superior faith amidst the pagan idolaters by whom they were surrounded. Soon there was added to these two groups, a third called in Arabic sources the *Ahlaq*, consisting apparently of fugitives from the blood-feud and needy emigrants from other parts of Arabia, who were glad to settle as clients of the possessors of such a settled civilisation.

The early history of Hira is lost in obscurity.[2] Legend tells of the amours of 'Adi ibn Rabi'a with Raqash,[3] sister of Jadhima, and of 'Amr the son of Raqash who was brought up by the Jinn and revenged Jadhima's death on Zenobia. Real history begins with the Lakhmid dynasty in the second half of the third century of our era. The first King whose name acquired celebrity was Imru'l-Qais I, whose name has fortunately been found in the Nemara inscription by René Dussaud[4] and thus gives us evidence of his existence independent of the Arabic historians. The inscription tells us that he ruled over the tribes of Asad and Nizar and Madhhij, and that he besieged Najran the city of Shamir. As we have been able to equate this King with the Shamir Yukhar'ish of the Sabaean inscriptions, we have another solid historical link in the early history of Hira, and the inscriptional date of his death (328 AD) gives us our first fixed point for the chronology of the Kings, and permits us to accept Tabari's list of the four successors of Imru'l-Qais I, whose 90 years of reign give us the exact period between the death of the former and that of Nu'man I (418AD)

---

[1] عباد of course only means 'servants', and probably should be 'Ibad Allah or 'Ibad al-Masih as Guidi suggests *L'Arabie anteislamique,* 1921, p11.
[2] The best account we have is that of Rothstein *Die Dynastie der Lahmiden al-Hira,* Berlin, 1899.
[3] See infra p74.
[4] It commences – *ti nafs Maralqays bar 'Amr malik al-arab Kullihā* – ie. "this is the tomb of Mara'l-Qays son of 'Amr, King of all the Arabs".

which is our next fixed point.[1] We may then state the chronology of the earlier period as follows:

'Amr I ibn 'Adi[2]	*272-300(?)AD*
Imru'l-Qais ibn 'Amr	*? -328*
'Amr II ibn Imru'l-Qais	*328-358*
Aus ibn Qallam	*358-363*
Imru'l-Qais II	*363-388*
Nu'man I ibn Imru'l-Qais	*388-418AD*

Nu'man I was the first of these Kings to attain any prominence. The Sasanian dynasty which succeeded the Arsacids in Persia quickly recovered its control over the Mesopotamian provinces, and the Kingdom of Hira almost from its commencement was under Persian control. It was at the instigation of the Sasanian monarch Yazdigird I that Nu'man carried out the work of building the famous castle of Khawarnaq[3] as a residence for Bahram Gōr the son of the Persian Monarch, who desired that he should live in a salubrious spot. Some legends say that he even trusted the education of his son to Nu'man, who was specially famed for his training of cavalry and had two troops called *Dausar* (two headed) and *ash-Shahba* (the brilliant). Legend also recounts how Nu'man sitting on the roof of the wonderful castle of Khawarnaq and contemplating the rich surrounding lands, was struck by the thought – 'today all this belongs to me, tomorrow it will belong to another, such is the vanity of life.' Impressed by the necessity of seeking refuge in the eternity of God, he left his realm secretly and became a wandering ascetic. The Arab writers count him as a Christian, but Nicholson doubts this,

---

[1] See Dussaud *Arabes en Syrie*, p36.
[2] (Ed. *Handwritten note:*) Herzfeld, *Paikuli*, 136ff; 140ff has suggested that this 'Amr b. 'Adi is the אמרו of the Paikuli inscription whose reign would then have been c272-300 AD and H. H. Schaeder, "Rezension von Schmidt und Polotsky, Ein Mani-Fund", Gnomon 9 (1933), 337–362 in *Gnomon* ix (1933) thinks that the same 'Amr is the Αμαρω of the new Coptic Manichaean documents.
[3] The word is Iranian: *huwarnaqa* = that which covers or protects well – (Guidi): *huvarna* = having a fine roof (Andreas): *hvarēno* = splendour or regal glory (Halévy) have been some of the suggested origins.

though there is reason to believe that he was well disposed towards it, and that his Christian subjects enjoyed complete religious liberty'.[1]

Nu'man was succeeded by his son Mundhir I, who was a faithful vassal of Persia, and is said to have used his military power to assist his old companion Bahram Gōr to attain the throne of his father, when the Mazdaean priesthood endeavoured to prevent him from succeeding. He seems to have been an unusually able Prince, and when war broke out between Rome and Persia, the Western historians relate the prowess of the bands of "Sarasins" who aided the Persians and who in the great defeat perished at the crossing of the Euphrates, in 412. He left his throne to his son Al-Aswad, who appears to have revolted against his Suzerain, who punished the disobedience by keeping him a prisoner in Persia. He was succeeded by his brother Mundhir II, who in his turn left the throne to the son of Al-Aswad, Nu'man II,[2] who married a princess of the tribe of Kinda[3]. He is renowned for the part he took in the battles against the Romans, in one of which he received a wound in the head from which he died.

The Persian King Qobadh now placed on the throne a ruler, Abu Ya'fur ibn 'Alqama, who was not of the royal family, but we know nothing of him save that two years later he was succeeded by one of the most brilliant rulers of Hira, Mundhir III, who died in 554 after a reign of about half a century and around whom an unusual cluster of legends has clung. The peace which had been concluded between Byzantium and Persia in 506, was broken again in 518, by Justinian refusing to pay the tribute. In reply Qobadh sent the Bedouin to ravage the Byzantine territories in Syria, and it was probably during one of these raids that they captured a monastery and

---

[1] *Literary History* 41: Guidi relates (*L'Arabie antesilamique*, p16) Nu'man was a pagan: he persecuted the Christian religion and forbade the Arabas to visit St Simon Stylites, the famous anchorite, and listen to his words. But the Saint appeared to him in a dream, bitterly reproached him and even beat him with his staff. Nu'man then permitted the practice of Christianity in Hīra, allowed them to build churches and receive priests and bishops.
[2] (Ed. *Handwritten note*:) For Nu'man II fighting with Qobadh against the Byzantines, see Malalas 398, Evagrius III, 37, Eustathius in *FHG*, iv 142, Joshua the Stylite cap, 50-57, Zacharius of Mitylene vii, 3-4. This was in 502-503.
[3] (Ed. *Handwritten note*:) This was Umm al-Malik, sister of al-Harith b Amr and granddaughter of the great Huja of Kinda, see Hamza p 104, Tabari 1. 900.

Mundhir sacrificed to Al-'Uzza some four hundred nuns.[1] It was also, in all probability, during Mundhir's absence on these raids that Harith ibn 'Amr the Kindite[2] invaded Hira and usurped the throne.[3] On Mundhir's return to power the raiding of Syria continued, and the Arabs are even said to have burned the suburbs of Chalcedonia. To combat them Justinian drew into alliance with himself the rising power of the Ghassanids of Syria, another Arab Kingdom whose history we shall have to investigate a little later. The Ghassanids then raided Hira as often as Hira raided Syria, and it was in the Ghassanid prince, Harith ibn Jabala that al-Mundhir found his match. Peace was made between Byzantium and Persian in 532 after the expedition in the East of Justinian's general Belisarius, but the Ghassanids and Lakhmids took no notice of the peace and continued to dispute the surpremacy in the desert along the long *strata* to Palmyra. It was in one of these raids that Al-Mundhir[4], whose own son Nu'man had been killed in the battle of Callinicus on the Euphrates in 531, captured a son of al-Hadrith and sacrificed him to Al-'Uzza (the Arabian Venus). Tradition tells also of an embassy from al-Mundhir to the king of Yemen, and this seems to be confirmed by a Himyarite inscription published by Glaser, but we really know little of the remainder of al-Mundhir's reign save that he was killed at al-Hiyar on the route from Aleppo in another raid in 554, when on the "day of Halima", the Ghassanids were amply revenged for the sacrifice of al-Harith's son.

---

[1] The Syriac text is published by Land, *Anecdota,* III.247 cf. also Procopius, *De Bello Persico* ii, 28 for his sacrifice of Harith's son.
[2] (Ed. *Handwritten note:*) Devreesse, "Arabes-Perses et Arabes-Romains Lakhmides et Ghassanides" in *Vivre et Penser,* 1942, p 275, however, thinks that it was in the 503 push, when al-Harith was at the head of the Tha'labites under Byzantine suzerainty. See Joshua Stylites, cap 57. In his note, however, he recognizes that the Arab .... kept him master of al-Hira till 531 when Chosroes came to the throne.
[3] Nicholson, *Literary History,* p42 thinks this temporary eclipse of Al-Mundhir may have been due to his thorough dislike of the communistic doctrines of Mazdak which at that time were the fashion in the Persian court. This would have earned him the enmity of his overlord, who may have instigated the rising Kindite power to invade al-Hira. With the accession of Anushirwan who massacred the Mazdakites in 528 AD and changed the court policy in Persia, al-Mundhir would have his chance to avenge his dishonour and win back his Kingdom.
[4] (Ed. *Handwritten note*:) He was the king to whom Dhu Nawas sent his famous letter telling of the slaughter of Christians of Najran, as is recorded in the letter of Simeon of Beth Arsham. Cf. Guidi in *MAL³ (Memorie della Reale Accademia dei Lincei,)* vii 481.

Before passing from al-Mundhir we should perhaps pause for a moment to read the legend which accounts for "al-Ghariyyan", the two obelisks erected at Hira. The *Kitab al-Aghani* (xix, 86ff) tells us that he had two drinking companions, Khalid and 'Amr. One night, angered in the midst of a drunken revel, he ordered them to be buried alive, but awoke next day from his drunken stupor with no remembrance of what he had done. On learning how they had died he was filled with remorse and erected over their graves these two obelisks. Two days every year he would come and sit by these obelisks. One day was the Day of Good Luck, and the other the Day of Misfortune. To whoever first met him on the day of Good Luck he would give a hundred camels, but whoever first met him on the day of Misfortune was immediately sacrificed, and his blood smeared on the obelisks, hence their name, *al-Ghariyyan* = blood smeared. He is said to have given up this evil custom through witnessing a case of Damon and Pythias[1] friendship between Ḥanẓala and Sharik.

Al-Mundhir was succeeded by three of his sons – 'Amr, Qabus and Nu'man III. 'Amr is always called 'Amr ibn Hind, and Hind was a Kindite princess daughter of the Harith who for a time had ruled in Hira. It is probable that she was taken prisoner when Mundhir regained his throne and kept as a concubine in his harim.[2] 'Amr had a taste for letters and Hira became during his reign the most important literary centre in Arabia, visited by the most famous poets and littérateurs of the day. He seems to have been an energetic prince who carried on the struggle with Byzantium and Ghassan, but he was morose, passionate and tyrannical, and the poets called him – *al-muharriq* – "he who burns fiercely". The great poet Tarafa is said to have been one of his victims. Legend says that Tarafa was sent with his uncle Mutalammis to 'Uman with letters to the governor of the province, which like the σηματαλυγρα[3] the Homeric Bellerophon, contained orders for them to be killed. Mutalammis opened his letter and escaped the danger, but Tarafa went on and perished.[4] 'Amr's passionate disposition was the cause of his death, for having insulted

---

[1] (Ed. Note: This refers to a Greek legend where two friends were willing to give their lives for each other.)
[2] She was a Christian and built a monastery at Hira: vide Nöldeke's *Geschichte der Perser und Araber*, 1879, .172.
[3] (AB: Unfamiliar reference: not enough context to clarify for me)
[4] See Nicholson *Literary History*, 108.

Laila the mother of the Taghlibite chief, 'Amr ibn Kulthum, the latter slew him with his own hand.

He was succeeded by his brother Qabus[1] another son of Hind, who was unfortunate in his efforts to continue the struggle with Ghassan. In 570 he was defeated by Mundhir ibn al-Harith in a battle from which he and a few of his companions alone escaped, but when Ghassan became involved in domestic trouble with Byzantium, Qabus took advantage of the opportunity and raided as far as Antioch. He died, however, in 573 and was succeded by al-Mundhir IV also a son of Hind.[2] The Ghassanid King Mundhir al-Harith, now reconciled with Byzantium, moved against Hira, captured and burned it in 578 and took numbers of the inhabitants away as prisoners. Mundhir IV disappeared about 580, probably in one of the numerous raids, and was succeeded by his son Nu'man III, the last Lakhmid King, and by far the most celebrated in Arab Legend.

Nu'man III is said to have been remarkably ugly and there are suspicions as to his birth, since there is reason to believe that he was the son of a Jewish girl, daughter of a jeweler of Fadak near Madina. For this reason, his succession was disputed, especially by al-Aswad another son of Mundhir IV. Nu'man had been brought up in the home of a noble Christian family in al-Hira, and the poet 'Adi ibn Zaid, the son of the head of this household was the companion of his youth. 'Adi was an unusual character and possessed of unusual accomplishments,[3] and it was his championing of his friend's cause that placed Nu'man on the throne, for 'Adi had a prominent position in the Persian court of Chosroes Parwēz, and had married Hind the little daughter of Nu'man. Nu'man however, repaid the help of 'Adi by casting him into prison and finally murdering him.

'Adi's son Zaid, however, succeeded his father in office at the Persian court, and planned vengeance on Nu'man. It is related that

---

[1] i.e. Καμβύσης = Cambyses.
[2] There was, however, apparently an interregnum of a year or so between the death of Qabus and the succession of Mundhir IV, when the Persians seem to have ruled the state through a governor. Huart, *Histoire des Arabes*, i.69 suggests that this was because the Christian inhabitants of Hira detested him. Cf. also Nöldeke, op. cit. 346, n.1.
[3] Nicholson, *Literary History*. 45ff gives some account of him.

he secured this by praising to the uxorious Persian King the beauties of the Arab women and having an embassy sent to the court of Hira to procure some for the Persian *harim*. This gave him opportunity to make trouble between Chosroes and Nu'man, who was brought as a prisoner to the Persian court and was trampled to death under the feet of elephants.[1] It seems more likely, however, that the trouble was in his series of misfortunes in the wars against Byzantium.[2]

Nu'man III appears to have been a tyrannical, debauched ruler, but like 'Amra patron of Letters. The great poet Nabigha Dhubyani was for some time attached to his court. There are also legends about Nu'man's conversion to Christianity. When we remember his upbringing we can quite believe that he may have formally accepted Christianity, but the accounts of his life that have been preserved to us show that the Christian faith must have sat lightly upon him as upon other members of the dynasty. There seems no reason to doubt the wide spread of Christianity in Hira, but it would seem to have been among the city population, rather than among the aristocratic families of the surrounding nomad Arabs.

The importance of Hira for our studies is two-fold. In the first place its close connection with Persia made it a channel for the dissemination of Iranian culture through Arabia. When we come to study the life of the Prophet, we are sometimes astonished at the amount of Persian legend and ideas we find in his teaching and wonder how a quiet citizen of Mecca could have acquired all this material. One source at least is revealed to us, when we remember how important a literary centre Hira was at this time, and how strong Persian influence was there. Secondly it was a centre for the diffusion of Christian learning and culture,[3] and also one may say, of the old Aramaic culture of Babylon. The 'Ibadites were the earliest among

---

[1] See this story in Nicholson op. cit. 48.
[2] So Huart, *Historie des Arabes*, i.69.70.
[3] *The religion and culture of the 'Ibād were conveyed by various channels to the inmost recesses of the peninsula ... They were the schoolmasters of the heathen Arabs, who could seldom read or write, and who, it must be owned, so far from desiring to receive instruction, rather gloried in their ignorance of accomplishments which they regarded as servile. Nevertheless, the best minds among the Bedouins were irresistibly attracted to Hīra.* Nicholson, op. cit. 19; cf. also p138.

the Arabs to learn the art of writing which spread from them to other parts of Arabia.[1]

The fall of Nu'man III brought the Lakhmid dynasty to an end. He was succeeded by one Iyas ibn Kabisa, a Christian of the tribe of Tayy, at whose court was a Persian resident. Iyas reigned for nine years, but during his reign the Bedouin came in conflict with his suzerain Chosroes, and the great battle of Dhu Qar was fought in which the Persians were routed, and the Arabs had their first taste of victory over the forces of the Sasanians. This defeat lost Iyas his government. He was replaced by a Persian governor who controlled the city till the Muslim conquest in 633.

We may complete the Lakhmid Dynastic table then:

Mundhir I, ibn Nu'man	*418-462*
Al-Aswad ibn al-Mundhir	*462-482*
Mundhir II b. Mundhir I	*482-489*
Nu'man II b. al-Aswad	*489-503*
Abu Ya'fur ibn 'Alqama	*503-505*
Mundhir III ibn Ma'as-Sama	*505-554*
'Amr ibn Hind	*554-569*
Qabus	*569-573*
Mundhir IV	*573-580*
Nu'man III, Abu Qabus	*580-602*

(e) **Ghassan**

The most famous of all the families who quitted Yemen to seek for safer and happier homes in North Arabia, is that known to the Arabs as the family of 'Amr ibn 'Amir al-Muzaiqiya',[2] some of whom are said to have settled near Madina, but the major portion of whom journeyed into Syria. Jafna ibn 'Amr was the eponymous ancestor of this Syrian group, which settled in the district around

---

[1] Cheikho, (Ed. Note: volume not indicated.) pp 155-157 with testimonies from Wellhausen, Rothstein, Goldziher and Berger.
[2] (Ed. *Handwritten note*:) Ibn Hisham 8 tells of the migration of the family of 'Amr b. 'Amir from Yemen when the dam at Ma'rib began to give way and he says that Jafna settled in Syria, 'Amr and Khazraj(?) at Yathrib, Khuza'a at Man and Azd divided into Azdz (?) as Sarat and Azd 'Uman.

Bosra and gradually drew into fellowship other Arab elements settled in the same district. Tradition makes them at first tributary to the Kingdom of Salih[1] already mentioned, but when they first appear on the stage of history we find them in relations with Byzantium and their leaders holding Byzantine titles of Phylarch and Patricius.

Whether they were Christians before leaving their Yemenite home we do now know, but when they appear before us in North Arabia they appear as Christians and their leading family, that of Ghassan, is given recognition by the Emperor Anastasius (491-518). It is curious that the Arabs gave to some of the Kings of Ghassan the title *al-muharriq* which we have already seen used for the Kings of Hira.

We have already seen that Justinian, in order to balance the Persian use of the Arabs of Hira for raiding purposes, had to ally to himself and strengthen the power of this Kingdom of Ghassan, and the first date of which we are historically sure is that of 528, when al-Harith ibn Jabala[2] of Ghassan defeated al-Mundhir King of Hira. This al-Harith[3] fought under Belisarius in the campaign in Mesopotamia in 541, and apparently fell under suspicion of disloyalty to the Byzantines because he returned home to Syria by a different route from that of the main army and had no success to report. The *day of Halima*[4] in June 544, when he won a decisive victory over al-Mundhir of Hira,[5] we have already mentioned in our account of the latter Kingdom. In 563 he appears to have visited the court at Constantinople to settle the question

---

[1] (Ed. *Handwritten note*:) Ibn Rashiq *'Umdah* ii, 177 says *Salih ruled there under Byzantine control till the coming of 'Amr b. 'Amir. See* Ibn Qutaibah *'Kitab al-Ma'arif'* (?) 215.

[2] (Ed. *Handwritten note*:) Jabala(h) was concerned in the Palestinian insurrection of 496. Cf. Theophanes *Theophanis Chronographia*, ed. de Boor, p 141.

[3] (Ed. *Handwritten note*:) Ἀρέθας τοῦ Γαβάλα: He must be the Ἀρέθα of the inscription of 559 from Qasi al Khair in Syria (? *Inventaire des inscriptions palmyréniennes de Doura-Europos* Robert Du Mesnil du Buisson, Revue des études juives Année 1935, RES 2, pp. 17-39.)

[4] This is probably a place name (so Schliefer in *EI* ii, 143) but tradition says it was so called because before the battle of Halima, the daughter of al-Harith, with her own hands anointed the warriors with the perfume *Khalug*.

[5] (Ed. *Handwritten note*:) This Mundhir is referred to as the Patricius al Mundhir in a Christian inscription at Heyat date 578 (?) in Waddington no 2110. In Waddington 2562 he is Φλ(άβιος) Ἀλαμούνδαρ[ο]ς, [ὁ] πανεύφημυς

of succession to his office.[1] He died in 569 or 570. Like all his dynasty, he was a staunch partisan of the Monophysite church,[2] and on his visit to Constantinople, he is said to have secured the appointment of James Baradeus and Theodor as Bishops for the Syro-Arab territory.

There is a curious story told among the Arabs that the great poet Imru'l-Qais when he went on his journey to Constantinople, left his magnificent cuirasses in charge of the Jew as-Samau'al ibn Adiya, at his castle of Ablaq in Taima'. Al-Harith coveted these cuirasses and when as-Samau'al refused to betray the trust, al-Harith besieged him in his castle and slew his son.

He was succeeded by his son Mundhir ibn Harith, who carried on the war against Hira, and as we have already seen, defeated Qabus in 570 at the battle of 'Ain Ubagh, and it was only Justin II's refusal to send further financial assistance that prevented him from carrying the war further into the enemy's territory. This caused trouble between the Byzantines and al-Mundhir which resulted in the latter being called to Constantinople and the Kingdom in Syria left to practical anarchy from which it never fully recovered. The four sons of Al-Mundhir ravaged Byzantine territory for some time, but an expedition suppressed them, though it served but to spread further the anarchy in Syria. The Kingdom of Ghassan finally came to an end by the capture of Syria by Chosroes Parwiz in 613 or 614. Ghassanid princes are said by Muslim historians to have fought with the armies of Heraclius in the battle of Yarmuk in 635-636, but it is unlikely that the Kingdom was restored at the re-conquest of Syria by the Byzantines in 629.

Just as Hira was a channel for the dispersion throughout Arabia of Persian and Aramaeo-Babylonian culture, so Ghassan was the channel whereby Greek and Syrian culture came down to the Arabs of the rest of the peninsula.[3] We have called it the Kingdom of Ghassan, but it seems to have had no fixed capital, though the centre

---

[1] In the History of John of Ephesus, we read an account of the strange sensation produced in Constantinople by the appearance of this stalwart Bedouin phylarch from the desert.
[2] On the Christianity of the Ghassan see *Al-Mashriq*, i, 519, 554. According to Yaqut, iv. 652 they used to worship Manat before they became Christians.
[3] Hogarth *Arabia*, 1922, p10 thinks that they became the heirs of the earlier Palmyrene Civilisation.

of its power was round Damascus,¹ and the fact that its civilisation was not so stable as that of Hira is perhaps the reason for our knowing less about it. The list of its Kings as given by Huart² is –

'Amr ibn 'Arm Mozaiqiya	
Jafna	
Abu Khamir el-Harith ibn 'Amr	
Jabala	-528
Al-Harith ibn Jabala	528-569
Al-Mundhir	569-581
An-Nu'man	581-
Al-Harith the young	
'Amr ibn al-Harith.	

Their empire seems to have extended from the land of Hermon to the Gulf of Aqaba and the Romans held them responsible for the good behavior of the nomads who wandered in the Palestinia Secunda, Arabia, Phoenicia ad Libanus, and perhaps Palestinia Tertia and the provinces of Syria.³ How effective their control over the Arab tribes was it is difficult to estimate.

> 'Over the Arab tribes of the interior, says Bell,⁴ they would, if we may judge by analogy, only exercise real authority so far as they could make their power dreaded. But no doubt their indirect influence as wealthy and powerful princes of Arab race was considerable. There are indications that they were occasionally able to make themselves felt almost as far south as Medina.'

(f)   Kinda

We have already seen that early in the sixth century a Kindite prince⁵ invaded Hira and assumed the Government for a while, and that three later rulers of Hira were sons of a Kindite princess. Unfortunately, we know very little about the history of this

---

[1] Bell, *Origins of Islam in its Christian Environment* (London, 1926) p22 says "The main seat of their court seems to have been at Jabiya in the Jualan."
[2] Caussin de Perceval *Histoire des Arabes,* i.72.
[3] Margoliouth, *Mohammed,* p35. The only monograph on the subject is Nöldeke's *Die Ghassanischen Fürsten aus dem Hause Ǧafga's,* Berlin, 1887.
[4] op. cit. p23.
[5] (Ed. *Handwritten note*:) cf. Olinder, *The Kings of Kinda*.

interesting Kindite confederacy. It apparently was of Hadramaut origin and founded its Kingdom in central Arabia early in the fifth century, gradually extended its power to the Persian Gulf, and by 430 AD exercised considerable power in Central and North Arabia. The reputed founder of the Kingdom was Hujr 'Akil al-Murar, and in his time Kinda would seem to have held the same relationship to the Himyaritic Kingdom of the south, that Hira did to the Sasanians or Ghassan to the Byzantines. Harith ibn 'Amr was the most renowned of their Kings. It was he who conquered Hira. The vengeance taken by Mundhir on re-conquering his Kingdom in 529, when he slaughtered the captive Kindite princes, has been celebrated in the verses of the great Kindite poet, Imru'l-Qais.[1]

> 'Oh eyes will you not weep for me warm tears
> Weep for the princes who have perished.
> Princes of the house of Hujr ibn 'Amr,
> Led out at even to be put to death.
> Would that they had perished on the day of conflict
> (But now that they are killed in cold blood)
> In the land of the Beni Marina.
> Ablution water has not washed their heads
> Which remained soiled with their blood.
> The birds of prey are assembled round them
> To snatch out their eyebrows and their eyes.'

After the death of Harith, his two sons Salam and Sharahbil fell out with one another and there followed a period of feuds in which the Kingdom gradually declined. The poet Imru'l-Qais endeavoured to restore the broken fortunes of the Kingdom and even journeyed to Constantinople to beg help from Justinian as an hereditary enemy of Hira, but in vain.

---

[1] Ahlwardt's *Divans*, p158-159

و بكى لي الملوك الذاهبينا	الا يا عين بكى لي شنينا
يساقون العشية يقتلونا	ملوكا من بني حجر بن عمرو
و لكن في ديار بني مرينا	فلو في يوم معركة اصيبوا
و لكن بالدماء مرملينا	فلم تغسل جماجمهم
و تنتزع الحواجب و العيونا	تضلل الطير عاكفة عليهم

The importance of this little Kingdom of Kinda is twofold. As Guidi says,[1] this confederacy of Arab tribes under Hujr was the first attempt of the Arabs of the centre of the peninsula to group themselves round a common centre and under a common chief,

'it is a prelude to the movement that a century later was to reunite the different tribes under the founder of Islam.'

Moreover, Kinda was Christian and its capital Yamama[2] was a notorious pre-Islamic seat of Monotheistic teaching.[3] It is possible also that towards the end of its existence it came into some kind of relationship with the Byzantine power, but by the time of the Muslim conquest it had retired back into insignificance again near the old home in Hadramaut.[4]

C   THE OUTSIDE EMPIRES

We have already had occasion to mention the three great world powers which were influencing Arabia at this period, and which as a matter of fact possessed between them a large part of the small fringe of fertile land which Arabia possesses. It is now time for us to look at them a little more closely.

(a)   Byzantine Empire
To the North was the Roman power[5] which ruled over all Syria and Palestine, a large part of Asia Minor and the northern end of Mesopotamia and was pushing its influence steadily down the Hejaz coast. It also ruled Egypt and had considerable influence at this time in Abyssinian affairs.

---

[1] Guidi *L'Arabie antéislamique*, p30.
[2] يمامة Anciently called Jau جَو, was the residence of Muhammad's great rival prophet Musailama.
[3] Hogarth, *Arabia*, p1: *and Jamama, its Najdean seat, was notoriously an active seat of monotheism before Muhammad. began to preach. The Meccan Prophet is said even to have sat at the feet of the Najdean before Arabia grew too small for two Apostles of one God.*
[4] (Ed. *Handwritten note:*) A Sprenger, "Die arabischen Berichte über das Hochland Arabiens beleuchtet durch Doughty's Travels in Arabia Deserta", ZDMG, xlii (1888), pp321-340.
[5] Ar- Rum, in the Arabic Chronicles, always means the Byzantine Empire.

MAP 11: OUTSIDE EMPIRES ABOUT 600CE (AD)

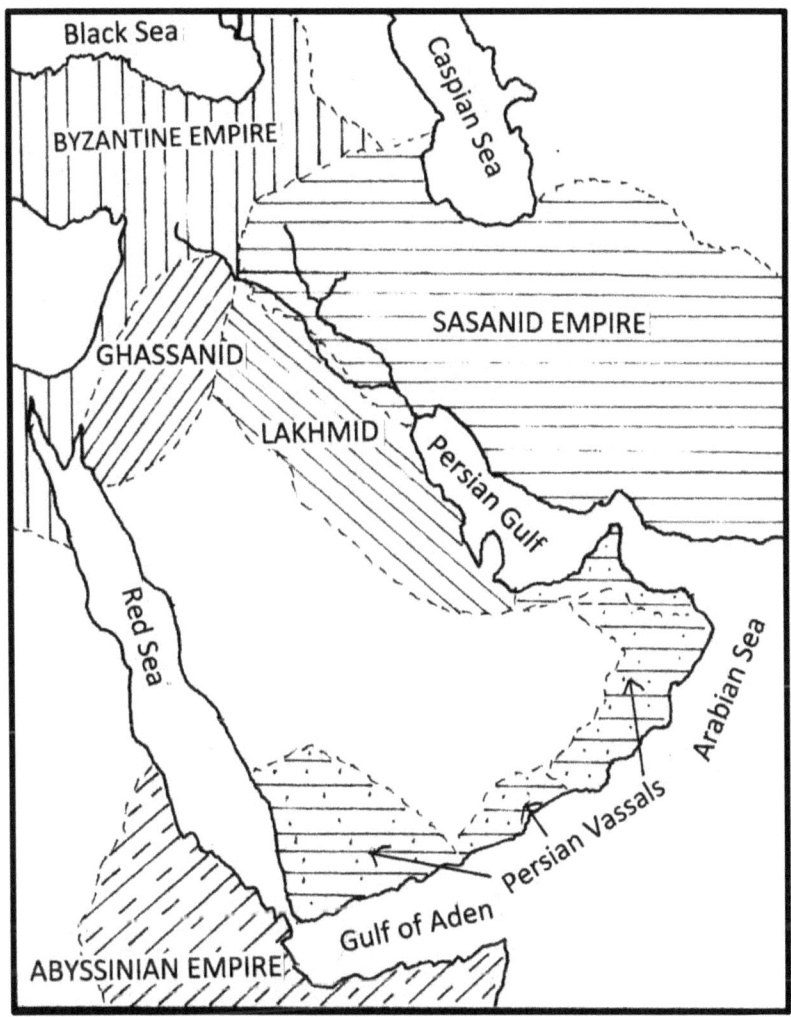

Ed. note: This map has been constructed from a number of sources. The boundaries are estimates and approximations only.

"Roman Empire" it was called, and followers of Gibbon are still wont to look on it as the continuation and decadence of the glory of ancient Rome. Recent writers, however, have been inclined to question this and look on it as little more than the inheritor of Rome's position and prestige. It was as Rambaud points out[1] "a mediaeval state situated on the extreme frontier of Europe on the edge of Asiatic barbarism," which was far from being a new Rome. The commencement of its greatness was the founding of the new town by Constantine in 330 AD[2] says Diehl[3]

> 'The day when Constantine founded Constantinople, and made of it the second Capital of the Roman Empire, — that day, 11th May 330 – the Byzantine Empire began. By its geographical situation at the point where Europe and Asia meet, Constantinople was the natural centre round which the Eastern world could gather. On the other hand, by its marked Hellenic characteristics, and above all by the new nature that Christianity gave it, the new capital 'New Rome', differed profoundly from the older, and symbolized the new aspirations and new characteristics of the Eastern world.'

From its foundation on to the time of Justinian, there was a gradual evolution along the lines mentioned by Diehl, its Hellenic character, use of the Greek language, and close connection with Oriental affairs, tending to separate it more and more from the Western Empire. In that time, moreover, there were three great events which set the current strongly in the direction of wider separation. First was the division of the Empire politically in 395 AD, at the death of Theodosius the Great, when his two sons, Arcadius and Honorius, divided the Empire between them. Secondly there was the barbarian invasion which came near blotting out the Western Empire while it left the Eastern practically intact. And thirdly there was the rise of Christian heresies which left the more somber Westerners unmoved, but which wrought havoc in the Eastern Empire.

---

[1] Rambaud, *L'Empire grec au dixième siècle,* pvii
[2] The old town, according to Greek legend, goes back as far as 657 BC, when it was founded by Megarians and Argives under one Byzas.
[3] *Byzance,* 1919, p4.

The reign of Justinian from 518-565[1] saw a valiant attempt to do away with this fatal separation of the two parts of the Empire. Justinian desired to be a Roman Emperor in the old sense, and ably assisted by his brilliant general Belisarius, carried his arms victoriously in all parts of the Empire in order to realize this dream. His fame came down to the Arabs through his preoccupation with the struggle against Persia, in which the Arab Kingdoms of Hira and Ghassan were involved, as we have already had occasion to see. But though Justinian's exploits both in the arts of war and of peace have left him a splendid name in the annals of history, his work really weakened the Empire most seriously, so that under his successors it became more and more difficult to resist the attacks of enemies in the East.

At the time of the rise of Islam, Heraclius was Emperor at Byzantium. With the fascinating study of his reign[2] we are not concerned save to notice the two great factors which were weakening the Empire at this time.[3] First was the Persian wars. There had been rivalry between Persia and Rome as far back as 385 AD but the bitter strife really began when Justinian commenced his eastern campaigns. The struggle became even more bitter under Justinian, continued on through the reigns of Tiberius Maurice, Phocas and Heraclius. In origin they were partly economic, due to the desire of the Byzantines for a trade route to the East free from Persian influence, and which made them ally themselves to the Turks[4], who were at that time Persia's enemies. Partly they were due to religious causes, arising from Byzantine determination to protect fellow Christians in

---

[1] On Justinian who is of unusual importance for affairs in the East, see particularly Diehl's essays in *Cambridge Mediaeval History* (ed Gwatkin,) vol ii, caps. i & ii; and the same scholar's *Justinien et la civilisation byzantine au vie siècle,* Paris 1901.
[2] On Heraclius, besides the essay by Baynes in *Cambridge Mediaeval History,* vol ii, cap ix: see Euangelides,'Ηρήκλειος ὁ Αὐτοκρατωρ τοῦ Βυζαντίος (Odessa, 1903); Penrice, *L'Imperatore Eraclio,* Florence, 1905 and the earlier work of Drapeyron, *L'empereur Héraclius et l'Empire Byzantin au vii. siècle,* Paris, 1869
[3] See on this the essay "Byzantino e decdadenza del Cristianesimo orientale all vigilia dell' invasion arabs", in Caetani's *Annali dell Islam,* ii, 997-1052
[4] Two embassies were sent in this connection. See on them Marquart's essay 'Historische Glossen zu den altturkischen Inschriften' in *Vienna Oriental Journal,* xii (1898)

Armenia from Sasanian oppression.[1] One may suspect, however, that the real cause of the struggle was the intense jealousy of these two rival powers, each wishing to see the other crushed.

The honours of war fluctuated. Under Maurice the Byzantines triumphed, but after his death the Persians overran Syria and Palestine, devastated Armenia, partially occupied northern Mesopotamia, and pressed far into Asia Minor.[2] In 614 came the crowning disaster, when Persian troops captured the Holy City and carried off the jewelled bauble that was reverenced by the whole of Christendom under the supposition that it was the Holy Cross.[3] Under Heraclius, however, the tide turned again, and by 629 the Byzantines were practically everywhere triumphant.[4] But this triumph was only won at the cost of tremendous sacrifice of both life and treasure, and though Heraclius had vanquished the Persians he had deprived the Empire of all strength to defend the Eastern provinces against a more determined foe.

Secondly there was religious strife. From Justinian onward there had been much strife between the Court at Constantinople, which considered that what it believed was orthodoxy and the only true and legitimate interpretation of Christian doctrine, and the mass of the inhabitants of the Eastern provinces, who held various other interpretations, particularly that known as Monophysite teaching. It is quite profitless here to enter into the history of these controversies;[5] our interest is in the fact that all teaching on Christian doctrine not in accordance with that of the Court, was branded as heresy, and the Court seemingly thought that physical violence was the choicest way of asserting orthodoxy and suppressing heresy. The result was that the provinces paid only half-

---

[1] In 571 Chosroes had attempted to force the Magian religion on the Armenians, who appealed to the Byzantines for help against him. See Görres article "Das Christentum in Sassanidenreich", in *ZWT*, xxxi, 449-68 and ibid xxxix, 443-59
[2] (Ed. *Handwritten note:*) see Bell, *Origins of Islam*, p12
[3] Clermont-Ganneau has an interesting essay on this in *Recueil d'-Archéologie orientale*, ii, 137-160.
[4] The simplest account of the period is in Baynes article *The Successors of Justinian* in *Cambridge Medieval History* ii but the student can profitably consult the early chapters of Butler's *Arab Conquest of Egypt*, Oxford 1902
[5] The student will find ample material in Harnack's *Dogmengeschichte*, or in Dorner's *Person of Christian*, Edinburgh, 1861

hearted allegiance at best to the Byzantine power, and often actually preferred the rule of pagans under whom they would be free to follow their own doctrinal convictions.

(b) **Sasanian Empire**[1]

To the East of Arabia lay the great Persian Empire of the Sasanians, the bitter enemy of Rome, and at this time supreme in authority along the southern Mesopotamia, and predominant in influence all along the eastern coast of Arabia as far as 'Uman.

It will be remembered that after the overthrow of the great Achaemenian Empire by Alexander the Great, the Parthians came into control and there was a Parthian dynasty in Persia for nearly five centuries,[2] rising to power at the expense of the Seleucids and falling when a genuine Persian party was strong enough to overthrow them. This revival of Persian nationalism placed the first of the Sasanian Kings on the throne in 226 AD in the person of the almost legendary Ardeshir.[3] This accession of a true Persian dynasty after so many centuries of rule by foreign oppressors had two important consequences. Firstly, it meant the revival of the Zoroastrian religion and the use by the reigning house of the power of the Magi (the Zoroastrian priests) to support the newly centralized government. Secondly, in some mysterious way which we cannot explain, nor even fully understand, it gave rise to a belief very firmly held by the common people, that the ruling house possessed a mysterious Royal Splendour, (*Farri Kayani*), a kind of Shekinah[4] which symbolized the divine right by which they alone, as descendants of the legendary Kayani dynasty, could legitimately

---

[1] Ed. Note: Jeffery added some handwritten notes on "Pre-Islamic Contacts with Persia", see Appendix, p242.
[2] It is a curious fact that although the period between the death of Alexander the Great and the commencement of the Sasanian dynasty is five and a half centuries, the Persian Chronicles (and the Arab historians who copied them) invariably reduce this period to 266 years, probably with a view to lessening the importance of the period of Parthian domination.
[3] His story is told in brief in Browne's *Literary History of Persia,* I, 137ff.
[4] Ed. Note: Shekinah is a Hebrew word used in the Old Testament (Bible – Exod. xl:34-35). It is first mentioned when on the completion of the Tabernacle (tent) of Worship it was covered by a cloud. According to the Biblical account this tent of worship was constructed at God's direction and in accordance with His design. The cloud was understood to represent God's glory coming to earth and indicated God's approval.

wear the Persian crown. It was because of this that they assumed the title of gods *Pahlbagh* and it made them so secure in their possession of the throne that any impostor or rebel who dared to make a claim to the throne was considered by the people as guilty of the most heinous of crimes.[1] As the student will see in his later studies, it had also enormous importance in the history of Islam in Persia, and explains the fanatical devotion of Persian Muslims to the descendants of 'Ali.[2]

The revival of Zoroastrianism and the attitude of the Sasanians to subjects of other faiths within their realms is of some importance to us. So far as one can decide amidst a mass of conflicting opinions, Zoroaster seems to have preached a little before the rise of the Achaemenian dynasty in Persia and to have died about 583 BC.[3] It is still disputed whether Zoroastrianism ever became the official religion of the Achaemenians, though the weight of authority of A.V. Williams Jackson[4] and J. H. Moulton[5] is on the side of its having been acknowledged as the national Iranian religion in the time of the later Achaemenians. Under the Parthian domination it declined, and the Sasanians posed as restorers of the old Iranian religion, and were apparently fanatical persecutors of those who would not accept its claims.[6] There is a curious contradiction as to the fate of Christianity under their rule, though we are probably right in concluding that there is a large element of truth underlying the numerous accounts we have of the bitter persecution of the Christians at their hands,[7] and which, as we have

---

[1] An interesting illustration is given by Browne, op. cit., I, 129
[2] See Zhukofski in *Zapiski* ii, on *Ali Ilahi of Persia* (ie. Valentin Zhukovskiy, Sekta "Ludey Istiny" - Ahli Hakk –[Persia], *Zapiski Vostochnogo Otdeleniya Imperatorskogo Russkogo Arheologicheskogo Obshestva*, Vol. II, (St. Petersburg, 1887), pp.1-24) and Huart's article in *EI*. i. 292-292: also Dussaud *Nosairis*, also passim and Gobineau, *Trois ans en Asie,* p 338. Shahrastani (ed Cureton) p 122 gives an account of their belief that God was incarnate in 'Ali.
[3] So Jackson *Zoroaster,* 1919 (following West)
[4] Op. cit p 134 and *JAOS* xxi, 164-184
[5] *Early Zoroastrianism*, 1913, Sect ii and cf. L. H. Gray in *ERE*, i. 69-72
[6] The Kings of this line were ardent, and only too frequently intolerant, upholders of this faith' – Castarelli in *ERE* xi, 201
[7] See Caetani's essay "I popli cristiani sottomessi ai Sassanidi" in *Annali,* ii 890-912, and Labourt's *Le Christianisme dans l'Empire Perse sous la dynastie sassanide* Paris,

seen, became one of the ostensible reasons for war between Rome and Persia.

Throughout the whole of the Sasanian period there was more or less extensive war with the Byzantine power, and there is an account of conflict successfully waged by Ardeshir, the founder of the dynasty, against the armies of Severus Alexander[1]. In our account of the Byzantine Empire we have given some account of the later struggles which are more important for our purpose, but it should be kept in mind that while these struggles may have been caused by some local troubles, they are in reality a continuation of the struggle between Hellas[2] and Persia, which began when the Great King Darius invaded Greece and was defeated by the immortals at Marathon. Besides war with Rome, the Sasanians had also become interested in South Arabia, and in 570 AD Chosroes I overthrew Abyssinian rule there and appointed a Persian Governor. Persian control lasted in South Arabia till in 628, on the death of Chosroes II, the Persian governor at the time, named Badhan, accepted Islam.

The Sasanians were a literary dynasty and letters flourished under their patronage. It is during this period that we have the development of the two very important movements of thought in Persia, that of Manicheanism[3] and that of Mazdakism,[4] the former a highly speculative religious philosophy savouring of Gnosticism, and the latter a form of religious communism. This was the period of the Pahlavi literature[5] and the writing of the great national epic.[6] Scholars thronged the courts of the Sasanian Kings, who gave refuge to the

---

1904. Christian sources may be consulted in the *Chronicles of Joshua the Stylie,* ed. W. Wright, Cambridge, 1882 and Hoffmann's *Auszüge aus syrischen Akten persischer Märtyrer*, Leipzig, 1880

[1] Sykes *Persia* 1922, p 32
[2] Ed. Note: The Greek name for Greece
[3] On Manicheanism see particularly *Burkitt, Religion of the Manichees,* 1925, le Coq *Manichaiea,* 1922, Cumont, *Racherches sur le Manicheisme,* 1908
[4] See Nöldeke's *Geschichte der Perser und Araber,* 1879. App iv. "Über Mazdak und die Mazdakiten" and the account in Browne's *Literary History of Persia,* I, 166-172
[5] See Browne op. cit. p102ff
[6] See Browne op. cit. p122

Greek philosophers¹ who were driven out from their native land by Justinian, and there is some evidence that some of these Kings themselves indulged in literary composition.²

There is some little evidence of Persian culture reaching Mecca in pre-Islamic times, and it will be remembered that one of Muhammad's rivals in prophecy was Nadr b Harith, who bitterly offended the Prophet by reciting to the Quraish the stories of Rustam and Isfaniyar as of great value as the stories of the Qur'an.³ But the main channel for the diffusion of Persian culture was undoubtedly the literary court of al-Hira.⁴ It is remotely possible that the Persian occupation of South Arabia may have opened another channel of influence during the early years of Islam.⁵

(c) <u>**Abyssinian Empire**</u>

Unfortunately, we know very little about the early history of Abyssinia. As we have already seen, the Semitic population would seem to have colonized Abyssinia at an uncertain period BC probably not long before our era. They centred their African settlement at the town of Axum (and are consequently sometimes known as Axumites) and are still strongest in that region. Though in the process of time they have become much mixed with Hamitic and Negro elements, they still maintained interest in the affairs of their old home in South Arabia. In their new home they became Christians⁶, probably about 450 AD⁷ and may have been the first to introduce Christian teaching into South Arabia.⁸ Towards the end of Tubba'

---

¹ See Gibbon, cap xl, ad. fin.
² Bar Hebraeus in his Syria *Chronieon* ii, 91ff, indicates that Chosroes Anoshervan was particularly interested in religious controversy.
³ See Muhammad's reply to him in Sura xxxi, 5,6
⁴ infra p81.
⁵(Ed. *Handwritten note:*) Ibn Hisham *Sira* 46 notes that the *Abna* who were in Yemen in his day were known to be the descendants of the Persian lords who had come over under Vahriz
⁶ That they were pagans when they came over to Africa is evidenced by the fact that some of the earliest inscriptions at Axum are pagan.
⁷ This date is deduced from the fact that before this date the ruler of Abyssinia appears on his inscription as a pagan, and after it as a Christian: vide Littman *ERE*, I, 57, This would only prove, however, that Christianity became the official religion then.
⁸ (Ed. *Handwritten note*:) On the Abyssinian expedition into South Arabia see the discussions by F. von Pretorius *ZDMG* XXIII, p642ff and XXIV p624ff.

Dynasty in Yemen we find them in possession of certain parts of the country,[1] but their effectual entry into South Arabian politics is apparently connected with the massacre of the Christians of Najran in 523 or 524 AD. The story is that the last King of the old Himyarite stock (Dhu Nawas), after having assassinated the usurper Lakhi'a and firmly seated himself on the throne to which he had been raised by public acclamation, suddenly turned Jew, and with all a proselyte's fiery zeal, proceeded to persecute the Christians of Najran. He marched with a huge army, into their territory, destroyed all their Churches, pulled down and burned all their crosses and then called on them to embrace Judaism. When they refused, he ordered an enormous ditch to be dug and filled with combustibles. The inhabitants were then brought before him one by one, and some twenty thousand who refused to accept Judaism, were cast into the pit and burned alive. The others fled. The memory of this event is preserved in the Qur'an, lxxxv.4ff.

> 'Cursed by the Masters of the Trench, of the fuel fed fire
> When they sat around it,
> Witnesses of what they inflicted on the believers:
> Nor did they torment them but for their faith in God,
> The Might, The Praiseworthy'[2]

The remnant who fled brought the news to the Abyssinians, and the Negus (Najashi) sent an army to the help of his co-religionists in their distress.[3] This army was commended by Aryat and Abraha, and defeated the Himyarites with heavy loss. Seeing that all hope of saving the day was gone Dhu Nuwas spurred his horse into the sea and disappeared from sight.[4]

---

[1] The story is in Tabari, i.926, and in a Syriac letter which Mordtmann (*ZDMG*, xxxv, 700) thinks is spurious, but which Nöldeke and most other authorities accept as genuine.
[2] Cf Pocock, *Specimen,* p62. It is to be noted, however, that Geiger, *Judaism and Islam,* p153, and Nöldeke, *Geschichte der Qoran* p77n take this passage as referring to Daniel iii (The Bible), which is hardly likely, especially as Grimme points out (*ZA*, xxvi.166) the word trench اخدود is probably Sabaean.
[3] Tradition said he was instigated by Byzantine intrigues; see Muir *Life,* pxciii.
[4] On Dhu Nawas see further, supra 214.

Aryat and Abraha[1] now fell out and fought a duel. Aryat was killed, and Abraha, though victor, carried forever in memory of the fight a great gash across his face, which gained him the nickname of al-Ashram "the split nosed".[2] Having put an end to the fear of Jewish supremacy, Abraha now commenced to raise a monument to Christian supremacy in the country, by building a great Cathedral at San'a called *al-Qalis,* the ruins of which remain to the present day, and proclaiming that this should be in future the centre of pilgrimage for all Arabia. The Meccans whose chief means of support came from the pilgrimages to their shrine were alarmed and angered at this report, so on the night before the great consecration ceremony a certain Meccan (Nafil al Hijazi of the family of Kenanah, so tradition says)[3], entered the Cathedral by stealth and rubbed ordures all over the high altar and cross.[4] One can imagine the wrath and indignation when this defilement was discovered next morning. Learning that the culprit was a Meccan, Abraha vowed to march on that city and utterly destroy the Ka'ba[5].

An army was immediately prepared, provided with huge war elephants[6] brought over from Abyssinia, and marched on Mecca. Muslim tradition, which however, is quite baseless, tells how that while Abraha lay encamped at Mughammas near Mecca, the grandfather of the future Prophet paid the Axumite leader[7] a visit to request from him some camels that had been taken, and to inform him that the Ka'ba has its own Master who would defend it without human aid. There would seem to have been some conflict with a

---

[1] (Ed. *Handwritten* note:) Story of Abrahi Qalis (ἐκκλησίκ) in Ibn al Kalbi *Aznam,* pp46,47; Hamdani *Sifat* p240; Tabari *Annals,* I, 934-9, Ibn Hisham *Sira,* p29: Yaqut *Mu'jam,* iv 170-172: Ibn Manr, *Lisan al'Arab* (The Arabic Lexicon) قلس
[2] See Tabari's narrative in Nöldeke's *Perser und Araber,* 1879, p195ff. It is interestingly written up in Zwemer *Arabia, the Cradle of Islam,* 1900, p307ff
[3] Tabari, however, says he was of the Banu Fuqaym, and one of those who arranged the calendar.
[4] Burton *Pilgrimage,* i.321 mentions that this form of defilement is by no means uncommon in Arabia: cf. his account of the defilement of the Ka'ba during the pilgrimage of 1674, in ii, 168 and Wavell's *Modern Pilgrim,* p109
[5] Nicholson *Literary History* p66 suggests that this story of defilement was a mere pretense and that Abraha's real object was to capture the trade of Mecca
[6] Ed. Note: See Jeffery's note on Ethiopian War Elephants in the Appendix, p238.
[7] Ed. Note: See also Jeffery's note on Byzantium and the Kings of Axum in the Appendix, p235.

defending army of Meccans who were routed, but then small pox broke out in Abraha's army, the remnants of which were compelled to retreat in disorder.[1] Stragglers from the stricken army were taken captive and lived on in Mecca as slaves. This expedition took place in 570 AD so tradition says, and the miraculous deliverance made so great an impression on the minds of the Meccans that it was known to future generations as the "Year of the Elephant". It was in this year that Muhammad was born.[2]

After Abraha's death he was succeeded in Yemen by his two sons, called in Arabic tradition Yaksum and Masruq, whose rule was so despotic and weighed so heavily upon the inhabitants that an ambassador from the old Himyarite aristocracy was sent to the capitals of the two great empires of the day, the Byzantine and the Persian. The Byzantines were in league with Abyssinia, so he got no encouragement there, but he was able to induce Mindhir of Hira to introduce him to the Persian court, where the King[3] was only too anxious to seize an opportunity of striking even an indirect blow at Byzantine authority. The tradition, however, is that he at first replied that Yemen was too far off for Persian interference, and too poor to be worth their trouble over it. When the ambassador pressed his point, however, one of the courtiers suggested that they might send an army of the criminals in the gaols who had been condemned to death, and whose loss would make no difference. In any case an army was sent under an old general named Vahraz and, joined by great hosts of Yemenites, defeated the Abyssinians and drove them out of

---

[1] Tradition has run wild over this retreat. The story can be read in d'Herbelot *Bibliotheque Orientale* i.63 S.V. Abrahah. *Sura* cv of the Qur'an refers to this event and illustrates the popular legend, rather than being, as Prideaux throught, the origin of it. Margoliouth, however, agrees with Prideaux that the whole expedition may be a myth of the exegetes who coupled *Suras* cv and cvi. It is curious that the accident which befell Abraha is the same as that which befell Sennacherib.

[2] This date can hardly be correct for the Persian conquest of Yemen was in 570, and as Nöldeke points out, op. cit. p205, this leaves no room for the rest of Abraha's reign and that of his sons. On this ground Wellhausen has conjectured that the attack on Mecca must have been an earlier episode in Abraha's career in South Arabia.

[3](Ed. *Handwritten note*:) He was Saif bin Dhu Yazān. See Nöldeke, *Sasaniden* (understood to refer to *Geschichte der Perser und Araber)* 220 n4, Hartmann *Die Arabische Frage,* 508, Möberg, *Himyarites,* plxx.

the country. From that time South Arabia became a province of Persia and remained so till the Muslim conquest.[1] [2]

An investigation of the foreign words that are used in the Qur'an reveals the fact that quite a number of them are of Abyssinian origin, and it is curious that early Muslim writers quoted by al Suyuti in his *Itqan* knew by tradition that not only were there Ethiopic words in the Qur'an, but also Zinji words, that is words of the language of the woolly haired blacks of Africa.[3] The only source from which these could have been learned is the band of Abyssinian and negro stragglers from the army of the Elephants whom we have already seen were used as slaves in Mecca, and among whom Muhammad grew up. When we remember also that Bilal the Habashi (Abyssinian) was the first muezzin of Islam, and remember that Muhammad advised his followers, who in the early years were feeling the stress of persecution, to emigrate to Abyssinia, where they were well received, we can see that this Christian Empire of Abyssinia exercised no small influence on the early development of Islam.

D   THE LEGENDARY TRIBES[4]

Another collection of legends which bulks largely in the work of the Arab historians is that concerning certain primitive, semi-mythical Arab tribes, whom the traditionists considered to represent the original inhabitants of the country, stories of whom lingered on in the verses of the poets and popular legends, and thus came down in post-Muslim times to the makers of history. While most of the material that has been preserved is obviously sheerest legend, there are embedded in it, historical facts which may give us some glimpse

---

[1] Ed. Note: See added handwritten note in Appendix, p240-241: Mordtmann "Persian Intervention in Yemen".
[2] Cf Ibn Hisham, Sura 46
[3] Ed. Note: An expression not considered today to be an appropriate form of identification or description.
[4] Ed. Note: In the notes transcribed for this work, Jeffery had used the word 'primitive' to denote these tribes, a term which today is not considered to be an appropriate form of reference. In Jeffery's day it reflected a notion, following that of Darwin that there had been an evolution from a basic style of living to more complex civilisations. He may also have used the term in the sense of 'primal' or 'early'.

of the historical conditions of earlier times, though outside Arabic tradition we know practically nothing of them.

(a) *'Ad*[1]

The Qur'an many times makes mention of a tribe of 'Ad who lived in earlier days and whose dreadful fate, due to their rejecting the Prophet whom God has sent to them, is held up as an awful example and warning to the people of Mecca and Madina who rejected the message of Muhammad. The reference to them in the Qur'an occurs so many times that we may be certain that the legend was one widely known in Muhammad's day, a conclusion which is strengthened by the fact that mention of them occurs in the poems of 'Umayya ibn Abi as Salt of Thaqif, one of the Hanifs, one of Muhammad's contemporaries.[2] Our early information about them may be summarized thus –

    i)   *Ancient Poetry*[3]
        a) They are referred to as a nation that has perished in past time by the Mufaddaliyat viii:40:[4], Tarafa i.8:[5]; Hamasa (ed Freytag) i:195.341[6]
        b) Their Kings are mentioned in the *Ash'aru'l-Hudhailiyyin*, lxxx:6[5]
        c) In the *Diwan of Nabigha* there is mention of their prudence (xxv:4.)[7]

---

[1] (Ed: *Handwritten note:*) The story in Ibn Hisham 134 (154?) assumes that the Jews in the Jahiliyya were familiar with the story of 'Ad and Eham but this may not be genuine.
[2] See the Indices of Schulthess, *Umayya ibn Abi as-Salt,* Leipzig, 1911
[3] Ed. Note: While Jeffery notes that much of pre-Islamic poetry is of later record some of the references can be collaborated with other sources. Daniel W. Brown in *A New Introduction to Islam* 2nd ed., Wiley-Blackwell, Chichester, 2009, p25 would suggest that later Muslim selectors focused on the 'ignorant' behaviour of the Arabs showing their need for Islam.

[4] بن اننى كنت من عاد ومن ارم

[5] Ed. Ahlwardt

راقد بدالى انة سغولنى ماغال عاد اوالقرون غاشحبوا
[6] من عاد كان معروفا لنا اسر املوك وفتلها وفتالها
[7] احلام عاد واجماد مطهرة من املعقة والاغات والاثم

d) An 'Adite by name Ahmar is mentioned both in Zuhair (*Mu'all* 32) and the *Diwan of the Hudhailites* (no(?):31)[1]

e) They are known to contemporaries of Muhammad such as 'Umayya ibn Ali 'Salt, 'Adi ibn Zaid (587 AD) and Al-Afwah al-Audi (570AD)[2],[3]

ii) Qur'an

a) A prophet named Hud was sent to them as a preacher of monotheism, but they rejected him (xxvi:123ff; vii:63; xli:13; xi:54ff; liv:18 etc.) calling his message a lie, much as the Meccans did that of Muhammad.

b) They had great buildings [4] (xxvi:129).

c) God punished them for their unbelief by destroying them (xxvi:140; xlvi:24; xi:62ff: liv:19,20: lxix:6-8).

d) They were tall of stature[5] (vii:67).

---

[1] Zuhair

قتنتج لكم غلمان اشام كلهم كاحمر عاد ثم عقرضع فتفطم

Hudail

فمن كان بز جو القلح فيه غانه كاخمير عاد از كليب لوآل

[2] On *'Umayya* see Schulthess, op. cit. p48 and on the others Cheikho *Christian Arabic Poets,* p71

[3] (Ed. *Handwritten note*:) Umayya xxxviii:7

فغال الا لا تجزعى دتكزبى ملانكة من رب عاد وجرهم

"So he said – 'No don't be hasty and falsely deny
An angel from the Lord of 'Ad and Jachum'
in a poem about Mary, the mother of Jesus.

[4] Sura lxxxix:6 ارم ذات العماد "Iram adorned with pillars" may refer to this, if it can be taken, as by some to refer to a kind of earthly Paradise built for them in their ancient home by their King Shaddad. This, however, is uncertain as some take it to mean that the men there were tall of stature (see next note), and others that they were nomads (see Loth in *ZDMG* xxxv.). More interesting is the tradition that the survivors of the destruction of 'Ad, i.e. the 'second 'Ad', were the builders of the great dam at Ma'rib under their King Luqman.

[5] وزادكم فى الخلق بسطة Interpreting lxxxix:6 in the light of this, some commentators have taken ذات العماد as referring to the stature of the 'Adites. Loth (*ZDMG* xxxv, 627) quotes Ibrahim b. Sa'd as interpreting the passage علولهم متل العماد يعنى and Isra'il as, لهم فى السما كان . Sprenger (*Leben,* i. 508) quotes the tradition "The Ardites were giants and the smallest men among them were sixty cubits in height while the biggest reached over a hundred", other traditions may be seen in Zaidan's *Al-Arab qabl al-Islam,* p10 and Mas'udi, i. 179

e) The destroying blast which came upon them reduced everything to dust (ii:41,42).

f) The agent of their destruction was a cloud (xlvi:23), a tempest (xli:12, 15) or a roaring wind (liv:19, 20; lxix:6).

g) They dwelt at Iram[1] (lxxxix:5, 6).

h) They were proud and unjust in the land (xli:14).

i) They were unlike the Arabs of Muhammad's day[2] (lxxxix:7).

j) They were badly in need of rains (xi:56; xlvi:25).

k) They inhabited the sand downs – *al Ahqaf* (xlvi:20).

l) Hud and those who believed in him were rescued from the destruction[3] (vii:70).

iii) Later Muslim Legend[4]

This is based on the Qur'an. It tells us that these giants of Ad were idolators and given over to every sort of abomination of which it is a shame even for man to speak. While they were in this condition, Hud was sent to them to preach the unity of God and repentance, and that they should give up their idols. The 'Adites, however, mocked him, saying that he had no evidence of his god, while they could plainly see theirs, and it was evident that a man who believed in a god of whom he had

---

[1] The identification of Iram is uncertain. The commentators were even uncertain whether it meant a place or not. Loth (ZDMB, xxxv.626) gives five variations from their words. (i) بلدة - a town: both Alexandria and Damascus are suggested: (ii) امت – a people (iii) قبيلة – a tribe; (iv) an ancestor of 'Ad: (v) ابها لل - .i.e. that which has perished. Hamdani 80 thinks it is the South, but says that some held it was Damascus. It is noteworthy that Hamdani knows three Irams other than that of the عمار. One is a فلاة (53) one a جبل (126) and one a بئر (129)

[2] This is a very unlikely point as it depends on Iram being taken as a people and not as a place.

[3] The problem of this prophet Hud is a very interesting one. See Appendix, p244, "The Problem of the Prophet Hud"

[4] The native sources are, Tabari *Chronicles* 1:231: tr. Zotenberg i,121-129; Khazin, *Tafsir* ii:205; Tabari, *Tafsir*, viii.142f: Baghawi, *Tafsir* on Sura vii.63: Tha'labi *Qisas al-Anbiya'* 43-46: Kisa'I, *Vita Propherarum* ed Eisenberg, 103-110; Mirkhond, *Rauzat us Safa*, tr. Rehatsek, i.98-106; Abu'l-Fida, i.12; See also Sprenger, *Leben* i.505-18; Caussin de Perceval, i.15; D'Herbelot *BO*, ii.263; Nicholson, *Literary History*. cap. i; Sale, *Preliminary Discourse*, pp.4.5; Geiger, *Judaism & Islam*, p89ff; Marruccio, *Refutationes*, p282.

no evidence, must be mad. As punishment for this God sent them three years' famine which reduced them to great distress, and though they made diligent supplication to their rain god Sakia[1], they got no relief. At last they decided to send an embassy on pilgrimage to the great sanctuary at Mecca, to pray for rain. There were some seventy men in the expedition but the leaders were Qail and Murthad and Luqman. When they arrived in the Hijaz they were entertained for a month by the Amalakite prince Mu'awiya ibn Bakr whose wine and singing girls were famous. Murthad was a seriously minded man, who had been greatly impressed by the preaching of Hud and all the journey he had been urging on his fellow pilgrims the folly of their going on to Mecca to pray for rain when the real trouble was their own unbelief. Luqman was won over to Murthad's opinion as were a few of the party, but Qail was a man of a different type and a confirmed lover of the old bad ways, so he intrigued with Mu'awiya to have these pious few kept in custody while he and the others went on to the sanctuary to make their prayer.

This was done, and Qail went on to the last stage of the journey. He arrived at the Holy Place and prayed, "O Lord! Send to the people of 'Ad such rain as may please you." Hardly had he finished speaking when three clouds appear in the sky, one white, one red and one black, and simultaneously a voice was heard from heaven, "Choose which of these three you wish". Qail chose the black one thinking that there would be more rain in it. Having made the choice they started back home, the cloud followed them, and when they arrived, all the people crowded out of their houses to meet Qail returning with the rain, all except poor Hud and a few who believed in him. Just as the two parties met the cloud burst but instead of rain they got a hot, suffocating dust storm, which blew for seven nights and eight days, passing in at their nostrils and through their bodies, and which destroyed all save the Prophet Hud and the faithful who had remained indoors. Murthad and

---

[1] The traditions about their divinities Sakia, Hafiza, Razika and Salima are nothing but inventions of the commentators. See Blochet, *Le Culte d'Aphrodite–Anahita chez les Arabes du paganisme,* 1904, p28.

those who remained behind in the Hijaz were also saved, and became the progenitors of the second 'Ad.[1]

From out of all this mass of confused material we may perhaps glean one interesting fact, viz that in this story which came down to Muhammadan times and lingered on in the old poems and legends, we have a dim reminiscence of the horror of the encroaching sands of the desert and the breaking up of the old civilisations.[2] Some scholars have doubted whether the 'Adites ever existed[3] but there seems too persistent a tradition not to have some basis in actuality. Who the 'Adites were and from whence they came, is a more practical question.

a.) Sprenger[4] imagined that the 'Adites would be found in the tribe of Wadites whom Ptolemy informs us lived in North West Arabia,[5] though in face of the unanimity of tradition that their home was in the South this is hardly likely. The only point would be that maybe a remnant of the tribe later settled in the North and preserved their old name.

b.) Wetstein in an essay on *The Monastery of Job in Hauran and the Tradition of Job* published as an Appendix to Delitzsch's

---

[1] The Arabian tradition places these people of the second 'Ad also in Hadramaut and connects them with the building of the great dam at Ma'rib, under Luqman b.'Ad, called Dhu'n-Nusur.

[2] The points to recapitulate are – (1) they suffered severely from drought (2) they lived near the 'sandy hillocks' (الا حقاف) which Khazin ii.05 says means الرمل and is situated between 'Uman and Hadramaut; (3) they had a special rain god; (4) they were destroyed by a great dust storm: (5) after the storm was over everything was reduced to dust.

[3] Eg. Franz Buhl in *EI.*, i.121, and Wellhausen in *G.G.A.*, 1902, p596. Wellhausen's argument is based on the fact that besides the expression in the poets "from this time of 'Ad" there is also the form "from the 'Ad" (من العاد) so he would take عاد as a noun meaning "ancient time" with its adjective عادى meaning 'ancient' and thus regard the tribe as a mythical outgrowth of a misunderstanding of the word. So Margoliouth in *ERE x, 541*. Horovitz *Koranische Untersuchungen* 127 however is against it.

[4] (Ed: *Handwritten note:*) Loth agrees with Springer, as does Moritz *Sinaikult*, 56 Ὀαδῖται vol vi.7.21 but in Nobbi text thus reads Θαδῖται with a Θ not O. In VI, vii, 21 there are, however, Ὀυδηνόι. (AB: Loth note looks nearly right, but AJ seems to have corrected Θαδῖται in the centre to Θαδεται.)

[5] See Appendix I to cap vi of the first volume of his *Leben* and par 199 of his *Alte Geographie Arabiens*. Some colour is lent to this by the fact that Hamdani (ed Müller, p 169) mentions a well Iram in Hisma,

وبحمسى بر ارم من مناهل العرب العروفة -

Hiob (1876) declares for a North Arabian site¹ and in this he is followed by O. Loth in an article in *ZDMG* xxv, on some points in Tabari's Commentary on the Qur'an. This theory depends on the identification of ارم with ארם (which is not at all sure, and the theory that only Aramaic traditions are associated with the name of Iram, (which is not true), but it fits in nicely with Yaqut's contention that ذات العمود is an appellation of Damascus. Loth also finds a point in the fact that the ʿAdites are often mentioned in connection with the Thamudites who are, demonstrably a North Arabian tribe and would thus think of the ʿAdites as their neighbours somewhere in North Arabia.² Having got so far, he concludes,

> "But who were the ʿAd? I believe that they are none other than – allowing for dialectial modifications – the double of the Iyad (اياد), the vanished ancient people of Arabian legend, whom Blau so brilliantly found again in the ידי (Ιαδ)³ of the Palmyrene inscriptions."⁴

c.) Arabian tradition both inside and outside the Qur'an has persistently held the view that the home of the ʿAdites was

---

¹ He writes: 'The topographical writings on Damascus trace these two names back to a Gerun ibn Saʿd ibn ʿAd ibn ʿAus (עוץ) ibn Iram (ארם) ibn Sam (שם) ibn Nuh, (נוח), who settled in Damascus in the time of Solomon', (one version of the tradition identifies him with Hadad: Josephus *Antiquities* viii.7), 'and built in the middle of the city a castle named after him, in which a temple to the planet (Kokeb) Mushteri, the guardian god of the city, was erected. That this temple, which is well known, under Theodosius, at the same time with the temple of the sun at Baʾalbek, passed over to the Christians was actually surrounded with a strong, fortified wall, is capable of proof even at this present day. In this tradition which has assumed various forms, a more genuine counterpart of the Biblical עוץ appears than that ʿAis which we have characterised above as an invention of the schools, viz an ʿAus (عوص), father of the ʿAdite tribe which is said to have settled in the Damascus district under that Gerun, and also ancestor of the Prophet Hud, lost to tradition, whose *makam* on the mountains of Suet rises far above Gerash the city of pillars, this true <u>Iram dhat-el-ʿImad</u>, the valley of the Jabbok and the Sawad of Gilead.
² Little weight, however, can be placed on this, for they are mentioned also in close association with the people of Noah. The point of connection is their treatment of the prophets, not their locality either in place or time.
³ (AB. Accords with the Hebrew).
⁴ Op. cit. p628. The reference to O. Blau is to his article 'Altarabische Sprachstudien', in *ZDMG* xxvii: See particularly p 340 for his identification of ידי and ידא.

in Hadramaut. The Qur'an as we have already noticed placed them at Al-Ahqaf (xlvi.20), and this the commentators say means the sandy country between 'Uman and Hadramaut in South Arabia[1] and this is confirmed by two pieces of evidence that are fairly conclusive —

(i) The form of the name Iram is South Arabian not Aramaean.
(ii) Beside the fact that Hamdani mentions two Irams in South Arabia, one on a hill and the other a well, there is the tomb of 'Ad b. Iram which has been discovered there.[2]

We may conclude then that the tradition of South Arabian origin is well founded, but the question still remains as to who they were. Is their story but a reminiscence of one of the peoples of the South Arabian Kingdoms which were blotted out by the encroaching sands? Hommel, in pondering over the tradition of the 'many coloured Iram', which was built by the great Shaddad, came to the conclusion that they were the remnants of a pre-Semitic civilisation *einer vorsemitischen in festen Städten sitzenden Cultur* – of whose magnificence the tradition of "Iram of the pillars" is the only survival.[3]

It may be mentioned also that Philby in his account of his exploration of the *Ru' al Khali,* the great southern desert, mentions the existence of ruined cities in some of the depressions of the desert, such as that found at Jafura, and these may well be ruins of the extinct civilisation to which the Arab tradition refers.[4]

---

[1] Khāzin ii.205: Tabari *Tafsir* on Sura xlvi*:* Tha'labi *Qisas* p43: Baidawi on xlvi.20: Jalalain on the same passage simply says it was in Yemen.
[2] The story is in D. H. Müller's "Südarabische Studien*", SBAW* lxxvi, 134ff, and see his *Die Burgen und Schlösser*, p 418. The main uncertainty is as to how primitive the tomb is.
[3] See his *Die Namen der Säugethiere bei den südsemitischen Völkern,* Leipzig, 1879, p344
[4] See Philby *Heart of Arabia,* 1922, vol ii. P100, 221

(b) *Thamud* [1,2]

In the Qur'anic passages dealing with the fate of the people of 'Ad we very frequently find the 'Adites coupled with the people of Thamud, who provided a similar example of the fate which befell those who rejected God's apostles, and from whom the Meccans were urged to take warning. In the case of the Thamudites however, we have independent evidence that they dwelt in North Arabia between the Hijaz and Syria, and were imagined to have lived in the houses which they had cut for themselves from the rocks, which can still be seen at Meda' in Salih. We know now from the Nabataean inscriptions there that these were sepulchral monuments, which apparently were mistaken in later times for human habitation.[3] In any case we have evidence of the existence of Thamudites in North Arabia down to the fifth century A.D.

We may summarize our information about them as we did of the 'Adites.

i.) European sources[4]

Both Diodorus Siculus[5] and Ptolemy[6] mention the *equites Thamudeni* who as late as the 5th century AD were attached to the cavalry arm of the Byzantine army[7] and they may be the *Tamud*[8] of Sargon's inscription of 8th Century, BC.

ii.) Early Poetry

There are frequent references to the slayer of the she-camel, which became proverbial.

> "more unlucky than the hamstringer of the she-camel,
> Than Ahmar of Thamud."

---

[1] (Ed. *Handwritten note*:) Sprenger *Leben* thinks of both 'Ad and Thamud as other communities ruined by the change of trade routes.

[2] (Ed. Jeffery's notes also included various handwritten notations taken from various sources relating to Thamud.)

[3] See particularly Doughty's account of them, *Arabia Deserta* I, caps iv & v

[4] (Ed. *Handwritten note*:) See classical references in article *Egra* in *Pauly*, Wissewa.

[5] Θαμουδηνοί, *Historica* iii.44 (AB. The Greek agrees with transliteration given above.)

[6] *Geography*(?) 6,7,9,21. See also Pliny *Natural History*, vi, 28, 32? Note: Horovitz, *Koranische Untersuchungen*, 184

[7] Caussin de Perceval, i.27

[8] (Ed. *Handwritten note*:) "amil Tamudi" *Annales*, 94.

iii.) Qur'anic Evidence[1]
  a. They had sent to them a Prophet named Sahil who preached monotheism, and produced a she-camel from a rock as miraculous evidence of his heaven sent mission. The Thamudites, however, rejected his teaching and hamstrung the camel. (vii.71ff: xi.64: liv.23ff).
  b. They lived in castles hewn out of the hills (vii.72; xxvi.149; lxxxix.8.
  c. They were destroyed by an earthquake (vii.76), a violent storm (xi.70; xli.12); thunder bolts (lxix.5)[2].
  d. After their destruction they appeared like dry sticks (liv.31).

iv.) Muslim Tradition[3]
As in the case of 'Ad, Muslim Tradition is mostly an amplification of the material contained in the Qur'an. The Prophet Sahil, we read, was sent of God to the tribe of Thamud which inhabited the country of Hijr,[4] but it was badly received. He urged his people to pray to Allah alone, but they said he was only a man like themselves, so how could he pretend to come to them with revelations from God. They would follow as they always had done, the religion of their fathers and not listen to a bewitched fool as he was. Some few, however, believed in him, and there was a schism among the people. As a proof of his mission by a single word he caused a great rock to open, from the opening of which appeared a she-camel, which at that very moment gave birth to a young camel. Salih advised them to cherish her, which they did for a while, allowing her to

---

[1] (Ed. *Handwritten note:*) Note also now the Thamudii inscriptions in Lidzbarski, *Ephemeris*
[2] Hamdani says (ed. Müller, p212)وانا ثمود فرماها بالدمالق واهلكها بالصواعق
[3] Arabic sources are Tha'labi *Qisas al Anbiya'* p46ff., Mas'üdi *Muruj al Dhahab* iii.85ff; Kisa'i *Qisas*, ed Eisenberg, p110ff, Tabari, *Chron* i.244ff:, (Zotenberg's *Tabari*, i.130ff: the Commentaries on Sura vii: European writes to be consulted are D' Herbelot, *BO*, article "Salah"; Sprenger *Leben*, i.518ff Grimme *Muhammad*, ii.80
[4] For a modern account of the place see Euting's *Tagebuch*, ii.215ff. Hamdani calls Hijr. موضح ثمود

drink from the well at which they watered their sheep and cattle, and as she drank a whole well full each time, they arranged that their cattle should drink one day and the camel the next.¹ As a regard for their consideration they were permitted to milk her, and from one side of her udder they drew milk and from the other honey. At last, however, a party of the Thamudites moved with envy determined to kill the camel. Qadar al-Ahmar hamstrung her and her young one, of which injury they died. Then they mocked at Sahil and his God, so God sent a great earthquake which threw down each man of them dead, on his face before his own house.

v.) Critical Conclusions

(a) A consideration of the evidence would seem to indicate that they too, like the 'Adites were victims of climatic changes in Arabia.

  i.) According to some Arabic authorities[2] the first home of the Thamudites was Yemen, whence they were driven to find homes in the north.

  ii.) The curious passage فطانعرا كهضىم اطحتفلر in the Qur'an liv.31, would seem to contain good tradition as to their condition as a result of their destruction.[3]

  iii.) Although the popular tradition is that their death was caused by an earthquake, there still persists in the Qur'an the variant tradition that it was by a great windstorm.[4]

  iv.) here is the curious fact that water is so frequently mentioned in connection with them.

---

[1] Cf Sura xxvi.155 - "This she camel shall have her drink and you your drink on a certain day."
[2] Vide Pococke *Specimen*, 37
[3] There is also the curious story that Sahil prophesied that their faces should turn yellow, then red, and then black, Vide *Rausat-us-Safa*, tr Rehatsek, i.116
[4] Sura xi.70: xli.12. This, however, may have originated from the tempest of 'Ad.

These are not sufficient indications on which to build a definite theory, but they at least point to a possible explanation lying in the gradual drying up of Arabia.[1]

(b) The question of the identity of Salih presents considerable difficulties. The name itself means "pious man", and it may be that this has merely been hypostatized into a proper name.

    i) D'Herbelot (op. cit.) follows the older tradition of equating him with שלח of Gen xi which identification is helped out by the fact mentioned by Geiger[2] that the Samaritan Arabic translation has in the passage mentioned صالح instead of the regular سالح.

    ii) Bochart's guess in *Geographica Sacra,* that he is the Peleg of Gen xi.16 is based on late Arabic tradition about the Thamudites and is worthless.

    iii) The most hopeful suggestion is that made by Palmer, who in his *Desert of the Exodus,* [p50] tells of a tomb of Sahil near al-Watiyeh which is a sacred spot for the Towara Bedouin of Sinai, where they have an annual festival, in which after camel races, the sacrificial victims are led to the mortuary chapel, their ears are cut off, and the posts sprinkled with their blood.[3] He also notes that near the summit of Jebel Musa is a rock with the semblance of a camel's foot print, always called the footprint of the Prophet's she-camel. Taking all this in connection with the striking of the rock, Palmer thinks the story is a distorted

---

[1] The fact that the story represents them as being forced to drop the favourite Arab pastoral life and hew out for themselves homes in the great stone hills, may also favour this explanation.
[2] *Judaism and Islam,* A. Geiger and F.M. Young, p94
[3] Goldziher *Muhammadanische Studien,* ii, 328ff thinks this festival described by Palmer was an ancient heathen festival grafted on to the Sahil legend.

reminiscence of the great Israelitish lawgiver, and the "pious Prophet", would thus be Moses.[1]

iv) Dussard, *Arabes en Syrie*, p119 makes the suggestion that the point in the offence of killing the camel was that it was the violation of a sanctuary. The camel was devoted to God and was killed on the hima'.[2]

(c) *Lesser Early[3] Tribes*
1. *'Amaliq.* The name املقة of course represents the עמלקי (Amalekites) of the Old Testament, who in Old Testament times appear as nomadic Arabian tribes wandering through the wilderness country now known as Et-Tih, between Sinai and the Southern borders of Sinai.[4] There are lengthy accounts of them in Arabic sources,[5] which look upon them as the remains of one of the most ancient Arab tribes. Nöldeke has carefully studied the whole question,[6] and his conclusion is that these Arab accounts have no historical value whatever save where they are actually based on Biblical material. The M[uslim][7] writers obviously had no clear ideas as to whom they were, and at different times we find Egyptians, Canaanites and Philistines classed as 'Amaliq'. It is to be noted also that the antiquarians of Islam differed considerably among themselves as to the correct genealogy of the tribe.[8]

---

[1] See also his *Qur'an* i.147n
[2] Ed. Note: Recognized protected pasture areas.
[3] Jeffery had used the word 'primitive' here as well. Legendary does not fit here as the Amalekites are frequently mentioned in the Old Testament.
[4] Grimme thinks they are meant by the Melukh of the Babylonian inscriptions, vide *EI* i.377
[5] Cf. Tabari i.213ff: Mas'udi, *Muruj*, iii, 83-91: 283-275 (Ed. 295?), Nawawi, p319-320: Yaqut, *Mu'jam*, ii.794: iii.634: iv.184, 238: vide also *Aghani*, iii, 12: xiii, 109: xix, 94
[6] *Uber die Amalekiter und einige andre Nachbarvölker des Israeliter*, Göttingen, 1864
[7] Jeffery had used the older term which is no longer acceptable.
[8] Vide Seligsohn in *EI* i.325

2. *Jadis*. According to Ibn Qutaiba[1] Jadis جديس was a descendant of Noah through Shem,[2] Aram and Ludh (a Lawidh) and the tribe which bears his name was placed by Hamdani in Yemen.[3] Other antiquarians differ as to the genealogy of the tribe, and as the genealogies have evidently been constructed under Jewish influence they have little value. Caussin de Perceval gives their story[4] which we will consider under *Tasm*.[5] Fresnel in *JA* 1840, p193, makes the plausible suggestion that the Jadisites may be referred to by Ptolemy[6] under the name Ἰοδυσίτα (Ἰολυσίτα), which would imply their existence about the period 125-130 AD. After their revolt from the rule of Tasm, they themselves were wiped out by the Himyarites from Yemen[7] under Tibba' Hassan.

3. *Tasm.* The genealogists claim that Tasm (طسم) was the brother of Jadis.[8] For some time the two tribes lived harmoniously together under the rule of the princes of Tasm, until one of these princes named 'Amtuq commenced to enforce the observance of an old tribal custom of *le droit du seigneur,* whereby every maiden of the Jadisites must be deflowered by him before her marriage.[9] When he insisted on this right over the young and beautiful Ghufaira, the sister of Aswad ibn Ghifar, one of the chief men of the Jadisites, the latter decided to put an end to the tyranny. They invited 'Amluq and members of his family to a great feast, in the midst of which, the Jadisites, who had concealed their swords

---

[1] Ibn Qutaybah *Kitab al Ma'arif* (ed Wüstenfeld), p14 see also Tabari i.771ff.
[2] (Ed. *Handwritten note:*) Others attempted to link him with Thamud. Ibn Hisham p5.
[3] ed. Müller, p 140,141. Tabari says they lived in Yamama.
[4] *Essai*, (Caussin de Perceval) i.28: see also Zotenberg's *Tabari*, ii.28ff. in Al Maidani i.192; ii.690 we have two proverbs coined from the Tasm and Jadis story

[6] *Geographia,* (ed Willberg) viii. p406.
[7] *Kitab al-Ma'arif*, p308ff: Pocock, *Specimen*, p547: *Aghani*, iii.15: Abul-Fida', *Historia Ante-Islam* p180: Tabari, i.
[8] *Kitab al-Ma'arif,* p14(?). Jeffery added a question mark here.
[9] That the custom is even now not extinct among the inhabitants of that area is witnessed by not a few modern travelers, e.g. Stevens *By Tigris and Euphrates*, 1923.

under the table, rose and massacred the prince, his family and his following. The only one who escaped was Ribah ibn Murra, who fled to Yemen and incited the Tubb' Hassan to invade the country and bring it under Himyaritic control.

Caussin de Perceval would date these events a little before 250 AD[1] but it is doubtful if we can attribute much historical value to the accounts that have come down to us.

4. *Hadhura*[2]. Ibn Khaldun tells us of a people of the tribe of Hadhura who lived in the country of Ar-Rass in Yemen, to whom was sent a prophet Shu'aib ibn Dhu Mahdam, who preached against their idolatry and revealed to them the truth about God, but his people called him an impostor and killed him.

The people of Ar-Rass who illtreated their Prophet, are twice mentioned in the Qur'an (xxv.40; 1.11), but the great variety of opinions found in the Commentators shows that no certain tradition had come down as to their identity.

Caussin de Perceval (*Essai*.i.30) notes that according to Ibn Khaldun, the Hadhurites were descended from Eber through Yoqtan and he thinks they may be the Hadoram (הֲדוֹרָם) of Gen x:27 (The Bible) who presumably represent a tribe somewhere in Yemen.[3]

5 *Wabar*[4] Also mentioned by Ibn Khaldun as among the descendants of Yoqtan and inhabiting the country around Aden. They sent to them the Prophet Hanzhala ibn Safwan, but they rejected and killed him. They may

---

[1] *Essai,* (Caussin de Perceval) i.100
[2] (Ed. *Handwritten note:*) Ibn Hisham p5 says he was the brother of 'Amluq son of Dawidh b. Shem
[3] See Schleifer's article, "Hadur" in *EI* ii, 210
[4](Ed. *Handwritten note*:) See article by Tkatch in *EI* 1073-1074

represent the Ophir (אוֹפִר) of Gen x.29 mentioned among the descendants of Yoqtan.

6 *Jurhum*. The traditional accounts of the origin of Mecca all tell of an ancient tribe - جرهم which was thought to have had some share in the building of the Ka'ba. There appear, however, to have been two ancient tribes of that name, known in Arabic tradition as the first and the second Jurhum. The first Jurhum were thought to have been contemporaries of the 'Adites.[1] The second Jurhum are said to have come from Yemen, driven out by the failure of the water supply.[2] Entering the Hejaz they settled in the valley of Mecca and in the Tihama, from whence, according to tradition, they drove the Amalekites. They became related to Ishmael by marriage,[3] helped in the building of the Ka'ba, over which they had authority for some time, until they were finally driven out by the Khuza'a.[4]

The legends about Jurhum[5] are probably mostly drawn from the imagination of Arabic historians but they would seem to enshrine some historical fact. Stephanus of Byzantium knows of Γοραμα,[6] as an ancient Arabian tribe, and this may seem to prove their existence independently of Muslim legend, and as a matter of fact some remnants of them seem to have lived on at the borders of Mecca as

---

[1] Cf. Ibn Hisham (ed Wüstenfeld), p468, and *Kamil* (ed Wright), p445
[2] Diyarbekri *Tarikh al-Khamis,* see Caussin de Perveval *Essai*, i.33
[3] Caussin de Perceval, op. cit.i.168
[4] Sources of the story are Tabari *Annales*, i.219, 283, 784, 904, 1096, 1131-34: *Kitab al-Aghani*, xiii, 110: texts in de Goeje, *Bibliotheca Geographorum Arabicorum* v.27:vii.29,60:viii, 82,185,202: Mas'udi, *Muruj*, iii 95-103: Azraqi *Chronicles*. (ed Wüstenfeld), 44-56: Ibn Hisham (ed Wüstenfeld),71ff: Ibn Qutaiba, *Kitab al-Ma'arif,* 313
[5] (Ed. *Handwritten note.)* See article by Tkatch in *EI* iv, 1073-1074
[6] Ed. Note: Jeffery left a space for details. Stephanus of Byzantium's work is *Ethnica*. (AB: The initial element is actually a capital gamma, I think, so Γοραμα, which makes sense in relation to Jurhum on the top line.)

late as the second century of the Hejira.[1] The list of their princes is given by tradition as[2]

1. *Jurhum*[3]   74-44 BC
2. *'Abd Yalil ibn Jurhum*   44-14 BC
3. *Jurhum ibn 'Abd Yalil*   14BC-16 AD
4. *'Abd al Madan ibn 'Abd Yalil*   16-46 AD
5. *Bakila ibn 'Abd al-Madan*   46-76 AD
6. *'Abd al-Masih ibn Bakila*   76-106 AD
7. *Mudhadh ibn 'Abd al-Masih*   106-136 AD
8. *'Amr ib Madhadh*   (136-170 AD
9. *Harith ibn Mudhadh*
10. *'Amr ibn Harith*
11. *Bishr ibn Harith*
12. *Mudhadh ibn 'Amr ibn Mudhadh*   (170-206 AD

The tradition of their connection with the building of the Ka'ba is very strong and we find it referred to in the early poets.[4] The legends may be read in Azraqi's *Chronicle*, pp45-56, and would seem to point to the fact of a Yemenite settlement there at an earlier date. Caussin de Perceval is probably right in concluding that there was only one people of Jurhum, and that the so called first and second Jurhums arise from a confusion of two streams of tradition about the same people.[5]

---

[1] See Nöldeke in *ZDMG*, xli.717 and Buhl in *EI* i.1066. Notice also the reference to them in the *Diwan* of Hassan b. Thabit (ed Cairo p 131)
[2] See Abulfida *Historia ante-Islamica,* p131: the dates are those calculated by Caussin de Perceval op. cit. p195
[3] (Ed. *Handwritten note.*: Dozy in *De Israëlieten te Mekka* took the first Jurhum to be Jews of the tribe of Simeon who came down into the Hijaz during the time of David, and the second Jurhum as the reinforcements that came to them at the time of the Babylonian captivity.
[4] Zuhair *Mu'allaqa* v, 16, al A'sha: (Ed. Note. No further details given in the footnotes.)
[5] Op. cit. i.34

TRIBAL ORGANISATION

The student who comes from the study of the Old Testament (The Bible) to the study of early Arabian history, is at once struck by the common love of genealogical tables in the written records. The Priestly writer in the Pentateuch loves to give his lists of family relationships, and the Arabian historians love to do the same. F. Wüstenfeld, an indefatigable explorer among the early records of the Arabs, published at Göttigen in 1852, a great work on these genealogies, entitled *Genealogische Tabellen der arabischen Stämme und Familien*, in which he collected all the information available at that time on the interconnexions of these Arab tribes.[1] The genealogists divide the Arabs into three great groups.[2,3]

(1) *Al-'Arab al-Ba'ida*
   Here they include the ancient tribes of Tasm, Jadis, 'Ad, Thamud, 'Amaliq, etc

(2) *Al-'Arab al-'Ariba*
   or the Banu Qahtan – or Yoqtan, comprising the South Arabian or Yemenite stock, which as we have already seen, in later times spread all over the Arabian peninsula.

(3) *Al-'Arab al-Musta'riba*

---

[1] The most important Arabic authorities are Ibn Duraid's *Kitab ul Ishtiqaq*, and Ibn Qutaiba's *Kitab al Ma'arif*
[2] Vide *al-Wasit* (Cairo, 1925)
[3] (Ed. *A Handwritten note:*) There are two forms of this threefold division-
  1. Some, as of Al-Suyuti give
      (i)   Al-'Arab al 'Arba = the ancient tribe
      (ii) Al-'Arab al Muta'arriba = the Qahtan group
      (iii) Al-'Arab al musta'riba = the Ishmaelite group
  2. Others with a Yemani bias as eg. Al-Hamdani gives
      (i)   Al-'Arab al Ba'ida – i.e. ancient
      (ii) Al-'Arab al 'Ariba' – i.e. Yemenite
      (iii) Al-'Arab al Muta'arriba, i.e. al Musta'riba

Or the Banu 'Adnan, - or Ma'add or Nizan, the North Arabian or Ishmaelite stock.

It seems probable that there was a fundamental racial difference between the North and South Arabian stocks,[1] a supposition which is strengthened by the fact that the new information gathered from the South Arabian inscriptions reveals these South Arabians as a peaceful, commerce-loving people, strikingly submissive to their gods.[2] There are considerable differences between the "Himyaritic" language and the Arabic of North Arabia, though both belong to the South Semitic group and would seem linguistically to have a common origin. It is possible that "Himyaritic" represents a Semitic language spoken by a non-Semitic people who had come across the sea and settled in South Arabia. The trackless desert, al-Rub al-Khali, which stretches across the peninsula from the Persian Gulf to the northern part of Yemen, must have formed in early days as an almost insuperable barrier to intercourse between the North and South. Arab tradition[3] says that the Banu Qahtan emigrated to Yemen from the fertile plains of the Euphrates valley and as we know that in later times the Persian conquerors came that way, it is very possible that the original population came that way. In some of the genealogies it is shown that Southern tribes are descended from Yaqtan who is identified with Qahtan and the Northern Arabs are sometimes referred to as the Nizarites or Ma'addites.[4]

It becomes obvious on the most cursory examination of the statements about the first group, *Al-'Arab al-Ba'ida,* that no certain tradition has come down to Islamic times, in fact the authors of *Al-Wasit* dismss them with the statement that no certain information about them has survived save what God revealed in his noble Qur'an and in the Traditions of the Prophet.[5] The genealogists nevertheless

---

[1] Vide Nicholson *Literary History,* pxvii.
[2] Goldziher, *Muhammedanische Studien,* i.3.
[3] Al-Wasit, p6
[4] (Ed. *Handwritten note:*) Ma'add being represented as the son, and Nizar a grandson of 'Adnan. See Robertson Smith, *Kinship,* 5, 6
[5] Op cit. p5

are able to give us their genealogical table, which links them up with the Banu Qahtan.[1]

The lack of fertility of the country keeps the tribes continually wandering about with their camels and herds in search of pasture, and the result is that when we come to Muslim times we find an extraordinarily complicated map of the position of the tribes. Many Yemenite tribes are now situated in the far north, and some northern tribes are away down in the South.

The theory of the genealogists is that the Arab tribes all go back to Abraham,[2] and their organisation was patriarchal. The theory as Robertson Smith summarises it is:

> The groups were all patriarchal tribes formed by subdivision of an original stock, on the system of kinship through male descents. A tribe was but a larger family; the tribal name was the name or nickname of the tribal ancestor. In process of time it broke up into two or more tribes, each embracing the descendants of one of the great ancestor's sons and taking its name from him. These tribes were again divided and subdivided on the same principle, and so at length that extreme state of division was reached which we find in the peninsula at the time of the Prophet. Between a nation, a tribe, a sept or subtribe, and a family, there is no difference on this theory, except in size and distance from a common ancestor. As time rolls on, the sons of a household become heads of separate families, the families grow into septs, and finally the septs become a great tribe or even nations embracing several tribes.[3]

---

[1] On the value of these genealogical lists see Nicholson, op cit. pxx, and in *ZDMG*, xl, p177. A curious light is thrown upon them by an examination of the equally detailed genealogical trees of their horses which can be traced back to the five mares of the Prophet. Vide Deville's *Palmyra*, 1898, p64

[2] (Ed. *Handwritten note*.) Robertson Smith's summary is *No one who has worked through any part of the material in detail, comparing Wüstenfeld's tables with the notices in the 'Aghani', the* "Ogd", *the* 'Hamasa', *the Hodhalite poems and similar sources can fail to conclude that the system of the genealogists and the methods by which traditional data are worked into the system are totally unworthy of credit. Kinship* p (not given)

[3] Robertson Smith *Kinship and Marriage in Early Arabia*, 1903, pp3,4

As a matter of fact this genealogical unity is nothing more than a fiction growing out of cases of local unity[1] and the great scheme of the tribes all coming from the common ancestor appears to be but a development of the Pension Lists of 'Umar, as Sprenger pointed out.[2] We have already met these lists in our account of the Shu'ubiyya movement.[3] When the Arabs asserted their supremacy in the new religion of Islam, as a privileged people, all members of which were to receive pensions from the state out of the spoils of conquest, and who alone were to serve in the great works of conquest and administration, it became very necessary to have authoritative lists of the Arab tribes.[4] 'Umar had these lists made. In one sense it was a military census and in another it was a pension list. And it was the cause of interminable fabrications of the most baseless genealogies[5] as well as a process which provided the later genealogists with abundance of material for linking up all the various Arab tribes into one great family tree whose root was Abraham.[6]

As Abraham plays such a big role in these traditions, it becomes necessary to examine what basis there is for this almost universal tradition among the Arabs that he was the founder of the sanctuary at Mecca and the father of all Arabs.[7][8]

---

[1] Vide Goldziher *Muhamedanische Studien*, I, 64: Margoliouth, *Mohammed*, p4; Sprenger, *Alte Geographie Arabiens*, p290
[2] *Leben*, III, ppcxxff. Robertson Smith largely agrees. *Kinship* p6,7
[3] Infra p53.
[4] (Ed. *Handwritten note*.) Robertson Smith *Kinship* p8,9 shows that another cause of fabrication of genealogies was the need of allies: tribal quarrels, as is illustrated in the case of Qoda'a who originally belonged to Ma'add but claimed kinship with Himyar to get help for the Kelhites against Kair. See also Hamdani, *Jazira*, 90
[5] *A pedigree is a luxury the need for which is only felt when men have attained to wealth and power ... when the need arises it can no longer in ordinary cases be ascertained: a flattering conjecture has therefore to serve in lieu of a possibly less flattering but quite unascertainable reality* — Margoliouth
[6] Accounts of 'Umar's work will be found in Tabari *Annales*, i.2749
[7] Muir *Life* plxii, cll-cv. Palmer *Qur'an*, pxiii records a tradition that there was a statue of Abraham in the Ka'ba at Mecca.
[8](Ed. *Handwritten note*.) *The backbone of the system was the pedigree of the Prophet — itself one of the most obviously untrustworthy parts of the whole scheme — and around this all the other Northern Arabs were grouped on the principle that every connection, real or imaginary between two tribes was explained by deriving them from a common ancestor who in turn was brought into the prophet's stemma as brother or cousin of some ascendant of Mohammed. 'Kinship'*, p11

In 1863 Renan wrote –

> For the rest, I cannot believe that the tradition by which the Arabs link themselves to Abraham and to Biblical genealogies, has any value. In my opinion this tradition is only a reflection of that of the Jews, who in the centuries preceding Islam, exercised so decisive an influence on the education of the Arabic people.[1]

Further research has shown the justice of Renan's judgment. Sprenger[2] pointed out that in the Qur'an there are presented two different views of Abraham in one of which he is only a Prophet like Muhammad, but in the other becomes the founder of the Ka'ba and the father of the Arabs. The suggestion was taken up by Kuenen in his *Hibbert Lectures* (p14ff) and later by Hurgronje[3] and their investigations showed that these two views represent a change in Muhammad's attitude toward the Jews. In the early Suras he is never called a Muslim nor is any hint given of his connection with the Arabs. In the Medinan Suras, however, we find Abraham made a Muslim, the founder of the Ka'ba, and linked with Ishmael as the father of the Arabs. The reason for this, these scholars find, is that at first Muhammad was anxious to gather the Jews into his movement and made no attempt to go further with their revered Abraham than to claim him as a fellow prophet.[4] But when Muhammad was ruler in

---

[1] *Histoire genérale des langues sémitiques*, p 40. Margoliouth notes, (Mohammed, p4) *The introduction of the Old Testament was a boon to the archaeologists when such arose, because in it they found the beginnings of genealogies, to which, by calculation of time and arbitrary insertions, they could attach the pedigrees with which they were acquainted.* (Ed.:*Handwritten note:*) Schwally I, 147-n3, Rudolph *Abhängigkeit des Quran* 49; Sprenger x, 279-284; Grimme, *Mohammed*, 64 and I, 60ff; Winckler *ASO* 106-109 thinks that Arabian Jews or Christians may have associated Abraham with the Ka'ba before Muhammad's time in order to take over the Ka'ba cult with their new faith.

[2] *Leben* ii, 276ff

[3] *Het Mekkaansche Feeste,* Hurgronje, 1880, p20ff

[4] Rudolph *Die Abhängigkeit des Qurans von Judentum und Christenum*, 1922, p48 interestingly indicates how opportune the figure of Abraham was for Muhammed at this period. He was a figure revered alike by Jews and Christians and yet not specifically Jewish or Christian for he lived before either the Torah or Gospel had been revealed.

Medina and realized the hopelessness of persuading the Jews as to the genuineness of his mission and especially his revelations, he adroitly turned the tables on them, and, by making Abraham the founder of the Ka'ba, could bring the prestige of his name into connection with Islam and could accuse the Jews of having departed from the true doctrine of Abraham which he had come to restore.[1]

The conclusive argument, however, against there being any basis in the fact for the legends of the connection of Ishmael and Abraham with the Ka'ba, is philological. Margoliouth puts it very succinctly –

> the inhabitants of the peninsula similarly had no knowledge of having sprung from either Ishmael or from Eber, the eponymous of the Hebrews. The epigraphy of Arabia contains no allusions to the pedigrees which the Jewish books assign to the tribes. The form wherein the Qur'an introduces the name Ishmael 'ISHMA'IL with an initial vowel, shows that it is taken from the Greeks or Syrians: the Arabian inscriptions in which this word figures frequently as a personal name, write it correctly with an initial consonant Y. Had the North Arabians had any tradition of Ishmael as their ancestor they would not have had to learn his name from the LXX or Peshitta. The form of the name Abraham which appears in the Qur'an also indicates that this personage was absolutely unknown before Muhammed's time, it was vocalized on the analogy of ISHMA'IL and ISRA'IL and has became IBRAHIM: these vowels must have been given it by conjecture: so utterly unfamiliar were the Northern Arabs with the name of the founder of their family.[2]

(cont. from p121) So claiming to preach the *milla* of Abraham he was claiming to go back behind both Judaism and Christianity to a more fundamental religion whose validity both Jews and Christians recognised. See also Bell, *Origin*, pp130ff

[1] So Demombynes writes in *Le Pèlerinage à la Mekke*, p 30 –
Sans prétendre à la dissiper, il importe au moins de rapporter ici les principales traditions relatives à l'histoire de la Ka'ba. On y distinguera sans peine celles qui sont des essais d'adaption juive et s'efforcent seulement, suivant la tendance générale de l'Islam, de rattacher la Ka'ba aux légendes bibliques et à l'histoire d'Abraham, et à en confirmer ainsi le caractère sacré; et d'autre part, celles qui cherchent à assurer aux Coréichites des titres privilégiés.

[2] *Schweich Lectures*, p12. Further on p23 he writes: (cont. p123)

The philological material is very simple to understand. The Hebrew form is ישמעאל which is correctly given in the Safaitic inscriptions יסמעל, the ס for ש being quite a normal change. Arabic, however, in the Qur'an gives the form إسماعيل which would correspond to a form אשמעיל which as a matter of fact we get in the Syriac ܐܝܫܡܥܝܠ and Greek Ισμαηλ.

It is clear then that the theory of Arab descent from Abraham has no greater authority than that given in the Qur'an.

Matriarchal Theory

The Patriarchal theory[1] which is assumed in all the genealogical schemes of the Arabs, has also not escaped scatheless from the fires of modern criticism. There can be no doubt that the tribes of Muhammad's time were organized on patriarchal lines, and perhaps had been for some considerable time previous to his day, but a critical investigation has brought to light traces of a much earlier and more primitive form of social organisation, viz the Matriarchate.[2] It must be admitted that as yet there is no unanimity among Semitic scholars on this point, and students must themselves go to the fundamental works on the controversy to form their own

---

When Muhammad gave the North Arabians Abraham and Ishmael for their founders and ancestors, there were no archeological objections as far as we know, because the people had no historically attested account to set against the new system. Similarly the ingenious Greek who first told the Romans that they were the descendants of Aeneas and the Trojans, could easily render his pedigree authoritative: for the Romans like other communities which had emerged slowly from savagery to a sort of civilization had no record from which this theory could be contradicted.

[1] (Ed. Handwritten note.) *The patronymic theory was no mere arbitrary hypothesis, no mere idea borrowed from the Jews: it was not even an arbitrary extension to all tribes of an explanation really applicable to some of them; it follows inevitably from the assumption that the tribal bond and the law of tribal succession had always been what they were at the time of the prophet.* "Kinship" p221

[2] (Ed. Handwritten note.) Robert Devreesse's article in the journal *Vivre et Penser*, 1942, p266 thinks something of matriarchal organisation, referring to such well known queens as Zeonbia, la Thalabanè, la Zèkiké and Mawia.

opinion:[1] all that can be done here is to outline the evidence on which the case for a primitive matriarchate rests.

In connection with the status of women and the ownership of children, there were among the Semites, as among other peoples, two main types.[2] The more common in historical times is that where the woman on marriage leaves her home, her kin or group, and enters that of her husband who becomes the natural guardian (*ba'al*) of her and her children. The other type, which would seem to be more primitive, is where the woman remains a member of her own family or group. Her husband or lover visits her there, and her children remain in her group, counting their descent through the mother and finding their natural protectors in the mother's family, particularly in the mother's brother. In this latter case the woman bears children for her own group not for her husband's and so the question of paternity is of secondary importance, and in many cases where polyandry is associated with the custom, it may even be quite uncertain.

These two types represent the patriarchal and matriarchal social forms. It has been suggested that the matriarchal form originates in conditions of tribal life where the hardy men are mostly engaged in hazardous enterprise and are unable to settle down to stable family life, or where economic conditions press so heavily that female infanticide is practiced and so women are scarce in the tribe. Whatever may be its origin, as we find it in history, it tends to pass into the patriarchal type whenever conditions for the tribe are stable and settled.[3]

---

[1] The main works are Robertson Smith, *Kinship and Marriage in Early Arabia* (2nd ed. 1903): G. A. Wilken, *Het Matriarchaat bij de oude Arabieren,* Amsterdam, 1884: Nöldeke, Review of Robertson Smith's book in *ZDMG*, xl, 148, 1871 and Review of Wilken's book in *Oesterreichische Monatsschrift für den Orient,* (journal) 1884, p301ff: Wellhausen, *Die Ehe bei den Arabern,* 1893: Barton, *Sketch of Semitic Origins*, cap ii, New York, 1902; Wetzstein in *Zeitschrift für Ethnologie (ZfE - journal)*, 1880

[2] Vide Cook in *Cambridge Ancient History,* i. 207. On the Israelitish matriarchiate see H. P., Smith, *Old Testament Writing,* p66n

[3] Full accounts may be consulted in River's article "Mother-right" in *ERE,* viii, and cap ii of Barton's *Semitic Origins.*

From what we know of the methods of Muslim writers in suppressing information about the pre-Islamic period which seemed out of harmony with Islamic claims, we will not expect to find much information surviving about matriarchal conditions. What has survived, however, is sufficiently startling.

    a) **Polyandry.** Modern Islam is characterized by polygamy, or one husband having many wives, a condition which possibly characterized the period immediately preceding Islam. There are traces, however, that in ancient Arabia, polyandry, or one wife with many husbands was not unknown.

        i) Strabo, in his *Geographica, xvi* (ed Kramer, iii, 340)[1] definitely states that polyandry was practiced in the South of Arabia. He writes

> *"Property is common among all the relations, the eldest being chief. There is one wife among them all and it is first come first served, he who first enters to her leaving at the door his staff, for it is the custom for everyone to carry a staff ... Hence the male children are all brothers.*

And then tells a curious story of a maiden of high degree, pestered by fifteen brothers, who worked a ruse by means of these same staffs to rid herself of their attentions.

        ii) Inscriptions gathered in South Arabia bear this out for we find, eg. a man listed as the son of three fathers, which can only be explained as a result of polyandrous unions.

    (b) **Primitive[2] Paternity in Arabia.** The pre-Islamic conception of paternity also provides interesting evidence,

---

[1] The passage reads "κοινὴ κτῆσις ἅπασι τοῖς συγγενέσι, κύριος δὲ ὁ πρεσβύτατος· μία δὲ καὶ γυνὴ πᾶσιν, ὁ δὲ φθάσας εἰσιὼν μίγνυται, προθεὶς τῆς θύρας τὴν ῥάβδον· ἑκάστῳ γὰρ δεῖν ῥαβδοφορεῖν ἔθος· νυκτερεύει δὲ παρὰ τῷ πρεσβυτάτῳ· διὸ καὶ πάντες ἀδελφοὶ πάντων εἰσί."
(AB. https://archive.org/details/strabonisgeogra02kramgoog/page/n362/mode/2up)
[2] Jeffery again uses the word 'primitive' which in this case could be expressed as 'early forms of'.

for we find that the custom of assigning paternity was very vague, the important point to the Arabs being that someone in the tribe was the father rather than any particular individual being settled on.¹ This state of things is unthinkable in a society organized on a patriarchal form where descent is traced through the individual father, but is quite intelligible in an organisation of the matriarchal form.²

(c) <u>Contract Wives:</u> There are a few traces still extant in Arabic literature, of partnerships being entered into between men, which included partnership in wives as well as goods. A condition of affairs which again is unthinkable save under a system when the old matriarchal type still left its influence.

(d) The phenomena met with in investigation of the relationships of the tribes, seem to indicate, as Robertson Smith has pointed out (*Kinship* cap.1) that in early times relationship counted through the female and not through the male (*Kinship*. p29)

(e) (Added later as a handwritten note). *Mut'a* Marriage. *mut'a* marriage, in short, is simply the last remains of that type of marriage which corresponds to a law of mother-kinship ..." ³

Totemistic Organisation

Another question of no little interest in regard to the primitive organisation of the tribes, is whether or not they were organized as Totem groups. Here again authorities differ. Robertson Smith, Wellhausen and Dussaud claim that the traces which have survived

---

¹ The three curious stories told by Al Biruni in his *India* cap x (ed Sachau, I, 108-9) are interesting illustrations of this point.
² In the matriarchal type of organisation the unit is not so much the individual as the group to which the individual belongs. The same principle holds good in blood-revenge. Vide further Wheeler Robinson's *Religious Ideas of the Old Testament*, p87
³ Roberston Smith *Kinship,* (1885), p69. (Ed. note:) While Sunnis believe that this practice has been abrogated, Twelver Shi'ites (Athna Ashria school) consider it is still valid. (cf. Q4:24)

are sufficient grounds for basing a judgment that Totemism was found among the ancient Arabs. On the other hand, so great a scholar as Nöldeke feels that the evidence is not sufficient to support any such weighty conclusion. So here again one can only set forth the evidence and let each judge for himself. It must again be remembered however, that such evidence as we have, consists of the fragmentary statements which have escaped the efforts of Muslim writers to suppress all information about early conditions in Arabia which were not in harmony with their Prophet's legislation.

Totemism may be defined, at least as regards its outward manifestation, as a form of social organisation in which all members of a group feel themselves to be of common blood with each other, and also with the animal, plant, or other natural object, whose name the group bears and to which certain forms of worship are paid. Some anthropologists claim that it is a stage through which all peoples have passed in their upward development,[1] and certainly the totemistic type of social grouping has been in past times, and is at present, very widely spread. Its best known developments at the present day are in Australia and America.

The characteristics of Totemism are very much the same everywhere, and include more particularly –

(1) The naming of the tribes by the name of the Totem animal, thus we find, Lion, Wolf, Hyena, Bear etc. tribe.
(2) Tattooed tribal marks, the mark generally being that of the Totem.
(3) Tabus connected with the Totem. It is a general rule that members of a totemic clan will not eat the flesh of their totem animal save on certain sacramental occasions. Sometimes we find they will not even use its skin for clothing.
(4) Worship connected with the Totem. On these sacred occasions the members of the tribe will frequently dress up to resemble their totem animal and will act like it.
(5) It is usually associated with some form of polyandrous or matriarchal organisation.

---

[1] Jevons, *Introduction to the History of Religion* (1896), p 117

Jevons has pointed out that the domestication of animals is fatal to Totemism,[1] and that it has survived only where the animals of a country are naturally of such a kind as cannot be domesticated; in other countries where such animals as can be domesticated come under the control of man and the others are more or less driven off to wilder parts, we only find traces of former totemistic conditions. This would lead us to expect then, that the traces of it among Semitic peoples would not be very numerous. The evidence for its existence has been carefully gathered together and learnedly expounded by Robertson Smith.[2] We merely summarize here.

(a) <u>Animal Tribal Names</u>
Lion – Banu Asad; Banu Farahid; Banu Labwan; B. Lab'
Dog — B. Kelb; B. Kolaib
Fox – B. Tha'lab; B. Tho'al
Serpent – B. Hanash; B. A'fa; B Araqin; B Hayya[3]
Wolf – B. Dhi'b; B. Sirham; B. Sid; B. Dhoaib

These are only a few out of the many that have been collected but are good examples which can be exactly paralleled with totemistic groups known elsewhere.[4]

(b) <u>Tattoo Marks</u>
The Arabic tribal mark (وَسْمٌ) was branded on cattle, and there is some evidence that these marks were of pictorial origin. There is no evidence of the markings ever being used on human beings, but the presumption is that anciently they were.

---

[1] Jevons, *op cit,* p120, 125, 127 ff.
[2] *Kinship and Marriage in Early Arabia* (new ed. by S. A. Cook, 1903), caps vii, viii: and in his article "Animal Worship and Animal Tribes among the Arabs and in the Old Testament" in *Journal of Philology,* vol. ix. Jacobs follows him in his studies in *Biblical Archaeology,* London 1894
[3] (Ed. *Handwritten* note:) On the serpent totem see H. P. Smith *Old Testament History* p259
[4] Nöldeke thinks that the giving of animal names was only a case of *bonum augurium*; see his article. "Einige Gruppen semitischer Personennamen" in his *Beiträge,* p 74ff. Dussaud, however, in *Arabes en Syrie,* p98, controverts his position.

(c) <u>Animal Worship</u>

The direct evidence for this is small, but we learn from the Qur'an (lxxi.23) of the lion-god Yaghuth[1], the horse-god Ya'uq, and the vulture-god Nasr. There was also the sacred dove sanctuary at Mecca.[2] Many of the Jinn reverenced in modern as well as in more ancient days among Muslims are possibly only old Totems transformed or transmuted.

(d) <u>Tabus</u>

Muhammad himself bears evidence to the sense of Tabu in regard to the eating of certain animals, e.g. the hare, the hyena and the lizard. Present day custom among the Bedouin bears similar evidence, and the only satisfactory explanation of this is the totemistic one. Specially interesting in this connection is the pig taboo, which has such practical consequences in the modern life of Islam.[3]

This is all the direct evidence there is from Arabia itself, but collateral evidence is borne by traces of Totemism found among other Semitic peoples,[4] for the religious and social bonds of this whole group are so close that we are almost always safe in arguing that a thing clearly evidenced in one Semitic group, must at some time have been common to others also.

---

[1] Yaghuth is also mentioned in an early poet quoted in Yaqut, iv.1023. Robertson Smith equates him with the יעוש of Gen xxxvi:14 (*Religion of the Semites*, p37 and 43) (AB: The term in Gen. xxxvi:14 is actually the subject of a kethiv-qere variant, but the qere would read (consonantally) יעוש. Again, discussion using the consonants only is quite familiar in this sort of context. I'm confident enough to change this one.)

[2] Vide Ibn Hisham 821: Nabigha 5:38, and Robertson Smith, *Kinship*, p229

[3] Vide Jevons *Introduction,* p118: Robertson Smith, *Kinship,* p307z

[4] Barton *Semitic Origins,* pp36ff: Jevons, op cit. p128

THE QURAISH

The great tribe to which Muhammad's family belonged, and which was the leading family in Mecca at the time immediately preceding Islam, was the Quraish. Its importance for the early history of Islam is thus obvious and demands some consideration from us here.

(a) **Traditional Account.**

The story as told in Arabic tradition[1] runs (with variants) as follows. When Abraham turned out Hagar and her son Ishmael, she wandered on in the desert till she reached the spot where Mecca now stands. It was there that the last pangs of thirst came upon her and she ran madly to and fro between the hills of Safa (صفا) and Marwa (مروه) vainly looking for water,[2] when suddenly from the ground under the feet of her son Ishmael, whom she had left lying on the sand, there bubbled up a spring of purest water.[3] This is Zemzem.[4] She built a little hut there, and was later discovered by wandering Amalekites and Yemenite Arabs, who were astonished to find there such good water. Gradually a little community grew up round the well, and it was there that Abraham found them when later he repented and came to look for them. It was at this post also that he attempted to offer Ishmael in sacrifice. Being grieved to find at this settlement no worship of the true God, with Ishamel's assistance, he built for them the Ka'ba[5], and instituted the practice of pilgrimage thereto.

---

[1] Vide Tabari, i.270ff: 1130ff: Ibn Sa'd i.21ff.
[2] Sura ii.154
[3] There is another tradition that Gabriel had caused it to flow for Adam: vide '*Omda*, ('Umda) iv.646; article "Hawwa" in *EI*, Demombynes *Mekke*, p72
[4] The origin of the name is doubtful. Renan parallels with זַמְזֻמִים = βαρβαροί (p35, n.2. *Langues Sémitiques*) (AB: This note looks to be a reference to 'זַמְזֻמִים' as in the one Old Testament (The Bible) occurrence in Deut. ii:20, despite the fact that Rahlfs has the Greek transliteration Ζομζομμιν at that point. I'm going to make the change here.)
[5] Sura ii.121-4: xxii.27: Another legend makes Adam its builder, and then to reconcile the two we find a statement that it was taken up to heaven and then rebuilt later by Abraham, Vide Nicholson, *Literary History*. p63: Tabari Comment 1, 408

The descendants of Ishmael[1] became the Quraishite tribe and were closely linked by blood with the Banu Khuza'a who also dwelt at Mecca.[2] Later they came under the domination of the Yemenite tribe of Jurhum who stopped there on their way up from the South, and who retained possession of the Ka'ba and directed the Pilgrimage for a considerable period. They were overthrown by an adventurer named Qusai, who established the Quraishite rule, which continued till the time of Muhammad.

(b) Criticism

Critical examination reveals that most of this account is pure legend.[3] The legend of Abraham has already been before us. It has no greater authority than Muhammad's own elaboration of Jewish legend. The same is true of the story of Ishmael. There is apparently no ancient tradition on the subject earlier than the Qur'an, and the tradition when it does appear is demonstrably based on Rabbinic material, and so quite valueless for the early history of the tribe.

The few historical facts embedded in the tradition are:

(i). That for some time previous to the coming of Muhammad, the Meccan sanctuary and the conduct of the pilgrimage had been in the hands of the Quraish, (the great name among whom was that of one Hisham[4]) but there was a consciousness

---

[1] (Ed. *Handwritten note:*) Muslim writers place statements indicating the acceptance of this Abrahamic theory in the mouths of pre-Islamic persons. Eg. in *Nur al Yaqin* 6th ed. p15-16 we find an account of a speech made by Abi Talib at the wedding of Muhammad and Khadija in which he praises God for his Abrahamic descent. وزرع امحد لله الزى جعلنان خريه ابراحيم اسمايل

[2] Ibn Hisham, 71ff: Margoliouth, *Mohammed,* p10; Ibn Qutaiba, *Kitab al Ma'arif,* p18

[3] "It is doubtful whether any actual history is to be got out of the lengthy series of fables dignified with the title *Chronicles of Mecca* - Margoliouth, op.cit. p10. These *Chronicles* have been edited by Wüstenfeld, - *Chroniken der Stadt Makka, 4 vols.* Leipzig, 1958-61

(Ed. *Handwritten* note.) "Everything that the Moslems tell about the pre-Islamic perogatives of the Cureish is suspicious." *Kinship,* p115

[4] *Of all the myths that seems to be nearest history which makes the head of the Kuraishite settlement at Meccah one Hisham, son of Mughira, of the tribe Makhzum.*

more or less definite among them that they had not always been in undisputed possession (see Diodorus, iii.43: Strabo)[1]. In fact there was still some lingering memory among them that once they had been a nomadic people.[2]

(ii). That there had been at some earlier period a settlement of Yemenites on the spot, and this was probably connected with the planting of Yemenite colonies in North Arabia.[3]

(iii). That the main source of revenue of Mecca in pre-Islamic days, was, as it is now, from the Pilgrimage crowds.[4]

(iv). That in the early days it was not uncommon to find Christians and Jews in Mecca.[5] Ibn Duraid (p172) tells us that the Quraish used to levy a tax on foreign visitors to the Ka'ba.

The question of the origin of the Quraish is an interesting one. As to the derivation of the name, Jahiz said it was derived from their trading and profit making, (التجارة والتضريش,) while Baihaqi has a tradition from Ibn 'Abbas that they were named from a sea monster called *Alqaish*,[6] which may have been a Totem. Certainly the name seems to be non-Arabic, and it would seem that they were foreigners who had settled in Mecca. There is a tradition said to be derived from 'Ali that they were Nabataeans from Kutha in Mesopotamia and Margoliouth thinks there may be some truth for this –

Traditions which seem valuable state that Hisham and Mecca were at one time interchangeable terms: and that at Hisham's death the people were summoned to the funeral of the 'lord'.

[1] Jeffery left a space, obviously to add the information later.
[2] Vide Jahiz, *Mahasin*, ed Van Vloten, p225
[3] Muir, *Caliphate*, p42 suggests that Mecca was largely Yemenite in the times of Abu Bakr. How strong this Yemenite influence was is evidenced by the South Arabian divinities such as Al-Ussa, Waad, Nasr etc. associated with the Ka'ba.
[4] Ed. Note: See "Revenue from Pilgrimage Crowds in Appendix, p243.
[5] The presence of non-Muslims at the Festival was forbidden first in the Prophet's own lifetime. *ERE*, viii. 512 Margoliouth (*Muhammed*, pp41, 42)
[6] Vida Caussin de Perceval, *Essai*, I, 231: Margoliouth. op cit. p9 says it was a "sword-fish".

i) The great god Hubal of Mecca was said to have come from Hit on the Euphrates.[1,2]

ii) Kutha was a name used for Mecca, or part of it.[3]

iii) The commercial and political ability of the tribe was unusual for Hijazis.[4]

This is in support of the suspicion that the cult of Mecca was of foreign origin[5] and may possibly be derived from that of the Sumerian Ishtar. The following points may be noted –

i. The Byzantine writers state that the Arabs adored at Mecca an idol on which was carved the image of Aphrodite.

 a) Nicetas of Khonia[6] in his form of malediction for converted Muslims, makes them say "and I anathematize the Meccan house of prayer … in the midst of which they say is a great stone on which is engraven the image of Aphrodite."

 b) Nicetas of Byzantium[7] says "the Arabs adore a very ancient idol which is found in the desert of Yathrib and

---

[1] Azraqi, (ed. Wüstenfeld) i.133. Other tradition, however, says he came from Moab.
[2] (Ed. *Handwritten note*:) W. Caskel, *Das altarabische Königreich Lihjan* (1950) points out that Hubal was a Nabataean deity and that Qurai, who is said to have secured the Quraish supremacy in Mecca is a Nabataean name, so probably the Quraish were a band of Nabataen conquerors. This would explain their aptitude for trafficking, See קצין in Cantineau *Lexique* p143. (AB: There is no biblical Hebrew word that would appear in a dictionary in the form in the note, and I don't have access to the recent dictionary by Clines right now, which would list extrabiblical Hebrew words (or my dictionary of Talmudic/Midrashic words), but I am wondering whether the rare word for 'leader', 'קצין' might be intended. It has the final nun rather than a final vav and appears in Prov. vi:7; xxv:15; Isa. iii.6-7; Dan.xi:18. However, I feel the lack of context for this one. I'm not sure whether this is our root or not.)
[3] Vida Yaqut iv.317: and *Hilal*, ed Amedroz
[4] Wellhausen, *Reste*, p93
[5] Robertson Smith *Religion of the Semites*, p113n
[6] *Thesaurus Orthodoxae fidei* in Migne *Patrologia.Graeca*. cxl. col 105. He says that they call her Χαμάρ which means 'the great'. This may stand for كبرى or as Blochet thinks (*Culte d'aphrodite-Anahita*, 1902, p6) for كعبة. Blochet notes that Vincent de Bauvais in his *Speculum Historiale* and Marino Sanute in his *Liber Secretorum Fidelium Crucis*, narrate the same story.
[7] *Refutatio Mohammedis* in Migne, *Patrologia Graeca*. vol. cv. col 793

Mecca, which as they say, has engraved on it the image of Aphrodite.

c) Bartholomew of Edessa[1] in his *Contra Mohammedem* says that the Saracens of the time of Heraclious were idolators worshipping Aphrodite whom they named Χαμάρ.

d) Glycas[2] in his *Annales* tells us also that at the time of Heraclius the Arabs worshipped Astarte, whom they called "the great".

e) Euthymius Zigabenus repeats the same statement.[3],[4]

(ii) The word Ka'ba كعبة, was obviously a divinity in the pre-Islamic period, for we find the personal name Abd el-Ka'ab.[5] The form of the word being feminine would point to the divinity being a goddess.[6] Moreover, the origin of the word would seem to point to Aphrodite or Ishtar, for though كعبة now is taken as connected with "cube", and referred to the shape of the building, the original meaning would seem rather to be connected with the sense كعب = development of a woman's breasts كُعُبٌ = breast, a young girl with fully developed breasts كعاب, كعبة = virginity. So كعبة would signify the goddess of the prominent breasts, i.e. Ishtar of Assyria.[7]

(iii) Herodotus tells us (iii.8) that the Arabs of his day worshipped a goddess Ἀλιλάτ whom he equates with Οὐρανίη. This is doubtless the Allat (اللات) who is mentioned in the Qur'an (liii:19) as the companion of Al-'Uzza and Manat, the 'daughters

---

[1] *Contra Mohammedem* in Migne, *Patrologia Graeca.* vol 1448, 1456 and in *Elenchus et confutatic Ägareni,* in Migne, *Patrologia Graeca.* vol civ, col 1385
[2] *Annales,* Bonn, 1836, p514
[3] *Panoplia Dogmatica,* in Migne, *Patrologia Graeca.* cxxx. Col 1333
[4] (Ed. Handwritten note:) Epiphanius in *Haereses* li.22 see Appendix p237.
[5] Tabari i.1073, 10. Cf. Wellhausen *Reste* 3. It is said that Abu Bakr bore this name before his conversion.
[6] Blochet, op cit p5. Margoliouth, however, thinks the word may be only the Ethiopic for 'double'. Cf. *ERE*, viii.511
[7] Vide Jastrow, *Religious Belief in Babylonia & Assyria,* 1911, p136. See also Epiphanius *Panarion,* li

of God". In the great text of the Descent of Ishtar[1], we find her associated with Allatu the queen, the consort of Nergal.

(iv) Al-'Uzza (العزى) is mentioned in the Qur'an along with Al-Lat, and Al-'Uzza is Venus[2] who resided in a sacred acacia tree[3] just as Ishtar (Ashtart) dwelt in an ashera.[4] That she was the special goddess of the Quraish is indicated by Yaqut, iii. 664 and Ibn Hisham i.93.94 connects her specially with the Ka'ba.[5] As to the licentiousness of the rites connected with her worship we have evidence from both ancient and modern times.[6]

(v) The only idol allowed to be actually inside the Ka'ba in pre-Islamic days was Hubal, whom we are told, was in the form of a man,[7] and whose name shows that he was considered as the husband of the goddess.[8] There is some reason for thinking that he was the chief god of Mecca.[9] And all the traditions state that he was a foreigner.[10] From the *Maghazi* [11]() we learn that his name was coupled with that of 'Uzza as the Meccan war cry at 'Uhud.

(vi) The Qur'an, Sura lxxi.22-23 mentions certain ancient divinities of the Arabs, Wadd, Suwa', Yaghuth, Ya'uq. and Nasr. Zamakhshari on this passage, along with many other commentators says that Wadd was in the form of a man, Suwa' in that of a woman, Yaghuth in the form of a lion, Ya'uq of a

---

[1] Vide Barton's essay "The Semitic Ishtar Gult" in *Hebraica*, ix, 143-47
[2] Vide Cheikho, *Le Christianisme en Arabie*, p10
[3] Yaqut *Mu'jam*, iii, 224ff. Vide also Barton *Semitic Origins, p88*: Huart, *Histoire des Arabes*, i.32
[4] *NSI*, 5094
[5] On her close connection with the Meccan sanctuary see Barton, op.cit. p133: Robinson Smith, *Kinship*, p 294: Wellhausen, *Reste,* p36: *Hebraica,* Barton, x, 64ff
[6] Ephraem Syrus (ii. 457-459) tells of sacrifices of chastity to her, and Isaac of Antioch (ed Bickell, pp220,224) mentions the licentiousness of her festivals. For the licentious character of her modern festival, see Hurgronje, *Mekka* ii, 59-61
[7] Cheikho, p (Ed. note: page number(s) not given.)
[8] Pococke *Specimen,* p98 suggeted (הַבַּעֲל) but הוא בעל (he is lord) is much more probable. Astarte also was wife of Baal.
[9] Wellhausen, *Reste,* p75: Demombynes, *Mekke, p43*: Wellhausen suggests his equation with Allah, and Nöldeke (*ERE*, i.663) hesitatingly agrees.
[10] *Shahrastani* ed Cureton, p295: Ibn Hisham p51; Margoliouth *Muhammad,*
[11] ed. Kremer, p237

horse, and Nasr of an eagle. Now in the Gilgamesh Epic we read that the four paramours of the goddess Ishtar were a man (Tammuz), a lion, a horse and a great bird.[1]

(vii)   In pre-Islamic times the Ka'ba was a dove sanctuary,[2] and Mecca is called by an early poet "a town in which the dove is safe".[3] Ibn Hisham (ed Wüstenfeld, p 821) tells us that when Muhammad entered Mecca as a conquerer and destroyed the idols, he removed from the Ka'ba a wooden image of a dove. The dove was sacred to Ashtoreth among the Northern Semites.[4]

(viii)   The pig was sacred at the Ka'ba, and we know from other sources that it also was sacred to Ishtar.[5]

(ix)   At the present time the Ka'ba is known as 'Arusa – the bride. She is given a new gown with great ceremony every year (the Kiswa), and only eunuchs attend on the Ka'ba.[6]

ix)   The sacred day of the Muslims is Friday. This was doubtless taken over from pre-Islamic days and is of course the day sacred to Venus.[7]

The most sacred relic in the Ka'ba is the black stone, which tradition says fell down from heaven.[8] In Philo of Byblos we read of the Phoenician Astarte, that she found a star falling through the air, which she took up and consecrated in the holy island of Tyre. (See also Sozomen *Ecclesiastical History.* ii.5) The kissing of this stone forms an important part of the rites of the Ka'ba, though not mentioned in the Qur'an.[9]

---

[1] See details in *AJSL* (Ed. Note: No further details given.)
[2] (Ed. *Handwritten note.*) Nabighah, *Mu'allaqat* 2:37
واملومن العابزات الطير تعسحها   ركبان مكه بين امغيل والسعد
[3] Vide eg. Richter *Kypros,* p 274: *Hebraica,* x, 49.
[4] See *EI* ii, 586: Demombynes in *RHR,* 1918. In *De Dea Syria,* (see Lucian of Samosata) 54 we read that Syrians would not eat the dove.
[5] (Ed. *Handwritten note:*) Note the boar in the Venus and Adonis story
[6] Vide Soubhy, *Pilgrimage,* p85
[7] It is the *dies Veneris*
[8] On the Black Stone see Demombynes *Mekke,* p41
[9] Burton, *Pilgrimage,* iii, 168ff

x) Ibn Hisham (ed Wüstenfeld, p94) tells a story of how 'Abd al-Muttalib, when cleaning out the well Zemzem, found two golden gazelles which he placed in the Ka'ba. The gazelle was also an animal sacred to Aphrodite.[1]

xi) The desacralization rite at the conclusion of the Pilgrimage, would seem to point to some connexion with the old licentious rites of the mother-goddess.[2]

xii) The regulation still survives in Islam of performing the ceremonies at the Ka'ba in a state of partial nudity, and there is reason to believe that the ceremony in pre-Islamic times was performed naked.[3]

---

[1] Robinson Smith, *Kinship,* p 227
[2] Vide Demombynes *Mekke,* p305ff
[3] Nöldeke in *ERE* I, 667d

MECCA

Our previous discussion will have made it clear that we know very little of the actual facts as to the early history of Mecca. As Nicholson has pointed out –

> "Mecca was the cradle of Islam, and Islam, according to Muhammad, is the religion of Abraham ... consequently the pre-Islamic history of Mecca has all been, so to speak, Islamised. The Holy City is made to appear in the same light thousands of years before the Prophet's time."[1]

How ancient Mecca may be we cannot guess. Ptolemy (vi.vii.32) refers to a Macorabe (Μακοράβω) an inland city of Arabia, which has been very generally supposed to refer to Mecca. If the identification can be upheld, it would probably point to a South Arabian origin of the city, for the name is apparently etymologically connected with the South Arabian *mukarrib*.[2] This supposition is supported by certain other facts —

1. The persistent tradition that Yemenites had some share in the building of the Ka'ba and ruled for some time in the city.[3]

2. The ancient name for the city, according to the Qur'an, (iii.90) was *Bakka*, and we know that *Bakka* in the South Arabian dialects occurs for the *Mecca* of North Arabia.[4]

---

[1] *Literary History*.p62. See also Margoliouth *ERE*, viii. He says "The *Chronicles of Mecca* of which the earliest extant is by Azraqi (245AH), so far as they treat of the pre-Islamic period, are collections of fables, in the main based on the Qur'an, but to some extent influenced by the later history also.
[2] Margoliouth, *HDB*, iv. 480 c.
[3] Vide infra p116 &132
[4] Blochet, *Culte d' Aphrodite-Anahita*, p7

3. The worship of al-*Uzza* at Mecca was very firmly established in the period when Muhammad came, and she is a South Arabian divinity.[1]

4. Wadd and Nase, divinities also mentioned in the Qur'an occur on South Arabian inscriptions.[2]

Several attempts have been made to establish other conjectures as to its origin.

(a) <u>Israelitish Theory</u>
In 1864, the Orientalist, Reinhardt Dozy in his book *De Israeliten te Mekka*[3] put forward a theory that the city was an old Israelitish settlement, first founded by a band of discontents from the tribe of Simeon, who migrated there in the time of Saul. They founded the Ka'ba there and instituted the great Meccan festival, and were later joined by a great crowd of Israelites at the time of the Babylonian captivity.

Dozy's theory originated in a certain inscription which was supposed to come from the Ka'ba, and of which Dozy thought he had the key. The working out of his theory led him to postulate that the primitive worship of Israel was not that of Yahweh but of Ba'al, and naturally the book roused a great storm of controversy. Dozy's theory now, however, has only an antiquarian interest.[4]

(b) <u>Zemzem[5] Theory</u>

---

[1] Her name occurs frequently in the South Arabian inscriptions and wherever South Arabian tribes are found in Arabia we find the worship of Al-'Uzza. A good example is Hira.
[2] Vide, Mordtmann, *Sabäische Denkmäler*, p69 & 90
[3] There is a German translation *Die Israeliten zu Mekka von Davids Zeit,* Leipzig, 1864
[4] (Ed. *Handwritten note:*) See particularly the case against Dozy put by Graf in *ZDMG,* 1868, pp348ff and G. Rösch in *Jahrbuch für deutsche Theologie,* 1865, pp344ff
[5] Alternate spelling: Zamzam

Sprenger[1] suggested that the town owed its origin to the fact that the famous well of Zemzem[2] is on the direct caravan route between Mecca and Syria. This suggestion has commended itself to many other scholars including Snouck Hurgronje.[3] Caravans are dependent upon good water supply being available at the end of each stage of the journey, and it was greatly to the interest of these caravans on the spice road to have this important well with its fairly abundant supply of water, kept clean and wholesome, and protected from the raiding Bedouin. Thus we can imagine the South Arabian merchants planting a little colony there. This would grow by accretions from other Arab tribes and soon become a considerable community. As at Palmyra, the ruling class would be a commercial aristocracy, the ruling motive of whose policy would be the maintenance of the caravan trade, with constant vigilance to prevent blood feuds or petty tribal wars from closing the trade routes. Now, as Robertson Smith has pointed out,[4] the most effective means of protecting commerce from these embarrassments was to place it under the sanction of religion, so Mecca was made into a centre of cosmopolitan worship for all Arabia, where all the tribes could have their idols, and where even Christian Arab tribes could set up an image of the Virgin and Child.[5]

The weaknesses of this theory are these. In the first place, as we have already seen, the commercial activity of Mecca has been exaggerated[6] and is hardly strong enough to bear the weight this theory puts upon it. Secondly, we have abundance of evidence that the water of Zemzem is of inferior quality,[7] whereas Nöldeke points

---

[1] *Leben,* ii, 346
[2] Burton *Pilgrimage,* ii, 164 thinks it is a reduplication of ... [Ed. Note: The remainder of this sentence is missing.]
[3] *Mekka,* i
[4] Article *Palmyra* in *Ency. Britt.* lxth ed. xviii.1999
[5] It was probably a picture of Mary with the child on her knee: vide Azraqi p112ff: Yaqubi, ii, 62: 'Umda, ('Umdat\'Omda) iv. 611: Palmer *Qur'an*, p.xiii and Demombynes <u>Mekke</u>, p56. It is said to have been on the central pillar to the right of the door and to have remained there till the reconstruction of the Ka'ba by Al-Hajjaj (AH 73). Nöldeke, thinks that it was probably painted there by the Christian artist Baqum (i.e. the Coptic Pachomios) who was employed at the building in the sixth Century AD. Margoliouth, however, thinks the story is without foundation (*Mohammed,* p41)
[6] Infra p132.
[7] Vide Burton's account *Pilgrimage,* ii. 163

out,¹ there are other excellent springs no great distance off, which most certainly would have been the centre of the community if water were the main consideration. Thirdly, although it is true that we have no early trace of a priesthood at Mecca, yet the religious character of this place seems to have been of primary importance. The prohibition of killing in the *haram,* e.g. seems quite primitive and must have originally been connected with the conception of the place as a sanctuary. There is a very curious statement in Jahiz (*Opuscular* ed. van Victen p62) to the effect that there was a time when Mecca was only inhabited at the two seasons of the year, the summer being spent at Jiddah and the winter at Ta'if.

(c)   Astronomical Theory

This leads us to the final theory, viz that the growth of the city was due to its religious character. What the origin was, we cannot at this time even guess, but the place seems to have been a very primitive sanctuary, connected maybe with the old Arabian mother goddess, where for long there survived a very decided objection to blood shedding. The ceremonies of the pilgrimage suggest that there were probably in the early days a number of sanctuaries, the visiting of which is now stereotyped into a single pilgrimage ritual. Margoliouth suggests that may be the word حجة is to be explained from the Hebrew חוג = to draw round, and so the Arab month, زوالحجة would mean "the month of going round", i.e. round these various sanctuaries.²

Wellhausen has pointed out³ a fact that has frequently been overlooked, viz. that the essential part of the pilgrimage would seem to have been the procession from Mt Arafat to the valley of Mina, and thus had originally nothing to do with the city itself. The association with the Ka'ba, however, must have been made in pre-Islamic times, for from the Qur'an (xxii.27) we should certainly infer that Muhammad was familiar with the circumambulation of the Ka'ba.⁴   Wellhausen's point also suggests certain features of

---

¹ *ERE,* I, 667 c. It would also seem that Zemzem had been choked up for some time and only opened up afresh by one of the immediate ancestors of Muhammad
² *ERE* viii,511. It is noteworthy also that Mecca is called ام قرى = mother of villages.
³ *Reste arabischen Heidentums,* Wellhausen, p79ff.
⁴ Vide Wensinch, in *EI* article *Ka'ba*

astronomical religion and that fits in with other astronomical features of the cult, notably –

i) The fact of the *sacred month* and the close connection of the festival with the old Arabian calendar.[1]

ii) The rites of circumambulation still practised during the Pilgrimage.[2]

iii) The fact that the famous Black Stone is apparently a meteorite.[3]

iv) The kindling of the lights on the hill Ilal; the fire at Quzah; the temporal limits set to the festival by the rising and setting sun; all of which point to a form of sun worship.[4]

Taking all this in connection with what we know of star worship among the Arabs in other parts of the peninsula[5] there seems ground for maintaining that Mecca in primitive times was a centre of early astronomical religion. Houtsma has even gone so far as to claim that the ceremonial ritual of the pilgrimage is the acting out of a complicated mythological drama with an astronomical motif.[6]

---

[1] Nöldeke in *ERE*, I 668
[2] An account of the actual ceremonies can be read in Burton's *Pilgrimage* ii.165ff, and the theory of them is given in Demombynes *Mekke*, p205ff. In connection therewith see the article *Circumambulation* in *ERE*.
[3] So Burton *Pilgrimage*, ii.300 n.
[4] Nöldeke *ERE*, i.669. cf. also the Jewish Festival of Lights: Gray *Sacrifice* p 270
[5] See supra p152ff.
[6] Vide his essay "Het Skopelisma en het Steenwerpen to Mina," in the *VMKA*, Amsterdam, 1904. The student should also consult an interesting article by Carl Clemen "Der Ursprüngliche Sinn des Hajj" in *Der Islam*, vol x.

RELIGIOUS BACKGROUND

The study of the Quraish and of Mecca has already led us into the heart of the problems of the religious environment of Muhammad and early Islam, problems which, it is obvious are even more vital than those that have been before us concerning the physical, social and historical backgrounds. One is safe in asserting that every religion owes much to those earlier religions among which it was born, and the influences of which played upon it in the early formative years of its life. In fact it is hardly possible to fully understand the development of a religion that has arisen in historical times, save in reference to its background. Mithraism is inexplicable save in terms of the Zoroastrian soil from which it sprang. Even in Christianity we bind together the Old and the New Testaments, not because we are still under the Law, still bound by the limited religious conceptions of the Old Testament, but because we sense that Christianity can only fully be understood when placed against the background of the Old Covenant of Judaism. As we read the New Testament, we find references to Abraham, Noah, Moses, and David, and others as well as to the numerous customs and points of ritual, which would be meaningless to us without the Old Testament background.

Similarly, when we come to Islam we find the Qur'an full of references to personages, places, rites and religious conceptions which were the property of various religions existing in Arabia at that time. Moreover, Islam, more than any other historical religion is a patchwork of multi-coloured fragments drawn from its religious environment, and thus like all Eclecticisms, such as Theosophy or Swedenborgianism is almost entirely explainable in terms of its sources, and quite inexplicable apart from a study of them. It thus becomes of the first importance for us to discuss in some detail the Arabian paganism of Muhammad's day and the state of the great external religions, Zoroastrianism, Judaism, and Christianity whose influence was widespread in the Arabia of that period.

ARABIAN PAGANISM

Our first and most obvious subject of investigation is the religion of the pagan Arabs[1] among whom Muhammad was born. This was the religion taught him in his youth: the religion he saw around him in the years of his early manhood, and the religion that he himself practised for many years before ideas of forming his own religion came to him.[2] It is true, as Hirschfeld[3] points out, that this old religion was gradually breaking down at the time of Muhammad, but there can be no doubt that very strong influence upon his own religious thinking came from this source.

Unfortunately we are faced at the outset with the fact which we have already encountered several times in our investigation, that the Arab writers have been obsessed with an endeavour, only too successfully carried out, in most directions, to draw a veil over the

---

[1] Nöldeke's article in *ERE* vol I is the best study available, but the older work of Wellhausen *Reste Arabischen Heidentums*, 2nd. ed. Berlin, 1897, is of the first importance, and the student may still consult with profit Krehl's *Über die Religion der vorislamischen Araber*, Leipzig, 1863, and Osiander's "Studien über die vorislamischen Religionen der Araber" in *ZDMG*, vol. vii.
(Ed. *Handwritten note*:) *"Arab authors are utterly unscrupulous in their attempts to minimize the ungodly practices of their ancestors". Kinship*, p18

[2] Muslims violently resent this statement and claim that Muhammad followed the religion of Abraham from the very first. There can be no doubt, however, of the accuracy of the statement in the text. Dr. Margoliouth mentions the following points in this connection (*Muhammad*, pp69,70).
    a.) The children of Muhammad and Khadija were named at times after the pagan gods: eg. 'Abd Manaf vide *Le Livre de la Creation*, (ed. Huart. iv. 130)
    b.) Muhammad confessed to having once sacrificed a grey sheep to Al-'Uzza: vide Wellhausen *Reste*, p34: Krehl p90 from Yaqut, *Mu'jam*, iii.664.
    c.) He and Khadija used to perform some domestic rite in honour of one of the goddesses each night before they retired to rest. vide *Musnad*, (Hanbal), iv.222.
    d.) In the *Musnad* (i.189) we have a story of his inviting Zaid ibn 'Amr to come and eat with him and his stepson of meat offered to idols and the refusal of the old man first inspired Muhammad with disgust for such food. See also *ERE*, vi, 249 and the *Dala'il an Nabbuwah*, al Bayhaqi, Haidarabad, 1324, p 59.

[3] *New Researches*, pp3,4. Hirschfeld thinks that this fact, coupled with the unsuitableness of either Judaism or Christianity to the Bedouin nature, may have suggested to Muhammad the advisability of preaching a new and simple national religion.

conditions of the "Times of Ignorance":[1] so that our courses for the study of pre-Islamic religion are none of the best, and as a consequence, not only must our picture of Arabian heathenism be incomplete, but frequently our reconstructions are far from certain.

Our Sources are –

(i) **Inscriptions**[2]
These fall into two groups –

(a) South Arabian, whose evidence is only valid for the Sabaean religion of the South Arabian Kingdoms, but which has frequently much light to shed on problems that meet us elsewhere in Arabia; e.g. in these South Arabian inscriptions we have found the names of gods previously known from other parts of Arabia, and whom we now know to be of South Arabian origin.

(b) North Arabian, both Greek and Semitic, give evidence for the tribes which had been settled in North Arabia. The inscriptions do not tell us very much. The numerous theophorus names[3] which occur in them and divinities mentioned, enable us to form the skeleton of the old Arabian pantheon. Frequently the inscriptions give us odd details as to the culture, such as the types of offerings made to the divinities, the particular seasons at which they were worshipped, sometimes the form of words by which they were involved, and such like. They are at times of particular value in revealing to us the area in which certain divinities

---

[1] Robertson Smith writes – *Religion of the Semites*, p 49 – "Arabian poetry has little to do with religion at all: it dates from the extreme decadence of the old heathenism, and is preserved to us only in the collection formed by Muhammadan scholars, who were careful to avoid or obliterate as far as possible the traces of their father's idolatry". So Margoliouth in *ERE*, vi. 247 "During the first century of Islam the very memory of the earlier condition was detested. Only enough then was retained to explain certain allusions in the Qur'an or the Prophet's biography: and even this is vague and contradictory."
[2] Berger made an attempt at gathering the results of epigraphy for our subject in his little work *L'Arabie avant Mahomet d'après les Inscriptions*, Paris, ... but the question needs further and more detailed study.
[3] On these theophorus names see Wellhausen, *Reste*, pp1-10.

were worshipped, although the scantiness of the inscriptional remains make it hazardous to infer that because a certain divinity does not occur in inscriptions from a certain locality, therefore that divinity was not reverenced in that locality.

(ii) Classical Authors

In the writers of classical antiquity, Greek, Roman, and Syrian, we have again a certain amount of information preserved about the early religion of Arabia. For example, Herodotus tells us of the Arabian worship of Ἀλιλά (Ἀλιττα) = Al-Lat. Uranius composed a treatise on Arabian affairs, some fragments of which are preserved by Stephanus of Byzantium. Nilus describes their worship of the morning star in sacrifice and Agatharchides as preserved in Didorus Siculus, tells of the ancient temples in Arabia. Porphyry bears witness to human sacrifice among the Arabs, and Ephraim Syrus mentions their worship of the planet Venus, and so on. Again it is not a great deal of evidence, but such as it is it gives us valuable information which helps to elucidate points which are known to us, but known imperfectly, from other sources.

(iii) Talmud

It might have been expected that the Jewish writers would have preserved much information for us about early Arabia, but S. Krauss' examination of the Talmud[1] was not very fruitful. It contains scraps of <u>information</u> about the Arabs, as e.g. that they used to worship Nasr, the eagle. It is possible, however, that further research will reveal more details that will be of help to us.

(iv) Qur'an

Muhammad's polemic in the Qur'an itself frequently bears witness to the existence of pre-Islamic divinities

---

[1] "Talmudische Nachrichten über Arabien" in *ZDMG*, 1916, 1 xx, 4321-323. (Ed. *Handwritten note*:) Krauss discusses names, political conditions, commerce and trade, linguistic matters and religious ideas.

and the practices of the ancient Arabs.¹ A typical passage is in sura liii.19

> Do you see Al-lat and Al-'Uzza and Manat the third besides? What! Shall ye have male progeny and God female? This were indeed an unfair partition. These are mere names: ye and your fathers named them thus: God hath not sent down any warranty in their regard.

(v) Pre-Islamic Literature

We have to thank the Islamic philologists and antiquarians for any material from this source that has been preserved to us. These writers were so keen on preserving material for their subjects that they have often preserved for us references to pre-Islamic religious customs in the old poems, references which would otherwise almost certainly have been glossed over. This glossing process, as a matter of fact, did invade even here, for there are several most interesting cases where a verse has come down to us in two recensions, one in what we may assume to have been the original form, and the other as glossed over by pious Muslims.²

The information, however, which we can gather from this source does not amount to a great deal. The early poets were not particularly interested in religion³ and rarely mention matters of religious interest in detail. Moreover, the question has recently been raised as to whether any pre-Islamic poetry has survived at all. A lot of material has come down to us that claims to be from the pre-Islamic era but these poems were not committed to writing till the 'Abbasid period (ie 750-99 AD), and certain scholars have expressed strong

---

[1] One must register a doubt, however, as to how accurate a picture of the pre-Islamic religion the Qur'an gives. On this point Margoliouth writes – "since the accounts of Judaism and Christianity given in that work are well known to be gross travesties of those systems, we have no guarantee that its treatment of Arabian paganism is any fairer or more intelligent." *ERE* vi 247

[2] It will be remembered that Muhammad himself started this process of glossing over, by renaming many of his followers who happened to be named after pagan idols. Vide Margoliouth *Muhammed*, p110.

[3] Robertson Smith *Religion of Semites*, p49

suspicions that most of this literature was manufactured by the antiquarians themselves.¹

(vi) Modern Islamic Practice

As great lumps of the pre-Islamic paganism were taken over undigested into Islam, and have survived as part of Islamic ritual to the present day, it will be seen that in modern Islamic practice we have a fruitful source of information, if carefully worked, for the practices of the pre-Islamic period. All the details of the Pilgrimage,² eg. the circumambulation of the Ka'ba, the running between Safa and Marwah, the sacrifice in the valley of Mina, the stoning of the pillars, the visit to the black stone, were taken over with practically no change from the pagan ceremonial that was practised in Mecca before Muhammad's birth.

(vii) Philology

Frequently a philological investigation into the significance of words used in the cult may help discern behind the present usage a more primitive conception. We have already seen an example of this case of the word كعبة ³ and Dr Margoliouth suggests other examples in عبادة and عكف etc.⁴

(vii) Types of Religion
(a) astronomical.

This is not the place in which to enter upon a discussion of whether all primitive Semitic worship was astronomical in character, but there is nevertheless no doubt that the predominant form in early Arab paganism was astronomical.

1) Sun Worship⁵.

---

¹ Vide Margoliouth *Schweich Lectures,* p72ff and a long article in *JRAS,* 1926. The conclusions of Margoliouth have recently been popularized in Arabic in a little volume by Taha Hussein *Fi'sh-Shi'r al-Jahili,* Cairo, 1926
² Vide Junyboll's article, "Pilgrimage (Arabian)" in *ERE,* x.
³ Infra p134.
⁴ See *ERE,* vi.249 and i.664
⁵(Ed. *Handwritten note:*) Moses of Kleorene (Moses of Chorene, Movses Khorenatsi) ii.27 mentions sun worship by the Arabs. So does Armenian Léroubna of Edessa. See Langlois *Collection,* i.328n

This was very widely spread all over Arabia. "They were worshipping it (ie. the sun)" says Cheikho[1]

> "... in the North of Arabia, and in the West and South-west in various forms and under different names, and because the sun was the wondrous shining one, its worship among the Arabs, surpassed that of all the others: it sometimes being made feminine, sometimes masculine."

Strabo tells us that the sun was the great divinity worshipped at Petra[2] and there were huge temples to the sun both at Baalbek[3] and Palmyra.[4] That this worship was very ancient in Arabia is evident from the fact that Tiglath Pileser in recounting his victory over an Arabian city, tells us his capture of its queen who was priestess of the sun-god,[5] and modern Bedouin according to Palgrave regard their God as

> "a chief, residing mainly it would seem in the sun, with which indeed, they in a manner identify him:"[6]

The great god of the Nabataeans was Dushara (דושרא)[7]; the Arabic *Dhu Shara* (دو الشرى), from which the Nabataeans were known to the Greeks as Δουσαρηνοί..[8] Special centres of his worship were at Petra, Bostra and Adra'a (עדרעי)[9]. There seems to be little doubt of his being the sun god, as Strabo states,[10] and there is some ground for thinking that he is the

---

[1] Chekho, p8
[2] Strabo xvi.7/41; vide also Arrian.vii.20 and Origen *Contra Olsum*. V.37
[3] Robinson, *Biblical Researches,* iii. 509ff
[4] Vide Chabot *Choix d'Inscriptions de Palmyra,* Paris, 1922, cap iii
[5] Layard *Inscriptions*, p72
[6] Palgrave *Central and Eastern Arabia*, 1866, i. 33
[7] Cooke *A Textbook of North-Semitic Inscriptions;* p218. (AB. It might be 'אָרְעִי', the town mentioned in Num. xxii21:33; Deut. i:4, and elsewhere.) *Dhu'l-Khalsa* (vide Bukhari iii.62, Tabari i. 1988: Cheikho, p12) may have been the same god.
[8] Vide Stephanus Byzantinus, so. Δουσάρη
[9] Buhl, *EI* i.965
[10] Baethgen, *Beiträge.* 95ff: Wellhausen *GGA,* 1905, p131: Strabo xvi.4.26: Buhl however is doubtful. op.cit.

Ὀροτάλ mentioned by Herodotus.¹ He is the son of the virgin mother-goddess Allat, whom Epiphanius (*Adversus Haereses* 51) calls Χααρου in his description of the great festival at Petra on December 25,² and when we learn that he was worshipped in the form of a black rectangular stone (Suidas, s.v. θιὸς Ἄρης)³ we are inclined to equate this Χααβου with كعبة, which would be the virgin goddess Ishtar. Among the Arab tribes he was worshipped by the Dawsites⁴ among whom the name 'Abu Dhu Shara is found. The territory of the Dawsites was quite near Mecca⁵ and the name Shara was known there, both as a place where water and gazelles abounded⁶ and where lions were found.⁷

Al-Lat of course was well known at Mecca in pre-Islamic days and is mentioned in the Qur'an (liii.19) as one of the daughters of Allah. Philologically her name means "the goddess"⁸ and she was the chief goddess of the ancient Arabs, being mentioned by Herodotus (i.131 and iii.8) under the forms Ἀλιλάτ and Ἀλιττα. Herodotus equates her with Οὐραγίη and when we remember that among the Sabaeans her counterpart has solar attributes⁹ we are prepared to agree

---

¹ iii.8: c.f. Clermont Ganneau. *Recueil d'Archéologie Orientale* v. Sect. 24: G.A, Cooke, *NSI* p239: Dussaud, *Arabes en Syrie*, p123. Ὀροτάλ may represent 'exalted light' in Aramaic אור העלה–as suggested by Cheikho, p7: or it may be A'ara (*ERE*.ix.122) which Lidzbarski *Ephemeris*, iii 90-93 thinks is connected with the Arabian Venus Ruda
(AB:
https://www.perseus.tufts.edu/hopper/text?doc=Perseus%3Atext%3A1999.01.0125%3Abook%3D3%3Achapter%3D8%3Asection%3D3.)
² Vide Robertson Smith *Religion of the Semites,* 57 n: *Kinship,* 292ff: Rösch in *ZDMG, xxxviii,* 643ff: Wellhausen, *Reste*, p50
³ Maximus of Tyre, xxxviii says that this black rock was 4ft high by 2ft wide. See also Huart *Arabes*, I, 32
⁴ Yaqut *Mu'jam*, iii, 268ff: Wüstenfeld *Genealogische Tabellen*, 10.20
⁵ *Bibliotheca Geographorum Arabicorum*, de Goeje, vii.316
⁶ *Diwan Hudhail* ed. Wellhausen, (*Skizzen und Vorarbeiten*, Vol.1) p276.
⁷ *Kamil*, ed. W. Wright, 33, 13: 54,3: 56,4.
⁸ *NSI* (Ed . note: no details given) Cheikho p10: Dussaud, op cit p122
⁹ *Sabaische Denkmäler*, Mordtmann, et al, 66ff

with Wellhausn (*Reste*, p33) that she was the sun-goddess.[1] She was the mother-goddess, the virgin mother, and mother of the gods, whose worship at Petra is described by Epiphanius[2] and in the Hauran and at Palmyra, it is curious to note, was equated with Ἀθηνη. She was the great divinity whose sanctuary was at Ta'if among the Thaqif, and Yaqut tells us that she was worshipped there as a square white rock, for which her devotees made a temple about which they were accustomed to circumambulate, and for which they had guardians.[3] It would thus seem that her cult was introduced into Nabataean Territory by the Arabs.

In Palmyra we find Al-Lat associated with Shamash,[4] and Shams (شمس) is well known as a divinity of ancient Arabia. The personal names 'Abd ash-Shams, Imru'l-Shams, are common, and Shams was the chief god of the Banu Tamim.[5] At Homs there was a great temple of Shams in which the sacred object was a black stone representing the god, which was made in human form with a fiery jewel blazing on his hand.[6] It was at this sanctuary that Heliogabalus[7] was for some time as priest. This 'house' of Shams at Homs was a great centre of pilgrimage and we are hardly likely to be in error when we infer that Shams is identical with Dhu Shara.

It is curious to note الاهة the feminine of الاه is said to mean "the sun" (*ERE* vi.248) which could point to an understanding that the earliest Arabian divinity was connected with the sun.

---

[1] (Ed. *Handwritten note:*) Winnett *MW*, Apr 1940 following G.A. Cooke *NSI* 222 wants to make her the moon goddess. However, Nielsen, *Handbuch* 197, 200; Hommel, *Grundriss* 149, Buhl *EI* ... take her to be the sun goddess, and ... take her to be another name for Al-'Uzza and Venus – cf Robertson Smith *Kinship* 295, Barton *Origins*, 218, Dussaud *Arabes in Syrie*, p131, Ryckman *Noms Propres*, I, 3: See Wellhausen *Reste* p44
[2] Robertson Smith *Religion Semites* p56
[3] *Mu'jam* iv. 36. Dussaud, op cit 118,119: Doughty, *Arabia Deserta*, ii.511-
[4] Le Vogué *Syrie centrale* no 8
[5] Huart, *Histoire des Arabes*, i.33. Yaqut says it was the idol of the people of 'Udlna.
[6] Cheikho p12, 15
[7] (Ed Note:) Marcus Aurelius Antoninus Augustus – Roman Emperor, 218-222CE, after his death was also known as Elagabalus

From this use there comes the verb *laha* "to shine" specially in the sense of mirage.

2) Moon Worship[1]

It is Nielsen's thesis[2] that moon worship was the foundation of ancient Arabian religion, and he even goes so far as to claim that the common Semitic *Il* was originally the moon god.[3] This position can scarcely be maintained, but it must not allow us to minimize the significance moon-worship had for the pre-Islamic Arabs. It had a special cult among the Banu Kinana.[4]

3) Star Worship.

The most important star deity[5] is Al-'Uzza, mentioned in the Qur'an (liii.19) and who is Venus.[6] A number of scholars think she was identical originally with Al-Lat, and it is certain that Al-Lat was worshipped as Venus.[7] Al-'Uzza[8] is generally Venus as the morning star, as the evening star was reverenced under the name Ruda among the Banu Rabi'a and also at Palmyra.[9] The name means *the mightiest* and is like Al-Lat but a title, so there can be little doubt that she represents the Arabian equivalent of Ishtar, the goddess of love and fertility, the primitive mother-goddess. She was known and reverenced in South Arabia,[10] and her cult was closely

---

[1] (Ed. *Handwritten note.*) Moses of Kleorene II;27 mentions moon worship of the Arabs. So does Armenian Léroubna d'Édesse: See Langlois, *Collection*, I, 326n. Winnett *MW*, Apr 1940 wants to make Allat the moon goddess – see his evidence.
[2] *Die Altarabische Mondreligion*, Nielsen, Strassburg, 1904.
[3] *MVAG*, xxi, 256: but see against it Margoliouth *Schweich Lectures*, p17.
[4] Bergmann, *De Religione Arabum*, p4: Pococke, *Specimen*, p4.
(Ed. *Handwritten note.*) Tribal names such as Banu Hilal (nous of crescent moon) and Banu Badr (nous of full moon) would seem to point to moon worship.
[5] (Ed. *Handwritten note:*) Nilus *Narriontes* represents them as worshipping Lucifer, star of the morning.
[6] Vide Isaac of Antioch i.247: Cheikho, p10: Ephraem Syrus, ii.457-459.
[7] Jerome, *Vita Hilaronis* c 25: Ephraem Syrus Ii.457-459: Huart *Arabes*: i.29: Dussaud *Arabes*, p123.
[8] (Ed. *Handwritten note:*) Abi Sahab: Muhammad's mule was called 'Abd el'Uzza
[9] Dussaud, *Arabes*, p132, 145.
[10] Derenbourg *Mem. Orient*, 1905, p33ff.

associated with Mecca.¹ In the valley of Nakhla she was associated with the acacia tree, just as Ashtart dwelt in an Ashera,² and Tabari has a curious story that she was an idol, out of which when it was destroyed, a naked Abyssinian woman tried to depart, but was slain by her captors.³

Manat, the third goddess mentioned in the Qur'an (liii.20) was apparently only another name for Al-'Uzza. The chief centre of her cult under this name was at the water of Qudaid, a station on the pilgrim road between Mecca and Medina⁴. She is also represented by a rock where sacrifices were offered,⁵ and the number of personal names compounded with Manat proves her worship to have been widely spread in Arabia.

Kuthra, the goddess of the Banu Ta'i in central Arabia seems also to have been a form of Al-'Uzza.⁶

Suwa' mentioned in Qur'an lxxi.22, whom the Commentators say was worshipped under the form of a beautiful woman⁷ among the Kinana and Banu Hamdan, and who had a great sanctuary in the territory of the Hudail⁸ was also a form of Al-'Uzza.

Atergatis of Syria is also another, as she was Venus as the evening star.

Sirius (الشعرى) the dog star is said to have been worshipped by the Khuza'a, though Nöldeke thinks the evidence for this

---

¹ Ibn Hisham, i. 93,94: Yaqut, *Mu'jam*, iii.664: Barton *Origins,* p236: Robertson Smith *Kinship*, 29; Wellhausen *Reste* p36.
² *NSI,* 50 sect. 4: Robertson Smith *Religion of the Semites* p185, p57n.
³ Tabari, I, 1648.
⁴ *NSI,* 219: Yaqut, *Mu'jam* iv. 337; Cheikho, p11.
⁵ Baidawi on liii,20: Yaqut, *Mu'jam* iv, 652.
⁶ Nöldeke, *ERE,* i, 660.
⁷ Razi, viii, 219: Nasafi on lxxi.22.
⁸ Nöldeke, *ERE,* I, 663: Tabari, *Tafsir,* xxix.54: Baghawi on lxxi.22.

is suspicious, as it apparently all depends on inferences drawn from the statement in Qur'an liii.50.[1]

Orion (الجوزا) was known under the name of Jabbar, and the name 'Abd al-Jabbar occurs,[2] which points to a cult of Orion.

The Pleiades (الثريا) were worshipped as rain makers. The name 'Abd al-Tharayya occurs,[3] and Nöldeke thinks that the name 'Abd an-Najm has the same reference[4] as the Pleiades are often called An-Najm.

Quzah whose name appears in قوس قزح the rainbow, was honoured near Mecca[5] though it seems to have been an Edomite god.[6] He was the divinity of the tempests[7] whose cult was attached to Muzdalifa in the Islamic pilgrimage rites. A fire was lit on the mountain here which seems to be referred to in the Qur'anic phrase " امشعر الحرام the sacred sign."

4) Pilgrimage Ceremonies

These, as had already been pointed out, had, according to Houtsma's theory, an astrological significance, possibly Zodiacal, which cannot be explained save as a relic of a former astronomical religious cult.

5). The Black Stone

The famous Black Stone at Mecca, reverence for which has taken such hold of the people of that city that even Muhammad, in spite of his iconoclasm, was forced to incorporate it in his system, is only one of many sacred stones known to us from various parts of Arabia. The stone of Al-Lat

---

[1] See Nasafi on this passage, and Nöldeke in *ERE*, i.660. See also Margoliouth, *Mohammed*, p50.
[2] Cheikho, p12.
[3] Cheikho p12. On the Hebrew Pleiades cult see Gray *Sacrifice*, p333.
[4] Nöldeke *ERE* i.660.
[5] Cheikho, p12.
[6] Vide article "Edomites" in *ERE* sect 2(e), Josephus *Antiquities,* xv, 255 apparently refers to this divinity – "one whose ancestors had been priests of the Koze (Koξί), whom the Idumaeans had formerly esteemed as a god'.
[7] Wellhausen *Reste* 87, Huart *Arabes,* i. 33: Nöldeke, *ERE,* I, 661.

at Ta'if,[1] and at the great temple at Homs (Emesa)[2] the stone of Manat and Dhu Shara have already met us, but there are many others in various parts of Arabia. There was *duwar* around which young women used to go in procession:[3] *Isaf,* and *Na'ila* on Mt. Safa and Mt Merwah, whom tradition says were a man and a woman of the Jurhumites who committed adultery in the Ka'ba and were turned to stone:[4] *Habhah,* the large sacred stone on which camels were sacrificed: *Dhu'l-Kaffain*[5] and *Dhu'r-Rijl* which Nöldeke takes to be sacred stones roughly carved into human shape: *Sa'd,* a high block of stone out in the desert reverenced by the Daws and Kinana[6]: *Dhu'l-Khalso* a great white stone surmounted by a sort of crown, venerated by the tribes of Hind, Buhila and Kath'am, and in the North of Yemen[7]: *Al-Fals,* a red rock jutting out of the black base of Mt. Adja and worshipped among the Ta'i:[8] *Jalsad,* the god of the tribe of Kinda in Hadramaut, which gave oracles, and was a white stone resembling a man's torso, surmounted by a black stone roughly resembling a man's head.[9]

Some have taken these facts as proof of stone worship by the ancient Arabs, but as the Black Stone in the Ka`ba is considered as a meteorite and of astronomical origin, so it would seem much more reasonable to connect the various stones revered in different parts of the country with similar astronomical relationships.

b. Totemistic

The evidence for this type of religion is not entirely dependent on our acceptance of the theory of a totemistic tribal

---

[1] Vide Robertson Smith, *Religion Semites* p210n and the references given there.
[2] Vide Athenaeus xv.48.
[3] Palmer *Qur'an,* p13.
[4] See Nasafi on ii.153: Baghawi on lxxi.23: Caussin de Perceval, i.199: Ya'qubi is evidence, however, that they were originally connected with the cult of the Ka'ba, and Barton *Origins,* p133 thinks they represented the original god and goddess of the Ka'ba.
[5] An idol of the Daws, see Cheikho, p15.
[6] Cheikho, p15; Huart, *Arabes,* i.33; Nöldeke *ERE,* i.662.
[7] Cheikho, p12: Bukhari, iii.62: Tabari, I, 1988: Huart, *Arabes,* ii.32.
[8] Huart, op. cit. i.33.
[9] Huart, op. cit. i.33.

organisation of the early Arabs. If they were organised totemistically, then we should expect on the analogy of totem groups elsewhere, that there would be some forms of religious cult connected with the totem animals of the various tribes. In fact, as Jevons points out[1] "totemism at present is the only satisfactory answer to the question why certain plants and animals are sacred."

Now we have a certain amount of definite evidence of animal divinities being worshipped in pre-Muhammad times.

<u>Nasr</u> the vulture god, who had the form of an eagle[2] and was worshipped in Himyar.[3] This god is mentioned in the Qur'an (lxxi.23), in the Talmud under the form נישרא [4] and in Addai[5] under the form (🕮). This god occurs also in the South Arabian inscriptions and may have been introduced to the rest of Arabia by the Yemenite migrations.

<u>'Auf</u> the great bird of prey, is known from the 'Abd 'Auf [6] which was fairly common. Nöldeke thinks it may be connected with Sa'd.[7]

<u>Yaghuth</u> whose name perhaps means *the helper* or *protector* was a deity of the Banu Madhhij and was in the form of a lion.[8] It is mentioned in the Qur'an lxxi.23 as an ancient god, and

---

[1] (Ed. note:) Details not mentioned in the footnotes.
[2] (Ed. *Handwritten note:*) The eagle god as adored by the Arabs is mentioned by Moses of Kleorene II 27 and in the Armenian Léroubna of Edessa, See Langlois Collection, I.322n.
[3] See the Commentators on lxxi.23 e.g. Nasafi; Razi (vol viii.218): Baidawi: Baghawi: c.f. Cheikho, p13.
[4] Tractate "Aboda Zara" (Talmud) 116; Buxtorf gives – "נישרא שבערביא": aquila in arabica, (🕮 Jeffery's writing here is difficult to decipher.) ii.B. Ar. scribit: "in Arabica est aedes idolatria, et in lad figura aquilae lapidi in sculpta, quam adorabant."
[5] *The Doctine of Addai*, p24 1.7: but see Cooke *NSI* p188. (Ed.: Note: *The Doctrine of Addai* is a Syriac Christian text which may be dated about 400 which relates to the conversion of Edessa.)
(https://www.catholic.com/encyclopedia/doctrine-of-addai cited 21 July, 2022).
[6] Cheikho, p 12.
[7] *ERE,* I, 663.
[8] See again the Commentators: Razi, Nasafi, Baidawi etc on lxx1.23.

names 'Abd Yaghuth 'Ubaid Yaghuth are known.[1] This idol originally stood at Yemen and became the object of an homeric context between the Banu Murad and the Banu al-Harith, in which the latter were finally victorious and took the idol a little before the time of Islam.[2] It is to be noted that the god-ancestor at Baalbek was worshipped in the form of a lion.

Ya'uq, the idol of the Banu Murad, had the form of a horse.[3] His cult would seem to be confined to Yemen[4], [5] where he was reverenced by the Hamdan and Khaulan. The name occurs in the Qur'an lxxi.23 and is possibly of South Arabian origin meaning 'the Preserver".[6]

It is well known that in Totemistic religion, animals and plants are associated with different divinities and there is reason for believing that all the above were originally associated with the primitive mother-goddess, the Arabian Ishtar. In the Gilgamesh Epic we read that among the lovers of Ishtar were an Eagle, a Lion and a Horse, which would explain the connection of these deities with the Ka'ba, which we have already seen was connected with this primitive Ishtar cult.

(c) Euhemerism

Euhemerus desired to explain all gods as the deification of mighty men of valour who had lived and striven here below and were then exalted. Euhemerism is common among all Semitic peoples. The Biblical student will at once recollect how rulers[7] are called *Elōhim* in the Old Testament (Exod. xxi:6; xxii·7-9; 1 Sam. ii:25; Ps lxxxii:1) and the same phenomenon occurs in

---

[1] Vide Khazin on lxxi.23: *Encycl. Bibl.*, iii.2804: Nöldeke *ERE* 1.662 thinks that 'Abd el-Asd can be quoted here for اسد is a more modern word for lion and may have replaced the older يغوث.
[2] Tabari *Chron* i. 1994 and article *Hamdan* in *EI*.
[3] See the Commentators again.
[4] Nöldeke in *ERE*, I, 663.
[5] (Ed. *Handwritten Note:*) Baladhuri *Futuh* p78 speaks of the Arbadhi people who were worshippers of horses in Bahrain.
[6] Nöldeke suggests the *Eth (Ethiopic)* = 'he who guards'.
[7] Also translated as judges in some versions.

the Tell-el Amana Letters. The Nabataeans also, we remember, deified their kings[1] and the great prevalence of Saint Worship all over Arabia, where the saints are practically deified,[2] would seem to point to a survival of Euhemerism.

Some of the deities who are mentioned as among the gods of the Ancient Arabs, would seem to be best explained as cases of the exaltation of mighty men of valour, who after their death were deified.

HUBAL, the great god of the Ka'ba at Mecca may perhaps be a case of this kind. He was a rain-maker[3] and was consulted by arrow-divination, and there was an image of him inside the Ka'ba.[4] There is some evidence that he was at one time the unique divinity of the Ka'ba and Wellhausen tentatively equated him with Allah.[5] It is said that his idol at Mecca was of red-carnelian in the form of a man, and that when the right hand got broken the Quraish replaced it by one of gold.[6]

Hubal, however, was not native to Mecca. The tradition is that he was brought down from the North.[7] As given by Shahrastani in his *Milal wa Nihal* (ed. Cureton, p295) it reads

> "Umr ... went to the land of Syria, and there a tribe of the Amalakites were worshipping idols. He said to them, "What are these images I see you worshipping?" They said "These are the idols that we worship. We ask help from them and help is given, we ask rain from them and rain is sent." He said, "Will you not give me an idol from among them that I may take it to the land of the Arabs, to the House of Allah, where the Arabs congregate?" So they

---

[1] *NSI*, 244.
[2] Curtiss, *Primitive Semitic Religion Today,* cap viii.
[3] Palmer, *Qur'an*, p xii.
[4] Demombynes, *Mekke*, p56.
[5] *Reste*, p75: Demombynes, *Mekke*, p43: Nöldeke in *ZDMG*, xli.715 hesitantly agrees with Wellhausen's equation.
[6] Cheikho (no reference given).
[7] Margoliouth *Mohammed,* p10, says he came from Hit on the Euphrates.

gave him an idol named Hubal and he brought it to Mecca and set it up in the Ka'ba."[1]

That he did actually come from the north would seem to be made certain by the fact that the name occurs in Nabataean inscriptions as הבלו [2], which would indicate an Aramaean origin and as Buhl has pointed out,[3] the etymologies given by Yaqut and others refute themselves.[4] Now the tribe of Kelb who lived in Syria knew the name as a clan name, and probably as a personal name[5] which may point to his being a deified ancestor.

BA'AL, which is really a title meaning 'lord' is frequently used of old Arabian gods and is found in personal names such as 'Abd al-Ba'li, Aus al-Ba'li, and Garm a-Ba'li. It is very possible that some if not all these Ba'al gods are euhemeristic.. It has been pointed out that the verb بعل and its derivatives which mean 'bewildered' very probably point to Ba'al worship.[6]

Ancestor worship among the early Arabs[7] may also be quoted as a link in the chain of development of euhemerism.

(d) Monotheism

It is frequently claimed that in spite of the prevalence of polytheism among all Semitic peoples in historical times, every Semite is nevertheless a potential henotheist if not

---

[1] Ibn Hisham also knows this story (ed. Wüstenfeld, p51), and says that the place was Ma'ab in the land of al Balqa. Some traditions would have it that he was the first idol in the Ka'ba, but following 'Amr's example the Arabs brought other idols and installed them along with them.

[2] (AB. From the *Dictionary of Deities & Demons*.)

[3] *EI* ii.327.

[4] Yaqut, *Mu'jam*, iv.949ff: Wüstenfeld, *Chroniken*, I, 58, 73,107,133: Tabari, I, 1075ff: Ya'qubi (ed Houtsma) I, 295: Pococke, *Specimen*, 98.

[5] (Ed. note:) details given in the footnotes.

[6] Margoliouth in *ERE*.

[7] See Goldziher *Muhammed Studies, i. 230* and his *Cults das ancetias chez les Arabes,* Paris, 1885.

(Ed. *Handwritten note:*) Note also the Arab idea of Asylum at a tomb. Smith (ed Cook) *Kinship*, p22.

monotheist.¹ Islam, of course, is the most rigid and barren of monotheisms, but careful study of pre-Islamic conditions shows us that monotheism did not spring forth suddenly and unexpectedly in Islam. There had been a strong tendency towards monotheism in certain quarters in Arabia long before the birth of Islam.

i). The development of the conception of Allah.
The common Semitic word for God is EL.² Thus we find in the different dialects –

Hebrew: אֵל, אֱלוֹהַּ, אֱלֹהִים, אֵל שַׁדַּי, אֵל עֶלְיוֹן
Aramaic: אֱלָה, אֱלָהָא, (Syriac word here ܐܠܗܐ), אֵילָה
Nabataean
Babylonian (cuneiform word here)
Sabaean   אלה
Phoenician   אל, אלו

The Hebrew אֱלֹהִים and the Syriac (ܐܠܗܐ) are thus the equivalent of the Arabic إِلَه or إِلٰه = god, divinity, and Allah (الله) is just a contraction of this used with the article i.e. Al-Ilah = Allah³. In the pre-Islamic inscriptions, particularly those of Safa, the name frequently occurs in personal names: thus we have:

Abdallahi (עבדאלהי),
Wahballahi (והבאלהי = وهب الله, cf *NSI*, 80, 93),
Halafallahi (חלפאלהי = خلف الله = cf *NSI*, 86, 89 חלפי),
Taimallahi (תימאלהי = تيم الله cf *NSI* 84 = Θεμάλλου cf Waddington, 2020⁴ which was common in Sinai, cf *NSI* 108:
Garmallahi (גרמאלהי cf Euting 79⁵ cf *NSI*, 104 = Euting 559:⁶
= Garmallae of *CIL*.x.2638. Note also גרמאלבעלי of

---

¹ Cook in *Cambridge Ancient History,* i, 198.
² On suggested meanings for 'El' see Davidson, *Old Testament Theology.*
³ Vide discussion in *ERE*, vi.248.
⁴ Waddington, *Inscriptions.*
⁵ Euting, *Nabatäische Inschriften aus Arabien.*
⁶ Op. cit.

NSI. 106), Sa'dallahi (שעדאלהי of *NSI* 107. 109 = سعد
الله),
Zabdallah (זבדאלה of *MFOB,* iv, 155 = Ζαββιλα, Ζαββιλαυ), and so on.

The name would thus appear to have become well known as an epithet "the God", i.e. the supreme, and so applied to the supreme god of a tribe or community. In the Nabataean inscriptions we frequently find the name of a deity accompanied by the title *Alaha* which leads us to conclude with Wellhausen that among the Arabs further south the word must similarly have been used as an epithet for any god[1] and later specialized as in the inscriptions of Safa, for the divinity considered in any place as supreme. Nöldeke has pointed out that the polemic of the Qur'an reveals that the Meccans were acquainted with the use of *Allah* in certain idiomatic forms of speech in constant use among the heathen Arabs.[2] There is also ancient tradition to the effect that the Quraish before Muhammad's day were called "the family of Allah"[3]. It would thus seem that in the use of the name for God we find proof of a strong tendency toward a monotheistic view in Mecca itself in pre-Islamic days,[4] closely associated with the "house"[5] which

---

[1] *Reste,* 218. It is curious that we have a precisely similar development in the case of Ba'al vide Jevons *Introduction,* p385.
[2] *ERE,* i.664.
[3] Ibn Duraid, p94 (and cf. *ZDMG,* xviii.226); Tirmidhi, I, 167: Azraki, 98. 155
[4] Palmer, *Qur'an,* p.xii suggests that Allah was the chief god of a vague local cult. It is noteworthy that Muhammad's own father was called 'Abd Allah. It has been pointed out (Margoliouth in *ERE,* vi. 248) that there is some evidence that Muhammad was at first unwilling to associate or identify his movement with this Allah of the local cult, but afterward changed his mind and welcomed the identification.
[5] Demombynes *Mekke,* p117, point out "le *masjid el haram* n'a rien d'une mosque; c'est un étroit enclos autour de la maison d'Allah, où une population peu nombreuse se reunit, où ses chefs vivent entre *dâr es siqâya* et *dâr en nadwâ,* à l'omble du temple." The name 'Abd ad-Dar has survived from pre-Islamic times, and Margoliouth says (*ERE,* vi, 249) "the god of the Meccans seems similarly to have been a 'house': their festival was 'the Feast of the House' (*hajjat al-bait* cf. hag *JHVH,* (Bible) Lev. xiii:39). In the Qur'an the word 'house' is used in some special theological sense where this phrase occurs, and we are told that the first 'house established for mankind is that in Bakka for a blessing guidance to the

has been preserved in Islam. It would thus seem that Muhammad took over this local element into his Islamic conception. As Nöldeke says[1]

> "In any case it is an extremely important fact that Muhammad did not find it necessary to introduce an altogether novel deity, but contented himself with ridding the heathen Allah of his companions, subjecting him to a kind of dogmatic purification and defining him in a somewhat cleared manner. Had he not been accustomed from his youth to the idea of Allah as the Supreme God, in particular of Mecca, it may be doubted whether he would ever come forward as a preacher of Monotheism."

i) Monotheistic Movements

Mas'udi *Muruji,* iii.256 tells us that Monotheism was not unknown among the Quraish in the days of Ignorance, and we have vague references to such monotheistic sects as the Rakusians,[2] but the great pre-Islamic monotheistic movement is that connected with the men known as the *Hanifs.*

When we open the question, however, as to who these Hanifs were, and what the word means, we are immediately involved in an apparently hopeless conflict of opinions. Wellhausen thought the term referred to the Christian ascetics[3] of Muhammad's day[4] for the anchorite monks with their ascetic days, the earnestness of their consecrated lives, their habits of vigil, and their preparation for the day of reckoning, were well known at that time,[5] and one of the Hanifs Abu 'Amir is expressly called a *rahib* or monk.[6] Margoliouth, on the other hand thinks that the word everywhere means Muslim[7]. De

---

worlds' (iii.90)." Notice also the oath – *by the Lord of the Ka'ba,* cf Muir, *Caliphate,* p82.

[1] *ERE* I, 664.
[2] Nicholson *Literary. History.* p149.
[3] (Ed. *Handwritten Note:*) Deutsch calls them "eine Phase jüdischen Christentums oder christlichen Judenthums", *Der Islam,* (Berlin, 1873) p38.
[4] *Reste,* p238: he is followed by Sell in his little pamphlet *The Hanifs,* Madras, 1912.
[5] Bell, *The Origin of Islam in its Christian Environment,* 1926, p43ff.
[6] Ibn Hisham, p411.
[7] *JRAS,* 1903, p467ff. So Nicholson *Literary History,* p149, 212.

Goeje says it is equivalent to 'heathen'[1] and Nöldeke is inclined to agree.[2] Grimme, at the period of his enthusiasm for South Arabian origins, saw a connection between the Hanifs and South Arabian religion[3] while Schulthess thinks it means *apostate*.[4]

If we begin our investigation with the Qur'an we find that the term occurs in general with reference to Abraham, or the religion of Abraham[5] and Sprenger in the first volume of his *Leben,* worked out a theory that the name referred to a sect of monotheists in Arabia, who, moved it may be by Jewish or Christian influence, had banded themselves together to oppose the worship of idols, labour for reform among their people, and maintain the ancient faith of Abraham. This theory, however, has been severely criticised on the assumption that as Caetani insists[6], the concept of a religion of Abraham was unknown before Muhammad. So Keunen says,

> "When we refer to the Hanifs of Tradition in explanation of the texts of the Qur'an, we are guilty of a ὕστερον πρότερον, and that in reality the name assigned in the Tradition to Muhammad's supposed predecessors in this faith is simply borrowed from the Qur'an. They are called Hanifs because Abraham is so called in the Qur'an, and because it is 'the milla of Abraham' they are represented as seeking, or even, like Zaid ibn 'Amr as actually finding and openly professing."[7]

Caetani[8] draws attention to the fact that the Tradition about the Hanifs is based on a single passage in Ibn Hisham[9] which he professes to quote from Ibn Ishaq, but which Tabari in quoting from the same source does not contain. The tradition

---

[1] *Bibliotheca Geographorum Arabicorum* in Glossary.
[2] *ZDMG*, xli.721 n.2.
[3] *Mohammed*, I.12ff.
[4] Nöldeke *Festschrift,* p86.
[5] Vide vi.79,162: xvi.121-4: ii.129: iii.89: xxii.32: iv.124: iii.60.
[6] *Annali,* i.183.
[7] *Hibbert Lectures,* 1882, p22.
[8] Op. cit. i.183.
[9] Ibn Hisham p143, 147 and see p822.

is thus held to be suspect, and one must agree that in the form in which it has come down to us it seems to bear evident traces of the influences of the Qur'an. At the same time it is difficult to believe that there is not an historical kernel in it.

This tradition tells us of four great Hanifs – *Waraqa b. Naufal,* supposed to be a cousin of Khadija, Muhammad's first wife: *'Ubaidallah b. Jahsh: 'Uthman b. Huwairith,* and *Zaid b. 'Amr.* It is said that the four came together at Mecca and said,

> "Ye know, by God, that your nation hath not the true faith, and that they have corrupted the religion of their father Abraham: how shall ye compass a stone that neither hears nor sees, neither helps nor hurts? Seek ye another faith for yourselves, for the one ye have is useless."

It may not be without interest to notice that information that has come down to us about each of these four men.

(a) Waraqa b. Naufal,[1] is universally recognised to be the most important of the four, and tradition makes him one of the first to recognise the prophetic mission of Muhammad.[2] Later authorities tell us that he studied deeply the Christian faith, or even that he had become a Christian, and had copied out some portions of the Gospel in Hebrew characters.[3] It appears that Khadija was very much attached to him, and he may have had great influence on Muhammad in his earlier years. He is said to have wandered far from Mecca in seeking the truth, and may not improbably have come in contact with Christians of Gnostic sects in Syria.[4]

---

[1] (Ed. *Handwritten Note:*) On Waraqa see Nöldeke *ZDMG* 1858, p703; Rösch "Die Jesusmythen des Islam, *ThStKr*, 49, 1876, p409-454.
[2] Ibn Hisham p143.
[3] Aghani iii.14 and see Sprenger, *Leben,* i. 128-134 also 533.
(Ed. *Handwritten Note:*) On this legend of the Gospel in Hebrew see besides Springer, Muir *Life* 156n: Caetani *Annali,* I. 187ff.
[4] Perhaps there may be a hint of this in the tradition that he copied the Gospel in *Hebrew* characters.

(b)   'Ubaidallah ibn Jahsh[1] remained in Mecca, dissatisfied with paganism but unable to decide on anything better. When Muhammad began his mission 'Ubaidallah is said to have hailed the new message with joy, joined the ranks of the Muslims, and in the first emigration, he went with his wife Habiba to Abyssinia. There he came in contact with Christianity, saw the fuller light of the Christian revelation and became a Christian.[2]

(c)   'Uthman b. al-Huwairith, whose story Caetani thinks is the least likely of the four to contain any truth.[3] He is said to have abandoned the ancient faith and to have become a Christian. Having political aspirations he made his way to Syria, and from there to the Imperial court at Byzantium, where he set forth to the Emperor the importance of Mecca and the advantages of its being under Byzantium sway, and succeeded in having himself appointed by the Emperor as Governor of Mecca in Byzantine interests, to offset the Persian victories in Yemen. Returning to Mecca he attempted to persuade the unwarlike Meccan merchants of the advantages of being under Byzantine protection and would have succeeded in having his appointment at Mecca ratified, had not Zam'a al-Aswad b. al-Muttalik raised a cry "O servants of God! A king from Tihama?" 'Uthman then returned to Byzantium where he died.[4]

(d)   Zaid b. Amr b. Naufal,[5] around whom an even greater mass of tradition has gathered. He renounced idolatry, the eating of the flesh of animals who died naturally, or flesh or blood that had been offered to idols. He strongly opposed the custom of exposing female infants. Refusing to embrace either Judaism or Christianity he claimed to follow the faith of Abraham and to be the only true believer of Mecca. One tradition says that he went to the Ka'ba but refusing to conform to the usages of his people

---

[1] Ibn Hisham, p143-144: Ibn Khaldin, *Prolegomenes* ii. app 4.
[2] Caetani, *Annali*, i. 188.
[3] See on him Ibn Hisham p144: Ibn Khaldun op. cit., Halabi *Insan al-'Uyun*.
[4] Ibn Hisham, p144-145: Ibn Khaldun, op cit. Halabi *Insan al-'Uyun* , i. 169.
[5] (Ed. note:) No details supplied in the footnotes.

there he cried out. "Oh God! Did I know what form of homage would be pleasing to you, that would I offer, but alas I know it not." In order to have peace he was accustomed to retire to Mt Hira' near Mecca and there in a cave, practise ascetic exercises and fasting. Some traditions say that in order to find out the real religion of Abraham, he made long journeys to Syria and Mesopotamia where he conversed long with Rabbis and Christian monks, all of whom, says Muslim orthodoxy, told him that they knew nothing, but that soon a great prophet was to arise in Mecca.

Others of whom mention has come down to us as Hanifs are – Abu 'Amir[1]; 'Umayya ibn Abis-Sait, the poet, some of whose verses are possibly incorporated in the Qur'an[2]; Urbab b. al-Bara[3]; Quss b. Sa'ida al-Iyadi[4]; Abu Qays Sirmah b. abu Anas[5]; Khalid b. Sinan b. Ghayth[6]; Qays Sayfi b. al-Aslat[7]; As'ad b. abu Harb al Himyari[8]. About none of these, however, have we any detailed account.

It does not seem possible to gather much as to what is meant by the term *hanif* from these accounts. Caetani seems certainly justified in his judgment that as they have come down to us they are late and tendential accounts. Perhaps all we are justified in concluding from them is that there were certain men of the period in Mecca, who revolted from the polytheism of the day, realized that their way to real religion lay in a monotheistic direction, and sought it either in or in association with the monotheistic faiths around them.

Let us next take up the word *hanif* itself and see what it can tell us. It is clear, to begin with, that *hanif* (حنيف) is not an Arabic word.

---

[1] Ibn Hisham, p411.
[2] Aghani xvi, 71-84; Ibn Qutaiba (Ed. No pages given); Aghani iii, 186-192. On his relation with the Qur'an see Schulthass *'Umayya*, 1911 and in Nöldeke *Festschrift*, p 71ff; and particularly the essay of Kamenetzky *Untersuchungen über das Verhältnis dem Umayya b. Abi-s-Sait zugeschriebenen Gedicht zum Qoran*, 1911.
[3] (Ed. Note:) Page numbers not given for this reference nor for the following three.) Ibn Qutaiba   *JRAS*, 1903.
[4] Aghani xiv. 41-44: Ibn Qutaiba p (number not given), *JRAS*, 1903.
[5] Ibn Qutaiba p.... *JRAS*, 1903.
[6] *JRAS*, 1903: ... Ibn Qutaiba p. ...
[7] Aghani xv. 161-168:
[8] Ibn Qutaiba, p 29: See also Abu Dhair cf. Muir *Caliphate*, p79.

Mas'udi in his *Tanbih* (ed. de Goeje *BGA*, viii) knows that it is the Syriac (☒) which is to be connected (with) the Canaanite Aramaic חֲנֵף, חָנֵיף, חֲנֵפָא, meaning hypocrite, ungodly, profane, godless, pagan, heathen person. Winckler[1], indeed proposed to derive it from the Ethiopic but it has been pointed out that this is probably a loan word in Ethiopic and Nöldeke[2] and Schulthess[3] notwithstanding, it seems clearly a borrowing from Syriac though even this Syriac-Aramaic form may ultimately be derived from the Hebrew חָנֵף = profane.[4] Now the abstract noun in Syriac ☒ is definitely used for Sabianism,[5] which suggests a possible way out of our difficulty. The main characteristic of Sabian religion was apparently star worship. Now Ya'qubi curiously enough calls the Philistines *hunafa* because he says, they worshipped stars[6] and Mas'udi in the *Tanbin*, expressly equates the *hanifs* with the *Sabians*.[7]

Now Sprenger had already held that the Sabians and the Hanifs were identical[8] and the most recent study of the question, that by the Danish scholar Jos Pedersen in E. G. Browne's *Festschrift*[9] shows that Sprenger's identification must be upheld. As we shall see when we come to discuss the Sabians, the evidence points to their being Gnostics, probably of Judaeo-Christian type.[10] So here we get a new point of departure for the interpretation of the Arabic stories of the Hanifa.

Buhl in his article on the Hanifs in the *Encyclopaedia of Islam* (ii.258-260) seems to favour the interpretation of the word which would make it signify

---

[1] *Arabisch-Semitisch-Orientalisch*, Winkler, p79.
[2] Nöldeke, *Neue Beiträge*, p72 thinks it is a genuine Arabic word.
[3] Cf. Nöldeke *Festschrift*, p86, where he agrees with Nöldeke that it is genuine Arabic.
[4] So Deutsch, and Lyall, *JRAS,* 1903, p (Ed. No number given.) Also Hirschfeld *New Researches,* pp 19, 26.
[5] See particularly Bar Hebraeus *Chronicon*. p176
[6] See also his *Muruj* (ed. de Meynard) i.73:11, 111; iii, 348; iv, 44.
[7] Ya'qubi *Historiae* (ed Houtsma) i.51ff.
[8] *Leben* i. p46.
[9] *Oriental Studies presented to E.G. Browne,* ed. Arnold, 1922, pp383-391.
[10] (Ed. *Handwritten Note.*) So Deutsch (*Der Islam*, Berlin, 1873) has called them 'eine arabe jüdischen Christentimes oder Christentimes oder christlichen.'

> "the original, innate, primitive religion in contrast to the particular which arose later, polytheism on the one hand, and the in part corrupt religions of the possessors of scriptures."

So he is disinclined to associate the term with any particular body of belief, but thinks that Muhammad simply took over a word which was fairly well known in his day, to denote those

> "people who, although influenced by Christianity had refused both Christianity and Judaism in favour of a simpler and more primitive religion."

But if *hanif* = *Sabian* = Gnostic, then we remember the numerous traces of Gnosticism which can be detected in the Qur'an,[1] and find ourselves inclining toward Sprenger's old view of a *haniferei* to which both Waraq and Zaid may have belonged, and from whence Muhammad may have drawn his conception of the *milla* of Abraham, as well as many other things we find in his teaching.

It becomes clear then, that there was at least a strong tendency toward monotheism working with more or less success in the milieu of Muhammad, and we must not forget to stress also the great importance of the presence of Jews, or at any rate Judaized communities in various parts of Arabia and the wide spread of Christianity there before Muhammad's day. Muhammad was thus introducing nothing novel when he preached such an insistent monotheism, and in this case again he was largely entering into the fruits of the labours of many unknown maintainers of the unity who had preceded him.

---

[1] Notice in particular (i) the Docetic view taken of Christ's person (ii) the theory that another was crucified in His place, (iii) The common name for Christians – Nasara (iv) The idea that the Virgin Mary was the third person of the Trinity, (v) the constant contrast between الدنيا and الاخرة. (vi) the plurality of heavens etc. (vii) John the Baptist was given a book. See on this whole question an article by Clemen, *Muhammeds Abhängigkeit von der Gnosis* in the Harnack *Ehrung*, 1921, pp 249-262 and Rodwell, p10.

The Cult

Turning now to the details of the cult, or organised expression of this pre-Islamic paganism, we find that it was –

(1) Sacrificial

In being associated with a sacrificial system, pre-Islamic Arabian paganism was in harmony with all primitive Semitic religion, for sacrificial systems are very pronounced among all branches of the Semitic people. In the earliest documents on Semitic religion coming from the Babylonians and Assyrians[1] we find evidence of a highly developed sacrificial system. The contracts frequently refer to the daily sacrifices and the great inscription of Tiglath Pileser (vii.16) speaks of the great annual sacrifice. It is somewhat curious that a primary purpose of sacrifice among the Babylonians would seem to have been divination.[2] For the importance of the sacrificial ritual among the Phoenicians the inscriptions of sacrificial tariffs are sufficient evidence,[3] and numerous sacrificial altars excavated in Syria and in South Arabia prove its prevalence among the Nabataeans and Sabaeans. The student hardly needs to be reminded of how highly developed a system of sacrifices there was among the Hebrews and Canaanites,[4] and we may be quite sure that primitive Semitic religion was sacrificial in type.

Controversy still rages over the question of the origin of sacrifice, at least of Semitic sacrifice. The two prominent views are (a) Ethical Theory, which sees the origin of sacrifice in man's sense of need of propitiating his God or gods. Put in the words of Dr. A. B. Davidson,[5] his theory runs –

---

[1] See the evidence for example in Schrader's *Die Keilinschriften und das Alte Testament,* Berlin, 1903, p594ff and the discussion in Zimmern's *Beiträge zur Kenntnis der babylonischen Religion,* Leipzig, 1901.
[2] Jastrow *Aspects of Religious Belief in Babylonia and Assyria,* 1911, p147ff.
[3] Vide *CIS,* i. 165: *NSI,* 112-122: Dussaud *in RHR,* lxix, 70ff "Les tariffs sacrificiels carthaginois".
[4] On sacrifice among the Hebrews see Buchanan Gray's recent study *Sacrifice in the Old Testament,* Oxford, 1925, and Dussaud's *Les Origines Cananéennes du Sacrifice Israelite,* Paris, 1921.
[5] *Theology of the Old Testament,* 1904, p312. The same theory is defended in Trumbull's books, *The Blood Covenant,* London 1893: *Threshold Covenant,* New York, 1906 and

Man's sense of evil, of his own inadequate service to God, and of God's holiness, made him feel that reparation was due to God, and that he deserved death. Hence, to express this feeling, he brought living creatures to God as his own substitutes, inflicting on them the penalty of death deserved by himself. Sacrifice was thus from the first piacular[1] and propitiatory"

There is no doubt whatever that many, if not most, sacrificial systems did, in the course of their development, tend to take on this form, which is so well illustrated for example in the Hebrew ritual detailed in the book of Leviticus (Bible), but it shows far too an advanced stage of religious reflection to be considered primitive. Moreover, it provides no explanation of the bloodless sacrifices.

The same criticism must be made of E.B. Tylor's variations of this theory[2] viz. that sacrifice was in the nature of a bribe to the deity just as might be offered to an Oriental potentate to secure favours or to avert anger. Moreover, as Hubert and Mauss pointed out,[3] this theory describes rather the moral development of the rite than the actual working of the rite itself.

(i) Sacramental Theory

The second theory as elaborated by Robertson Smith refers sacrifice back to the primitive life of the clan, where the members were not only blood brothers in the clan but blood brothers with the deity of the clan and with his totem animal. Now in primitive times existence depends on the unity and solidarity of the clan, and freedom from supernatural ills on the solidarity of the union between the clan and the deity. The symbol of this solidarity is the common meal which all share on an equality, and in which the deity naturally had his share set apart. It is noteworthy that the offerings of sacrifice, whether of blood or bloodless, which survived till later times, were

---

Studies in Oriental Social Life, 1894. A desperate but quite unsuccessful attempt to prove the same theory was made by Curtiss in his *Primitive Semitic Religion Today,* Tylor, Chicago, 1902.

[1] (Ed Note:) *piacular* – making or requiring atonement.
[2] Vide his *Primitive Culture* (4th Edition), ii.362.
[3] In *L'Année sociologique,* ii.30.

always of things edible, except in some cases of extraordinary solemnity when extraordinary sacrifices had to be offered.

But how did God share in the common meal? At first the share was just left for him and probably was eaten by the birds or animals as happens at the present day in India. Later there grew up the idea that in the blood was the life, and as God was the giver of life the blood was his share and should not in normal cases be partaken of by the human partner in the fellowship. This blood was poured out and absorbed by the sand, or later poured or smeared over the stones of sacrifice, which later became the altar.[1] Still later grew up the more subtle idea of the burnt offering, in which God's share ascended to him in the smoke of the altar as a sweet savour.

Typical examples of one development of this are seen in the covenant sacrifice. Macalister[2] quotes for instance the covenant of Laban and Jacob (Bible: Gen xxxi:46) where they have their common meal on the altar, or the covenant of Abraham with God, where the victims were divided, and God, typified by a torch, passed between them (Bible: Gen xv). A still further development is the covenant made by Moses on behalf of the people (Bible: Ex xxiv:4-8) where half the blood of the victims was poured on the altar and the other half sprinkled on the people.

Out of this primitive conception of the sacramental meal, it is no difficult matter to trace the growth of other conceptions of the meaning and object of sacrifice. Even human sacrifice becomes clear when we remember that among some primitive peoples cannibalism, i.e. the sacramental eating of a member of the clan, is indulged in in times of great calamity when they feel that the offering of animal blood is not sufficient.

---

[1](Ed. *Handwritten Note:*) On the altar or a sacred stone. See Smith *Old Testament History*, p162.
[2] *ERE*, xi.37.

Sacred blood-smeared stones of the character mentioned above have always been part of the cultus of Arabian religion[1] and are still common at the present day.[2] There is also abundance of evidence that in early times the eating of the sacrifices was an integral part of the ceremony.[3] Traces of human sacrifice have been found, but the common types were those both of blood and bloodless sacrifice as found among other Semitic peoples. It is curious to note that a custom of the Arabs has become common to Muslims everywhere, which makes every slaughter of an animal a sacrificial act, for the animal's head is turned toward Mecca and the Bismillah is pronounced as its throat is cut. It will be remembered how careful Muslims are not to eat meat which had not been killed in the correct orthodox fashion and all the blood poured out.

Muhammad took over the sacrificial rite into Islam as part of the Pilgrimage ceremony.[4] It is apparently not an obligatory rite but is recommended to be carried through in imitation of the Prophet. The sacrifice is offered in the valley of Mina on the tenth day of Dhu'l-Hijja, and is by Muslims treated as a memorial of the sacrifice of Abraham's redemption of his son Ishmael.[5] After this sacrifice the head is shaved, and there can be little doubt that this is also a survival of an ancient rite of sacrifice of hair to the divinity of the place.[6]

---

[1] Vide particularly the third volume of Musil's *Arabia Petraea*, Vienna, 1908. The best ancient account of Arabian sacrifice is that of Nilus (410 AD): vide *Nili opera quaedam,* Paris, 1639, pp28,117: cf. Cheikho, pp16,17.
(Ed. *Handwritten note.*) In *Patrologia Graeca*, vol. LXXIX, 612-613.
[2] Cases will be found in Jaussen, *Coutumes des Arabes au Pays du Moab*, Paris, 1908. passim and in Curtiss, *Primitive Semitic Religion Today.* See also Palmer *Desert of Exodus*, 1872, p218.
[3] See Nilus, op cit.; Macalister, op cit. Nöldeke's conclusion is *Originally every sacrifice, properly so called, was regarded as food consumed by the god, or at least as a means of gratifying his sensations. ERE,* i.666.
[4] The fullest account of the matter will be found in Demombynes' *Mekke*, p277ff. On the legal side see Sell's *Faith of Islam*, 3rd ed., pp367ff.
[5] Burton gives a description of the actual rites in his *Pilgrimage,* ii.140, 217, 218.
[6] On hair offerings see Jevons, *Introduction*, 193: Frazer *Golden Bough*, i.28ff.

The 'Aqiqa ceremony[1] which is preferred in Muslim households on the seventh day after a child's birth, is another survival of expiatory sacrifice in Islam, whose origin goes back to pre-Islamic days. It may be remarked that in this case also the ceremony is frequently accompanied by a ritual shaving of the hair of the child.

(2) <u>Idolatrous</u>

One of the most vivid pictures in early [Muslim] history is that which shows us Muhammad entering Mecca as conqueror in the year 630AD and commencing the overthrow of the three hundred odd idols which adorned its sacred place.[2]

In their love of idols the ancient Arabs were again at one with the rest of Semitic antiquity. The huge images erected by the Babylonians and Assyrians for the adornment of their temples are still objects of wonder in our Western Museums, and the images that once adorned the sacred fanes[3] of the Phoenicians were only less great and magnificent. The historical records in the Old Testament (Bible) bear ample witness to the fondness of the Hebrews for graven images and tell of the images which some of the Israelitish Kings erected for their Canaanitish wives. It is not improbable that Jehovah himself was primitively worshipped in the high places in association with images such as the golden calf.

There is no evidence that the idols of the pagan Arabs were in any way different from those known to us among other Semitic peoples, save that they were apparently always very simple. Many of the idols would seem to have been little more than rough blocks of stone and the word *nusub* used for idol (نصب pl. أنصاب) means rather the flat stones used for sacrifice than an actual idol.[4] It is to be noted

---

[1] Zwemer has a chapter on this in his *Animism in Islam*, 1920, p87ff.
[2] See the story in Muir's *Life of Mahomet,* cap xxiv: and the following chapter for the destruction of the idols in other parts of Arabia.
[3] (Ed Note:) temple, shrine.
[4] (Ed. *Handwritten note:*) Robertson Smith *Kinship* p59 thinks the انصاب were like the Hebrew מצבות originally *baetylia,* or god-boxes.

that both the Qur'anic words for idol, *sanam* and *watham* are borrowed into Arabic from Aramaic.¹

Sacred stones still play an important part in the popular religion of Syria and Arabia, and many examples have been quoted by Curtiss.² It would seem that they were associated with the most primitive forms of Semitic worship. The common form was the pillar, fine examples of which have been found at the entrance of the sanctuary at Petra and at Megiddo.³ Among the Phoenicians they became finely carved pillars.⁴ The Israelites borrowed these pillars or *mazzeboth* from the Canaanites and previous to the Deuteronomic reformation they had become an integral part of the worship of Yahweh so that Hosea could refer to as to a great calamity the day when they should be without sanctuary and without mazzebah.⁵ Sacred pillars of this kind were erected by Jacob at Bethel⁶ (Gen xxviii:18: cf xxxi:13) and Shechem (Gen xxxiii:20)⁷ and at Gilead (Gen xxxi:52); by Joshua (Josh xxiv:26: cf Jud ix:6) and by Samuel (1 Sam vii:12). They were well known at Gibeon (II Sam xx:8), Enrogel (I Ki i:9) and Michmash (I Sam. xiv:33), and the stones Jachin and Boaz in the temple (I Ki vii:21) which have acquired curious importance in modern Free-Masonry, were doubtless similar mazzeboth.

Among the ancient Arabs the cult of these sacred stones was so common and widespread that Clement of Alexandria⁸ looks on stone worship as characteristic of the Arabs. The blood of sacrifice

---

¹ Vide the discussion in Fraenkel *Aramäische Fremndwörter*, Leiden, 1886, p273. وثن however, may be S. Arabian וָתָן but see Margoliouth in *ERE*, vi.249.
(AB. There is no term anything like this in biblical Hebrew, but the Buxtorff lexicon has an entry for וָתָן with a centre *tav*, which would be closer to the transliteration *watham* in the text.)
² *Primitive Semitic Religion Today,* pp84-89.
³ (Ed. *Handwritten note:*) Smith, *Old Testament History* p48 notes that mazzeboth as residences of the deity. See also his remarks on p182.
⁴ See illustration in Benzinger, *Hebräische Archäologie* and for Tyre, see Heroditus, ii.44.
⁵ Hos. iii:4 (The Bible), cf. x:12.
⁶ (Ed. Note:) All the following references in this paragraph are to be found in the Bible.
⁷ We should read here מצבה instead of מזבה.
⁸ *Exhortation,* iv.*ad init.*

was originally poured out on the tops of these stones, later they were anointed with oil, and there seems very good reason for holding that the altar developed out of the sacred stone, which however was kept alongside the altar even when the two had become separate[1]

It is to be noted that a conical stone was sacred as the symbol of Astarte of Ishtar the goddess of love, and many of the Phoenician mazzeboth are apparently phallic images,[2] and this taken in connection with the custom of anointing the top with blood or with oil, suggests that they were in primitive times at least associated with the primitive Semitic worship of the Mother-Goddess.

In Islam, beside the Black stone at the Ka'ba, which is still fervently caressed and kissed by the worshippers at the Pilgrimage, we have surviving the three pillars in the valley of Mina which are still stoned under the name of Satans, in the Pilgrimage ceremony.[3] This is the *jamrat al-aqaba*[4] which van Vloten connected with some snake ritual,[5] and which Chauvin thought was intended to cover the ground with stones as to render it useless for cultivation[6] but which Houtsma thinks it to be connected with a ritual of stoning the sun-demon.[7] It is possible however that these pillars may have been *mezzeboth* connected with the old fertility cult.

(3)   <u>Non-Sacerdotal</u>
Sir Richard Burton finds it a point to commend in Muhammad, that 'he did his best to abolish the priest and his craft ... and he severely condemned monkery and celibacy'.[8] The point of this praise becomes blunted, however, when one realises that there does not seem to have been any developed sacerdotal system among the Arabs before his time. As Margoliouth points out,

---

[1] See especially Benzinger op.cit: Lagrange *Études*, p191, and his essay "Enceintes et Pierres sacrées" in *Rev. Bibl* for April,1900 (1901), Vol 10, No. 2. p216-251.
[2] Cf. those set up in the temples at Paphos and Hierapolis, and the representation on coins of Byblos.
[3] See Burton's description *Pilgrimage,* ii.203ff.
[4] On which see Demombynes *Mekke,* p268ff.
[5] Vide his essay in the *Feestbundel aan de Goeje ann geboden,* M.J. de Goeje" 1891, p33.
[6] *Annales de l'Académie Royale d'Archéologie de Belgique,* 5th Se. vol.1v. p272ff
[7] "Het Skopelisme en het steenwerpen te Mina," 1904, in *VMKA, iv. P185ff.*
[8] *Arabian Nights,* v185 n. (Burton Club Edition)

the love of, and pride in offspring, which is so characteristic of that country would have a tendency to render monastic institutions unpopular, even before they were branded by Muhammad as a wicked innovation.[1]

There is early evidence, however, that there was some sort of priesthood connected with the early Arabian religion, though it never became an office or institution of any great importance. Greek writers bear witness to the existence in North Arabia of ministrants at shrines. If the grove near Poseidium mentioned by Strabo (xvi. 4. Sect 18) is to be taken as a sacred grove connected with the fertility cult, his next sentence –

προεστήκασι δὲ τοῦ ἄλσους ἀνὴρ καὶ γυνὴ διὰ γένους ἀποδεδειγμένοι, δερματοφόροι, τροφὴν ἀπὸ τῶν φοινίκων ἔχοντες

may refer to a priest and priestess of the grove. Diodorus Siculus[2] also mentions this place and says that there was an ancient stone altar there on which was graven an inscription in antique characters and guarded by a priest and priestess for the duration of their lives.

The title of priest occurs with personal names on some of the Sinaitic inscriptions[3] and Dr Margoliouth[4] in discussing the word سادن a title borne by the ministrants at several sanctuaries,[5] connects it with σινδών = a sheet of fine linen, the word used of a garment used in the Bacchic mysteries.[6] There is some evidence too that priesthoods were

---

[1] *Mohammed* p40. That it was not always very important among other Semitic people is pointed out by Davidson in his *Theology of the Old Testament'* p242.
[2] Diodorus Siculus. iii.42
[3] Euting *Sinäitische Inschriften,* Berlin, 1891, nos. 249, 348, 223a, 550, in all of which the word is כהן.
[4] *ERE,* vi, 249.
[5] Nöldeke in *ERE,* i.667 thinks that the term originally meant "one who holds the curtain".
[6] Cf Strabo xvi.58 and Suidas (Ed. Title of a Greek lexicon-encyclopedia) under σινδονιάζων διογυσιάζειν; Angus *Mystery Religions.* p90 notes it. The word may be originally Egyptian, vide Parthey *Vocabularium* p572 and Fränkel *Fremdwörter,* p41, suggests a connection with 🖹 Egypt, *schens, schenti.* Boissacq *Dictionnaire étymologique,* gives σινδών as an eastern borrowing and refers to Lewy's

hereditary.¹ It is doubtful how much reliance can be placed on statements that have come down to us in writers such as Yaqut, about the priesthood of some of the ancient deities among the Arabian tribes, though as Wellhausen points out, the fact that we are told of ministrants at a sanctuary being of other tribes than the one actually in possession, would seem to point to genuine tradition, for this phenomenon can only be explained by the fact that members of the original tribe which was driven out would be retained as the only suitable ministrants at the old shrine. Margoliouth suggests that the priests were also treasurers at the shrines.²

In connection with the matter of Priesthood there is the problem of the *kahin,* or soothsayer. The word is the Semitic term for priest,³ and it retained this sense among the Sinai Arabs, though in the rest of Arabia even in pre-Islamic times, it has come to mean the soothsayer or diviner. We shall have to consider the importance of these men under a later heading but it is to be noted here (1) that they gave their utterances in the short sentences of rhythmic prose with single rhyme, known as *saje,* in which Muhammad couched his early revelations: (2) that they had the habit of commencing their utterances with striking oaths⁴ such as by the earth and sky, sun and moon and stars, light and darkness etc. much as Muhammad does in the Qur'an.

(4) Sanctuaries
Unlike the Babylonians, Phoenicians and Sabaeans, the Arabs seem never to have developed the temple building appetite.

Early references to the Ka'ba at Mecca, all speak of its extreme simplicity, and (save in Yemen) in the rest of Arabia we find no evidence of great temples except up on the Syrian border, where in all probability they were due to non-Semitic influence. The sanctuary

---

Fremdwörter, 84ff. It may be from Assyrian *Sudinnu* vide *Cambridge Ancient History* iii, 249.
¹ See Nöldeke, *ERE,* I, 667n.
² *ERE,* vi. 249.
³ Cf. Heb כהן Syriac ⌂, Ethiopic ⌂. Nöldeke thinks the Arabic word is an Aramaic borrowing (*Neue Beiträge,* p36 n.6). But Fishher (*EI* ii.625) thinks it is original Arabic. See the discussion in Gray *Sacrifice* 220ff and note particularly his remarks on p219 on the function of the priest as an organ of revelation.
⁴ For examples of their utterances see Mas'udi *Muruj* iii. 387ff; Ibshihi, *Al-Mustatraf,* Cairo, 1321 cap. ix: *Aghani,* xi.164.

of the *sanam* among the primitive Arabs was not necessarily enclosed by walls, but marked off by boundary stones, and thus it developed the very important concept of the *haram*.

The origin of the sanctuary must probably be sought in the primitive thought that the god must be a possessor as well as the worshipper.[1] The things that the god possesses will thus vary with the stage of culture of the worshippers. Thus nomadic people make their gods the possessors of cattle, town dwellers invariably build for him a house which they exercise themselves to adorn much as they adorn their own dwellings, agriculturists give the god, lands. All evidence of what possessions were given the gods by the early nomadic Semites has been lost, but wherever they settled down to agricultural life we find them giving the gods lands[2] marked off by boundary stones as were their own lands.[3]

Now the land that was given to the god belonged exclusively to him: it was separated for his special use, and the common Semitic root for this idea is QDS (cf. Hebrew: קדש, Arabic قدس: Syriac ▭ Ethiopian ▭, Assyrian qadasu)[4] from which is developed the conception of holy. A holy thing is a thing separated to the use of the god. Thus in the Hebrew ritual the instruments of service are *holy unto the Lord*[5] and in Canaanitish worship the temple prostitutes are "holy

---

[1] There is a different theory, however, of the origin of sanctuary, which thinks that primitively all fertile, well-waterd places were inhabited by jinn and so were more or less sacred. It thus became a pious act to build on such areas a house for the divinity. See Wellhausen *Reste,* p106*:* Robertson Smith, op.cit. p115.
[2] Palmer, *Qur'an*, p132 n.2 gives a note on the setting apart of portions of produce for the gods.
[3] So Robertson Smith says – 'almost every holy place at the time of Muhammad was a little centre of settled agricultural life'. *Religion of the Semites,* p113. Margoliouth in *ERE*, vi.249, Sura iii.90 suggests that in the case of local cults there was confusion between the soil, the god who dwelt there, and something which marked the place.
[4] The best discussion is still that in Baudissing's elaborate monograph 'Der Begriff der Heiligkeit im Altan Testament', in the second volume of his *Studien zur semitischen Religionsgeschichte*, Leipzig, 1878. The student may also consult Davidson's *Theology of the Old Testament*, p252ff; Wheeler Robinson's *Religious Idea of the Old Testament*, London 1938, p130ff; Keunen, *Religion of Israel*, i.43ff; Smend, *Alttestamentlichen Religionsgeschichte*, p333ff; and cap xii of Curtiss, *Primitive Semitic Relgion*
[5] So in Exodus xxx.22ff,:we find reference to "holy" oil and "holy" perfume.

women": קְדֵשָׁה and even Sodomies are called "holy".[1] The idea has thus originally no moral signification, but applies to anything and everything that belongs exclusively to the god or is dedicated for his use. Thus everything that grew on the lands of the god was *holy* and could not be put to profane usages. The pasture there was his, and as all the members of the tribe were equally interested in the god being propitious to them so they were all equally interested in resisting any encroachments on the territory of the god.[2] Here then we have the *haram*.

Sanctuaries of this sort were fairly numerous in pre-Islamic Arabia[3] but we have little information about any of them save that of Mecca. There long before Muhammad's time, it was forbidden to take life within the *haram,* or to pluck any herb save certain noxious weeds.[4] Muhammad claimed the power to suspend this privilege of sanctuary as one of his prophetic endowments, but he took over that of Mecca, and endeavoured to extend it to the whole of Arabia. Arabia was to be Allah's territory and none but Allah's worshippers were to be allowed thereon. Thus Jewish and Christian communities either had to accept Islam or move elsewhere.[5] This plan failed, but the sacredness of Mecca was intensified, and to this day it is death for any non-Muslim to enter the precincts of the city.[6]

(5)   <u>Festivals</u>

---

[1] Robertson Smith, *Religion of the Semites,* p 148; Montefiore, *Hibbert Lectures*, 1887, p88.
[2] A further and interesting development of this was that guilty persons could fly for asylum to such places. That is, they came under the protection of the god once they were on his property and the guest-law would compel the god to protect them. Originally in Israel this right of asylum belonged to all altars (Exod. xxi.13ff - Bible) and on the abolition of the local altars it was limited to certain 'cities of refuge' (cf Roberston Smith, *Religion of the Semites* p148ff: and Ibn Duraid, p235). A remnant of this survives in the old Abyssinian sacred city of Axum (Aksum), (ie. Wylds *Modern Abyssinia,* 1901, p157 and Bent *Sacred City of the Abyssinians*.p162).
[3] It will be remembered what a spirited attempt the people of Ta'if made to preserve their sanctuary.
[4] The whole question of these interdictions is discussed by Demombynes in the first chapter of his *Mekke*.
[5] Wensick *Joden te Medina*; Leszynskys *Die Juden in Arabien*, Berlin, 1810.
[6] On the similar sanctuary of the temple at Jerusalem see Kay *Semitic Religions,* p78 & Davidson op. cit. p158.

The discussion of sanctuaries inevitably raises the question of feasts and festivals, and sacred times and seasons, for in primitive times it is almost impossible to think of a sacred shrine without its accompanying festival. The early Semites were no different from other primitive peoples in this respect, and in the various Semitic groups we find a developed system of sacred seasons and festivals, some of them common Semitic and doubtless going back to the earliest period of common nomad life, and others individual developments within the different groups.

Among the early Arabs the most important festivals were apparently connected with the primitive worship of the mother-goddess, as the goddess of reproduction and fertility. Not only Arabic writers but also the Greeks[1] tell us that for three autumn months and one spring month, a truce was very generally observed among the tribes, who laid down their arms and came under an injunction to shed no blood. During these seasons they visited the shrines and celebrated their feasts. These sacred months corresponded with those of the birth of domestic animals and the harvesting of fruit. The more important festival was that in the autumn month, and Margoliouth suggests[2] that the reason for the three months truce being observed then instead of just the one month for the festival was that the month previous and the month after were instituted to enable distant visitors to arrive and return in safety. How deep Arab feeling was about the sacredness of these months is evidenced by the consternation caused by Muhammad's violation of the truce in order to provide for his needy followers in Medina.[3]

As far as one can gather there were no ascetic practices associated with these sacred months and Muhammad's introduction of the month of fasting was in all probability in imitation of the Jews[4] or possibly of the Sabians.[5]

The sacred months of course meant the year's fairest opportunities for trade, for with hostilities suspended the merchants

---

[1] Eg. Nonnosus and Procopius.
[2] *Muhammad*, p5.
[3] See the story in Muir *Life of Muhammad* (ed. Weir) cap xi.
[4] Bell, *Origins of Islam in its Christian Environment,* London, 1920, p145.
[5] Vide supra p190ff.

might in safety venture large caravans, so it is not to be wondered that fairs became common in the neighbourhood of these sanctuaries.[1] The most famous of these in pre-Islamic days was the fair of 'Ukaz, held somewhere between Ta'if and Nakhla, within easy reach of Mecca, commencing on the first day of Dhu'l-Qa'da at the beginning of the autumn festival, and lasting twenty one days. This great fair was not only a place of trading but was the occasion for the poetical contests of the Arabs. Lane-Poole describes it as *the press, the stage, the pulpit, the Parliament, and the Académie Française of the Arab people.*[2] It was the only rival of Hira as a cultural centre of the Arabs.[3]

The ecclesiastical writer Nonnosus,[4] who completed his mission to Abyssinia by a visit to Arabia, where he had unusual opportunities for studying the manners and customs of the people,[5] was particularly struck by this fact that the Arabs had a sacred place to which they repaired in large numbers during certain months of the year for worship, and during these months kept a universal peace.

6   Eschatology

As to the Eschatology of the pre-Islamic Arabs it is impossible at present to speak with any certainty. M[uslim] eschatology has never yet been worked at in detail by scholars[6], and without an historical account of the development of Islamic eschatology it is almost impossible to critically examine the sources and from them reconstruct a picture of the eschatological beliefs of the pre-Islamic period. Nor has sufficient work yet been done on the wider question

---

[1] The classical account is in Wellhaused *Reste,* p88-91.
[2] Ed. Note: See Appendix, p239 for Lane-Poole's - Poetic contests.
[3] (Ed. *Handwritten Note.*) Die vorislamischen Poeten bestätigen den Eindruck, den uns die koranische Predigt gibt, dass die eschatologischen Anschauungen der Schriftreligionen den Arabern gänzlich fremd waren. Mit dem Tode ist alles aus. Selbst der Ruhm, sonst das Höchste, was der arabische Held erstreben konnte, verliert angesichts des Todes allen Wert. Tor Andrae, *Der Ursprung,* p43.
[4] In Photius, *Bibliotheca,* iii. p6ff.
[5] So Thomas Wright, *Early Christianity in Arabia,* p88.
[6] For recent publications on the topic, see *Islam and the Last Day*, Occasional Papers vol 5, ed. Brett Neely and Peter Riddell, Melbourne, MST Press, 2015; *Death, resurrection, and human destiny: Christian and Muslim perspectives*: a record of the Eleventh Building Bridges Seminar convened by the Archbishop of Canterbury, King's College London and Canterbury Cathedral, 23-25 April 2012, Washington, DC Georgetown University Press 2014.

of comparative Semitic eschatology, to enable us to decide with any definiteness what is really Semitic and what is due to outside influences. One fact that stands out strongly is the very great influence of Persian conceptions on Semitic eschatology, and this Persian influence is very marked on much of the material that comes to us from Arabia.

(a) <u>The Future Life</u>
Hirschfeld suggests that the primitive Arabs like the primitive Hebrews had advanced but very little in conceptions of the future life.

> The common pre-Islamic view recognised a kind of shadowy after existence. Otherwise the materialistic opinion is valent, that death is the end of everything.[1]

It is possible that this is so, but it must be remembered that in the Qur'an there are a great number of passages detailing the delights of heaven and the pains of hell, and even if Muhammad was indebted for these to foreign sources, it is doubtful if the debt was immediate, for in his preaching he assumes familiarity among his hearers with the language he uses, and Horovitz has recently pointed out that practically all the details of his description of Paradise are to be found in the old poets.[2]

If, however, we take the old poetry as our starting point we find that a great number of important technical words denoting the conditions of the future life are of foreign origin. So, it would seem as though Arabia, at some little time before Muhammad, had become permeated with escahatological ideas partly from Persian and partly from Judaeo-Christian sources. Thus the abode of the blessed is الجنة which is Aramaic[3], or فردوس which is

---

[1] *New Researches*, p40. A few lines further on he refers to a pre-Islamic view of the transmigration of souls.
[2] *Das Koranische Paradis*, Jerusalem, 1923: see also Jacob, *Altarabisches Beduinenleben*, Berlin, 1897, p107, who points out that Qur'anic passages are often little more than transcriptions of verses of the heathen poets. Margoliouth (*Mohammed*, p114) states that the Qur'anic description of Paradise is taken in part from the picture of the city Ta'if where many wealthy Meccans had gardens.
[3] Fränkel *Fremdwörter*, p148. Nöldeke *Neue Beiträge p42*.

Persian,¹ and the curious place اعراف (vii. 44,46) is apparently Ethiopic,² عدن of course is Hebrew.³ The abode of the wicked is جهنم which is Ethiopic.⁴

At present then, we must be content to confess our ignorance of the early Arab conception of the future life. Nöldeke thinks that from the polemic of the Qur'an itself we would gather that the Arabs had little conception of a future life at all, seeing that they seemed to ridicule Muhammad's teaching of resurrection and a future life.⁵

(b) Angelology
The Qur'an clearly recognises the existence of angels, even perhaps hierarchies of angels in the heavenly places, but this seems to have been a borrowing from religions with more advanced eschatology. Thus the names of the great angels Gabriel and Michael are Hebrew⁶ and the very word for angel itself is Ethiopic.⁷ The beautiful females of Muhammad's Paradise are of Persian origin,⁸ though apparently the word was borrowed into Arabic before Muhammad's day.⁹ Harut and Marut are also apparently of Persian origin,¹⁰ while Shaitan and Iblis were borrowed from the Christians.¹¹

Demons, however, seem to have been well known in pre-Islamic times, for beside the gods we meet with as Nöldeke points

---

¹ Perhaps it came into the Arabic through the Syrian [illegible], but note the Persian فراديس – παράδεισοι as Hoffmann pointed out *ZDMG*, xxxii.761. See also Horovitz op.cit. p7. (AB. Form in note is good as the plural, if that's intended.)
² Ludolf, *Historia Aethiopica: et, Commentarius*, 208, sec. 36 and see Horovitz op. cit. p8.
³ Geiger, p32.
⁴ Nöldeke, *Neue Beiträge*, p47.
⁵ Nöldeke in *ERE*, I, 672.
⁶ Vide Eiekmann *Angelology*, 29ff: Pautz, *Offenbarung*, p39.
⁷ Bell, *Origin of Islam*, p 52. See also Pautz, op.cit. p69: Nöldeke *Neue Beiträge*, p34.
⁸ Tisdall, *Sources*, p237ff.
⁹ See Horovitz, *Paradies*, p10,13.
¹⁰ Littman in *Andreas Festschrift*, 70-87: Margoliouth *ERE*, viii.252: Wensinck, *El*, ii 273: Geiger, 104: Grunbaum in *ZDMG*, xxxi.
¹¹ Nöldeke *Neue Beiträge*, p34 & 47: Pautz, 48: Rudolf, *Die Abhängigkeit* 35, n i: Eickmann *Angelologie*, p24-27 and 43.

out,¹ "a great mass of shadowy beings everywhere yet nowhere distinctly perceived, the demons or as the Arabs call them, the Jinn". These Jinn are crafty mischievous beings, as a rule to be greatly feared. They are invisible, but at times may take the form of a snake, or a lizard, or some other loathsome creeping thing. We can see here that they are largely personifications of the terrors of the desert. The Jinn haunted barren and unhealthy places and on occasion can enter into a man and usurp the place of his reason.²

Robinson Smith thinks that there is probably a totemistic origin for the Jinn³ and it is very probable that many of the old totemic deities were later degraded into Jinn with animal-like qualities,⁴ just as under Islam, Muhammad classed the ancient gods among the demons.⁵

Some of the demons had sufficiently definite characteristics to be given special names. Thus, we read of the *Ghul,* a feminine noun from a root meaing *to destroy*. She assumes various forms and lures men away to lonely places where she destroys them. Another female demon is the *Si'lat:* and the *Khabal* and *Banu Uqaish* represent what may be conceived of as tribes of demons.

(c) <u>Soothsayers</u>

The Kahin we have already met. He corresponded to the μάγτις⁶ of the Greeks or the *vates* of the Romans, and was popularly supposed to give his oracles under the inspiration of a demon,⁷ who is called تابع (follower) ضاحب (comrade), وای (familiar)

---

¹ *ERE,* i.670: see also Van Vloten in *WZKH* vols vii and viii.
² Nöldeke op cit. p 671 thinks, however, that this was an idea borrowed from their neighbours.
³ *Religion Semites* p 119ff: See also Wellhausen *Reste,* p135.
⁴ (Ed. *Handwritten note:*) H. P. Smith, *Old Testament History,* p 14 notes how to Semites all animals were somewhat demonic. See his note also on p15 on the marriage between Jinn and humankind.
⁵ Cf. Qur'an xxxvii, 158 Just so Lev xvii:7(The Bible) calls the gods of Northern Semitic heathenism שעירים and the gods of Greece and Rome became devils to the early Christians.
6 (AB: Not familiar to me and not readily findable.)
⁷ (Ed. *Handwritten note:*) On trance as associated with prophecy see Smith *Old Testament History,* p109.

or رَئ (seer).¹ They gave their oracles in the *saj'* form of short sentences of rhythmical prose accompanied by a curious humming sound known as *zamzama*.² They apparently played quite an important role in early Arab tribal life, for they were consulted before all important tribal occasions where their oracles frequently decided action,³ and they seem also to have acted as judges in cases of legal disputes where their oracles could give final and authoritative verdicts.⁴

In the literature we also read of the *Hazi*⁵ with his feminine counterpart the Haziya, who was as the name indicates, a *seer, presager,* or *diviner* but who, as Fischer points out,⁶ enjoyed a lower degree of inspiration, and generally depended on some technical means to give his decision.

It is more than probable that Prophecy, which developed such a wonderful flower among the Hebrews had its origins in the work of the soothsayers⁷ and poetry also probably had the same origin, for the شاعر was originally one who uttered inspired sayings.⁸

(d) <u>Magic</u>
Babylonian magic, as it has been rediscovered from the inscriptions, has revealed to us how old Semitic magic is.⁹ There is much evidence in the Old Testament also to show how widely spread was the practice of magic arts among the Hebrews¹⁰ and

---

[1] Note the equivalence of this with the Hebrew רָאָה.
[2] Fischer (*EI*) suggests that the *saj'* may originally have meant the purring or chirping of the demon's voice as he spoke to the *Kahin*.
[3] (Ed. *Handwritten Note:*) Smith *Old Testament Prophecy,* p92 points out how naturally the prophet becomes an arbiter.
[4] There were also female soothsayers, or sybils on whom ... see Margoliouth, *Mohammed,* p18.
[5] The حازى corresponds with the Hebrew חֹזֶה, a word, however, which is not used save in later Hebrew cf 1 Chron.xxi:9: xxv:5 (The Bible) and which seems almost equivalent to נָבִיא. Fischer (*EI* ii.25) argues that it is a genuine Arabic word but this is doubtful.
[6] *EI* ii.626.
[7] See Montefiore, *Hibbert Lectures,* London, 1897, p77.
[8] Nöldeke in *ERE* i.671.
[9] See Campbell Thompson, *Semitic Magic,* London, 1903.
[10] See particularly Blau, *Das altjüdische Zauberwesen,* Strassburg, 1898.

Isaiah xlvii:5-11 (The Bible) connects this with Babylon[1]. Magic was freely and widely practised in pre-Islamic Arabia and there is even an authoritative tradition (*Muslim,* ii.180-183), to the effect that Muhammad himself sanctioned the employment of spells or magical prayers for the treatment of snake-bite, evil eye and various bodily complaints.

Divination was extensively practised, whether by the casting of arrows[2], (i.e. rhabdomancy), or by the examination of the entrails of slaughtered animals (haruspicy) or observation of the flight of birds, (called in Arabic *zajr* or *'iyafah,* divination with sand *(abacomancy,* called in Arabic *darb ar raml,* or with small nuts or pebbles.[3]

The names of some of the various types of magicians have been preserved for us. Thus *sahir* is the general term for any kind of a magician who practises *sihr* or magic.[4] The *'arraf* or sage, was one well acquainted with hidden things, also known as the *mu'arrif,* or water diviner; the *raqi* was an enchanter, the *zajir* read the flight of birds (also called *'a'if*): the *hazir* (also called *hazzar* or *qa'if*) read foot prints and the *murajjim,* read the stars: the *nazir fi asrar al-Kaff,* read fortunes by palmistry, and the *darib* read it by casting stones.

(e) <u>Cosmology</u>
In the Qur'an we meet with a very definite cosmological scheme of the heavens and the earth, but as this is obviously based on Jewish material and decked out with Iranian elements which may also have come to Muhammad through Jewish channels, it does not help us much to arrive at pre-Islamic conceptions. The ancient poetry has no very definite evidence to

---

[1] So too the classical writers look on Babylon as the headquarters of magic, cf. Lucan's lines in the *Pharsalia,* vi, 449ff.
      Tunc Babylon Persea licet, sacretaque Memphis
      Omne vetustorum solvat penetrale Magorum.
[2] Eg. At the shrine of Hubal in Mecca.
[3] On these various forms see Ibn Khaldun, *Prolegomena* (tr de Slane, 1862-68), i.218.
[4] On this term see Margoliouth in *ERE* viii, 252.

give, and the later elaborate cosmological treatises of Muslim authors are almost entirely of borrowed material, so we shall have to confess that at present we can say nothing definite about early Arabian cosmological ideas. It would seem, however, that Jewish and Iranian ideas were commonly known in Arabia at least some time before the birth of Muhammad, for he assumes some familiarity among his audience with the terms he uses in the cosmological passages of the Qur'an.

(7)   Minor Points

Some minor points connected with pre-Islamic religion may finally occupy our attention before we proceed to examine the more developed religious systems that were known in Arabia before the coming of Muhammad.

a) Tahannuth

It has been frequently pointed out that the Muslim month of fasting, *Ramadan* was probably instituted under Judaeo-Christian influence[1] but it would seem that in his choice of the month Muhammad was guided by the fact that during that month every year the Meccans were wont to practise a form of asceticism known to us under the name *tahannuth*. It was in connection with this practice that Muhammad used to retire annually to a cave on Mt. Hira on the way to Ta'if, some three miles from Mecca, and indulge in ascetic observances.[2]

It is quite uncertain what this word means. Hirschfeld[3] and Lyall[4] think it is simply the Hebrew pural תְחִנּוֹת prayers, and would look on it as another proof of the influence of Judaism on the more spiritually minded people of Arabia. Nöldeke in his *Geschichte des Qorans* (1860), p67, was inclined to think that حنث has the meaning 'to lead a solitary life' but in his *Neue Beiträge* p72 he prefers to derive it from *tahannuf*, thus connecting it up

---

[1] Bell, *Origin of Islam in its Christian Enviroment*, 1926, p145.
[2] It is noteworthy that Muhammad has been practising this *tahannuth*, when the angel appeared to him and gave him his first call to be a prophet. See Ibn Hisham, p152 and Margoliouth, *Mohammed*, p91.
[3] *New Researches*, p19, n.
[4] In *JRAS*, 1903, p77.

with the religion of the Hanifa¹. There is justice, however, in Hirschfeld's remark, that if it were an Arabic word, the Commentators and Traditionists would have had no difficulty with it, so it would therefore seem to have a foreign borrowing.

Remembering the ascetic practices of the Judaeo-Christian Gnostic sects, that a similar month of prayer and fasting was known among the Mandaeans² and that the Syriac ⌂ is a technical word for such fervent prayer, intercession, and supplication, the present writer is inclined to think that it is another indication of Gnostic influence in *Arabia*.

(b) Prayer

The Islamic ceremonial prayer or *salat* is apparently borrowed from Jews or Christians,³ and the ceremonial itself is a combination of Jewish and Christian custom in prayer⁴. How far prayer of any sort formed part of the ceremonial of the old Arabian religion, however, is doubtful. From the *Musnad*, iv.222, it would appear that in the days before his call to Apostleship, Muhammad was accustomed to perform with Khadija some domestic rite to the great Goddesses of Mecca, which may have been in the nature of prayer. Then there have been preserved to us some of the cries of welcome used in pilgrimage and associated with the various gods, which cries are more or less in the nature of prayers.⁵

(c) Food Regulations

Muhammad's food regulations which have become so important for Muslims of the present day, were largely influenced by Jewish

---

¹ With which Buhl agrees *EI* ii.259. It will be remembered that Wellhausen *Skizzen und Vorabeiten* iv. 156 pointed out that *tahannuf* apparently means the exercise of the purer type of religion during the pagan period. Ibn Hisham explains *tahannuth* by *tahannuf,* saying that *th* and *f* interchange in Arabic. (ed. Wüstenfeld p152).
² See Brandt's article *Mandaeans* in *ERE,* viii. and supra p191ff
³ Bell, *Origin,* p91: Mittwock, *Zur Entstehungsgeschichte des Islamischen Gebets und Kultur, 1913.*
⁴ von Kremer *Streifzüge,* p15.
⁵ Cheikho, p15.

and Christian usage[1], but there is no doubt that food regulations were well known to the pre-Islamic Arabs. Food was commonly offered to the idols[2] and certain animals were sacred to certain divinities, e.g. the pig at the Ka'ba, which is doubtless the origin of the Muslim objection to swine flesh[3]. Wellhausen gives some further indications of ritual food prohibitions among the tribes.[4]

---

[1] Margoliouth *Mohammed*, 126. *Mohammed's conversations with Jews and Christians had taught him to assign a far higher importance to that subject than the pagans are likely to have assigned it. All his life he had a hankering after the Jewish regulations on this subject, only as the Jewish system forbade the use of camel's flesh, he could not well adopt it, he preferred therefore that of the Christians.*
[2] See Margoliouth op. cit. p111 for a curious tradition. In the *Isabah*, ii.963 Ibn Hajr Asqalani we read of a prisoner at Mecca who implored his guards not to give him to eat of food offered to idols.
[3] If this represents a primitive (early) conception of the swine as sacred to the Semitic mother goddess, it would explain why swine's flesh was forbidden in other Semitic religions. See H. P. Smith, *Old Testament History*, p334, and Usener *Sintfluthsagen*, p93.
[4] *Reste*, p125 n.1 See also Nöldeke, *Sasaniden*, (*Geschichte der Perser und Araber*) p203.

SABIANISM

Three times in the Qur'an[1] there is mention, included among the People of the Book, the Sabians (الصابؤن) who like Jews, Christians and Magians are to receive specially favourable treatment at the hands of the Muslims.[2] The Qur'an itself gives us no hint as to the identity of this community, nor does it give us any information about them other than their name, and the fact that they were a People of a Book. It would seem that Muhammad himself, was at times called *Sabian* by his contemporaries[3], which would seem to indicate that it was a community of a fairly definite character, well known to him and to them, to whose tenets or practice, Muhammad's early preaching bore some resemblance.

When we come to examine more closely the question, we plunge at once into difficulties. Bell[4] thinks it is nothing but a reference to the Christian Sabaeans of South Arabia the difference in spelling being due either to a mistake or to a play on names. This seems a little difficult to accept, however, and the majority of scholars seek for a community other than the Christians, at least of the orthodox or semi-orthodox variety. The etymology of the word is uncertain, the Muslims themselves being uncertain on the matter: Shahrastani[5] derives it from صَبَا = to long for, which would probably give it a Syrian origin. Tabari[6] takes it to be from a root صَبَا' = to change one's religion: ie. it would mean 'apostate'.[7] Wellhausen[8],

---

[1] ii.59; v.73: xxii. 17.
[2] (Ed. *Handwritten note:*) Abd Al-Razzaq al-Hasani, *Iraq; Old and New*, Sidon, 1948.
[3] Cf. Bukhari (ed. Krehi) i.96,07: ii. 296, 387, 388. Ibn Hisham (ed. Wüsterfeld) 299. (Ed. *Handwritten note:*) In Ibn Sa'd I, 120 – the old woman from whose she-kid, he draws milk says, "I imagine this must be that Sabian who is in Mecca." Bukhari I, 96, 97 has a similar story.
[4] *Origin of Islam*, pp64, 148.
[5] *Milal*, ed Cureton, p203.
[6] *Tafsir* on ii:59.
[7] (Ed. *Handwritten note:*) So Bukhari I.97 says "to change one's religion".
[8] *Reste*, 257 So Nicholson, *Literary History*, 149 n.i: Margoliouth *Mohammed*, 117. The identification however appears to go back to Norberg and Michaelis (see *Browne Festschrift*, ed Arnold & Nicholson, p283).

with much more likelihood derives it from צבא = צבע and meaning 'baptist'.

The Commentators do not help us much. Tabari eg. in his *Tafsir* i.242ff on ii.59 gives a variety of opinions which had come down to the learned of his time, such as,

i) that they were a people who had changed from one religion to another
ii) that they were people who had no religion
iii) That they worshipped angels and prayed towards a Qibla
iv) That they were the people whose sacred book was the Zabur.

None of which is very helpful and would seem to show that nothing much was known of them in his day. Baghawi in the *Ma'alim at-Tanzil* on ii.59 narrates an interesting tradtion from Al-Kalbi to the effect that they were a people midway between Jews and Christians, which would suggest to our minds that they might possibly be Judaeo-Christian Gnostics. He also quotes from Qalada that they used to take 'from every religion a little'. Later writers have the idea that they were star worshippers.[1]

The first Western Scholar to take up the investigation of the Sabians, was the Russian Semitiest, Chwolsohn, who in his monumental work *Die Ssabier under der Ssabismus,* published in St. Petersburg in 1856, collected most of the information that was available at that time. He identified the Sabians with the Mandaeans; Margoliouth, however, thinks that they were Harranians,[2] and Brandt, that they are Elkesites.[3]

(i) <u>Mandaeans</u>
In historical times these curious people are found in little communities scattered among the towns and villages of

---

[1] This is given by Khazin, eg. As the most probable explanation (*Tafsir* i.57): see also Fakhr ad-Din Razi, *Tafsir,* viii.21.
[2] *ERE,* vi.519.
[3] See Brandt, *Elkasai, (Elchasai)* passim.

Mesopotamia[1] and are peculiarly interesting in having preserved to the present day their old religion[2] and their old language.[3] There has been much controversy over their origin. Hilgenfeld and Wellhausen take them to be a Judaeo-Christian sect, Kessler considering them to be Manichaeans, and others taking them for Parsis or Gnostics. The truth seems to be that they were a remnant of followers of the old Babylonian religion, who had at different times absorbed much of Hellenism, Judaism, Gnosticism, Christianity, and it may be of Zoroastrianism.

There is such a confusion of heterogeneous elements from various sources in their theology, and so little has been attempted at arranging this material chronologically, that it is exceedingly difficult to decide what is primitive and what is not. Certain features which interest us, however are:

1 Their religion was largely astronomical.
   Its monotheistic teaching was associated with its doctrine of the *Heavenly Man,* the *exalted King of Light*, who dwells far beyond the heaven of the planets in a world of light and splendour. Below it is the planetary world with which are associated the leaders of the different religions, thus Judaism is said to have been created by "Shamesh the sun, whom all people call Adoni" and Jesus is identified with Mercury.

2 It was closely associated with Baptism and emphasized ceremonial purity. This is associated with the teaching of the heavenly Jordan, and the rivers which descend from the celestial world of light.

---

[1] An interesting account of their modern settlement will be found in Petermann's *Reisen im Orient* ii.53-137 and 447-465 (Leipzig, 1861). See also Zwemer, *Arabia the Cradle of Islam,* cap xxviii. Stevens, *By Tigris and Euphrates,* 1923 cap xxii.
[2] The most important studies are Brandt's *Die mandäische Religion* and *Die Mandäischen Schriften*, Göttigen, 1893 Siouffi's *Études sur la Religion des Soubbas*, Paris, 1880: and Lidzbarski's three substantial volumes *Das Johannesbuch der Mandaer,* Giessen, 1915: *Mandaische Liturgien,* Berlin, 1920, *Ginza: das grosse Buch der Mandaer,* Göttingen, 1925. Vide also Brandt's article on "Mandaeans" in *ERE,* viii.
[3] Nöldeke, *Mandaische Grammatik,* Halle, 1875.

The idea of purity says Brandt was recognised in the sense of a relation to the world of light so intimate that it carried with it exclusion from every object and condition antipathetic to it.

Some of their washings are curiously like those which have come down in Islamic practice.

3 Prayers were obligatory.
In the earliest documents we find that believers must arise to pray thrice in the day-time and twice at night, but in later passages this is reduced to three, one in the morning, one at the seventh hour, and one at sunset. The connection with Islam is obvious.

4 It was a religion of a Prophet and a Book.
At least in its later forms it seems to gather around the personality of John the Baptist. Whether this was original or not it is difficult to say but at the time of Muhammad these were the people who held John to be the great Prophet, to whom had been given a book the *Sidra d'Yahya*.

Chwolsohn identified the Mandaeans with the Sabians of the Qur'an on the following grounds.

i   They are a monotheistic people of a book, and alone of the sects we know were sufficiently important to be classed by Muhammad with the Jews, Christians and Magians.

ii   They were identical with the *Mughtasila* of whom we learn from the *Fihrist* that they dwelt in the swampy regions around *Wasit* and Basra[1] and were known to him as the Sabians of the swamps.

---
[1] *Fihrist* ed Flügel, p340.

iii   They have always, so far as our records go, been known to their Arab neighbours as *Subba*.[1]

iv   They are identical with the Elkesites whom we know from the writings of Hippolytus and Epiphanius. The founder of the Elkesites is said to have given his book to one named Sobiai.[2]

Chwolsohn's authority was so great that he was followed by nearly all later writers, and even down to the present time his conclusions are generally followed.[3] Brandt, for example in his article *Mandaeans* in *ERE* viii says "The passage in the Qur'an and the name Sabians would apply most approximately to the Mandaeans" and Carra de Vaux in *Encyclopaedia Islam* article "Sabi'a" says that the Sabians "mentioned in the Kor'an ... are apparently the Mandaeans". Details of Chwolsohn's argument, however, have come under criticism, and the most recent research would seem to indicate that his identification must be given up.   Nöldeke in his *Mandäische Grammatik* (Halle, 1875, p.xix) decides against the identification of the Mandaeans with the *Mughtasila*[4] and as Pedersen points out[5] the *Mughtasila* like the Manichaeans were ascetics who frowned on marriage, but the Mandaeans set marriage high. Nor can the Elkesites be Mandaeans for they considered fire as an evil element whereas it was worshipped by the Mandaeans.[6] Moreover, it does not appear, says Pedersen, that the Mandaeans were a sect of any special importance in North West Arabia.

ii.   <u>Harranians</u>
The Harranians were a Syrian community having headquarters at Harran (the Old Testament הרן and classical

---

[1] *ERE* viii.390: Siouffi, *Étude sur la Religion des Soubbas,* passim, Stevens, *Tigris and Euphrates,* p204.
[2] *Philosopheumena,* (Hippolytus) 447.
[3] Eg:. In most Encyclopaedia articles on the Sabians.
[4] With reference to his article in *Göttingische Gelehrte Anzeiger,* G.G. A., vol 1, 1869, Vol. 1, p484. Cf. also Brandt *Eichasai,* 1912, pp141-144.
[5] *'Ajeb Namen* 384 (Ed. Note: Jeffery also refers to this work later in this volume and appears to associate it with an article in the volume of Oriental Studies presented to E. G. Browne.)
[6] Pedersen, op. cit. (*'Ajeb Namen*).

Carrhae) who in 833A.D. under Muslim rule, publicly took the name *Sabians* so as to come under the Muslim regulations for the protected cults. The Syrian writers who first mention[1] them call them pagans. Muslim writers such as Shahrastani[2] and Mas'udi[3] speak of them rather as philosophers. Chwolsohn judged that they were a little community who still retained some of the old Babylonian religion[4] largely mixed, however, with Hellenic elements (mostly Gnostic) and glossed over with a veneer of Neoplatonic philosophy. He thinks it was their taking the name Sabians which led this name to be given as a general name to all communities of star worshippers.

The points we should note about their religion are:

1 That it was decidedly astronomical in character.
All accounts agree on this point, and fragments of their calendar have been preserved to us in which there seems a strange blending of Babylonian with Greek elements.[5] Ibn Hazm[6], who wants to make them disciples of Abraham[7] whose religion was identical with that afterwards restored by Muhammad, suggests that this star worship was a survival which even Abraham was not able to abolish.

2 They had a thirty day fast every year.

---

[1] Cf. Dionysius of Tell-Mahre in his *Chronicle*; ed Chabot.
[2] *Kitab al Milal wa-n-Nihal,* ed. Cureton, London, p203.
[3] *Muruj,* i.73: ii.111; iii.348: iv.44ff and in his *Tanbih,* passim.
[4] One very curious Babylonian survival among them was the worship of Taus, who was the late Babylonian Du'uz = Tammuz. See Langdon, *Tammuz and Ishtar,* 1914, p2 n3 and E Burroughs in *Orientalia* vii.55.
[5] See the text published by Dozy in *Actes du sixiéme Congress des Orientalistes,* Leiden, 1888, ii.285.
[6] *Kitab al Fisal; wa'l Milal,* i.35 (ed. Cairo, 1317).
[7] It is curious that Maimonides knows a tradition that Abraham was a Sabian, for in his *More Nevochim* iii.c29 we read:
(AB: Replaced Hebrew from Thomas Wright, *Early Christianity in Arabia* (London: Bernard Quaritch, 1855), p. 27 n. 9, with

(ידוע שאברהם אבינו עליו השלום גדל באמוגת הצאבה ודעתם שאין אליה רק הככבים.

Ibn Hazm equates this with Ramadan, but this cannot be so, as we learn from other sources that it was distributed over December, February and March.[1]

3   They had prayers accompanied by prostrations.
Ibn Hazm says they turned to the Ka'ba in prayer but there are reasons for thinking that their qibla was the north[2], which is again a suggestion of astronomical religion.

4   They had a Prophet or Prophets.
They claimed that Hermes and Agathodaemon were their Prophets[3]. This would suggest Gnostic influence[4].

5   Their worship was sacrificial in character.
All the accounts seem to agree in this, though as Margoliouth points out[5], some of the stories particularly those of human sacrifice, are incredible.

6   They had a system of food restrictions.
Ibn Hazm again relates this to the system of Qur'anic prohibitions of unlawful meats but without justification, for they forbade the use of the flesh of the camel, which was allowed in Islam.

It will be noticed that some of these points would seem to link them at times with the Mandaeans, as Chwolsohn is inclined to do. Margoliouth, however, thinks they were quite distinct and that they were the Sabians referred to in the Qur'an and the Traditions. His grounds are –

a) Tabari in his *Tafsir* (i.243) locates the Sabians in the Jazira of Mosul, which though somewhat vague is a correct enough location for Harran, but does not suit the Mandaeans.

---

[1] *Kitab al Fisal.*
[2] Margoliouth, *ERE,* vi.
[3] Shahrastani (tr. Haarbrücker ii 76) These according to Shahrastani (ibid.ii.61) were to be equated with Idris and Seth, which would again suggest Gnostic influence.
[4] Vide Gilbert Murray, *Four States in Greek Religion,* 1918.
[5] *ERE* vi, 520.

b) The oldest geographer, Istakhri, mentions Harran as the city of the Sabians[1] and we may assume that it had been known as such for long enough before his time.

c) Muhammad and his early followers were called Sabians by their enemies, and this name, as Sprenger saw[2] was somehow connected with the word *hanif,* a word which Muhammad connects with the religion of Abraham. Now Abraham came from Harran[3], and Christian writers refer to the Harranians as *hanpe,* which as we have already seen is connected with *hanif.* [4]

d) Ibn Hazm[5] seems to have no doubt about the Harranians being the Sabians of the Qur'an, and he is a writer who usually has very accurate information about such matters, though the deductions he draws from his information do not always commend themselves to our judgment.

It may be noted that the Harranians are included among the Sabians by other Arabic writers. Thus Mas'udi in the *Tanbih*[6] speaks about the Sabians of the Egyptians whose remnants are the Sabians of the Harranians. So[7] mentions the Harranians along with the Sabians of Central Asia. Chwolsohn thinks that all this evidence, however, does not help us, for it is apparently all later than the actual adoption of the name Sabians by the Harranians. Chwolsohn thinks that the Harranians originally had nothing to do with the Sabians, but fraudulently usurped the name in order to come under the toleration extended to the People of the Book. Writers writing after this event, and not knowing of earlier conditions, naturally referred to them as among the Sabians.

---

[1] ed. De Goeje, *Bibliotheca Geographorum Arabicorum* p76.
[2] *Leben,* i.46.
[3] Acts vii:4 (The Bible) -κατῴκησιν ἰτ Χαρράς.
[4] Infra p194ff.
[5] *Fisal wa-Milal* i. 35.
[6] ed. de Geoje in *Bibliotheca Geographorum Arabicorum* viii 19 and 116.
[7] ed Sachau, pp204-207.

ii) Elkesites

Here we have another Mesopotamian sect whom an-Nadim in the *Kitab al Fihrist* calls *mughasila* and reckons among the Sabians.

We have interesting evidence about the Elkesites from Christian sources, for missionaries of the faith crossed from Syria to Rome about 220 AD and preached there, so that Hippolytus[1] and Epiphanius[2] both give some account of the teaching in their Refutations of Heresies. Elkesai is considered by Brandt, the leading authority on the sect[3], to be an historical figure[4] to have exercised considerable authority in Transjordania, where Essenes, Ebionites and Judaeo-Christian communities seem to have accepted his teaching in large numbers. The facts to be noted about the religion are:

1 *It was a religion of a Prophet and a Book.*
   Some curious problems are raised by this book which is so often referred to in the sources and from which we apparently have quotations in Hippolytus and Epiphanius. We learn that Elkesai wrote nothing but allowed his followers to copy down oracles on loose leaves or any fragments of other material that were at hand, and these were circulated among his followers and after his death collected into book form. The curious parallel to Muhammad will be immediately recognised. Another curious parallel is the story of how Elkesai got his call to preach and his first revelation. The "book" tells us that two

---

[1] *Philosopheumena,* ed. Miller pp 292-297 and 300.
[2] *Adversus Haereses* xix, xxx, lxxx: *Epitome* xix.xxx. Theodoret's account (*Haereticarum fabularum compendium* ii.7) is based entirely on these two writers.
[3] *Elchasai: ein Religionsstifter und sein Werk*, Leipzig, 1912 and his article 'Elkesaites' in *ERE* v.
[4] Others, however, think the name belongs not to the man but to the book. The origin of this name is difficult. Hippolytus writes it Ἠλχασαι: Epiphanius as Ἠλξαι: while he calls his followers Ἐλκεσαῖοι: Origen calls them Ἐλκεσαῖται. The Semitic form used by Theodore bar Khuni is Syriac ﷽. Epiphanians suggests that it may be Aramaic כסי, 'hidden' and 'חיל' "power" but the ה here is very difficult. Brandt's suggestion (*ERE* v.263) is better, viz כסי and אל, ie. "hidden god", but he is here depending on the Arabic form given in the *Kitab al Fihrist* which is doubtful in itself and has been given a different solution by Pederson (*Ajab Nameh,* 386).

huge figures appeared to him out among the hills and called him to his mission, just as Gabriel is said to have called Muhammad.[1]

2 *It had a baptismal system.*
This seems to have been the essential point in the cultus. Hippolytus (p45) gives us a description of that way in which Alcibiades baptised his converts in Rome, and as Brandt points out, this baptism, which has for its object the remission of sins, and for its preliminary condition the pledge of a changed life, reminds us much of John the Baptist.[2]

3 *It had an eschatological colouring.*
Brandt points out[3] that the founder was impressed greatly with the coming of the Last Day and cherished the expectation that on that Last Day his personal testimony would be accepted as decisive before the great Tribunal. Thus he gave to his converts a secret watchword

אנא מסהר עליכון ביום דינא רבא

= "I am a witness over you in the Day of the Great Judgment", Elkesai also taught much about the different classes of angels good and evil.

4 *Its qibla for prayer was Jerusalem*
Doubtless, Jewish influence, maybe through the Essenes, affected this.

In the *Kitab al Fihrist,* as we have already noticed, the Mughasila are called the Sabians of the swamps. The passage reads[4]

---

[1] Thus we find the book of Elkesai spoken of as that 'revealed by the angel' – ὑπὸ ἀγγέλου. Elkesai apparently taught that of these figures, one was male and called the Son of God and the other female called the Holy Spirit. It may be that here we have a suggestion of the origin of the strange نصرى who meets us in the Qur'an, and the even stranger identification there of the third person of the Trinity with the Virgin Mary.
[2] *ERE* v. 264.
[3] *ERE* v. 264.
[4] *Fihrist,* ed Flügel p 340.

These people live in large numbers in the regions of the swamps, and are the Sabians of the swamps. They hold that people should wash themselves and everything they eat. Their head is called Al-Hasih and he it was who founded their religion. He maintains that the two principles of existence are the male and the female, that the herbs belong to the male principle while the mistletoe belongs to the female, the trees being its roots. They have some detestable notes that can only be called nonsense. He had a disciple named Sham'um. They agree with the Manichaeans about the two principles but otherwise their religions differ. Among them are some who worship the stars up to the present day."

Taking the statements of this passage along with that in Hippolytus which tells us that Elkesai gave his book into the custody of one Sobiai[1], Brandt would identify the Sabians of the Qur'an with these Elkesites.[2]

Pederson, however, in his essay on the Sabians in the volume of Oriental Studies presented to E. G. Browne (*Ajab Nameh*, 1922, pp383-391) would reject all these identifications.

a) He agrees with Nöldeke's rejection of the identification of the Mughasila with the Mandaeans.[3]

b) He claims that though the Harranians took the title Sabians, yet as it is used in Muslim authors, the term is a much wider one and includes many others besides the Harranians.

c) He reads the difficult name الحسيح or الحسح of the *Kitab al-Fihrist* as السيح and thinks of them as a Gnostic sect, thus cutting away all connections between the Mughtasila and the Elkesites.

---

[1] *Philosopheumena,* Hippolytus 447.
[2] *ERE,* v, 268.
[3] *Mandäische Grammatik,* Nöldeke, xi, xv.

d) He thinks that Sprenger was right in identifying the Sabians with the Hanifs[1] and claims that our examination of the use of the word in the Arabic literature, leads us to the conclusion that it was the general word used to cover the various Gnostic sects of the East of that day.

Thus the word Sabian may have covered the Mandaeans and Harranians and Elkesites, but is too wide a term to be confined to any one of them. Only further research into the history of the Oriental Gnostic Movement will enable us to decide with any more certainty whether any particular group of Gnostics influenced the early history of Islam and is at the root of the Gnostic element that we have noticed in the Qur'an[2] and that can be found in the Traditions of the life of the Prophet.

---

[1] *Leben* i.46.
[2] Infra p168.n iii.

SABAEAN RELIGION

The state of uncertainty as to results in connection with attempts to reconstruct the history of South Arabia, is even more noticeable when we come to consider the religion of Minaeans and Sabaeans. The little investigation that has been done has made it clear that here again the Arabic accounts are practically worthless and we must base our work entirely on the epigraphic material. This material, unfortunately, is not as copious as we could desire, and it will only be after considerably more inscriptions are published that we shall be able to sketch in even approximately the outlines of South Arabian religion.

On the basis of material at present available we may tentatively suggest certain features as apparently characteristic of Sabaean religion.[1]

i.)   It was largely Astronomical
Numerous astronomical deities have been recognised in the inscriptions, and certain details of the cult seem to point to star worship.

(a) <u>Shams</u> was a goddess revered alike by Minaeans, Sabaeans, Qatabanians and Hadramites and Shams is obviously the sun goddess. It is curious that while in North Arabia, Shams appears as a god, it appears as a goddess in South Arabia. Shams also appears under other names and forms.

(b) <u>Sin</u> is the moon-god[2] and is apparently the same deity as the Babylonian Sin, so well known as the chief god of the great temple at Ur. He appears to have been particularly reverenced in Hadramaut. Sin also appears

---

[1] There is a sketch of South Arabian religion in Grimme's *Mohammed*, 1914 pp29ff. The most completet account, however, is that by Tritton in *ERE*, x 880ff.
[2] Nielsen has a thesis that moon worship was the most primitive form; see his *Altarabische Mondreligion*, Strassburg, 1904.

in other forms, eg. Haubas, "the drier" is the moon as cause of the ebb tide and 'Amn is another form.

(c) 'Athtar is the Babylonian Ishtar, the Semitic Venus. Curiously 'Athtar in South Arabia is masculine, whereas the North Semitic Ishtar is feminine. 'Uzza, so well known as Venus in pagan Arabia appears also in the South Arabian inscriptions.

(d) Almaquh, whom Hamdani identifies with Venus was also apparently a celestial deity though we cannot be certain.[1]

ii.) Euhemerism

Certain gods of clans who seem never to have reached full divine rank, but to have been rather patrons of their people,[2] are apparently to be classed as cases of euhemerism, and the curious 'month of fathers', would probably point in the same direction.[3] Such gods as Wadd[4] and Sumuh-'Ali may also be of this type.

iii.) Totemism

Nasr, the eagle god, known to us also in North Arabia appears in the inscriptions, and Ta'lab of Mt Itwa may have been sacred to certain deities, such as the antelope to 'Athtar, which would again point to a totemistic background for the religion. Moreover the polyandrous organisation of society so frequently found in connection with totemism is well evident in connection with the people of South Arabia.

iv.) Monotheism

The question whether South Arabian religion ever approached monotheism is of exceeding interest but very difficult to resolve. Margoliouth says in his *Schweich Lectures,* p39:

---

[1] cf. Nielsen, *Der Sabäische Gott Ilmukah,* Berlin, 1910.
[2] Such examples as Ta'lab of Riyam, whose temple was on Mt Itwa.
[3] Praetorius points out (*ZDMG* xxvii. 645ff) that among them the dead were sometimes deified.
[4] The 📷 (uncertain as to language here) of the El-Öla inscriptions and the ودّ of Sura lxxi.22.

> These kingdoms were not monotheistic: there is nothing in the monuments hitherto discovered which indicates the existence of any theory of creation and administration of the world by a single power

and that is true of the earlier period. But when we come to the the consideration of the god Rahman[1], who appears later in the inscriptions, we seem to find at least the germs of monotheism. Possibly the development of Rahman was under Jewish influence, but whether this can be maintained or not, we certainly find in some of the Rahman inscriptions very curious anticipations of Muhammadan theology[2] so that Dr. Margoliouth says:[3]

> this evidently contains doctrines which approach the monotheism of Muhammad. Forgiveness of sins, acceptance of sacrifice, 'association' in the sense of polytheism, a near and a distant world, and the ascription of both evil and good to God are all contained in this tablet ... Was Muhammad's theology, not, as the Qur'an so emphatically represents it, a fresh start in Arabia traceable, as tradition suggests, to contact of the Prophet with Jews and Christians on his travels or at Meccah, but merely the introduction into North Arabia of a system which had possibly for some centuries been, if not actually dominant, yet at least current in the South?

v.)   *Sacrificial System*

This was apparently well developed. Oxen and sheep were offered in large numbers, and we should naturally expect among people whose business interests lay largely in the spice trade, they burned incense as part of their worship. In the inscriptions we find the ordinary Semitic זבח used for sacrifice, and so far as we can judge their sacrificial system differed in no important particular from that of the rest of the Semites. Like

---

[1] The name however seems to be Aramaic. (Ed. *Handwritten note:*) In one of the (inscriptions) beside the name *Rahm'n* for God we find the word(s) 🕮 *Kaffara* and this nearer world contrasted with farther world.

[2] The important text is that edited by Mordtmann and Müller in 1896 in *WZKM,* x. 287.

[3] op cit. p68

the Jews their preferred day for sacrifice was the seventh, and they were very particular about sound animals being offered.[1]

vi.)   Pilgrimages

Pilgrimages apparently were common. The inscriptions contain references to pilgrimages to the temple of Ta'lab on Mt. Itwa, and from fragments of their calendar we gather that there was a particular month called "The month of Pilgrimage". Possibly Abraha was counting on the prevalence of this custom when he built his cathedral at San'a to be a great pilgrimage centre. The pilgrimage to Barahut which has continued to the present day may be a survival of the old rite.[2]

vii.)   Temples

Numerous remains of temples have been found, and from the inscriptions it would appear that the gods often took their titles from their temples. That there were priesthoods connected with these temples seems fairly certain. It is most remarkable that there has been nothing yet discovered to suggest that there were ever in use images of the divinities worshipped.

---

[1] It would also seem as though one of the technicalities of the Jewish altar of sacrifice has been satisfactorily explained by a Minaean text. See Weber in *MVAG,* vi 8 on עזרה and Margoliouth *Schweich Lectures,* p21. (AB, I made a conjectural emendation to the Hebrew name Ezra)

[2] See Schleifer in *EI* i. 654.

ZOROASTRIANISM[1]

The official religion of the Sasanian Empire of Persia, whose influence was pressing in on the East and South of Arabia was Zoroastrianism. So far very little attention has been given by scholars to the question of Zoroastrian influences in early Arabia. We suspect that both pre-Islamic and Islamic eschatology was very largely coloured by Persian thought, but whether this influence was direct from Persia or through Jewish channels has never been fully investigated. In the early poems and in the Qur'an there are very many Persian words but again, how many are direct borrowings, and how many came through Syriac is a problem yet to be solved. So, too, with other problems. Persian influence we know was very strong at the time of Muhammad's birth,[2] both at Hira and its surroundings in Mesopotamia and to a less extent in South Arabia. Shortly after the Arab conquest of Persia we find Persian scholars taking the foremost places in the development of Islam. The Islamization of Persia we know, was by the sword, not by conviction, and most of the Persians who so quickly became doctors in Islam, were the heirs of the old Zoroastrian civilization, and it is the present writer's conviction that a careful study of Zoroastrianism in relation to Islam would reveal that of Islamic theology and practice, considerably more could be traced to Zoroastrian sources than is at present recognised.

For our purposes we have not to deal with the old original Zoroastrianism, but with the modified form of it practised in the Sasanian Empire. There are three stages in this development.

(a) <u>Achaemenian Period</u>
Early Persian religion, or Magianism, was a form of the polytheism common to the primitive Indo-Iranians. Somewhere in

---

[1] See Appendix, p248, *Zoroastrianism* for additional handwritten notes.
[2] (Ed. *Handwritten note:*) In *Aghani* viii 63 we read how Qubaid enlisted the governor of al-Itira and the neighbouring territories, al-Mundhir to Ma'ai Sama' to embrace like himself the doctrines of Mazdak.

this Achaemenian period, possibly about 500BC there came a great religious reformer Zoroaster. It is possible that many elements of the reform that he preached had been striving for expression before he came, but his was the religious genius which gave its stamp to the reform and its first form to the religion afterwards known by his name. Some scholars, particularly Moulton[1], hold that Zoroastrianism then became an officially recognised religion in Persia, at least for a time, but this is uncertain. What seems to be certain is that, at least for the great mass of the people, there was a compromise between the abstract doctrine of the Zoroaster and the polytheistic animism of the old Magianism.[2] This was known as Mazdaeanism.

(b) <u>Avsacid Period</u>[3]
In this period under the Parthian usurpers we find Mazdaeanism fully developed, and religion in general formal and lifeless. Many elements from surrounding religions were absorbed into the system until Mazdaeanism became largely a syncretism. The teachings of Zoroaster survived and developed, but as an esoteric cult rather than as a recognised religion.

(c) <u>Sasanian Period</u>
With the overthrow of the Parthians and the installation once more of the true Persian dynasty in 211AD we find Zoroastrianism elevated to the position of the official state religion. The Sasanians were vigorous champions of the faith and bitter persecutors of the adherents of other religions.[4] The great literary development of Zoroastrianism belongs to this period, and from it dates the final recension of the Zend Scriptures.

As to the nature of the religion we need only notice the following points which are of interest from the point of view of its relation to early Islam.

---

[1] *Early Zoroastrianism,* London, 1913.
[2] It is as Magians that the Zoroastrians are known in the Qur'an vide Sura xxii.7
[3] Ed. Note: Also known as the Parthian Empire.
[4] For the persecution of the Christians see Labourt's volume, *le Christianisme dans l'Empire perse sous la dynastie Sassanide,* Paris, 1904 and more briefly the essay "I popoli cristiani sottomessi ai Sassanidi" in Caetani's *Annali,* ii. 890-921.

(a)   *Dualism.*

Its theological system was a dualism built up from the contrast between Ahura Mazda, the god of light and goodness and Angrato Mainyu, the god of darkness and evil[1] but approaching closely a Trinitarianism in its conception of Vohu Manah, the Right Reason or Logos.[2] It is very possible that the Allah of orthodox Islamic theology who is the source of both evil and good, and in so many ways seems to take up into Himself the attributes of both Ahura Mazda and Angra Mainyu, is really the creation of theologians imbued with the old Zoroastrian dualism, who on becoming Muslim monotheists conceived of their One God as the combination of the two.

(b)   *Revelation*

It was the religion of a Prophet and a Book. In Sasanian times Zoroaster had come to occupy for the Persians much the same position as Moses occupied for the Jews, and the book that corresponded to the Taurah or the Injil was the selection of Zoroastrian Scriptures known to us as the *Zend Avesta,* some parts of which apparently go back to Zoroaster himself, though the greater part of the collection is much later.

These facts about the Persian religion were apparently well known at Mecca and Medina, for Muhammad apparently recognised sufficient likeness between it and the religion of the Jews and Christians, to include the Persians among the People of the Book[3], with the full understanding of his contemporaries.

(c)   *Eschatology*

The eschatological system of Zoroastrianism was highly developed, and it was this feature of Persian belief which exercised the profoundest influence on other religions. Its

---

[1] *Yasna* xxx (Ed. Note: The text of the Zoroastrian worship – also the name of the worship rite) reads "The two primal spirits who reveal themselves in vision as twins re the Better and the Bad in thoughts, word and action. And between these two the wise knew to choose right, the foolish not so".
[2] It is possible that here is the origin of the curious روح of the Qur'an.
[3] xxii:17.

influence on Jewish eschatology is well known[1]: it affected Gnosticism also[2] and exercised no little influence on Arabia.

Zoroastrianism taught a very picturesque doctrine of Heaven and Hell, peopled with Spirits of all sorts – amesha spentas, fravashis etc. and in the latter case ruled by a devil – Aka Manah – of the most realistic and powerful kind.

The most obvious contacts of Zoroastrianism with Islam are found in this eschatological sphere, a few examples of which must suffice.[3]

i. The Houris, the beautiful maidens of the Qur'anic Paradise, who figure so largely in the Muslim descriptions of the bliss of the hereafter that awaits the faithful[4], are apparently nothing but the starry light-spirits of the Zoroastrians. The Arabic word is حور, a plural of حوراة which commentators would derive from خَوِرَ = to have the black and white strongly delineated. It is hardly possible, however, that it can be from an Arabic root. Sale in his *Preliminary Discourse*[5] suggested that it was from Persian origin,[6] referring to the Paradise Behisht "where they believe the righteous shall enjoy all manner of delights, and particularly the company of the *Hurani behisht* or black-eyed nymphs of Paradise". His reference to *Sadder* paragraph 5, however, was unfortunate, for Dozy pointed out[7] that the Parsi source was of later date than the Qur'an and probably borrowed from it. Carra de Vaux suggested a Christian origin for the houries, thinking that Muhammad or his teachers may have seen Christian miniatures of mosaics representing Paradise, and

---

[1] Vide particularly Stave's *Einfluss des Parsismus auf das Judenthum,* Haarlem, 1898.
[2] Particularly among the Ophites, Vide Mansel's *Gnostic Heresies*, Lect vii.
[3] See further in Tisdall's *Sources of the Qur'an,* London, 1911, Chap v.
[4] Sura lvi.22ff: 34FF: and the description in *Mishkat al-Masabih,* Al-Tibrizi, xxiii par 13. Ghazali's *Ihya* iv.464. Bukhari *Sahih,* par. Sifat al-Janna, Wensinck's article "Hur" in *EI.* II. 337, excellently summarizes Muslim opinions.
[5] Edited Denison Ross, p 108.
[6] (Ed. *Handwritten note:*) Amir 'Ali recognises this Persian origin, vide *Spirit of Qur'an,* p394.
[7] *Het Islamisme,* Haarlem, 1880, p101.

mistook the angels for young women[1]. This, however, does not explain the word حور so that Tisdall goes back to a Persian source for its origin[2] and suggests that حور is equivalent to the modern Persian خور = sun, from an earlier sense "light, brightness". This is represented by the Pahlavi *hur*[3] and the Avestic *hvara* [4].

ii. The Bridge Sirat, which stretches over the abyss of fire and which all have to cross in their journey to the other world. The word صراط is used in the Qur'an many times but always in the sense of the "Right Way" in religion. Tradition, however, applies it to the bridge, which is said to be finer than a hair and sharper than a sword and hedged about with briars and thorns. When true believers come they pass over it quickly and in safety, but the unbelievers miss their footing and fall into the infernal fires. This is doubtless the Avestic *chinvatō – peretush*, the "bridge of him that reckons up" the deeds of good and bad, across which the spirits of the departed go after the funeral ceremonies to be judged whether worthy of admission into Paradise or to be cast in the fires[5]. The Arabic صراط, Tisdall would thus equate with the Avestic *chinvat*.[6]

iii. The *mi'raj* or the famous Night Journey of the Prophet, detailed in the Commentaries on the opening verses of Sura xvii and in many Traditions[7], which tells how he was taken to Jerusalem and then on the back of the fabulous steed Buraq up through the various heavens and into the very presence of God, seems to be founded in the main on the Zoroastrian story of Arta

---

[1] *EI*. I, 1050: Wensinck apparently approves of this suggestion: see his article "Hur" in *EI*, II.337. Grimme *Einleitung in den Koran,* Münster, 1895 p100 n.9 also thinks they are of Christian origin, but he suggests Muhammad's fancies about Paradise were due to a too literal interpretation of the images in the Hymns of Ephraem Syrus.
[2] *Source of the Qur'an,* p23.
[3] Vide Horn, *Grundries der neupersischen Etymologie,* par.505.
[4] Bartholomae *Altiranisches Wörterbuch,* p 1847ff.
[5] In the *Midrash Yalqut,* Reubeni, par. Gehinnom, we read of a bridge in hell no thicker than a thread over which idolators have to pass, but as this Midrash was only written in the Middle Ages, we cannot be sure that this particular feature is older than Islam.
[6] *Sources of the Qur'an,* p253. There is reason to think, however, that it is from Latin *strata* cf Fränkel *Vocabulis* sub voc.
[7] See collections in Sprenger, *Leben,* ii, 527ff.

Viraf[1], though the legend has apparently in its growth drawn in elements from various sources. In this story we read how Arta Viraf in a trance ascended into the heavens, where, under the guidance of the archangel Sarosh he passed from storey to storey, going up and up until at length he reached the very presence of Ormazd (ie. the later form of the name Ahura Mazda), who commanded him to return and tell all he had seen to the Zoroastrians.

iv. The Light of Muhammad which plays so important a role in Shi'ism and in the 'Alid sects that at different times have sprung up in Islam[2], would seem to find its origin in the *Kavaem Hoarene* or "Royal Brightness" of the Avesta.

---

[1] The story can be seen in Pope's *Ardai Viraf Nameh*, London, 1816, translated from the Persian and Gujrati verions: or with the Pahlavi text and translated in Haug and West's *Arda-Viraf Namah,* 1872.
[2] A simple account of these sects will be found in Sell's *Cult of Ali,* Madras, 1910, *(in the Islam Series).*

JUDAISM

The story of the Jews in Arabia is a complicated question which we are yet far from having satisfactorily elucidated. As one might expect from their geographical position, Jews for commercial and other reasons early penetrated into North Arabia. The theory of the Islamic antiquarians was that the settlement of the Jews in this area began at the time of Moses. In the *Kitab al-Aghani,* xix.94, we read how an expedition was sent by Moses to slay the Amalekites who were living at Yathrib. The expedition carried out these instructions, but supposing Moses to have paederastic tastes they saved alive as a gift for Moses a beautiful youth whom they found there. Moses was dead by the time they returned to Syria, and his successor, to punish them for not completely carrying out Moses' commands, drove them out of Syria[1]. Remembering the delights of the land of those Amalekites whom they had exterminated, they decided to return there and so formed the earliest Jewish settlement at Yathrib which was later joined by other bodies of exiled Jews[2] at the time of the Roman conquest of Syria[3].

Dozy, it will be remembered,[4] claimed that a body of Israelites in the time of Saul came down into the Hejaz and founded the Ka'ba. While there is nothing to be said in favour of Dozy's arguments, there is no a priori reason why Jews should not have penetrated so far even at that early period.[5] They seem to have

---

[1] Margoliouth *Schweich Lectures,* p60 takes this to be a confused eminiscence of the story of Saul and Agag in (The Bible) I Sam. xv. Notice the curious word מַעֲדַנֹּת (voluptuously) in v. 32.
[2] (Ed. *Handwritten note*:) Reinaud imagined that bodies of Jews had sought refuge in Arabia at the time of the Egyptian and Assyrian invasions of Palestine. In his *Notice zur Mahomet* Paris, 1860, p2 he says 'De bonne heure les Israélites, lorsque la terre qui leur avait été promise par Dieu lui-même fut envahie par les Égyptiens et les Assyriens, cherchèrent un refuge dans ces contrées d'un accés si difficile ...'.
[3] That the Jewish elements in Arabia received reinforcement at the Fall of Jerusalem is very probable. Vide Caetani *Annali,* I 383. Leszynsky *Die Juden in Arabien,* 1910, p6: Hirschfeld in *REJ* vii, (1883), p168.
[4] *De Israeliten te Mekka,* 1864, see infra p139.
[5] (Ed. *Handwritten note*) The story of Salman in Ibn Hisham 1(i) 40 assumes the presence of Jews at Wadi'i-Qina.

settled themselves mainly, however, in the oases of the North West at Hejra, el-'Ola (which is the ancient Dedan)[1] Taima,[2] Khaibar, Yathrib and Fadak.[3] The earliest references we have to Jewish settlements in Arabia are in the Mishna (Shabbat. vi. 6: Ohalot viii.10)[4] and from this source we learn that there were considerable settlements in the Hejaz shortly after the destruction of the Second Temple.[5] Palmer thinks that there were further considerable accessions in the time of Hadrian.[6]

From their settlements in the North West they appear to have followed the trade route southwards until they came to Yemen[7], though it is very likely that Jewish traders gained a footing in Yemen from the Egyptian side at an early period[8],[9] The problem of the Jews of Yemen is a complicated one.[10] The Ecclesiastical historians Philostorgius (*Ecclesiastical History* iii.5)[11] and Theodorus Lector (in Migne's *Patrologia,* lxxxv.211) know of Jews in South Arabia in the fifth century AD though whether they were

---

[1] On this question see Lidzbarski *Ephemeris,* iii, 273.
[2] Doughty *Arabia Deserta* I, 287ff mentions traces of the old ruins al Taima. Rösch, *Theologische Studien und Kritiken*: 1876, p412 calls Taima the 'syrisch-arabischen Grenzstaft'.
[3] Janssen et Savignac, *Mission* I, 150: 242ff.; Hartmann, *Der Islam,* 1909, p2.
[4] (Ed. Note): Jefffery's manuscript read Shab which is assumed to be short for Shabbat. Both Shabbat and Ohalot are sections within the Mishnah.
[5] (Ed. *Handwritten note:*) Nöldeke does not seem inclined to admit that these settlements of Jews could have attained any considerable size or importance before the invasion of Palestine by Titus and Hadrian. See his *Beiträge zur Kenntnis der Poesie der alten Araber,* Hanover, 1864. In *ZDMG* xli 720 he checks Wellhausen for overlooking the fact that we have express statements that the Jews of Medina were for the most part converted Arabs. Ya'qubi II 49 tells us the Nadir and on p52 that the Qainuqa belonged to the Jewish community. Jeffery added a further note, but it has not been possible to definitively decipher his writing.
[6] *Qur'an* (Ed. note. No details given of edition being referenced.) pxv.
[7] Grimme, *Mohammed,* p24.
[8] Caetani, *Studi di Storia Orientale,* I,261. For the Muslim account see Ibn Hisham pp13-15, and further *Aghani,* xiii, 119.
[9] (Ed. *Handwritten note.*) Nöldeke *ZDMG* xli insists that it is not impossible that the Jewish groups in the Yemen, in Abyssinia and among the Khazari may have carried on some propaganda in the Hijaz.
[10] Winckler has an important essay "Zur Geschichte des Judentums in Yemen" in AOF I p329-336.
[11] (Ed. *Handwritten note.*) ed. Bidez p 33 οὐκ ὀλίγον δὲ πλῆθος καὶ Ἰοθδαίων αὐτοις ἀναπέφυρται.

genuine Jews or only proselytes is a question still in dispute.[1] Later legend tells how, taking advantage of opportunities provided by the struggle between the Sabaean nobility and the crown, they gradually edged their way into positions of power and influence, so that eventually South Arabian Kings even accepted their religion. Thus at the beginning of the sixth century of our era we find in South Arabia a Jewish King named Dhu Nawas[2], who persecuted the Christians of Najran and was thus the cause of Axumite interference in South Arabian affairs. As there are Greek, Syriac and Ethiopic accounts of this Jewish persecution of Christians[3] and it is even referred to in the Qur'an[4], it would seem to have a sufficiently certain historical basis[5], though we cannot place any reliance on the details of the Arabic stories.

The main settlements of the Jews, however, which are referred to in Islamic times, are those around Yathrib, which later became Medina. The polemic of the Qur'an is over and over again directed against Jews who apparently formed part of the community in which the Prophet was living, and whom he assumes to be fairly well acquainted with the stories of Old Testament characters with whom he deals in the Qur'an. One would also gather from the Qur'an that they were a considerable and well-organized body within the community. The Muslim historians tell us particularly of three important Jewish tribes settled at or near Medina — the Banu Qainuqa[6], and the Banu Nadir in the north and the Banu Quraiza in the East.[7] They would appear from these accounts to

---

[1] Hartmann *Die Arabische Frage,* p45 seems to think they were proselytes.
[2] Vide *Religion in Geschichte und Gegenwart (RGG),* i.650: Leszynsky, *Juden in Arabien,* p8: Margoliouth *Schweich Lecutres*, p65ff.
[3] Fell in *ZDMG* xxxv.
[4] lxxxv.4ff.
[5] Havély, however, in *REJ* xviii (1889) doubted the story and the very existence of the King. Strong confirmation has recently been given to the history by the discovery of Syrian fragments published by Axel Moberg, *The Book of the Himyaritas,* Lund, 1924.
[6] (Ed. *Handwritten note.*) For the Hadal (هدل) see Ibn Hisham *Sira* 135 (Ed. Note: Banu Hadal, according to Ibn Ishaq, was a Jewish tribe (a sister tribe of Banu Quraizah).)
[7] Careful studies of the Arabic material have been made by Wensinck in his thesis *Mohammed an ed Joden te Medina,* Leiden, 1908 and by Hirschfeld in his "Essai sur

have been both agriculturalists and artisans, being specially mentioned as skillful jewelers and armourers. They had built forts and castles for themselves, and were of considerable influence, though apparently, they were not of a very high grade of intelligence.[1]

When we come to examine, however, this Arab account of the Jewish tribes, we are immediately in confusion. The Jews of whom we are told all bear Arabic names, and it is at least curious, that if they were real Jews and emigrants from Palestine, they should bear names containing the characteristic Arabic consonants.[2] Moreover these accounts represent them as divided into tribes like the Arabs, whereas when we meet with real Jews among the Muslims in Islamic days, there appears no consciousness that there had ever been any such tribal organisation among them. In the accounts we do not find any hint of peculiarly distinctive Jewish practices among them, and it seems hardly likely that Jewish emigrants would have so soon sunk to the level of the civilization of the Arabs around them. The great Jewish poet, Samau'al[3],[4] whose *Divan* has come down to us, apparently knows nothing of Judaism but talks like an Arab, even like a Muslim. Two solutions are possible. One is favoured by Winckler[5] and would suggest that these Medina Jews were not Jews by birth, but Arabs who had become proselytes to Judaism, and while accepting many of the higher ideas

---

l'histoire des Juifs de Médine" in *REJ*, vii and x. The student should also consult Leszynsky's *Die Juden in Arabian zur Zeit Mohammeds,* Berlin, 1910 and the section "Juden und Christen in Arabien" in Wellhausen's *Reste*, pp230-234, with Nöldeke's criticism in *ZDMG* XLI. 720 (This is to the first edition of Wellhausen but should be consulted nevertheless.)

[1] That is if we can believe the story of this futile kind of magical revenge they took on Abu Jubaila the Ghassanid, who defeated them in battle. Vide Hirschfeld in *JE* ii.42. On the other hand they are credited with having poets of their own of no mean order.

[2] (Ed. *Handwritten note.*) Nau, *Les Arabes Chrétiens* 114ff argues this question. Cf. also Bernard Heller, *REJ*, vol.84, 1927, pp.113-37.

[3] His *Divan* has been published by Cheickho, Beirut, 1920. On it see Margoliouth in *JRAS,* 1926.

[4] (Ed. *Handwritten note:*) Nöldeke *ZDMG* xli, 720 points out that though his name is clearly Jewish, he was of Arab blood according to the Arab traditon. *Kamil* 89. (Ed. Note:) There are several works by this name. Jeffery does not specify the work to which he is referring. Ibn Duriad 259, Hamara 54, cf *Aghani,* xix, 98.

[5] *MVAG,* vi, 222.

of the new faith, still kept up many of the old customs and habits of life, and continued to use the old names. The polemic of the Qur'an, however, would hardly fit in with this theory, for Muhammad assumes that his opponents are real Jews, acquainted with the Scriptures, observed the Sabbath and food regulations and paid undue reverence to their Rabbis. The second theory is that favoured by Margoliouth[1], which would solve the difficulty by admitting that they were real Jews, but that by the time the Traditions began to grow, the Jews had been driven from Arabia, all exact knowledge of them had been lost, and the Traditionalists in seeking to draw the picture of earlier times, had drawn the Jews on the model of the Arabs they knew, so that in the traditional accounts that have come down to us, the Jews of Medina speak and act and are named like Arabs.

It is unfortunate that we have so little information about the religion of these Jewish or Judaised communities of Arabia, for the influence of Judaism on early Islam was profound. The briefest examination of the Qur'an makes evident how very much Jewish material is embedded there and how strong the Jewish colouring of the whole book is. Earlier writers were so impressed by this that they treated Islam as though it were fundamentally a corruption of Judaism adapted to Arab mentality and needs. Some of the Jewish writers still tend to make Judaism the main sources of Muhammad's borrowing[2] though a more exact examination of the evidence has provided philological as well as historical reasons for thinking that a great proportion of the Jewish material in the Qur'an came through Christian channels.[3]

---

[1] *Schweich Lectures,* 1924, pp60-63.
[2] For example, Hirschfeld in his *Jüdische Elemente im Koran,* 1878, and *New Researches into the Composition and Exegesis of the Qoran,* 1902.
[3] The philological argument is conclusive. Many of the names of Old Testament (The Bible) characters must obviously have come through Christian channels and not directly from the Hebrew. Jonah is a good example. The Arabic يونس having come not from the Hebrew יוֹנָה but by some form influenced by the Greek Ἰωνᾶς. (Ed. Note. In this section Jeffery refers to both Syriac and Ethiopic words.) So اسرائيل is from Syriac 🕮 rather than from the Hebrew יִשְׂרָאֵל and ابراهيم from Syriac 🕮 rather than from אַבְרָהָם so with other words of a religious connotation. شيطان is obviously from the Ethiopian 🕮 and not Hebrewשָׂטָן : فرقان from 🕮 (Syriac) and not as Geiger and others have held

From general considerations based on the history of Jewish religion we should expect the form of Judaism exemplified by these communities in Arabia to be that labelled Talmudism. An examination of the Jewish material in the Qur'an confirms this judgment. It is well known that the question of *Tradition* is as important in the history of Jewish religion as it is in Islam, and as has often been pointed out, the study of *Tradition* as it existed and developed among the Jews, is of primary importance for the understanding of Muslim *hadith*.[1] Just when the traditional supplement to the Old Testament began among the Jews cannot now be ascertained, but, it was probably very early.[2] In the Old Testament itself, of course, we have the first results of an even earlier collection of oral traditions, as they are now embodied in the historical books. It was after Prophecy ceased, however, that these records became themselves the subject of traditional interpretation. Pious stories founded on hints in the stories of the Patriarchs or intended to 'fill out' the story by providing detailed information on points passed over in silence by the Biblical writers; collections of legal decisions deduced by Rabbinic subtlety from the somewhat vague legislation of the Pentateuch; fanciful creations exegesis working on difficult or obscure, or contradictory passages of the Book, all grew with rank luxuriance during the "night of Legalism", until as this great body of floating tradition became more and more unwieldy it was at last crystallized into the Mishna and Gemara. All this was later gathered together into the two Talmuds, the Babylonian and Jerusalem, which were compiled between the third and fifth centuries A.D.[3]

---

from פרקו: جهْنم from ﷺ and not (Pace, Geiger), גיהנם. (AB. I could probably solve the last two given a transliteration of the Syriac and Arabic terms. Very hard without.)

[1] Vide Margoliouth *Early Development of Mohammedanism*, 1914, p 67, Goldziher in *ZDMG* lxi, 865 and *Vorlesungen* (ed. Babinger 1925) p36, 37.
[2] Funk, *Entstehung des Talmuds,* Berlin, 1919 inclines to think it goes back to a very early age.
[3] The fundamental introduction to Talmudic study in Strack's *Einleitung in den Talmud*, 1894, 5th edition of which (München '21) is of even wider scope and bears the title, *Einleitung in Talmud und Midrash*. Fränkel's work above mentioned is a very useful little summary but it is too brief for any serious work. Zachariah Frankel's *Beitrage zur Einleitung in den Talmud*, 1861 *MGWJ*, 10, 1861, pp. 186-94, 205-12, 258-72 is still useful, but it deals only with the Babylonian collection.

From the time of its completion the Talmud became the great religious book of the Jewish communities, and we might thus naturally expect that it would be Talmudic lore which was most familiar to the communities of Jews with whom Muhammad was in contact. A very brief examination of the Jewish elements in the Qur'an suffices to show that this was so. It seems practically certain that Muhammad had no access to written sources,[1] and such oral sources as have left their results in the pages of the Qur'an and early Tradition are overwhelmingly of Talmudic or Midrashic character. Very little of Muhammad's Old Testament information comes directly from the Bible; in practically all its details it is drawn from Rabbinic sources.[2]

---

[1] The question is discussed in detail in Rudolph's *Abhängigkeit des Qorans von Judentum und Christentum,* Stuttgart, 1922, pp10-25.

[2] Details are given in Geiger's *Judaism and Islam,* Madras, 1898. We may quote here Tisdall's conclusion – "very much of the Qur'an is derived from Jewish books, not so much from the Old Testament (The Bible) scriptures as from the Talmud and other post-Biblical writings. Although the Arabian Jews doubtless possessed copies of their Holy Books they were not distinguished for learning, and then, as now, for the most part, they practically gave greater heed to their Rabbinical traditions rather than to the Word of God. It is not surprising therefore to find little real knowledge of the Old Testament in the Qur'an, though as we shall see, it contains a great deal of Jewish legend.", *Sources, p61-62*

CHRISTIANITY

The history of Christianity in Arabia is quite as obscure and far more complicated than that of Judaism and has received even less attention from scholarship. Thos. Wright in 1855 devoted to the subject an interesting essay, *Early Christianity in Arabia,* but he based his account on sources that are now known to be largely untrustworthy, his treatment was only partial, and he had no access to many other and better sources of information which are at present in our hands. His work is thus of mere antiquarian interest at present. The only other work exclusively devoted to the question is that of Jesuit scholar Cheikho's *Histoire du christianisme et de la littérature chrétienne en Arabie préislamique,* Beirut, 1912-22, written in Arabic, save for the French Prefaces. This work has gathered together a great mass of material, but this has been treated uncritically, and as a consequence many of the author's conclusions fail to carry conviction. As a matter of fact it may be doubted whether we are yet in a position to seriously undertake the work of writing a detailed history of Christianity in Arabia, for so many possible sources of information in the writings of Oriental Christians have hardly been explored, and at any time new accessions of material may profoundly alter our conclusions.

Christianity would appear to have penetrated Arabia from three sides, from Syria, from Mesopotamia and from South Arabia. We may perhaps quote the New Testament (The Bible) as evidence of Christian penetration from Syria as early as apostolic times, for though Paul's journey there was only a private one[1] it at least shows the Christian touch.[2] De Vogué found a Christian Chapel (*Kalybē*) in the Hauran, which is dated by its inscription as founded in the seventh year of the Emperor Probus, ie. 282AD[3] and it would show

---

[1] So McGiffert *History of Christianity in the Apostolic Age,* 1899, p161.
[2] Assuming that the Ἀραβία mentioned in Gal i:17 (The Bible) was to the South West of Damascus and not as Lightfoot (*Galatians,* 6th ed. 1880, p37 ff.) would have us believe, in Sinai.
[3] Vide Merrill, *East of Jordan,* p7.

that Christianity was widely recognised and firmly established in that region. By the time of the Council of Nicaea (325AD) Arabian Christianity was important enough to be represented by several Bishops.[1]

South Arabian Christianity was of Abyssinian origin in all probability, though Philostorgius tells us of one Theophilus being sent to Himyar by the Emperor Constantius (349-361) and who founded churches there.[2] From South Arabia it spread northward and was not unknown at Mecca and Medina. It will be remembered that Muhammad sent his persecuted followers to Abyssinia for refuge and there is a tradition that his earliest nurse, named *Umm Aiman*, was an Ethiopian slave.[3] The great centre of South Arabian Christianity seems to have been Najran, and it was the Christian community of Najran which suffered so much at the hands of the Jewish persecutor Dhu Nawas.[4]

Christianity would seem to have been widely spread among the Arabian tribes, for we hear of many of them as being nominally Christian. We have already noticed the spread of Christianity among the great pre-Islamic Arab Kingdoms of Kinda, Ghassan and Hira[5], and noticed that the 'Ibadites of Hira may be considered to have given the Arabs their alphabet. Information about these Christian communities would have gone further still into the peninsula, for the early poets not infrequently refer to the lonely hermits in the deserts.[6] The Qur'an bears witness to the division of Christians into sects[7] and to the undue authority exercised by the monks among them[8] and the indolent lives of ease led by these same monks.[9] Their priests are mentioned with approbation[10], and we

---

[1] Details are given by Wright, op cit. p73.
[2] *Compendium Historiae Ecclesiasticae*, iii. 4.
[3] Abulfeda *Vita Mohammedis* p2.
[4] The Christian sources for this story are discussed by Möberg in his *Book of the Himyarites*, Lund, 1924, pxxivff.
[5] Infra p76ff.
[6] See quotations in Bell *Origin of Islam in its Christian Environment*, (no page given).
[7] xix.38; ii.254; v.17.
[8] ix.31.
[9] lx.34: the passage lvii.27 would seem to show that he thought Monasticism contrary to the spirit of Jesus.
[10] v.85: *ZDMG.* xlvi. 44.

hear of their converts and churches.¹ The presence of a picture of the Virgin and the Child in the Ka'ba mentioned by Agraqi², is probably to be explained as having been brought by some Christian tribe as its contribution to the national pantheon of Arabia.³

Still though widely spread in pre-Islamic Arabia, Christianity there does not seem to have been of a very high type. Margoliouth refers to it as "seed sown on stony ground, whose product had no power of resistance when the heat came".⁴ Jacob has made the very interesting suggestion that Christian ideas and customs were spread through Arabia by the curious channel of the liquor traffic and wine shops.⁵ It is certain at any rate that a large number of the Arabic words connected with wine and wine traffic were borrowed from Christian sources.⁶ It was also spread by means of literary culture, for not only would the spread of the alphabet from the home of the 'Ibadites help in this direction, but there were apparently many Christian poets,⁷ and scholars of the rank of von Kreme, Wellhäusen and Sir C. Lyall, think that the poetry of the pagan Arabs has been very largely influenced by Christian ideas.⁸

---

¹ صوامع = convents and بيع = churches in xx.41.
² (Ed. note)– Jeffery did not indicate the work to which he was referring.) Wüstenfeld p112; also Ya'qubi, ii.62. The picture was of Mary with Jesus on her knee and was on the central pillar to the right of the door. It is said to have remained there until the time of the reconstruction of the Ba'ba by Al-Hajjaj. It is held by Demombynes (*Mekke*, p113) that the Sacred Mosque itself is architecturally but an adaptation of a Christian church.
³ Infra p140.
⁴ *Mohammed*, p35: see also his remarks on pp37-39.
⁵ *Das Leben der vorislamischen Beduiner*, 1895, p99: cf also Wellhäusen *Rests*, 231: Winckler, *Arabisch-Semitisch orientalisch*, 1901, pp47, 50, 129: and Grimme, *Mohammed*, 1904, p47.
⁶ Eg. حانوت wine shop from Syriac ▦ (cf. Nöldeke *Neue Beiträge* p48: عنب grape from Syriac ▦. Cf. Hebrew עֵנָב Schwally *Idioticon* p70; Fränkel, *Fremdwörter*, p156: Lagarde *Übersicht*, p51ff, p153); خمر wine, from Syriac ▦ related to the Aramaic חַמְרָא and Hebrew חֶמֶר (cf. Guidi *Sede*, p42; *Fremdwörter* of Fränkel, pp160, 161: Bell *Origin of Islam*, p43n, p145.)
⁷ Imru' l-Qais of course is the best known. Cheikho in his *Christian Arabic Poets* has diligently collected material but all that he has gathered can hardly be accepted as Christian.
⁸ Vida Nicholson, *Literary History*, p139: Wellhausen *Reste* p233: Lyall *Ancient Arabian Poetry*, p61-73 in "Ancient Arabian Poetry as a Source of Historical

North Arabian Christianity was probably Nestorian, and it is doubtful whether any save[1] heretical sects were represented in Arabia. Hirschfeld even thinks that it was the eternal quarrelling of these different Christian sects that prevented Christianity from making any headway among the Arabs. In any case it is certain that the Christian communities in Arabia were not exempt from the general corruption of the Church in the East at this time. Mosheim[2] writing of this period says –

> During this century true religion lay buried under the senseless mass of superstitions, and was unable to raise her head. The earlier Christians had worshipped only God and His Son: but those called Christians in this century worshipped the wood of a Cross, the images of holy men, and bones of dubious origin. The early Christians placed Heaven and Hell before the view of men: these latter talked only of a certain fire prepared to purge away the imperfections of the soul. The former taught that Christ had made expiation for the sins of men by His death and blood: the latter seemed to inculcate that the gates of heaven would be closed against none who should enrich the clergy of the Church with their donations. The former were studious to maintain a holy simplicity and to follow a pure and chaste piety: the latter placed the substance of religion in external rites and bodily exercises.

The morality of the people would appear to have been almost as degraded as their religious cult. The Christian cities of Syria and Palestine were often sinks of iniquity and the monkish chronicler[3] of the horrors of the Persian conquest of Palestine in 614AD after giving a black picture of the sins and wickedness of the age, proceeds to demonstrate that the Persian conquest with all its horrors was a divine visitation on the Christians to punish them for their iniquities.

Information", *The Journal of the Royal Asiatic Society of Great Britain and Ireland*, 1914, Jan., pp. 61-73
[1] (Ed note:) Jeffery's use of 'save' in this context follows the traditional meaning of 'except'.
[2] *Ecclesiastical History,* Mosheim, ed Maclean(e), 1833, p164
[3] *Acta Martyrii S. Athanasii Persae*

Moreover, just as contemporary Arabian Judaism was Talmudic rather than Biblical[1], so Arabian Christianity would seek to have fed on the Apocryphal writings rather than on the New Testament. Consequently, we find that the Christian material included in the Qur'an is almost entirely taken from Apocryphal sources[2] and even from ecclesiastical legend.[3]

The trend of recent scholarship is to consider that the Christian influence on Muhammad, was far more profound than that of Judaism, and not on Muhammad only, but also on the early development of Islam.[4] It is therefore all the more tragic that Muhammad was apparently unable to come into contact with pure Christianity. Christianity had a wonderful opportunity in Arabia at the birth of Muhammad. Even a witness so prejudiced against Christianity as Gibbon, testifies that had there been a strong, vigorous, spirited Christian life in the East at that time, there would have been no Islam beyond the confines of Arabia, nor we venture to suggest, within them either. As it was, Muhammad found a Christianity divided against itself, one party persecuting to the death another party over points of creed or ritual, a Christianity superstition-ridden, honouring the creature more than the creator, and more interested in this world than in the next. Accordingly, though profoundly influenced by its teaching and accepting very much of its religious organisation of life, he preferred to strike out a new line of the religion of the Arabs, a line more suited to the accomplishing of his ends and in accordance with his own nature. Thus it is not untrue to say that the present Muslim problem is really

---

[1] Leveen, referring to this in an article "Mohammed and his Jewish Companions" in *JQR*, xvi, 399ff says – *"In reading the Koran one cannot help feeling – so gross is the ignorance Mohammed displays when he touched on Jewish matters – that some of the Jews in Mecca and Medina must have indulged in rather malicious leg-pulling. One can hardly explain the distortions of the Bible and rabbinical literature in the Koran otherwise."* (p401).
[2] Rudolph classifies all the possible contacts with the New Testament (The Bible) in pp13-17 of his *Abhängigkeit*. Among the Apocryphal sources used are the *Gospel of the Infancy, Proto-evangelium of James, Gospel of Thomas*.
[3] As in the case of the Legend of the Seven Sleepers. Sura.xvii
[4] Vide Goldziher *Muhammedanische Studien,* for the large Christian elements in the Hadith: Becker *Christianity and Islam,* 1909 for Christian influences on the later development of the system: Tor Andrae "Der Ursprung des Islams under das Christentum" in *Kyrkohistorisk Årshrift*, vol xxiii, Upsala, 1924, pp149-206: Bell's *Origin of Islam in its Christian Environment*, London 1926

the result of the failure of Eastern Christianity in the seventh and eighth centuries to witness truly to the light and truth it had known.

APPENDICES

TABLE of CONTENTS

APPENDICES

A COMPARATIVE TABLE	229
TIMELINE	231
BYZANTIUM AND THE KINGS OF AXUM	235
EPIPHANIUS COMMENT	237
ETHIOPIAN WAR ELEPHANTS	238
LANE-POOLE – POETICAL CONTESTS	239
PERSIAN INTERVENTION IN YEMEN	240
PRE-ISLAMIC CONTACTS WITH PERSIA	242
REVENUE FROM PILGRIMAGE CROWDS	243
THE PROBLEM OF THE PROPHET HUD	244
ZOROASTRIANISM	248

A COMPARATIVE TABLE
OF EARLY SOUTH ARABIAN KINGDOMS

Date / Kingdom	1000	900	800	700	600	500	400	300	200	100	100	200	300	400	500	600
	Before Common Era BCE (Before Christ BC)										Common Era CE (Anti Domini AD)					
KINGDOM																
MINAEAN				?						150?						
SABAEAN	?	*1										275?				
KATTABANIAN				?						110?						
HADRAMAUT				?												
HIMYRAT									*2	110?	*3?				*4	?

? indicates date is uncertain.

[1] Queen of Sheba (Saba'?) visits King Solomon whose dates are estimated to be 970 to 931 BCE.
[2] Himyrat was part of the Kattabanian Kingdom till about 110BC
[3] Dhu Nawas died (525/7)
[4] Estimated to have ended about 520CE

TIMELINE

The following table is a combination of the historical details given by Jeffery in the course of his notes on the Prolegomena with several other important dates added. The various empires or dynasties that he mentioned are identified by the bracketed letter after the name. Rather than indicate the beginning and ending of a reign, the span of a ruler's influence has been kept.

(A) Abyssinian: (G) Ghassan: (L) Lakhmid:
(J) Jurham: (S) Sasanian

BC\BCE

74-44	Jurhum (J)
44-14	'Abd Yalil ibn Jurhum (J)

COMMENCEMENT OF Anno Domini (AD) or COMMON ERA (CE)

AD\CE

16 (CE)	Jurhum ibn 'Abd Yalil (J)
16-46	Abd al Madan ibn 'Abd Yalil (J)
46-76	Bakila ibn 'Abd al-Madan (J)
76-106	'Abd al-Masih ibn Bakila (J)
120	Dam of Marib (Yemen) bursts
106-136	Mundhir ibn 'Abd al-Masih (J)
136-170	'Amr ib Madhadh (J)
?[1]	Harith ibn Mundhir (J)
?	'Amr ibn Harith (J)
?	Bishr ibn Harith (J)
170-206	Mundhir ibn 'Amr ibn Mundhir (J)

---

[1] Ed. Note: Question marks indicate that there is some uncertainty concerning the relevant details.

192(?)	First Arab migration to Hira
226	Ardeshir (S)
272-300(?)	'Amr I ibn 'Adi (L)[1]
325	Council of Nicea (B)
349-361	Constantine (The Great) (B)
? -328	Imru'l-Qais ibn 'Amr (L)
328-358	'Amr II ibn Imru'l-Qais (L)
330	Constantinople founded (B)
337-361	Constantine II (B)
358-363	Aus ibn Qallam (L)
363-388	Imru'l-Qais II (L)
386 – 450	Nestorius (B)
395	Death of Theodosius: Byzantine Empire Divided (B)
388-418	Nu'man I ibn Imru'l-Qais (L)
418-462	Mundhir I, ibn Nu'man (L)
431	Council of Ephesus (B)
431-518	Anastasius (B)
451	Council of Chalcedon (B)
462-482	Al-Aswad ibn al-Mundhir (L)
475	Eastern Roman Empire (Byzantine)
482-489	Mundhir II b. Mundhir I (L)
489-503	Nu'man II b. al-Aswad (L)
(?) 500	Amr ibn 'Arm Mozaiqiya Jafna (G)
503-505	Abu Ya'fur ibn 'Alqama (L)

---

[1] (Ed. *Handwritten note.*) Herzfelt, *Paikuli,* 136ff; 140ff has suggested that this 'Amr b. 'Adī is the אמרו of the Paikuli inscription whose reign would then have been c272-300 AD and H. H. Schaeder, "Rezension von Schmidt und Polotsky, Ein Mani-Fund", Gnomon 9 (1933), 337–362 in *Gnomon* ix (1933) thinks that the same 'Amr is the Αμαρω of the new Coptic Manichaean documents.

505-554	Mundhir III ibn Ma'as-Sama (L)
517-525(?)	Dhu Nawwas, Ruler of Himyar Kingdom
518-565	Justinian
521	Himyarites revolt against Abyssinian control
523/524	Massacre of Christians at Najran
525	Christian Kingdom of Axum in Ethiopia invades Yemen to redress killing of Christians (A)
(?) – 528	Abu Khamir el-Harith ibn 'Amr Jabala (G)
528-569	Al-Harith ibn Jabala (G)
541	Al Harith ibn Jabala (G) defeated al Mundhir, King of Hira (L)
554-569	Amr ibn Hind (L)
569-573	Qabus (L)
569-581	Al-Mundhir (G)
570/1	**Birth of the Prophet**
570	Chosroes overthrew Abyssinian rule in S Arabia (S)
570	Al-Mundhir (G)
570	Battle of the Elephants
573-580	Mundhir IV (L)
581	An-Nu'man (G)
558(?)	Harith the young, 'Amr ibn al-Harith. (G)
580-602	Nu'man III, Abu Qabus (L)
610(?)	**Prophet receives revelations**
613	**Prophet begins to proclaim his message**
613/614(?)	Ghassanid Empire ends: Syria captured by Chosroes Parwiz (S)
614	Sasanians captured Jerusalem (B) (S)
622	**Emigration to Medina**

628	Chosroes II (Sasanian) control of South Arabia ended
629	Heraclius triumphed over Persian army (B) (S)
632(?)	**Prophet Muhammad dies**

BYZANTIUM AND THE KINGS OF AXUM

At the time of Justinian, Ethiopia had a long coastline on the Red Sea. The Byzantine emperor at that time, being no longer in a position to spare ships for the patrolling of the Red Sea to keep down the pirates who had almost inaccessible haunts in the difficult inlets along the reef-bound coasts, to whose entrance they alone had the secret, caught the idea of using the Ethiopians subject to the Axumite Kingdom as his auxiliaries to undertake the policing of the Red Sea[1], at least in its lower end.

In 522 Justinian urged the king of Axum, Hellesthaeus, to extend his control to the Arabian kingdoms on the eastern side of the Red Sea, that this policing might be the more effective for being exercised over the harbouring places of the pirates on both coasts. He also urged him to extend his power northward on the Arabian side till he dominated the trade route that passed through Mecca, thus providing a check against Persian influence which was already supreme on the eastern coast, and had pushed into the south, and was likely to endeavour to extend around from the south to the Red Sea coast.

One Julian, was sent by the Emperor, as his envoy to Axum, and he was successful in inducing the king to undertake the South Arabian expedition.

Muslim tradition tells that the deciding factor was the desire to avenge the slaughter of the Christians of Nejran by the Jewish tyrant Dhu Nawas, who slaughtered the governor Arethas and numerous citizens. When news of this reached Justinian he instructed Timothy III, the Patriarch of Alexandria, to instruct Caleb, king of Axum, to invade the Arabian territory in a punitive expedition. This was done and a son of the murdered Arethas placed upon the throne. This narrative assumes that the king of Axum was a Christian and recognized Byzantine overlordship.

---

[1] (Ed. Note:). The Red Sea extends from the Cape of Muhammed on the Sinai Peninsula to the Bab el-Mandeb on the Arabian side or the Horn of Africa on the African side.

In Nicephorus Callistus, however, we have quite another story. Here we learn that the king of Axum was a pagan, but on hearing of the atrocities of Dhu Nawas, he swore that if the Christian God would help him to overthrow this tyrant, he would become a Christian. Both John of Asia and the Letter of Simeon of Beth Arsham refer to such a vow, so there may be some truth of an Ethiopian pagan chieftan being concerned in the matter.

It is noteworthy that after this date the Byzantines withdrew entirely from the patrolling Red Sea, and left that absolutely in the hands of the Auxumites, so that from 522 or thereabouts onward Axum is the dominant naval power in the Red Sea, and as such practically controlled the seaborne trade with India and the East.

EPIPHANIUS COMMENT

A copy of Jeffery's handwritten note.

Note that Epiphanius (....)[1] in *Haereses* li.22 after telling of the festival in Alexandria for Κορή (Kore) who gave birth to the Aion, says,

Τοῦτο δὲ καὶ ἐν Πέτρᾳ τῇ πόλει (μητρόπολις δέ ἐστι τῆς Ἀραβίας), ...ἐν τῷ ἐκεῖσε εἰδωλίῳ οὕτως γίνεται, καὶ Ἀραβικῇ διαλέκτῳ ἐξυμνούσι τὴν παρθένον, καλοῦντες αὐτὴν Ἀραβιστὶ χααβού,[2] τούτεστιν Κόρην, εἴτ᾽ οὖν Παρθένον, καὶ τὸν ἐξ αὐτῆς γεγεννημένον Δουσάρην, τουτέστιν Μονογεγῆ τοῦ Δεσπότου.

---

[1] It would appear that Jeffery was going to add further details later.
[2] (Checked by AB – Greek editor) This I will leave as it is, as probably intentional, despite my source reading 'χααμοῦ'.
Source is
https://www.google.com.au/books/edition/Librorum_adversus_haereses_prooemium

ETHIOPIAN WAR ELEPHANTS

They were used as shock assault troops in the Ptolemanic armies. Under Ptolemy Philadelphus and Ptolemy Euergetes, we learn that there was a special effort to recruit these elephant auxiliaries. There was a place Ptolemais in the land of the Troglodytes (Troglodytica)[1] where the elephant hunters had their rendezvous. The great beasts were embarked in special vessels. This was concentrated at the port of Berenice on the Arabhaitos Gulf (Red Sea[2]). This traffic in elephants is witnessed by the papyrus, the inscriptions and the geographers but little by little fell into disuse.

See note of Abel in *RB*, 1938, p517

---

[1](Ed. Note:) Berenice or Berenice Troglodytica, also known as Baranis, is an ancient seaport of Egypt on the west coast of the Red Sea. It is situated about 825 km south of Suez and 260 km east of Aswan in Upper Egypt. (Wikipaedia)

[2] (Ed. Note:) It would appear that the Arabhaitos Gulf is more frequently known as the Red Sea.

LANE-POOLE – POETICAL CONTESTS

Taken from *Studies in a Mosque*, London, 1883, p21. He writes of it –

It served as a focus for the literature of all Arabia: everyone with any pretensions to poetic power came, and if he could not himself gain the applause of the assembled people, at least he could form one of the critical audience on whose verdict rested the fame or the shame of every poet. The Fair of 'Okadh was a literary congress, without formal judges, but with unbounded influence. It was here that the polished heroes of the desert determined points of grammar and prosody: here the seven golden songs were recited ... and here a magical language, the language of the Hejaz was built out of the dialects of Arabia and made ready to the skilful hand of Mohammad ... the Fair of 'Okadh was not merely a centre of emulation for Arab poets: it was also an annual review of Bedawy virtues. It was there that the Arab nation once a year inspected itself so to say, and brought forth and criticised its ideals of the noble and the beautiful in life and in poetry. For it was in poetry that the Arab expressed his highest thoughts, and it was at 'Okadh that these thoughts were measured by the standard of the Bedawy ideal. The Fair not only maintained the highest standard of poetry that the Arabic language has ever reached, it also upheld the noblest ideal of life and duty that the Arab nation has yet set forth and obeyed'. op cit p20.

PERSIAN INTERVENTION IN YEMEN

Quoted from J. H. Mordtmann's article [1]
"Miscellen zur himjarischen Alterthumskunde", p69
Zeitschrift der Deutschen Morgenländischen Gesellschaft
Vol. 31, No. 1 (1877), pp. 61-90 (30 pages)

    Diese nahmen aber mit dem bald darauf erfolgten Starz der abessycischen Herrscaft durch die persische Occupation ein rasches Ende. Unter Justinus II (565-578 AD) geland es Chosroes II, den Sanaturces, König der Homeriten, gefangen zu nehmen (Theophanes Byz. FHG. T. IV p 279). Johannes Epiphaniensis (ib. p 273) redet von den Versuchen der "Meder", die Homeriten abtrünnig zu machen. Es gab dies den Römern Anlass den Persern den Krieg zu erklären, während diese andrerseits den Römern vorwarfen, die Homeriten gegen sie zu interstützen und zu dem Zecke den Julianus an Arethas, König von Aethiopien (see footnote for name in script.)[2] der Königslisten?) abgesandt zu haben (Theophanes I, 377). Es ist wohl keinem Zweifel unterworgen, dass diese versprengten Notizen der Byxantiner sich auf den behannten Zug des Vahraz وهرز, Feldherrn des Anuschirvan gegen die Abessynier in Jemen richten; der Commentar der himjarischen kaside und Bekri in dem angeführten Werke geben richt ausführiche und interessante Date über diese Zeit.

See account in Tabari I, 946-958

(Translation of the above with thanks to Michael Bräutigam[3]
However, this came to a swift end with the rise of Abyssinian rule through the Persian occupation. Under Justinus II (565-578 AD) it was possible for Chosroes II to capture the Sanaturces, king of the Homerites (Theophanes Byz. FHG. T. IV p. 279). Johannes Epiphaniensis (cf. p 273) speaks of the attempts of the "Medes" to make the Homerites apostate. This gave the Romans an opportunity to declare war on the Persians, while on the other hand they accused the Romans of supporting the Homerites against them and sending Julianus to Arethas, King of Ethiopia (the lists of kings?) (Theophanes I, 377). There is no doubt that these scattered notes of the Byzantines refer to the known procession of Vahraz وهرز*, general of Anuzhirvan against the Abyssinians in Yemen;*

---

[1] This quote was handwritten in Jeffery's manuscript.
[2] (Ed. Note:) Jeffery had included the Ethiopian script here.
[3] Director Centre for Theology and Psychology, Melbourne School of Theology

the commentaries of the Himjarian 'kaside' and Bekri in the cited work give very detailed and interesting dates about this period.

PRE-ISLAMIC CONTACTS WITH PERSIA

Meccan merchants carried their business ventures into Sasanian territory
> *Aghani* vi:93
> Abri Sufyam sent caravans with merchandise of the Quraish *Ila auf al 'Ajam*

Ibn Hisham 938 1.2 seems to be aware of military excursions into Persian territory

> Al A'sha, the poet journeyed in Sasanian territory and there were doubtless others

> Al Hira thought it was an Arab court 'im veritable tableau de la vie persani.'

A great many Persian words and expressions are to be found in the old Arab poetry.

> Also, there is contemptuous rejection of the Persian way of life, which shows acquaintance with it.
> See G. Jacob, *Altarabisches Beduinenleben*, p239, Goldziher, *Muhammedanische Studien. vol 1,* p102

> 'Adi bin Hajar (Hujr) (ed Geyer no. xxiv 1 (line?) 2 uses the term *farisiyya* as an insult to his enemy

> On brother-sister marriage as a wrong - see E Kuhn in *ZDMG,* xliii, p618

Also, Persian merchants had established themselves in Arab Territory

We know of Persians exploiting the gold mines in Arabian Territory. Glaser, *Skizze,* II, p193

Some Arab tribes in the Persian Gulf region had accepted Persian nationality. See Goldziher, *Muhammedanische Studien.* Vol 1, p102 n4

REVENUE FROM PILGRIMAGE CROWDS

Various little things point in this direction, though we have no actual economic details preserved to us.

Note

(1) The story of Meccan jealousy of Araha's cathedral at San'a, and their state of panic when the Abyssinian general marched on the Ka'ba to destroy it, even if it is only a story, yet illustrates the consciousness of the Arabs of that time of the dependence of Mecca in pre-Islamic days on the Pilgrimage, and they were in a position to know.

(2) The phrasing of Sura cvi seems to point to Mecca being kept in plenty by the Pilgrimage.

(3) The inability of pious Khalifas to abolish the taking of dues from pilgrims in Islamic time, is fairly sure proof that the custom was established long before the rise of Islam. When one remembers the barrenness of the situation any suggestion of wealth from agriculture is impossible, and Margoliouth has pointed out (*Mohammad*, p13) that it was only the sanctity of the neighbourhood of the temple that rendered it a suitable place for the arts of peace. There is, however, continuous tradition as to the wealth of the Quraish from trading, and it has been suggested it was this trade that tempted Abraha to attempt its conquest. Margoliouth. (op cit. p 393) points out that it was the Prophet by his interference with the Calendar, who ruined Mecca trade. (But see also *ERE* viii. 511, where he considers that their carrying trade must have been on a small scale.)

THE PROBLEM OF THE PROPHET HUD

The problem of this Prophet Hud is a very interesting one. In the Qur'an we find Muhammad claiming that no other Prophet had been sent to the Arabs before himself (xxviii.46: xxxii.2: xxxiv.43: xxxvi.5) which makes it the more remarkable that we find such frequent mention of Prophets like Hud and Salih. There have been many conjectures as to the identity of Hud.

1   Muir suggested that both Hud and Salih were contemporary and local Jewish or Christian reformers who had been rejected by their people, and whose experiences were fresh in Muhammad's mind when he was brooding over his own rejection by the Meccans.

An objection to Muir's hypothesis is, how, that Muhammad refers to the people of 'Ad to whom Hud was sent, as a people in the distant past, like the people of Noah who are sometimes mentioned along with them.

2   Geiger in *Judaism and Islam,* pp 88-92 equates him with the Biblical Eber. The grounds he gives for this identification are:

(a) among the Arabs هود or يهود is the equivalent of the late Hebrew יהודי which represents an earlier עִבְרִי from עֵבֶר = Eber, as says the Midrash Rabba on Genesis, par 42, commenting on Genesis xi: 14-17 (The Bible).

(b) Marraccio (*Prodromus ad Refutationem Alcorani,* iv.92) quotes the author of the work اعلام الهدى as saying distinctly that "Hud is عابر" so the Arabic tradition supports the identification. (We might add to Geiger's evidence here that of Mirkhond *Rauzat us-Safa* (tr Rehatsek) i.98. There is a tradition, however, that he was the son of عابر vide Tha'labi *Qisas,* ed. Cairo ١٣٣٩ p43 also Kisa'i, *Qisas* (ed. Eisenberg, Leiden, 1922) p103 gives quite a different origin.

(c) The circumstances of Eber's life correspond with those of Hud as described in the Qur'an.

i. He was a Prophet guided by the Holy Spirit. Seder 'Olam in Midrash Yalqut. Cap.lxiui on Gen x.25 (The Bible) says

נָבִיא גָדוֹל הָיָה עֵבֶר שֶׁקִּרֵא אֶחָד־שֵׁם בְּנוֹ פָּלֶג בְּרוּחַ הַקֹּדֶשׁ שֶׁכְּ׳ כִּי בְיָמָיו נִפְלְגָה הָאָרֶץ[1]

ii. He lived in a time when God sent a second punitive expedition to punish men for their bold and impudent behaviour. The Torah reads כִּי בְיָמָיו נִפְלְגָה הָאָרֶץ and this division is taken to be the dispersion of the peoples (the דּוֹרהֵפְלָגָה of the Rabbis) at the building of the tower of Babel. So, the words of Sura xxvi.128

تَبْنُونَ بِكُلِّ رِيعٍ آيَةً تَعْبَثُونَ

may refer to the building of the tower.

iii. The builders of Babel were idolaters, for the Rabbis tell us that they desired to put an idol on the top of their tower. (Vide Gen. R[2] xxxviii.2 70: *Tanhuma*,[3] Noah, xxvii). The people to whom Hud went were also idolaters (Sura xi.54ff)

iv. The people of 'Ad according to Sura xi.63 were to be followed by a curse both in this life and the next:-

وَأُتْبِعُوا فِى هَذِهِ ٱلدُّنْيَا لَعْنَةً وَيَوْمَ ٱلْقِيَامَةِ

so the Rabbis say in *Mishna Sanhedrim,* that because the dispersion from Babel is twice mentioned, it seems that they have no part in the next world as well as being cursed in this:

דּוֹר הַפְּלָגָה אֵין לָהֶם חֵלֶק לָעוֹלָם הַבָּא שֶׁנֶּאֱמַר וַיָּפֶץ ה׳ אוֹתָם מִשָּׁם עַל פְּנֵי כָל־הָאָרֶץ. וַיָּפֶץ ה׳ אוֹתָם, בָּעוֹלָם הַזֶּה. וּמִשָּׁם הֱפִיצָם ה׳, לָעוֹלָם הַבָּא[4]

v. Nimrod is connected with the building of the tower (D'Herbelot *B.O.* sub voc.) and there is perhaps a reference to this

---

[1] Checked by AB with aid of Gen. x:25 (The Bible) & https://www.sefaria.org/Radak_on_Genesis.10.25.3?vhe=Presburg_:_A._Schmid,_1842&qh=%D7%A4%D6%B6%D7%9C%D6%B6%D7%92%20%D7%91%D6%BC%D7%A8%D7%95%D6%BC%D7%97

[2] (Ed. Note:) Have not been able to trace this reference.

[3] (Ed. Note:) Apparently there are several *Tanhuma*. We have not established which of the *Tanhuma* refers to Noah.

[4] Checked by AB: reference: https://www.sefaria.org/Mishnah_Sanhedrin.10.3?lang=bi

Nimrod in Sura xi.62. In Gen x:25 (The Bible) Nimrod is described as גִּבּוֹר which would equate with the Arabic جبار.

Geiger's arguments from this Rabbinic material strike us as very artificial. Note

(i) The extreme artificiality of the equation עֵבֶר = هود. It is more probable also that עִבְרִי is not from עֵבֶר but from עָבַר to pass over (see Geden, *Introduction to Hebrew Bible*, p47).

(ii) The impossibility of the phrase "the earth was divided in his day" bearing the weight of the structure Geiger builds on it. It is doubtful, indeed, if the division there mentioned has any reference at all to Babel. Driver (*Genesis*, 1920, p130) thinks it may refer to the spread of Noah's descendants over the earth after the flood: Ryle (*Genesis* 1914, p243) sees it in reference to the separation of the Northern Semites from the Southern: and Sayce (*Expository Times*, 1897), from an identification of פלג with the Assyrian *palgu* = *canal*, would look on it as a reference to the division of Babylonia under Hammurabi into a number of canal zones.

(iii) Rabbinic tradition is a very unsafe guide at the best, and the tradition of Eber being a prophet is not of any great weight even among the Jews, eg König in his article on *Eber* in *JE* does not even mention it.

(iv) Not all Arabic sources give the genealogy in the Biblical form: eg. Baidawi gives

بن عبد الله بن رباة بن خلود بن عاد بن عوص بن ارم

then going on to Shem and Noah.

(3) Hughes (*Dictionary of Islam*, art *Hud*) equates him with the Biblical Heber of Judges iv:11 (The Bible). He quotes D'Herbelot as the authority for this identification, but this is a mistake, for D'Herbelot in his art. *Houd* (*B.O.* 263) takes him, as Geiger does, as equivalent to the Eber of Gen x:25. This is also Pocock's view, vide *Specimen* 36.) This Heber חבר was a Kenite, the husband of the famous Jael (King of Hazor), left his family and pitched his

tent in the plain of Zaanain. There does not seem to be anything to support this identification.

(4) Hirschfeld considers him a mythological figure. In his *Beiträge zur Erklärung des Koran,* Leipzig, 1886, he writes (p17, n.4) –

> *Vergleichen mit ii, 105 scheint Hud ursprünglick kein Eigenmame, sondern vielleicht nur eine allego rische Figure zu sein".*

His point is that in this and parallel passages the word هود is used for the Jews as a race, and the root هَوَدَ is used with the meaning "to profess Judaism" (eg in iv. 48). It looks as though the name is Muhammad's own invention made up from these lexical elements. The meaning of the name he gives in his *New Researches*, p62, as "penitent", هود being plural of هائد. The later traditional identification of هود with عابد would seem to point to some consciousness of the connection between هود with يهود. Wensinck in *EI*, ii, 327 agrees with this.

(5) Von Kremer in his essay *Über die südarabische Sage,* Leipzig, 1866, p21, suggests that the crater of Barahut in Hadramaut, with its strong sulphurous smell may be the origin of the whole story.

It is at least interesting to note that local tradition says that the souls of unbelievers gather here at night and wail: that the alleged tomb of Hud is nearby this spot at Qabr Hud.[1]

Other traditions, however, say that his tomb is at Damascus, or near the Ka'ba: It is the most important centre of pilgrimage in South Arabia, where people gather to make remembrance of the Prophets Noah, Abraham and others.

---

[1] (Ed: *Handwritten* note:) Ibn Sa'd i.25 says that the tombs of only three Prophets are known. That of Muhammad; that of Ishmael in Mecca, the tomb of Hud which 'lies among the sand dunes' beneath a mountain in Yemen on which is a tree and it is the hottest place on earth.

ZOROASTRIANISM

Called المجوسيه *al-majusiyya* in Ibn Hisham 137, in the story of Salman al Farisi. But this name is derived from the Qur'anic مجوس.

He uses the term قطن النار for one who served the sacred fire to keep it from going out.

Baladhuri *Futuh* 69 assumes the existence of Magians in the Yemen.
    ibid 71 the Prophet collected poll tax from the Magians of Hajar and the Magians of al Yaman.
    ibid 77 assumes the presence of Magians in 'Uman.
    ibid 78, 79 discusses the poll tax for the Magians in Bahrain & 79ff for the Magians of Hajar whom some thought were not people of the Book.
    ibid 85 many Magians who had assembled in al Qalif that had refused to pay tax.

Ibn Qutaiba *Ma'arif*, (Eg. ed. p305) says it had spread among Tamun and mentions the name Zararah b 'Adi and his son Hajib, Al-Aqra' b Hadris, Abi Siid the grandfather of Watii b Hassan.

The story of Khalid b Sinan al 'Abri in Mar'udi *Muruj* i. 131, 132 suggests the spread of Magianism among the Arabs.

The story of the poetical context between 'Imru'l Qais and al Yashkuri shows that the poets had a knowledge of the Zoroastrian fire ever burning. See Ibn Rahiq, *'Umda,* I, 135; Shariqati *Inshad* p11.

Zoroastrians in Arabia (from an additional sheet included by Jeffery)

'Umar would not accept *jizya* from a Magius (majus) till he heard the testimony of ' Abd ar Rahman b. 'Arif that the Prophet had accepted it from the Magian of Hijz.
Al Tayalisi no. 225

BIBLIOGRAPHY

NOTES

Both the Western (CE/AD) and Muslim dating systems (AH) are used.

There has been no attempt to Anglicise the names of towns or publishers where these differ from their English equivalents.

In addition, there has been no attempt to standardize Arabic transliterations. While most names and titles have been taken from Jeffery's work, the details of most of these references have been copied from various internet sources, though mainly from archive.com or world catalogue. It is not clear if Jeffery used one of the standardized forms of transliteration such as those adopted by modern publishing houses.

* indicates that there appears to be no further details available regarding this work or the edition to which reference is being made.

? indicates that there is uncertainty as to whether this is the edition of the volume that Jeffery referenced. A question mark in front of the author's name indicates that there is uncertainty regarding the author and the full name of the work

(xxxx) A date in brackets indicates that there appears to be a discrepancy between the date of publishing as mentioned by Jeffery and that which appears in current catalogues or on the various internet sites.

Further:
Since this is a work of historical relevance, the Bibliography has been set up by author, with the date of publication occurring first. That is, an author's works have been listed on the basis of the date of publication.

While every attempt has been made to accurately reproduce Jeffery's reference material, it has not always been possible to ensure the work has been correctly identified. In some cases, the information is incomplete.

"A"

Abd Al-Razzaq al-Hasani
  1948, *Iraq; Old and New*, Sidon
Abu al-Fida' Isma`il ibn `Ali `Imad al-Din
  *The Concise History of Humanity or Chronicles (**Tarikh al-Mukhtasar fi Akhbar al-Bashar*) or *History of Abu al-Fida*
  1723, *De vita, et rebus gestis Mohammedis: moslemicae religionis auctoris et imperii saracenici fundatoris,* ed. Jean Gagnier; Sheldonian Theatre, Oxoniae: E theatro Sheldoniano
  1831, *Historia ante-Islamica,* trans. Heinrich Lebercht Fleischer, Lipsiae: F.C.G. Vogel
  1888, *Actes du sixième Congrès International des Orientalistes,* Leiden, E. J. Brill
* *Acta Martyrii S. Athanasii Persae*
Aghani, Kitab al- (The book of Songs), see Al-Isfahani
Ahlwardt, Wilhelm, ed.
  1870, *Diwans of the Six Ancient Arabic Poets:* Nābigah al-Dhubyānī; Antarah ibn Shaddād; Ṭarafah ibn al-`Abd.; Zuhayr ibn Abī Sulmá. London, Trübner & Co
Ahmad ibn Hanbal
  *Musnad
Al-A`sha or Maymun Ibn Qays Al-A`sha
  *(no work named)
Al-`Ayni, Badr al-Din
  1308/1890-1, `*Umdat al-qari fi sharh al-Bukhari,* (11 vols.) Cairo
Al-Baghawi, Husayn b. Mas'ud
  Tafsir al-Baghawi also known as *Ma`alim al-Tanzil*
Al-Baidawi (Qadi Baydawi (also known as Naṣir ad-Din al-Bayḍawi, or Baidawi, Bayzawi and Beyzavi)
  Anwar al-Tanzil wa-Asrar al-Ta'wil
Al-Baladhuri, 'Aḥmad ibn Yaḥya
  *Kitab Futuh al-Buldan
Al-Balkhi
  1899-1919, *Book of Creation* ed Marie-Clément Imbault-Huart *Le livre de la création et de l'histoire* (ed. and trans. of *Ketab al-bad' wa'l-ta'rik* of Moṭahhar b. Ṭaher Maqdesi [Moqaddasi], 6 vols., Paris,

Al-Baladhuri, 'Ahmad ibn Yahya
**Kitab Futuh al-Buldan*
Al-Balkhi
1899-1919, *Book of Creation* ed Marie-Clément Imbault-Huart *Le livre de la création et de l'histoire* (ed. and trans. of *Ketab al-bad' wa'l-ta'rik* of Motahhar b. Taher Maqdesi [Moqaddasi], 6 vols., Paris,
Al-Bayhaqi, Shaykh Imam Abi Bakr Ahmad
1324, *Dalail -un- Nubuwwah - 3 Volumes,* Haidarabad
Al-Biruni, (alt spelling Beruni or Birunis, Muhammad ibn Ahmad)
1879, *The Chronology of Ancient Nations: An English Version of the Arabic Text of the Athar-ul-Bakiya of Albîrûnî, Or "Vestiges of the Past".* Trans. Eduard Sachau, London, W. H. Allen and Co.
1910, *India* Vol. 1-2, ed. Edward C. Sachau, London, Kegan Paul, Trench & Trubner
1910 (?) *Kitab al-Biruni, (Alberundi)* ed Edward C Sachau, London, Kegan Paul, Trench, Trübner
Al-Bukhari, Muhammad ibn Isma`il
**Sahih*
Al-Fakhri
1895, *Histoire du khalifat et du vizirat, depuis leurs origines jusqu'a la chute du khalifat `Abbaside de Bagd adh* (II-656 de l'hégire=632-1258 de notre ére), avec des prolégomènes sur les principes du gouvernement, ed Hartwig Darenbourg, Paris, É. Bouillon
Al-Fihrist, see ibn Ishaq
Al-Ghazali, Ahmad
Ihya' `ulum al-din (The Revival of the Religious Sciences)
Al-Hamdani, Abu Muhammad al-Hasan ibn Ahmad
Sifat Jazirat ul-Arab
1884, *Sifat Jazirat ul-`Arab,* (Geography of the Arabian Peninsula), Alte Geographie Arabiens, ed. *D. H. Müller,* Leiden,
(?)Ali ibn al-Athir
*1231(AH), *Tareekh Kamil (The Complete History)*
Al-Isfahani, Abu al-Faraj `Ali b. al-Husayn
**Kitab al-Aghani* (The book of Songs)
Al-Khazin

Tafsir al-Khazin with Tafsir al-Nasafi
Al-Kisa'i
   1922-23, *Vita prophetarum: auctore Muhammed ben `Abdallah, ex codibus qui in Monaco, Bonna, Lugd. Batav., Lipsia et Gothana asservantur. Kisa'i, Muhammad ibn `Abd Allah, 11th cent.*, ed., I. Eisenberg, Leiden, E.J. Brill
   Qisas al-anbiya,
Al-Mahalli, Jalal al-Din and Jalal al-Din al-Suyuti
   Tafsir al-Jalalayn
Al-Maidani, 'Ahmad b. Muhammad
   (1892?) *Majma` al-Amthal*, Cairo, A.H. 1310.
Al-Mas`udi, Ali ibn al-Husayn
   Kitab al-tanbih wa al-ishraf (The Book of Notification and Verification)
   1861-1877, *Murūj al-dhahab wa ma`ādin al-jawhar*, ed. and trans. C. Barbier de Meynard and Pavet de Courteille as *Les prairies d'or*. 9 vols. Paris: Imprimerie Imperiale and Imprimerie Nationale
Al-Nabighah, (al-Nabighah al-Dhubiyani, or Nabighah al-Dhubyani; real name Ziyad ibn Muawiyah)
   Mu`allaqat
Al-Nasafi, Najm ad-Din Abu Hafs 'Umar ibn Muhammad
   (no indication as to work being referenced.)
Al-Nawawi, Abu Zakaria Yahya Ibn Sharaf
   (?)*
Al-Qalqashandi, Ahmad ibn `Ali
   Nihayat al-Arab
   1879, *Die Geographie und Verwaltung von Ägypten*. trans. Ferdinand Wüstenfeld
Al-Samaw'al Bin `Adiya
   1920, *Diwan al-Samaw'al riwaayat Abi `Abd Allah Niftawayh*, ed. Louis Cheikho, Beyrouth (Beirut) Imprimerie Catholique
Al-Shahrastani, Taj al-Din Abu al-Fath Muhammad ibn `Abd al-Karim
   1846, *Kitab al–Milal wa al-Nihal* (lit. *The Book of Sects and Creeds*) ed William Cureton in Books of *Religions and Philosophical Sects*. 2 vols. London, Society for the Publication of Oriental Texts
   1851, *Abu-'l-Fath Muhammad asch-Schahrastani's*

Religionspartheien und Philosophen-Schulen, trans. Theodor Haarbrücker. - Theil 2: *Die Sabäer, die Philosophen, die alten Araber und die Inder*: Halle, Schwetschke
Al-Shinqiti, Ahmad b. al-Amin
 *c. 1329 (AH), *al-Mu`allaqat al-`ashr awi 'l-qasa'id al-`ashr al-tiwal*, later reprinted with the title *al-Mu`allaqat al-`ashr wa-akhbar shu`ara'iha*, C. 1345
 *1331 (AH), *Al-Mu`allaqat al-`Ashr wa-Akhbar Qa'iliha*, Cairo
Al-Suyuti, Jalal al-Din
 Itqan fi `ulum al-Qur'an (Mastery in the Sciences of the Qur'an)
Al-Tabari, Abu Ja`far ibn Jarir
 Tarikh al-Rusul wa'l-Muluk (Annals)
 Jami` al-bayan `an ta'wil ay al-Qur'an, popularly Tafsir al-Tabari
 1869, *Chronique de Tabari,* Abu-Ǧa`far Muḥammad Ibn-Ǧarir Ibn-Yazid aṭ-Ṭabari, trans H. Zotenberg, Paris, Imprimerie impériale
Al-Tabrizi (at-Tabrizi)
 Mishkat al-Masabih
Al-Tha'labi, Abu Isḥaq Aḥmad Ibn Muḥammad Ibn Ibrahim
 1339 (AH) (1920), *Ara'is Al-Majalis Fi Qisas Al-Anbiya* (Lives of the Prophets), Cairo
Al-Tirmidhi, (?) Al-Ḥakim al-Tirmidhi
 (?) Abu `Isa Muḥammad ibn `Isa as-Sulami ad-Darir al-Bughi at-Tirmidhi
Al-Wasit
 (?)1925, Cairo
Al-Ya`qubi, Ahmad ibn Abu Yaqub ibn Ja`far ibn Wahb ibn Wadih
 1883, *Historiae*, ed. M. T. Houtsma, vols. 1–2. Leiden
Ali, Syed Amir (Ameer)
 1889, *A Short History of the Saracens,* London, Macmillan
 1902, *The Spirit of Islam,* or the Life and Teachings of Mohammed, Calcutta, S K Lahiri & Co
Antara (Antarah) ibn Shaddad
 ? *Mu`allaqa*
Amedroz, Henry F., ed.
 1904, *The Historical Remains of Hilal al-Sabi'*: first part of his Kitab al-wuzara (Gotha Ms. 1756) and fragment of his

history, 389 - 393 A.H. (B.M. Ms, add. 19360) by Hilal Ibn-al-Muḥassin al-Sabi', Leiden, Brill
Ameer Ali Syed, see Ali Syed Amir
An-Nadim (al-Nadim), see ibn Is'ḥaq Ibn al Nadim
Andræ, Tor Julius Efraim
1926, *Der Ursprung des Islams und das Christentum,* Uppsala: Almquist & Wiksell
Andreas, Friedrich Carl
1916, *Festschrift Friedrich Carl Andreas zur Vollendung des siebzigsten Lebensjahres am 14. April 1916,* Leipzig: O. Harrassowitz
Angus, Samuel
1919, *Environment of Early Christianity,* Duckworth, London
1925, *The Mystery Religions and Christianity, A study in the religious background of early Christianity,* London
Appian of Alexandria
Civil Wars, see White
Arnold, T.W. & R.A. Nicholson, ed.
1922, *A Volume of Oriental Studies Presented to E. G. Browne on His 60ᵗʰ Birthday,* Cambridge University Press
Arrian
*The Anabasis of Alexander
Athanasius
*Historia Arianorum
Athenaeus
(no indication of work being referenced)
Autran, Charles
1925, *Sumérien at Indo-Européen, L'aspect morphologique de la question,* Paris, Geuthner
Azraqī, (Azraki) Muḥammad ibn `Abd Allāh
1858-1861, *Kitab akhbar Makkah wa ma ja'a fiha min al-athar,* trans. H. F. Wüstenfeld, *Chroniken der Stadt Makka,* iv vols, Leipzig

"B"

Baasten, Martin F.J.
2003. A Note on the History of "Semitic". In *Hamlet on a Hill: Semitic and Greek Studies Presented to Professor T. Muraoka*

on the Occasion of His Sixty-Fifth Birthday, eds. M.F.J Baasten and W.Th. van Peursen, 57–72. Leuven: Peeters
Babinger, Franz Carl Heinrich, see Goldziher
Baethgen, Friedrich
    1888, *Beiträge zur semitischen Religionsgeschichte: der Gott Israel's und die Götter der Heiden,* Berlin: H. Reuther's Verlagsbuchhandlung
Baghawi, see Al-Baghawi
Baidawi, see Al Baidawi
Bakker, Frederik Lambertus
    1922, *De Verhouding tusschen de Almacht Gods en de zedelijke Verantwoorde lijkheld von den Mensch in dem Islam,* Amsterdam, Drukkerij Holland
Baladhuri, see al-Baladhuri
Ball, Charles James
    1913, *Chinese and Sumerian,* London: Oxford University Press
(?)Bar Hebraeus (Barhebraeus or Gregory II, Abu'l-Faraj bar Ahron)
    **Chronicon Syriacum* (*Chronieon*)
Bartholomae, Christian
    1847, (1904), *Altiranisches wörterbuch,* Strassburg, Trübner
Barton, George Aaron
    1902, *Sketch of Semitic Origins, Social and Religious,* New York, Macmillan Co
Baudissin, Wolf Wilhelm, Graf von
    1878, *Studien zur semitischen Religionsgeschichte*, vol II, Leipzig, W. Grunow
Becker, Carl Heinrich
    (?)1909, *Christianity and Islam* (*Christentum und Islam*) (1907) transl H. J. Chaytor, London, Harper & Brothers
Bell, Richard
    1926, *Origin of Islam in its Christian Environment,* London, Macmillian and Co
Bent, James Theodore
    1896, *The Sacred City of the Abbyssians: Being a Record of Travel and Research in Abyssinia in 1893*
Bent, J. Theodore, Müller, David Heinrich, Garson, J. G.
    1896, *The Sacred city of the Ethiopians*, Longmans, Green and Co

Benzinger, Immanuel
    1907, *Hebräische Archäologie,* Tübingen, Mohr
Berger, Phil
    1885(?) *L'Arabie avant Mahomet, d'après les inscriptions,* Paris
Bergmann Friedrich Wilhelm (Frédéric Guillaume),
    1834, *De religione Arabum anteislamica.* Argentorati: Typis F. G. Levrault
Bezold, Carl
    1894, *Semitistische Studien Ergänzungshefte zur Zeitschrift für Assyriologie,* Berlin: Emil Felber
Bezold, Carl, ed.
    1906, *Orientalische Studien, Festschrift Theodor Nöldeke* zum 70 Geburztstag gewindmet, vol 1&2, A. Töpelmann
Bezold, Carl, Budge, E. A. Wallis, Sir
    1892, *The Tell el-Amarna tablets in the British Museum with autotype facsimiles,* London
Bickell, Gustav, ed.
    1873–77, *Sancti Isaaci Antiocheni, doctoris Syrorum, opera omnia,* 2 vol., ("Complete Works of Holy Isaac of Antioch, Doctor of the Syrians"), Giessen
Bidez, Joseph Marie Auguste, see Philostorgius
Berundi, (Birundi) Muḥammad ibn Aḥmad, also see Al-Berundi
    1910 (?) *Kitāb al-Bīrūnī, (Alberundi)* ed. Edward C Sachau, London, Kegan Paul, Trench, Trübner
Blair, John C.
    1925, *The Sources of Islam,* The Christian Literature Society for India, Madras
Blau, Lajos
    1898, *Das Altjüdische Zauberwesen,* Strassburg, K. Trübner
Blochet, (Gabriel Joseph) Edgard
    1902, *La Culte d'Aphtoditā – Anahita chez les Arabes du Paganism,* Paris
Bochart, Samuel
    1646, *Geographia Sacra seu Phaleg et Canaan,* Caen
Boissacq (Boisacq,) Émile
    1916, *Dictionnaire étymologique de la langue grecque, étudiée dans ses rapports avec les autres langues indo-européennes,* Heidelberg, C. Winter
Brandt, Wilhelm

1889, *Die Mandäische Religion: Eine Erforschung der Religion der Mandäer in theologischer, religiöser, philosophischer und kultureller Hinsicht dargestellt.*, Leipzig
1893, *Mandäische Schriften*, Göttingen: Vandenhoeck und Ruprecht
1912, *Elchasai: ein Religionsstifter und sein Werk; Beiträge zur jüdischen christlichen und allgemeinen Religionsgeschichte*, Leipzig, J.C. Hinrichs

Breasted, James Henry
c1909 (1920), *History of Egpyt from the earliest times to the Persian conquest,* New York, Scribner

Brinton, Daniel G.
1890, *Cradle of the Semites, Two papers read before the Philadelphia Oriental Club.* Philadelphia
1901 (1890 – New York), *Races and Peoples: Lectures on the Science of Ethnography*, Philadelphia, David McKay

Brockelmann, Carl
1908/1913, *Grundriss der vergleichenden Grammatik der semitischen Sprachen.* Band 1–2, Berlin, von Reuther & Reichard
1916, *Semitische Sprachwissenschaft*, Berlin: G.J. Göschen

Browne, Edward Granville
1908, *A Literary History of Persia,* London, T. F. Unwin
see Arnold also for volume on Oriental Studies

Brünnow, Rudolf-Ernst, and Alfred von Domaszewski
1904-1909, *Die Provincia Arabia: auf grand Zweier in den Jaahren 1897 und 1898 üntornommenen Reisen und der berichte früherer Reisender,* vol 3., Strassburg: Trübner

Bryce, James
1922, *International Relations*, New York, Macmillan

Budge, E. A. Wallis, Sir and Bezold, Carl
1892, *The Tell el-Amarna tablets in the British Museum with autotype facsimiles,* London

Bukhari, see al-Bukhari, Muhammad

Burkitt, Francis Crawford
1925, *The Religion of the Manichees: Donnellan Lectures 1924. Cambridge*, Cambridge University Press

Burton, Richard Francis
(?) *The Arabian Nights,* Club Edition

1855, *Personal Narrative of a Pilgrimage to Al-Madinah and Meccah,* London, Longman, Brown, Green and Longmans
1879, *Gold Mines of Midian,* London, C. Kegan Paul & Co.
Bury, J. B. et al., ed.
1911, *Cambridge Ancient History,* vol 1 & 2, Cambridge, Cambridge University Press
(?)Bury, J.B., Gwatkin, Henry Melvill, Mary Bateson, and G.T. Lapsley (Eds)
1911-1936 *Cambridge Medieval History* vol 9-11 Cambridge University Press and Macmillan
Butler, Alfred J.
1902, *Arab Conquest of Egypt,* Oxford, Clarendon Press
Buxtorf, Johannes
(?) *Lexicon Chaldaicum, Talmudicum, et Rabbinicum*

"C"

Caetani, Leone
1907, *Annali dell'Islam,* (multi volumes) Milano, U. Hoepli
1911, *Studi di storia orientale Vol. 1 Islám e Christianesimo - l'Arabia preislamica, gli Arabi antichi,* Milano Hoepli
(Ed. Note: It is assumed that this is the version of Caetani's words to which Jeffery is referring.)
Caldwell, Robert
1856, *A comparative grammar of the Dravidian, or South-Indian family of languages,* London: Harrison; Reprinted London, K. Paul, Trench, Trubner & Co., Ltd., 1913
Cambridge Medieval History,
1913, *The Rise of the Saracens and the Foundation of the Western Empire,* Vol. II, Cambridge, University Press
Cantineau, Jean
(Ed. note:) There are records of several books attributed to Cantineau using the word *Lexique* in the title. Jeffery does not indicate to which book he is referring.)
Caskel, Werner
1950, *Das altarabische Königreich Lihjan,* Krefeld, Scherpe Verlag
Caussin de Perceval, Armand Pierre

1847, (1902) *Essai sur l'histoire des Arabes avant l'Islamisme, pendant l'époque de Mahomet, et jusqu'à la réduction de toutes les tribus sous la loi musulmane,* Paris F. Didot
Chabot, Jean -Baptiste; J F Loubat,
1922, *Choix d'Inscriptions de Palmyra,* Paris, Publié aux frais Du duc de Loubat
Chabot, Jean -Baptiste; Charles Clermont -Ganneau
1905, *Répertoire d'épigraphie sémitique,* Académie des inscriptions & belles-lettres (France) Commission du Corpus inscriptionum semiticarum
Cheesman, Major R.E.
1926, *In Unknown Arabia,* London, Macmillan
Cheikho, Louis (born Rizqallah Cheikho)
(?) 1888, *Les poètes arabes chrétiens.* (Arab Christian Poets) *Poètes antéislamiques. Qouss, évêque de Najran,* dans *Études religieuses...,* Paris, [s.n.]
1912-22, *Histoire du christianisme et de la littérature chrétienne en Arabie préislamique,* Beirut, (written in Arabic)
1912-1923 *L'Histoire du Christianisme dans l'Arabie pré-islamique,* vol 1 - 3, Beyrouth: Imprimerie Catholique
1912, Volume 1 - *L'histoire du Christianisme dans l'Arabie préislamique.* Beyrouth: Imprimerie Catholique
1913, 1919, *Le Christianisme et la littérature chrétienne en Arabie avant l'Islam,* (3 vol.), Beyrouth, Imprimerie Catholique
1923, Volume 2 - *La littérature chrétienne dans l'Arabie préislamique.* Beyrouth: Imprimerie Catholique
Chwolson (also Khvol'son), Daniil Avraamovich
1856, *Die Ssabier und der Ssabismus,* St. Petersburg: Buchdruckerei der Kaiserlichen Akademie der Wissenschaften
Clay, Albert Tobias
1819 (1919) *The Empire of the Amorites,* New Haven, Yale University Press
1822, *A Hebrew Deluge Story in Cuneiform,* New Haven, Yale University Press
1909 (1915) *Amurru the Home of the Northern Semites,* Philadelphia, The Sunday School Times
1923, *The Origin of Biblical Traditions: Hebrew legends in Babylonia and Israel,* lectures on Biblical archaeology delivered at

the Lutheran theological seminary, Mt. Airy, Philadelphia, New Haven, Yale University Press
Clement of Alexander
*Exhortation to the Heathen
Clermont-Ganneau, Charles
1888, *Recueil d' Archéologie Orientale,* Paris, E. Leroux
Cook, S.A., W. Robertson Smith, Ignaz Goldziben, new ed., 1907(?) 1903, Kinship and Marriage in Early Arabia, London
Cook, S. A., J.B. Bury, F.E. Adcock (Eds) Vol 1-8, 2nd ed.
1928, *Cambridge Ancient History,* Cambridge, University Press
Cooke, George Albert
1903, *A Textbook of North-Semitic Inscriptions; Moabite, Hebrew, Phoenician, Aramaic, Nabataean, Palmyrene, Jewish,* Oxford, Clarendon Press
Compendium Historiae Ecclesiasticea
1680, *Prostat apud Salomonem Reyherum exscriptus à Christophoro Reyhero*
Contenau, Georges
1922, *La Civilisation Assyro-babylonienne,* Paris, Payot
Cosmas Indicopleustes
(?)1909, *Topographia Christiana* [*Christian Topography*]: Edited with Geographical Notes by E.O. Winstedt, University Press
Cumont, Franz Valéry Marie
1908, *Recherches sur le manichéisme,* Brussels
Cureton, William (ed)
1846, *Kitab al-milal wa-l-nihal,* by Muhammad al-Shahrastani; Book of religious and philosophical sects, London
Curtiss (also spelt Curtis), Samuel Ives
1902, *Primitive Semitic Religion Today,* Chicago, Fleming H. Revell

"D"

d'Herbelot, Barthélemy

(?)1776, *Bibliotheque orientale*, Maestricht: J.E. Dufour & Ph. Roux
(?)1777, *Bibliotheque orientale*, La Haye: J. Neaulme & N. van Daalen
Dalman, Gustaf
   1908, *Petra und seine Felsheiligtümer*, Leipzig, J.C. Hinrich
Davidson, Andrew Bruce
   1904, *The Theology of the Old Testament*, Edinburgh, T & T Clark
de Bauvais, Vincent (Vincent of Beauvais (Latin: *Vincentius Bellovacensis* or Vincentius Burgundus)
   Speculum Historiale
de Faye, Eugene
   1913, *Gnostiques et Gnosticisme, Etude critique des documents du Gnosticisme chrétien aux IIe et IIIe siecles* Paris, Ernest Leroux, Editeur
de Goeje, Michael Jan
   1870-1893, *Bibliotheca Geographorum Arabicorum*, Leiden, E. J. Brill
de Lacouperie, Terrien, ed.
   1886-1887, *Babylonian and Oriental Record, vols I & ii*, London, Nutt
de Lagarde, von Paul
   1889, *Uebersicht über die im Aramäischen Arabischen und Hebräischen übliche Bildung der Nomina*, Göttingen, Dieterich,
Delaporte, Louis-Joseph
   1923, *La Mésopotamie, les civilisations babylonienne et assyrienne*, Paris: La Renaissance du Livre
Delitzsch, Freidrich
   1881, *Wo lag das Paradies? Eine Biblisch-Assyriologische Studie*, Leipzig: J. C. Hinrichs'sche Buchhandlung
   1902, *Das Buch Hiob*, Leipzig, J. C. Hinrichs
Delitzsch, Friedrich & Paul Haupt, ed.
   1881–1933, Assyriologische Bibliothek, Leipzig, J. C. Hinrichs'sche Buchhandlung (a multi-volume work)
   1882, *Het Vaderland der Semitische Volken*, (307th Dies Natalis Lecture, University of Leiden)
   1891, *Feestbundel aan prof. M. J. de Goeje op den 6den October*1891 *aangeboden door eenige oud-leerlingen*, Leiden, E.J. Brill

de Meynard, C. Barbier and Pavet de Courteille, ed. and trans.
> 1861-1877, *Murūj al-dhahab wa ma`ādin al-jawhar*, Al-Masudi, Ali ibn al-Husayn ibn Ali as *Les prairies d'or*. 9 vols. Paris: Imprimerie Imperiale and Imprimerie Nationale

Demombynes, Maurice Gaudefroy-Demombynes
> 1923, *Le Pèlerinage à la Mekke: étude d'histoire religieuse*, Paris, P. Geuthner

de Morgan, Jacques, Daniel Fouquet; Alfred Wiedemann; Gustave Jéquier, ed.
> (?) 1897, *Recherches sur led Origines de l'Egypte*, Paris, Ernest Leroux, vol ii

de Perceval, see Caussin de Perceval

Derenbourg, Hartwig
> 1905, *Recueil de mémoires orientaux:* textes et traductions publiés par les professeurs de l'École Spéciale des Langues Orientales Vivantes à l'occasion du XIVe Congrès International des Orientalistes réuni à Alger, Paris: Impr. Nationale

de Slane, William MacGuckin, see Ibn Khaldun

Deutsch, Emanuel
> 1873, *Der Islam,* Berlin, F. Dümmler

Deville, Louis-Georges
> 1894 (1898), *Palmyre: souvenirs de voyage et d'histoire*, Paris, E. Plon, Nourrit et Cie

de Vogüé, Melchior, Marquis
> 1909, *Florilegium: ou, Recueil de travaux d'érudition dédiés à monsieur le marquis Melchior de Vogüé à l'occasion du quatre-vingtième anniversaire de sa naissance, 18 octobre 1909,* Paris:

de Vogüé, Melchior, marquis and Waddington, W. H.
> 1865, *Syrie centrale. Architecture civile et religieuse du Ier au VIIe siècle*, Paris, J. Baudry

Dictionary of Greek and Roman Geography, ed, William Smith
> 1878, London, J. Murray

Diehl, Charles
> 1901, *Justinien et la civilisation byzantine au vie siècle,* Paris, Ernest Leroux
>
> 1919, *Byzance, grandeur et decadence*, Paris, Flammarion

Dillmann, Christian Friedrich August
> 1857, *Grammatik der Äthiopischen Sprache,* Leipzig, T.G. Weigel (Ed. Note: assumed as the text being referenced)

Dio Cassius
   Roman History (History of Rome)
Diodorus Siculus
   Bibliotheca historica
Dionysius of Tell-Mahre
   1895, *Chronicon Pseudo Dionysianum Vulgo Dictum* vol I & 11, ed, J. B. Chabot, Paris
   1927, *Chronicle* ed. J. B. Chabot, *Chronicon Pseudo Dionysianum Vulgo Dictum I & II.* Louvain: L. Durbecq
Diyarbekri, Husayn ibn Muhammad
   1884, *Tarikh al-Khamis* (Tareekh Khamees and Tareekh-e-Khamees), Cairo
Dorner, Isaak August and William Lindsay Alexander
   1861, *History of the Development of the Doctrine of the Person of Christ*, Edinburgh, T & T Clark
Double, Lucien
   1877, *Les Césars de Palmyre,* Paris, Sandoz et Fischbacher
Doughty, Charles Montagu
   1921, *Arabia Deserta,* London, Philip Lee Warner
Dozy, Reinhardt
   1864, *De Israelieten te Mekka* ("The Israelites at Mecca"), Haarlem, A.C. Kruseman
   1864, *Die Israeliten zu Mekka* von Davids Zeith, (German translation), Leipzig
   1888, *Acts du sixiéme Congree des Orientalistes,* Leiden, E.J. Brill
   1880, *Het Islamisme*, Haarlem, Willink
   1912, (1913) *Spanish Islam, A History of the Moslems in Spain*, London, Chatto Windus
Drapeyron, Ludovic
   1869, *L'empereur Héraclius et l'Empire Byzantin au vii. siècle,* Paris, E. Thorin
Driver, Samuel Rolles
   1874, (1881) *A Treatise on the use of Tenses in Hebrew*, Oxford, Calrendon Press
   1920, (1905) *The Book of Genesis*, London, Methuen
Duchesne, L. (Louis),
   1905, *Églises séparées,* Paris, A. Fontemoing
Dussaud, René
   1900, *Histoire et religion des Nosairîs,* Paris, É. Bouillon

1907, *Les Arabes en Syrie avant l'Islam*, Paris, Ernest Leroux
1921, *Les origines cananéennes du sacrifice Israélite*, Paris, Ernest Leroux

"E"

Eichhorn, Johann Gottfried
    1781, *Repertorium für biblische und morgenländische Litteratur* Vol. VIII, Leipzig: Bei Weidmanns Erben und Reich
Eickmann, W,
    1908, *Die Angelologie und Dämonologie des Korans in Vergleich zu der Engel – und Geisterlehre der Hl Schrift,* Leipzig
Eisenberg, Isaac, ed
    1922-23, *Vita prophetarum: auctore Muḥammed ben `Abdallah al-Kisāʾi,* ex codibus qui in Monaco, Bonna, Lugd. Batav., Lipsia et Gothana asservantur. *Kisāʾi, Muhammad ibn `Abd Allāh, 11th cent.*, Leiden, E.J. Brill
Ephraem Syrus
    (Ed. Note: no indication as to which work has been referenced)
Epiphanius of Salamis
    Epitome (?)
    Panarion (*Adversus Haereses*)
Eratosthenes
    (Ed. Note: no indication as to which work has been referenced.)
Erman, Adolf
    1894, *Agyptische Grammatic, mit schrifttafel, litteratur, lesestücken und wörterverzeichnis,* Reuther & Reichard
Essai sur l'histoire des Arabes, see Caussin de Perceval
Euangelides
    1903, Ἡρέκλειος ὁ Αὐτοκρατω του Βυζαντίος Odessa
Euhemerus also spelled Euemeros or Evemerus
    (Ed. Note: no indication as to which work has been referenced)
Eusebius of Caesaria
    Historia Ecclesiastica (*Church History*)
Eusthathius, Epiphaniensis

1841-1873, *Fragmenta Historicorum Graecorum,* (ed Karl Mueller, Theodor Mueller and Victor, Paris, Editore Ambrosio Firmin Didot), iv, 142
Euting, Julius
    1885, *Nabatäische Inschriften aus Arabien*, Berlin
    1891, *Sinäitische Inschriften.* Berlin
    1896, *Tagebuch einer Reise in Inner-Arabien* (Diary of a Journey to Inner Arabia)
    1896, Part I, Leiden
    1914, Part II, Enno Littmann, Leiden
Evagrius, Scholasticus
    Ecclesiastical History

"F"

Fakhr ad-Din Razi
    (no information as to work being referenced.)
Farquhar, J.N.
    1915, *Crown of Hinduism,* London
Florus (?)
    (?) *Epitome of Roman History*
Flügel, Gustav, see Ibn Is'haq
Frankel, Zacharias,
    1859, *Darke ha-Mishnah*, Leipzig
Fränkel, Siegmund
    1880, *De vocabulis in antiquis Arabum carminibus et in Corano peregrinis: Dissertatio inauguralis,* E.J. Brill, Lugduni Batavorum
    1888, *Die Aramäische Fremdwörter in Arabischen*, Leiden, E.J. Brill
Frazer, James George
    1890, *The Golden Bough: A Study of Magic and Religion,* London, Macmillan
Freytag, Georg Wilhelm Friedrich
    (?) 1928, *Hamasae Carmina cum Tebrisii scholiis integris* by Abu Tammam Ḥabib ibn Aws al-Ṭa'i
Funk, Salomon
    1919, *Die Entstehung des Talmuds,* Berlin: Walter de Gruyter

"G"

Ganneau, see Clermont Ganneau
Gauthier, Léon,
   1900, *La Philosophie Musulmane,* Paris, Ernest Leroux
Geden, Alfred S.
   1909, *Outlines of Introduction to the Hebrew Bible,* Edinburgh, T. & T. Clark
   1913, *Studies in the Religions of the East,* London, Charles H Kerry
Geiger, Abraham, and F. M. Young
   1898, *Judaism and Islam. A prize essay,* Madras, M.D.C.S.P.C.K. press
Ghazali, see al-Ghazali, Aḥmad
Gibbon, Edward
   1776 – 1788, *The History of the Decline and Fall of the Roman Empire*
Glaser, Eduard (also see O. Weber)
   1897, *Zwei inschriften über den Dammbruch von Marib. Ein Beitrag zur geschichte Arabiens im 5. u. 6. Jahrhundert n. Chr.,* Berlin, W. Peiser
   1890, *Skizze der Geschichte und Geographie Arabiens, von den ältesten Zeiten bis Propheten Muhammad,* Berlin, Weidmannschebuchhandlung
   1906, *Altjemenische Nachrichten,* München, F. Straub
Glycas, Michaelis
   1836, *Annales,* Bonn, Impensis E. Weberi
Gobineau, Joseph Arthur
   1859, *Trois ans in Asie, 1855 à 1858,* Paris, Hachette et c
Goldziher, Ignaz Isaac Judah
   1885, *Cults das ancetias chez les Arabes,* Paris
   1890, *Muhamedanische Studien,* vol 1, Halle, M/Niemeyer.
   1925, *Vorlesungen über den Islam,* (Zweite, ungebearbeite auflage von Dr Franz Babinger) Heidelberg, Winter's Universitätesbuchhandlung
Graetz, Heinrich
   1888, *Geschichte der Juden: von den ältesten Zeiten bis auf die Gegenwart,* Leipzig, Leiner
Gray, George Buchanan

1925, *Sacrifice in the Old Testament: its theory and practice,* Oxford, Clarendon Press
Grimme, Hubert
1895, *Einleitung in den Koran. System der koranischen Theologie.* Münster: Aschendorff
1904, *Mohammed: Die weltgeschichtliche Bedeutung Arabiens.* Munich, Kirchheim'sche verlagsbuchhandlung
Guidi, Ignazio
1879, "Della Sede primitive dei popoli Semitici", Memorie della Reale Accademia dei Lincei, Ser.III vol. iii
1921, *L'Arabie anteislamique,* Paris, Geuthner

"H"

Haddon, Alfred Cort
1927, *The Wanderings of Peoples,* Cambridge, Cambridge University Press
Halabi
Insan al-`Uyun
Halévy, Joseph
1872, *Études sabéenes*: Examen Critique et Philologique des Inscriptions Sabéennes, Paris, Imprimerie Nationale
Hall, Harry Reginald Holland: Arthur S Peake et al, ed.
1925, *The People and The Book, Essays on the Old Testament,* Oxford: Clarendon, 1925
Hamdani, see Al-Hamdani
Hamza, Hamza ibn al-Hasan [ibn] al-Mu'addib al-Isfahan
Annales
Harnack, Adolf von Harnack
1888, *Lehrbuch der Dogmengeschichte,* Freiburg, J. C. B. Mohr
1921, *Harnack-ehrung; beiträge zur kirchengeschichte,* Leipzig, J.C. Hinrichs
Harris, Rendel
1925, *Contemporary Review,* August
Hartmann, Martin
1909. *Die Arabische Frage emit einen versuche der Archäologie Jemens*, Leipzig, Rudolf Haupt
1909, *Der Islam, geschichte--glaube--recht; ein handbuch,* Leipzig, R. Haupt

1909, *Der Islamische Orient, Berichte und Forschungen,* Berlin, W. Peiser

Hassan b. Thabit
**Diwan* (Cairo edition)

Haug, Martin, & Edward William West, trans
1872, *The book of Arda Viraf,* Bombay: Government Central Book Depot

Haupt, Paul, Carl Bezold, Johann Nepomuk Strassmaier
(?) *Assyriologische Bibliothek, herausgegeben von Friedrich Delitzsch und Paul Haupt:* Leipzig, J.C. Hinrichs

Heck, J.G., ed., Spencer Fullerton Baird trans.
1852, *Iconographic Encyclopaedia of Science, Literature and Arts,* vol. 1, New York, R. Garrigue

Heeren, Arnold Hermann Ludwig
1832, *Historical Researches into the Politics, Intercourse, and Trade of the Carthaginians, Ethiopians, and Egyptians,* Oxford, D.A. Talboys

Hein, Heinrich
1919, *Sumerisch-Indogermanisch?* (Steindruck?), Altona

Heroditus
**The Histories*
(?) 1908, *Herodoti Historiae. Tomus prior: Libros I-IV continens. & Tomus alter: Libri V-IX continen,* ed. C. Hude, Oxford

Herzfeld, Ernest
1924, *Paikuli: monument and inscription of the early history of the Sasanian empire,* Berlin, Dietrich Reimer

Hilsprecht, Hermann Vollrat
1903, *Explorations in Bible lands during the 19th century,* Philadelphia, A. J. Holman

Hippolytus
1851, *Philosopheumena (Elenchus - Refutation of All Heresies)* ed. Miller (wrongly attributed to Origen), Oxford

Hirsch, Leo
1897, *Reisen in Süd-Arabien, Mahra-land und Hadramaut,* Brill, Leiden

Hirschfeld, Hartwig
1886, *Beiträge zur Erklärung des Koran,* Leipzig, O. Schulze
1878, *Jüdische elemente im Ḳoran. Ein beitrag zur Ḳoranforschung,* Berlin, Im Selbstverlag

1902, *New Researches into the composition and exegesis of the Qoran,* London, Royal Asiatic Society
Hoffmann, Georg
    1880, *Auszüge aus syrischen Akten persischer Märtyrer,* Leipzig: Brockhaus
Hogarth, David George
    1915, *The Ancient East,* New York, Holt & Co.
    1922, *A History of the Arabs (Arabia),* Oxford, Clarendon Press
Hommel, Fritz
    1879, *Die Namen der Saugsethiere bei den Südsemitischen Völkern, als Beitrag zur arabischen und äthiopischen Lexicographie, zur semitischen Kulturforschung und Sprachvergleichung und zur Geschichte der Mittelmeerfauna; mit steter Berücksichtiung auch der assyrischen und hebräischen Thiernamen und geographischen und literaturgeschichtlichen Excursen,* Leipzig, J.C. Heinrichs'sche Buckhandlung
    1883, *Die Semitischen Völker und Sprachen,* Leipzig, Otto Schulze
    1892-1901, *Aufsätze und Abhandlungen arabistisch-semitologischen Inhalts.* 1-III., München, G. Franz
    1893, *Südarabische Chrestomathie,* München, G. Franz
    1897, *The Ancient Hebrew Tradition as illustrated by the old monuments,* New York, E. & J. B. Young & co.
    1897, *Die altisraelitische Überlieferung in inschriftlicher Beleuchtung,* München, H. Lukaschik
    1898 (1908) *Geschichte des alten Morgenlandes,* Leipzig, G.J. Göschen
    1904 – 1926, *Gundriss der Geographie und geschichte des Alten Orients,* 2nd ed., Munich, Beck Publishing House
Horn, Paul
    1893, *Grundrise der neupersischen Etymologie,* Strassburg, Trübner
Horovitz, Josef
    1923, *Das Koranische Paradies,* Scripta Universitatis atque Bibliothecae Hierosolymitanarum. Orientalia et judaica, Bd. 1.2, Jerusalem
    1926, *Koranische Untersuchungen,* Berlin und Leipzig: Walter de Gruyter
Houtsma, Martijn Theodoor, see Ya`qubi

Huart, Clément
    1912-1913, *Histoire des Arabes,* Paris, Librairie Paul Geuthner
Huart, Clément, ed. also see Al-Balkhi,
    1903, *Le Livre de la Creation,* Paris, Ernest Leroux
Hughes, Thomas Patrick
    1885, *A Dictionary of Islam,* London, W.H. Allen
Huntington, Ellsworth
    1907, *The Pulse of Asia: a journey in Central Asia illustrating the geographic basis of history,* London: Houghton Mifflin
Hurgronje, Christiaan Snouck
    1880, *Het Mekkaansche Feeste,* Leiden, Brill
    1931, *Mekka in the Latter Part of the 19th Century,* trans. J. Mohanan, Leiden, Brill
Hussein, Taha
    1926, *Fi al-Shi`r al-Jahili,* فى الشعر الجاهلى, Cairo

"I"

Ibn a-Athir
    *al-Kamil
Ibn al-Kalbi (Abu al-Mundhir Hisham bin Muhammed bin al-Sa'ib bin Bishr al-Kalbi)
    *Kitab Al-Asnam
Ibn Duraid
    (Ed. Note: Ibn Duraid wrote several works, Jeffery does not always indicate the work to which he is referring.)
    *Kitab al-Ishtiqaq
Ibn Hajr Asqalani
    al-Isabah fi tamyiz-is-sahabah
Ibn Hazm
    Al-Fisal fi al-Milal wa al-Ahwa' wa al-Nihal ("The Separator Concerning Religions, Heresies, and Sects"). Cairo, 1317 edition
Ibn Hisham, (Ibn Hisam), `Abd al-Malik, Muḥammad Ibn Isḥāq
    Sira
    The Life of Muhammad, a translation of Isḥāq's Sīrat Rasūl Allāh, trans. Heinrich Ferdinand Wüstenfeld
Ibn Is'ḥaq Ibn al Nadim (Abu'l-Faraj Muhammad bin Is'haq al-Nadim),

1872, *Kitab Al-Fihrist,* ed. Gustav Flügel, Leipzig, F. W. Vogel

Ibn Khaldun, (Khaloun)
*Kitab al-`Ibar wa-Diwan al-Mubtada' wa-l-Khabar fi Ta'rikh al-`Arab wa-l-Barbar wa-Man `Asarahum min Dhawi ash-Sha'n al-Akbar
1863 – 1868 (?), *Les prolégomènes d'Ibn Khaldoun,* trans. & ed. William MacGuckin Slane, Paris, Imprimerie Impériale

Ibn Manr, Muhammad ibn Mukarram
*1232-1311 or1312, Lisan al-`Arab,* Bullag Misr al-Matb`ah al-Kubra al-'Amiriyah

Ibn Qutaybah (Ibn Qutaiba) Abu Muhammad Abd-Allah ibn Muslim ibn Qutayba al-Dinawari al-Marwazi
?*Kitab al-Ma`arif, (Ibn Coteiba's Handbuch de Geschichte,* ed. Ferdinand Wüstenfeld, Gottingen, 1850)
(Ed. Note: Jeffery does not always indicate to which of Ibn Qutaiba's many works he is referring. He also refers to an Egyptian(?) edition.)

Ibn Rashiq
* *Kitab al-`Umdah fi sina`at al-shi`r wa-naqdih*

Ibn Sa`d, (Abu `Abd Allah Muḥammad ibn Sa`d ibn Mani` al-Basri al-Hashimi)
* *Kitab aṭ-ṭabaqat al-kabir*

Ibn Thabit, Hassan
(?) *Diwan,* Cairo

Ibrahim b. Sa`d

Ibshihi, Muhammad ibn Ahmad
1321, *al-Mustatraf fi kull fann mustazraf,* Cairo

Indicopleustes, Cosmas
(Ed. Note: no reference as to work cited)

Isaac of Antioch
Sancti Isaaci Antiocheni, doctoris Syrorum, opera omnia, 2 vol. ed. G. Bickell, (1873–77; "Complete Works of Holy Isaac of Antioch, Doctor of the Syrians"), Giessen

"J"

Jackson, Abraham Valentine Williams

1899 (1919?) *Zoroaster, the Prophet of Ancient Iran,* New York, Macmillan

Jacob, Georg

1895, *Studien in arabischen Dichtern, Bd. III: Das Leben der vorislamischen Beduinen nach den Quellen geschildert,* Berlin: Mayer & Müller

1897, *Altarabisches Beduinenleben nach den Quellen geschildert,* Berlin, Mayer & Müller

Jacobs, Joseph

1894, *Studies in Biblical Archaeology,* London, David Nutt

Jahiz, Abu `Uthman `Amr Ibn Bahr Al-Jahiz

1898, *Kitab ul-Mahasin wa'l-Addad,* ed. G. van Vloten as *Le Livre des beautes et des antitheses,* Leiden, Brill

1903, *Tria Opuscula auctore Abu Othman Amr Ibn Bahr Al-Djahiz Basrensi,* ed. Michael Johan de Goeje and Gerlof van Vloten, Lugduni Batavorum, Brill

Jastrow, Morris

1911, *Aspects of Religious Belief in Babylonia & Assyria,* New York G.P. Putnam's Sons

Jaussen, Antonin Joseph

1908, *Coutumes des Arabes au pays de Moab,* Paris, Gabalda

Jaussen, Antonin Joseph RR. PP et Savignac

1922, *Mission archéologique en Arabie*, Paris: E. Leroux

Jerome

*Vita Hilaronis

Jevons, Frank Byron

1896 (1902?), *Introduction to the History of Religion,* London, Methuen & Co

John of Ephesus

**Ecclesiastical History*

Johns, C.H.W.

1914, 'The Relations between the Laws of Babylonia and the Laws of the Hebrew Peoples', *Schweich Lectures on Biblical Archaeology,* 1912, London, Oxford University Press

Josephus, Flavius

**Antiquities of the Jews*

*Contra Apion

Joshua the Stylite (possible edition)

1882, *The Chronicle of Joshua the Stylite: composed in Syriac A.D. 507,* trans. W. Wright, Cambridge University Press

"K"

Kamenetzky, Israel Frank-Kamenetzky,
    1911, *Untersuchungen über das Verhältnis der dem Umajja b. Abi s. Salt zugeschriebenen Gedichte zum Qoran,* Kirchhain: Max Schmersow

Kay, David Miller
    1923, *Semantic Religions: Hebrew, Jewish, Christian, Moslem,* Edinburgh, T & T Clark

Keane, Augustus Henry
    1896, *Ethnology. In Two Parts: I. Fundamental Ethnical Problems. II. The Primary Ethnical Groups,* Cambridge, University Press
    1899, *Man Past and Present,* Cambridge, University Press

Keunen, Abraham
    1882, *National Religions and Universal Religion,* Hibbert Lectures
    1874, *The religion of Israel to the Fall of the Jewish State,* vol 1, (vol 2 & 3, 1875), London, Williams and Norgate

Khazin, see Al-Khazin

Khuda Bukhsh, S.
    1912, *Essays Indian and Islamic,* London, Probsthain & Co

Kiepert, Heinrich
    1878, *Lehrbuch der alten Geographie,* Berlin, D. Reimer

Kisa'i, see al-Kisa'i

Kitab al-Aghani, see al-Isfahani

Krall, Jakob
    1899, *Grundriss der altorientalischen Geschichte,* Wein

Krauss, Samuel
    (Ed. Note: no reference given to work cited.)

Krehl, Christoph Ludolf Ehrenfried
    1862, *Kitāb al-Jāmi` al--sahīh,* Leyden: E.J. Brill
    1863, *Über die Religion der vorislamischen Araber,* Leipzig, Serig

Kremer, see von Kremer

Kuenen, Abraham
    1882, *National Religions and Universal Religion,* Hibbert Lectures

1874-75, The Religion of Israel to the Fall of the Jewish State," 3 vols., tr. *Godsdienst van Israël,* 2 vols., London, Williams and Norgate

"L"

Labourt, Jérôme
    1904, *Le christianisme dans l'empire perse sous la dynastie Sassanide,* Paris, V. Lecoffre
Lacouperie, see de Lacouperie
Lagarde, von Paul de, see de Lagarde
Lagrange, Marie-Joseph
    1905, *Études sur les Religions Sémitiques,* Paris: V. Lecoffre
Lammens, Henri
    1922, *Arabia,*
    (*L'Arabie Occidentale*) Beyrouth, Imprimerie Catholique, 1928. (Ed. Note: This appears to be the nearest reference to the one mentioned by Jeffery.)
    1914, *Le Berceau de l'Islam: l'Arabie occidentale la veille de l'histore,* Rome: Pontificii Instituti Biblici
Land, Jan Pieter Nicolaas
    1870, *Anecdota syriaca: collegit, edidit, explicavit,* 4 Volumes, Leiden, E.J. Brill
Lane, Edward W.
    *1842, *Manners and Customs of Modern Egyptians,* Everyman's Edition
Lane-Poole, Stanley
    1883, *Studies in a Mosque,* London, W. H. Allen
Langdon, Stephen
    1911, *Sumerian Grammar and Chrestomathy,* Paris, Librairie Paul Geuthner
    1914, *Tammuz and Ishtar: a monograph upon Babylonian religion and theology containing extensive extracts from the Tammuz liturgies and all of the Arbela oracles,* Oxford, Clarendon Press
Langlois, Victor
    1869, *Collection des historiens anciens et modernes de l'Arménie,* Paris, Firmin Didot frères, fils et cie.
Layard, Austen Henry

1860, *Inscriptions in the Cuneiform Character, from Assyrian monuments, discovered by A. H. Layard,* London, Harrison & Son

Le Coq, Albert von
1922, *Türkische Manichaica aus Chotscho,* Volume 3, Berlin: Verlag der Akademie der Wissenschaften

Le Vogüé, see Vogüé

Lenormant, François
(Ed. Note: the work to which Jeffery referred was not mentioned)

Léroubna d'Édesse
1880, *Histoire d'Abgar,* in V. Langlois: *Collection des historiens anciens et modernes de l'Arménie,* Paris

Leszynsky, Rudolf
1810, (?1910) *Die Juden in Arabien zur zeit Mohammeds,* Berlin, Mayer & Müller

Lewy, Heinrich
1895, *Die Semitischen Fremdwörter im Grischischen,* Berlin, Gaertner

Lexa, Frantiek
1925, (1922) *Comment se revèlent les rapports entre les langues Hamitiques, Sémitiques et la langue Egyptienne dans la grammaire des pronoms personnels, des verbes et dans les numéraux cardinaux 1-9,* Prague

Lidzbarski, Mark
1905 - 1915, *Johannesbuch der Mandaer,* Giessen: Töpelmann
1908, *Ephemeris für semitische Epigraphik,* Giessen, J. Ricker
1920, *Mandaische Liturgien,* Berlin, Weidmannsche Buchhandlung
1925, *Ginzā, der Schatz: oder das Grosse buch der Mandäer,* Göttingen: Vandenhoeck & Ruprecht

Lightfoot, Joseph Barber
1880, (? 1896) *Saint Paul's Epistle to the Galatians,* a revised text with introduction, notes and dissertations, London, MacMillan and Co

Littmann, E., in
1916, *Festschrift Friedrich Carl Andreas zur Vollendung des siebzigsten Lebensjahres am 14. April 1916,* Leipzig, O. Harrassowitz

Lucan

Pharsalia
Lucian of Samosata (attributed to)
    1913, *De Dea Syria:* The Syrian goddess; being a translation of Lucian's De dea Syria, with a life of Lucian by Herbert A. Strong. Edited with notes and an introd. by John Garstang: London, Constable
Ludolf, Iobi (Hiob)
    1681, *Historia Aethopica*, Frankfurt am Main, Zunner
    1699, *Historia Aethiopica: et, Commentarius* ad suam Historiam Aethiopicam; Appendix prima ad Historiam Aethiopicam atque Commentarium; Appendix secunda ad Historiam Aethiopicam, dissertationem de locustis continens, Francofurti ad Moenum: J.D. Zunner

"M"

Maclean, Arthur John (ed)
    Ecclesiastical History, see Mosheim
Maidani, see Al-Maidani
Maimonides (Rabbi Moshe ben Maimon)
    *(c) 1190, *More Nevochim (The Guide for the Perplexed)*
Malalas, John (Ioannis Malalae)
    1831, *Chronographia,* Impensis E. Weberi
Mansel, Henry Longueville
    1875, *The Gnostic Heresies of the First and Second Centuries,* London: J. Murray
Manzoni, Renzo
    1884, *El Yèmen tre anni nell'Arabia felice; escursioni 1877-1880,* Roma, Tipografia Eredi Botta
Margoliouth, David Samuel
    1905, *Mohammed and the Rise of Islam*, New York, G. P. Putnam's Sons
    1914, *The Early Development of Mohammedanism,* New York, Charles Scribner
    1923, *The Homer of Aristotle*, Oxford: Basil. Blackwell
    1924, 'The Relations between Arabs and Israelites prior to the Rise of Islam', *The Schweich Lectures Biblical Archaeology, 1921,* London: Oxford University Press
Marraccio, Ludovico

(?) 1698, *Alcorani textus universus*: Ex correctioribus Arabum exemplaribus summa fide, atque pulcherrimis characteribus descriptus, eademque fide, ac pari diligentia exArabico idiomate in Latinum translatas; appositis unicuique capiti notis, atque refutatione: His omnibus praemissus est Prodromus totum priorem Tomum implens, Vol. 1, Padua
(?) 1691, *Prodromus ad Refutationem Alcorani* in quo Mahumetis vita, ac res gestae ex probatissimis apud Arabes sriptoribus collectae referuntur. De Alcorani nominee, auctore, idiomate, stylo, summa apud Mahumetanos veneration, aliisque similibus ad integram illius, absolutamque notitiam pertinentibus agitur. Denique per quatuor verae religionis noas sectae Mahumetanicae falsitas ostenditur, et Christianae Religionis veritas comprobatur. In quator partes divisus, Rome
1759, *Prodromus ad Refutationem Alcorani,* London, Dreweatts

Mas`udi, see Al-Mas`udi

Maximus of Tyre
The Dissertations

McGiffert, Arthur Cushman
1899, (?1914) *History of Christianity in the Apostolic Age,* New York, Charles Scribner

Meinhof, Carl
1912, *Die Sprachen der Hamiten,* Hamburg, L. & R. Friederischsen

Meissner, Bruno,
1913, (1915) *Die Keilschrift,* [Rezension] by: Rudolf Zehnpfund, Berlin, Vereinigung wissenschaftlicher Verleger

Merrill, Selah
1881, *East of Jordan,* New York, C. Scribner's sons

Meyer, Eduard
1907 (1906), *Sumerier und Semiten in Babylonian,* Berlin
1907, *Geschichte des Altertums,* Stuttgart, J.G. Cotta

Migne, J. G., ed.
1857–1866, *Patrologia Graeca (or Patrologiae Cursus Completus, Series Graeca),* vols1-161, Paris, Imprimerie Catholique

Mirkhond (Mir Khvand (Mir Khwand) Muḥammad ibn Khavandshah)

1891(?) *Rawżat as-safa' (Rauzat us-Safa) fi sirat al-anbiya' w-al-muluk w-al-khulafa'* 'The Gardens of purity in the biography of the prophets and kings and caliphs', tr. Edward Rehatsek, London: Royal Asiatic Society

Mittwock, Eugen
    1913, *Zur Entstehungsgeschichte des islamischen Gebets und Kultus*, Berlin: Verl. der Königl. Akad. der Wiss.

Moberg, Alex, ed. & trans.
    1924, *The Book of the Himyarites, Fragments of a Hitherto Unknown Syriac Work*, Leipzig, Lund

Montefiore, Claude Goldsmid
    1897, *Lectures on the Origin and Growth of Religion*, as Illustrated by the Religion of the Ancient Hebrews, *Hibbert Lectures,* London: Williams and Norgate

Mordtmann, J.H. and Müller, David Heinrich,
    1885, *Sabäisches Denkmäler*, Wein

Moritz, Bernhard
    1916, *Der Sinaikult in heidnischer Zeit,* Berlin: Weidmann
    1923, *Arabien,* Hannover

Moses of Kleorene (Moses of Chorene, Movses Khorenatsi?)
    (Ed. Note: no details of work referenced)

Mosheim, Johann Lorenz, von
    1824, *An Ecclesiastical History, Ancient and Modern, from the birth of Christ, to the beginning of the present century*, ed. Archibald Maclaine (MacLean(e), New York, Duyckinck

Mott, John R.
    1925, *The Moslem World Today,* London, Hodder & Stoughton

Moulton, James Hope,
    1913, *Early Zoroastrianism,* (Lectures delivered at Oxford and in London, February to May, 1912), London, Williams and Norgate

Mubarrad, Muḥammad ibn Yazīd
    1864-1892, *Kamil*, trans. William Wright, and M J de Goeje, Leipzig

Mufaddal al-Dabbi
    Mufaddaliyat

Muir, William

(Ed. Note: Jeffery does not specify either the volume or edition of *The Life of Muhammad* (*Mahomet*) to which he is referring.)

(Ed. Note: There appears to be several books by Muir that contain "the Calipate" in their titles. Jeffery does not specify to which book he is referring.)

 1881, *The early Caliphate and rise of Islam,* London, Smith, Elder & Co

 1883, *Annals of the Early Caliphate, from originals sources,* London, Smith, Elder & Co

 1891, *The Caliphate: its rise, decline and fall,* Oxford

Müller, August

 1885, *Der Islam im Morgen- und Aberdland,* Berlin, G. Grote

Müller, David Heinrich

 1878-1881, *Die Burgen und Schlösser Südarabiens, nach dem Iklil des Hamd ani,* Vienna

 1888, *Epigraphische Denkmäler aus Arabien,* Wein, F. Tempsky

 1899, *Südarabische Alterthümer im kunsthistorischen Hofmuseum,* Wein, Hölder

Müller, David Heinrich, ed.

 1884–1891, *Al-Hamdani's Geographie der arabischen Halbinsel,* 2 vols. Leiden

Müller, David Heinrich and Mordtmann, J.H.

 1885, *Sabäische Denkmäler,* Wein

Müller, Fredrich

 1884, (1876-1888) *Grundriss der Sprachwissenschaft,* Wien, Hölder

Murray, George Gilbert Aimé

 1912, *Four States in Greek Religion,* New York, Columbia University Press

Musil, Alois

 1908, *Arabia Petraea,* Wien, Hölder

"N"

Nabigha, see Al-Nabighah
Nasafi, see Al-Nasafi
Nau, François

1933, *Les Arabes Chretiens de Mesopotamie et de Syrie du VIIe au VIIIe Siecle,* Paris, France: Societe Asiatique
Nawawi, see Al-Nawawi
Nicephorus Callistus Xanthopulus
*Historia Ecclesiastica
Nicetas of Byzantium
(? *Refutation of the Error-Directed Book of Muhammad the Arab*)
Nicetas of Khonia (Choniates)
*Thesaurus Orthodoxae Fidei
Nicholson, Reynald A.
1907, *Literary History of the Arabs,* New York, Charles Scribner's Sons
Niebuhr, Carsten (also Karsten)
1772, *Beschreibung von Arabien, aus eigenen Beobachtungen und im Lande selbst gesammieten,* Copenhagen, Clemens
(Ed. Note: Niebuhr wrote a number of works on Arabia. Jeffery does not always indicate the work to which he is referring.)
Nielsen, Ditlef
1904, *Die altarabische Mondreligion und die mosaische Ueberlieferung,* Strassburg, Trübner
1920, *Der sabäische Gott Ilmukah,* Leipzig, J.C. Hinrichs
1922, *Der dreieinige Gott in religionshistorischer Beleuchtung,* København Gyldendal Nordisk forlag
Nielson, Niels
1906, *Handbuch der theorie der gammafunktion,* Leipzig, Trübner
Nilus, Saint or Nilus of Sinai
?*Narrationes*
1639, *Opera quaedam nondum Edita,* Parisiis: Apud Sebastianum Cramoisy, Typographum Regium, via Iacobaea, sub Ciconiis
Nöldeke, Theodor
1860 (? 1919) *Geschichte des Qorans,* Leipzig: Dieterich
1864, *Beiträge zur Kenntniss der Poesie der alten Araber,* Hanover, Carl Rümpler
1864, *Uber die Amalekiter und einige andre Nachbarvölker der Israeliter,* Gottigen
1875, *Mandäische Grammatik,* Halle, Buchhandlung des Waisenhauses

1879, *Geschichte der Perser und Araber,* zur Zeit der Sasaniden aus der arabischen Chronik des Tabari: Übersetzt und mit ausführlichen Erläuterungen und ergänzungen Versehn, Leyden, Brill

1887, *Die Ghassanischen Fürsten aus dem Hause Ğafga's,* Berlin, Akademie der Wissenschaften

1899, *Die Semitischen Sprachen,* Leipzig, C. H. Tauchnitz

1906, *Festschrift Orientalische Studien Theodor Nöldeke ed* C. Bezold, Giessen

1910, *Neue Beiträge zur semitischen Sprachwissenschaft,* Strassburg: K.J. Trübner

Nonnosus

(Ed. Note: Possibly referred to in *Chronicle of Ioannis Malalas* (Book 18.457) and *Chronicle of Theophanes.*)

Norris, Frederick A, Howard Crosby Butler, Enno Littmann, Edward Royal Stoever, David Magie

1907, *Publications of Archaeologial Expedition to Syria,* Leyden, E.J. Brill

"O"

Olinder, Gunnar

1912, *The Kings of Kinda: The Family of Akil Al Murar,* Lund, Hakan Olsson

Oppert, Jules Julius, MM. Fulgence Fresnel, Félix Thomas,

1863, *Expédition Scientifique en Mesopotamie, Exécutéé par ordre du gouvernement de 1851 à 1854,* Impremerie Imperiale

Origen

*248(?) *Contra Olsum (Against Celsus).*

"P"

Palgrave, William Gifford

1868, (1908) *Personal Narrative of a Years Journey through Central and Eastern Arabia,* London, MacMillan

Palmer, Edward Henry

1871, *The desert of the Exodus: journeys on foot in the wilderness of the forty years' wanderings: undertaken in connexion with the*

ordnance survey of Sinai, and the Palestine exploration fund, Cambridge, Deighton
Palmer, E. H., trans.
    1880, *The Qur'an,* Oxford, Clarendon Press
Parthey, Gustav
    1844, *Vocabularium Coptico-Latinum et Latino-Copticum e Peyroni et Tattami lexicis,* Berolini: Prostat in Libraria Fr. Nicolai
Paton, Lewis Bayles
    1901, (1902) *The Early History of Syria and Palestine,* New York, Charles Schribner & Sons
Paulys Realencyclopädie der classischen Altertumswissenschaft, see Wissewa
Pautz, Dr Otto
    1898, *Muhammeds Lehre Von der Offenbarung,* Leipzig, J.C. Hinrichs'sche Buchhandlung
Penrice, Angelo
    1905, *L'Imperatore Eraclio. Saggio di storia bizantina,* Firenze. Tip. Galletti e Cocci
Penrice H.M. and J.P. Whitney, eds
    1913, *The Cambridge Medieval History* (vol-ii), Cambridge, Cambridge University Press
Petermann, August Heinrich
    1855(+) *Geographische Mitteilungen,* (Journal) vols xxxiv & xxxvi
Petermann, Julius Heinrich
    1861, *Reisen im Orient,* 1. Ausgabe, Leipzig
    1865, *Reisen im Orient, 1852-1855,* 2. Ausgabe, Leipzig
Petrie, William Matthew Flinders et al.
    1894, *History of Egypt,* London, Methuen & Co.
Philby, H. St. J. B. (Harry St. John Bridger)
    1922, *The Heart of Arabia, a Record of Travel and Exploration,* London, Constable
Philo of Byblos
    **Phoenician History*
Philostorgius
    425? *Ecclesiastical History (Ἐκκλησιαστικὴ ἱστορία)*
    ?1913, *Philostorgius kirchengeschichte, mit dem leben des Lucian von Antiochen und den fragmenten eines Arianischen Historiographen,* ed. Joseph Bidez, Leipzig, J.C. Hinrichs

Photius
*Bibliotheca (*or *Myriobiblos)*
Pliny, Gaius Plinius Secundus
*Naturalis Historia (*Natural History*)*
Pocock (Pococke), Edward, trans.
?1806, *Specimen historiæ Arabum;* Bar Hebraeus, 1226-1286. Silvestre de Sacy, A. I. (Antoine Isaac), 1758-1838, translator, White, Joseph, 1745-1814, editor, Oxford University Press
Pollio, Trebellius
(?) Historiae Augusta
Pope, J.A., trans.
1816, *The Ardai Viraf Nameh; or the Revelations of Ardai Viraf,* London: Black, Parbury & Allen
Porphyry
(Ed. Note: No indication as to which work has been referenced.)
Prideaux, Humphrey
(?) 1697, *Life of Mahomet*
Procksh, Otto
1899, *Die Blutrache bei den vorislamischen Arabern,* Leipzig, B.G. Teubner
Procopius
(Latin) De Bello Persico
Ptolemy, Claudius
1838-1845, *Geographiae libri octo: graece et latine ad codicum manu scriptorum fidem,* trans Friedrich Wilhelm Wilberg; Essendle, G.D. Baedeker
Pumpelly, Raphael
1906, (1908) *Excavations in Turkestan,* Washington, Carnegie Institution of Washington

"Q"

Qalqashandi, see Al-Qalqashandi

"R"

Rambaud, Alfred Nicholas
    1870, *L'Empire grec au dixième siècle; Constantin Porphyrogénète,* Paris A. Franck
Razi
    (Ed. Note: no indication of work being referenced.)
Rehatsek, Edward, see Mir Khvand
Reinaud, Joseph Toussaint
    1860, *Notice sur Mahomet,* Paris, 'F. Didot frères et fils
Renan, Ernest
    1863, *Histoire Générale et Systéme Comparé des Langues Sémitiques,* Paris, Michel Lévy Frères
    (Ed. Note: There appear to be a number of volumes to this work. There also appears to be a 1928 edition printed by Calmann-Levy)
Reubeni
    1660, *Midrash,* Prague
Rhodokanakis, Nikolaus
    1908, *Der vulgärarabische Dialekt im Dofar (Zfar)* Wien, Hölder
Richter, Ohnefalsch-Richter, Max Herman
    1893, *Kypros, the Bible and Homer,* London, Asher & Co
Ripley, William Z.
    1899, *The Races of Europe: A Sociological Study,* New York, D. Appleton and Co
Roberstson Smith, William
    1885, *Kinship and Marriage in Early Arabia,* Cambridge, University Press
    (See S. A. Cook for a new edition)
    1889, *Lectures on the Religion of the Semites. Fundamental Institutions. First Series,* London, Adam & Charles Black
Robinson, Edward
    1841, *Biblical Researches in Palestine,* Boston
Robinson, Henry Wheeler
    1938, *Religious Ideas of the Old Testament,* London, Duckworth
Rodén, Karl Gustaf
    1913, *Le Tribu dei Mensa, storia, legge e costume,* Asmara, Evangeliska forterlands-stiftelsens förlags-expedition
Rodwell, John Medows

1911, *The Koran,* translated from the Arabic, London, J.M. Dent & Sons, Ltd
Rothstein, Gustav
    1899, *Die Dynastie der Lahmiden in al-Hîra. Ein Versuch zur arabisch-persichen Geschichte zur Zeit der Sasaniden* Berlin: Reuther & Reichard
Rudolph, Wilhelm
    1922, *Die Abhängigkeit des Qurans von Judentum und Christentium,* Stuttgart, Vohlhammer
Ryckmans, Gonzague
    1934-1935, *Les noms propres sud-sémitiques.* Louvain, Bureaux du Muséon
Ryle, Herbert Edward
    (?)1900, *The Early Narratives of Genesis,* Macmillan and Co.
    1914, *The Book of Genesis in the Revised Version with Introduction and Notes;* The Cambridge Bible for Schools and College Series, Cambridge

"S"

Sachau, Edward C., ed.
    1910, *Alberunis India* Vol. 1-2, London, Kegan Paul, Trench & Trubner
Sale, George
    1921, *The Preliminary Discourse to the Koran* with an introduction by Edward Denison Ross, London: F. Warne
Samau'al (Samaw'al), see Al-Samaw'al
Sanuto, Marino (Sanudo the Elder of Torcello)
    *Liber Secretorum Fidelium Crucis
Sayce, Archibald Henry
    1872, *Assyrian Grammar for Comparative Purposes,* London, Trübner & Co
Schrader, Eberhard et al.
    1836-1908, *Keilinschriftliche Bibliothek: Sammlung von assyrischen und babylonischen Texten im Umschrift und Übersetzung,* Berlin,
    1872, *Die Keilinschriften und das Alte Testament,* (KAT) Giessen: J. Ricker

(Ed. Note: There is a latter revision of this work in 1903, by Heinrich Zimmern, Hugo Winckler and Friedrich David Heinrich, Berlin, Reuther und Reichard
Schultens, Albert et al.
    1740, *Monumenta vetustiora Arabiae*, Apud Johannem Luzac
Schulthess, Friedrich
    1911, *Umayya ibn Abia-Salt*, Leipzig, J.C. Hinrichs'sche Buchhandlung
Schürer, Emil
    1898, *Geschichte des Jüdischen Volkes im Zeitalter Jesu Christi*, 3 Aufl., Leipzig
Schwally, Friedrich
    1893, *Idioticon des Christlich palästinischen Aramaeisch*, Giessen, J. Ricker
Seetzen, Ulrich Jasper
    1810, *Travels in Yemen*
    (Ed. Note: It appears that these may have been published posthumously by Kruse and Fleischer (1854-59) but further details have not been found. Below is a major work by Seetzen which includes his travels through Arabia)
    1859, *Reisen durch Syrien, Palastina, Phonicien, Die Transjordan – Lander, Arabia. Petraea und unter-Agypten*, (Four Volumes), Verlagt bei G. Reimer
Sell, Edward (Canon)
    1880, *Faith of Islam*, Trübner & Co
    1909, *Battles of Badr and Uhud*, The Islam Series, London, Christian Literature Society
    1910, *The cult of `Ali*, The Islam Series, Madras
    1911, *Ghazwas and Sariyas*, The Islam Series, London Christian Literature Society
    1912, *The Hanifs*, Madras
    1913, *Al-Khulafa ar-rashidun or the four rightly guided Khalifas*, London, The Christian Literature Society
Sergi, Giuseppe
    1909 *The Mediterranean Race: a Study of the Origins of European Peoples*. London: Walter Scott
Shahrastani, see Al-Shahrastani
Siculus, Diodorus
    Bibliotheca historica
Siouffi, Nicolas

1880, *Étude sur la Religion des Soubbas*, Paris, Imprimerie Nationale
Smend, Rudolf
 1899, *Lehrbuch der alttestamentlichen Religionsgeschichte*, Freiburg, J.C.B. Mohr
Smith, George Adam
 1915, *Atlas of the Historical Geography of the Holy Land*, London, Hodder and Staughton
Smith, Grafton Elliot
 1923, *The Ancient Egyptians and the origin of Civilization* London/New York, Harper & Brother.
Smith, Henry Preserved
 1903, *Old Testament History,* New York, S. Scribner's sons
Smith, Robertson, see Roberstson Smith
Smith, William, ed.
 1878, *Dictionary of Greek and Roman Geography,* London, J. Murray
Soubhy, Saleh
 1894, *Pèlerinage à la Mecque et à la Médine,* Cairo
Sozomen, (Sozomenus)
 Historia Ecclesiastica
 ?1855, *Sozomen, The ecclesiastical history of Sozomen: comprising a history of the church from A. D. 324 to A. D. 440,* London, Bohn
Sprenger, Aloys
 1861, *Das Leben und die Lehre des Muhammad vol i,* Berliö, Nicolai'sche Verlagsbuchandlung,
 1864, Die Post und Reiserouten des Orients, Leipzig
 1875, *Die Alte Geographie Arabiens als Grundlage der Entwicklungsgeschichte des Semitismus,* Bern, Huber
Stave, Erik
 1898, *Über den Einfluss des Parsismus auf das Judentum; ein Versuch,* Haarlem, E.F. Bohn
Stephanus of Bysantium,
 *Ethnica (Ἐθνικά)
Stevens, Ethel Stefana (E S Drower, Lady)
 1923, *By Tigris and Euphrates,* London, Hurst & Blackett
Strabo
 *Geography
Strack, Hermann Leberecht

1908, *Einleitung in den Talmud*, Leipzig, J.C. Hinrichs
1921, *Einleitung in Talmud und Midras* (5th Ed), München: O. Beck
Suidas
 *? Suidas
Suyuti, see Al-Suyuti
Sykes, Percy Molesworth
 1922, *Persia,* Oxford, University Press

"T"

Tabari, see Al-Tabari
Tarafa, Ṭarafah ibn al-`Abd ibn Sufyan ibn Sa`d Abu `Amr al-Bakri al-Wa'ili
 (Ed. Note: No mention of which work has been referenced.)
Thabit, Hassan ibn, see Ibn Thabit
Tha'labi, see Al-Tha'labi,
Theodore Bar Khuni
 (Ed. Note: No mention of which work has been referenced.)
Theodoret
 Haereticarum fabularum compendium (*Compendium of Heretical Accounts*)
Theodoros Anagnostes
 Historia Tripartita
Theophanes
 1883, *Theophanis chronographia*, ed Carl de Boor, Lipsiae: B.G. Teubnneri
Theophrastus
 Historia Plantarum (Enquiry into Plants),
 1916, *Theophrastus Enquiry into Plants and minor works on odours and weather signs* trans. Arthur Hort, London and New York: William Heinemann and G. P. Putnam's Sons
Thompson, Reginald Campbell,
 1905, *Semitic Magic: its Origins and Development,* London, Luzac
Tirmidhi, see al-Tirmidhi
Tisdall, W. St. Clair
 1905, (1911?) *The Original Sources of the Qur'an,* London, Society for Promoting Christian Knowledge

Tor Andre, see Andræ
    (1893), *The Blood Covenant: A Primitive Rite and Its Bearings on Scripture,* London
    (1894), *Studies in Oriental Social Life,* London, Hodder and Stoughton
    1906, *The Thresholod Covenant or The Beginning of Religious Rites,* New York, Scribner
Tylor, Edward Burnett
    1871, *Primitive Culture,* Vol. 1&2, London: John Murray

"U"

Uranius
    See Stephanus of Byzantium
Usener, Hermann
    1899, *Die Sintfluthsagen, Untersucht,* Bonn, F. Cohen

"V"

Van den Berg, Lodewijk Willemm Christiaan
    1886, *Le Hadhramout et les colonies arabes dans l'archipel Indien,* Batavia, Impr.du gouvernement
Van Vloten, Gerlof, see Jahiz
    1891, *Feestbundel aan prof. M. J. de Goeje*
    1891 Aangeboden door eenige oud-leerlingen, Leiden, E.J. Brill
    1898, *Kitab ul-Mahasin wal-Addad,* ed. G. van Vloten as *Le Livre des beautes et des antitheses,* Leiden. Brill
Vogüé, see de Vogüé
Volz, Paul
    1903, *Jüdische Eschatologie; von Daniel bis Akiba,* Tübigen, Verlag von J.C. B. Mohr
von Kremer: Alfred, Freiherr von
    1866, *Uber die suïdarabische Sage,* Leipzig: Brockhaus
    1873, *Culturgeschichtliche Streifzüge auf dem Gebiete des Islam,* Leipzig, F.A. Brockhaus
von Kremer, Alfred, and Marsden Jones ed.

1856, *Kitab al-maghazi*, by Muḥammad ibn `Umar Waqidi, *'Abu 'Abd Allah Muḥammad ibn 'Umar a Waqidi,* Maṭba` Babtist Mishin

von Maltzan, Heihrich Freiherrn
> 1873, *Adolph von Wrede's Reise in Hadhramaut, Beled Beny 'Yssà und Beled el Hadschar,* Braunschweig, Friedrich Vieweg

Vopiscus, Flavius(?)
> (?) *Historiae Augustae*

"W"

Waddington, William Henry
> 1870, *Inscriptions Grecques et Latines de la Syrie: recueillies et expliquées,* Paris, Didot frères, fils et Cie.

Wavell, Arthur John Byng
> 1918, *A Modern Pilgrim in Mecca,* London, Constable

Weber, von Otto
> 1907, *Forschungsreisen in Süd-Arabien bis zum Auftreten Eduard Glasers.* Leipzig, J.C. Hinrichs
> 1909, *Eduard Glasers Forschungsreisen in Südarabien,* Leipzig, Hinrichs
> 1922, *Mitteilungen aus der Vorderasiatischen Abteilung der Staatlichen Museen zu Berlin,* Berlin, Curtius H. I.
> 1904, *Arabian vor dem Islam,* Leipzig, J.C. Hinrichs
> 1908, *Studien zur südarabischen Altertumskunde,* (multiple volumes) Berlin, W. Peiser Verlag

Weidner, Ernst Friedrich
> 1922, *Die Assyriologie, 1914-1922, wissenschaftliche Forschungsergebnisse in bibliographischer Form,* Leipzig, Hinrichs

Wellhausen, Julius
> 1884, "Lieder der Hudhailiten, arabisch und deutsch", Prt II in *Skizzen und Vorarbeiten,* Berlin: Georg Reimer
> 1884, *Skizzen und Vorarbeiten,* Berlin: Georg Reimer
> 1893, *Die Ehe bei den Arabern,* Dieterich
> 1897, *Reste Arabischen Heidentums,* Berlin, Georg Reimer
> 1902, *Das Arabische Reich under Sein Sturs,* Berlin, Georg Reimer

Wellsted, James Raymond
   1838, *Travels in Arabia,* vol 1 & 2, London
Wensinck, A.J.
   1928, *Mohammed en de joden te Medina,* Leiden, E.J. Brill
Wheeler Robinson, see Robinson, Henry Wheeler
White, Horace, trans.
   1899, *Appian Civil Wars,* London, Bell
Wilberg, Friedrich Wilhelm, trans.
   1838-1845, *Claudii Ptolemaei Geographiae libri octo: graece et latine ad codicum manu scriptorum fidem,* Essendle, G.D. Baedeker
Wilken, George Alexander
   1884, *Het Matriarchaat bij de oude Arabieren,* Amsterdam, J. H. de Busy
Winckler, Hugo
   1889-1890, *Der Thontafelfund von el-Amarna,* Berlin, W. Spemann
   1892, *Geschichte Babyloniens und Assyriens,* Leipzig, Eduard Pfeirrer
   1898, *Geschichte Israels.* Leipzig: E. Pfeiffer
   1899, *Völker Vorderasiens,* Leipzig: J.C. Hinrichs
   1893-1906, *Altorientalische Forschungen,* Vol I- III Leipzig: Verlag von Eduard Pfeiffer
   1901, *Arabisch, Semitisch, Orientalisch: kulturgeschichtlich-mythologische Untersuchung,* Berlin: W. Peiser
Winckler, Hugo and Heinrich Zimmern, eds.
   1903, *Die Keilinschriften und das Alte Testament,* von Eberhard Schrader. 3. Auflage, mit Ausdehnung auf die Apokryphen, Pseudepigraphen und das Neue Testament, neu bearbeitet, Berlin, Reuther und Reichard
Wissowa, Georg Otto August, ed.
   1894, *Paulys Realenzyklopädie der klassischen Altertumswissenschaft,* vol 1&2, Stuttgart, Metzlersher, Verlag
Wood, Robert
   1829, *Les ruines de Palmyre, autrement dite Tedmor au désert,* A Paris, Lugan, Libraire, Passage du Claire
Wright, Thomas
   1855, *Early Christianity in Arabia: a historical essay,* London: Quaritch

Wright, William, ed.
    1882, *Chronicles of Joshua the Stylie*, Cambridge
    1890, *Lectures in the Comparative Grammar of Semitic Languages*, Cambridge, University Press

Wright, William and M.J. de Goeje, trans.
    1864-1892, *The Kamil of El-Mubarrad*, author Muḥammad ibn Yazīd Mubarrad, Leipzig

Wüstenfeld, Heinrich Ferdinand trans (see also Ibn Hisham)
    1857-60, Muḥammad Ibn Ishaq `Abd al-Malik Ibn Hisham; *The Life of Muhammad,* a translation of Ishaq's Sirat Rasul Allah
    1858-1861, *Chroniken der Stadt Makka*, iv vols, Leipzig, trans Muḥammad ibn `Abd Allah Azraqi, *Kitab akhbar Makkah wa ma ja'a fiha min al-athar*
    1852, *Genealogische Tabellen der arabischen Stämme und Familien*, Göttigen

Wylde, Augustus B.
    1901, *Modern Abyssinia,* London, Methuen

"Y"

Ya`qubi, see Al-Ya`qubi
Yaqut Shihab al-Din ibn-`Abdullah al-Rumi al-Hamawi
    Mu`jam ul-Buldan

"Z"

Zacharius of Mitylene (Z Scholasticus or Z. Rhetor)
    (Ed. Note: No indication as to which of his works is being referenced.)

Zaidan, Jurji
    1907, *Al`Arab qabl al-Islam*, Cairo

Zimmern, Heinrich
    1885, *Babylonische Busspsalmen, umschrieben, übersetzt und erklärt*, Leipzig, J. C. Hinrichs

Zimmern, Heinrich

1901, *Beiträge zur Kenntnis der babylonischen Religion. Die Beschwörungstafeln Surpu, Ritualtfeln für Wahrsager, Beschwörer und Sänger*, Leipzig J.C. Hinrichs
Zosimus, Historicus
*Historia Nova
Zotenberg, Hermann
1869, *Chronique de Tabari, Abu-Ǧa`far Muḥammad Ibn-Ǧarir Ibn-Yazid aṭ-Ṭabari*, Paris, Imprimerie impériale
Zuhair
*Mu`allaqa
Zwemer, Samuel Marinus
1912, *Arabia, the Cradle of Islam*, London & Edinburgh, Oliphant, Anderson and Ferrier
1920, *The Influence of Animism on: an account of popular superstitions*, London: Central Board of Missions and Society for Promoting Christian Knowledge

www.ingramcontent.com/pod-product-compliance
Lightning Source LLC
Chambersburg PA
CBHW062056290426
44110CB00022B/2607